John Randolph of Roanoke

for Cousin Billy

with best regards

David Johnson

22 May 2012

SOUTHERN BIOGRAPHY

Andrew Burstein, *Series Editor*

John Randolph, by Gilbert Stuart, 1806. Andrew W. Mellon Collection, image courtesy National Gallery of Art, Washington.

John Randolph
of Roanoke

DAVID JOHNSON

 LOUISIANA STATE UNIVERSITY PRESS
BATON ROUGE

Published by Louisiana State University Press
Copyright © 2012 by Louisiana State University Press
All rights reserved
Manufactured in the United States of America
First printing

Designer: Laura Roubique Gleason
Typeface: Warnock Pro
Printer: McNaughton & Gunn
Binder: Acme Bookbinding, Inc.

The epigraphs at the head of each chapter are taken from the poem "Randolph of Roanoke" by John Greenleaf Whittier.

Library of Congress Cataloging-in-Publication Data

Johnson, David E., 1961–
    John Randolph of Roanoke / David E. Johnson.
        p. cm. — (Southern biography series)
    Includes bibliographical references and index.
    ISBN 978-0-8071-4397-1 (cloth : alk. paper) — ISBN 978-0-8071-4398-8 (pdf) —
ISBN 978-0-8071-4399-5 (epub) — ISBN 978-0-8071-4400-8 (mobi)
    1. Randolph, John, 1773–1833. 2. Legislators—United States—Biography. 3. United
States—Politics and government—1783–1865. 4. United States. Congress. House—
Biography. I. Title.
    E302.6.R2J59 2012
    328.73'092—dc23
    [B]
                                                                        2011039037

For Aloma Hindman

Contents

Prologue   1

1. Keep Your Land   8

2. Macbeth Hath Murdered Sleep   25

3. Ask My Constituents   42

4. Master of the House   53

5. An Evil Daily Magnifying   68

6. Yazoo Men   75

7. The *Tertium Quid*   88

8. Mystery of Affection and Faith   106

9. House Cynosure   118

10. Of Roanoke   134

11. An Irreclaimable Heretic   150

12. Dying, Sir, Dying   165

13. The Moral Authority of My Heart   176

14. Two Souls   182

15. A Fig for the Constitution   192

16. The Puritan and the Blackleg   206

17. Remorse   216

Epilogue   229

Acknowledgments   235

Appendix 1. Randolph Genealogy   239

Appendix 2. Randolph's Contemporaries   241

Notes   245

Bibliography   319

Index   335

John Randolph of Roanoke

Prologue

John Randolph of Roanoke defied indifference.

There had never been seen a man quite like him—so eloquent and so acerbic, so shrewd and so troubled. A man as facile with words as he was handy with a pistol. An "object of admiration and terror," John Randolph both attracted and repelled.[1]

His first public debate was with Patrick Henry. He was Jefferson's ally, then opponent; the bitter enemy of Madison; critic of Monroe; unrelenting antagonist of "King John" Adams, then of John Quincy Adams, who had "outdone his [father's] out doings"; curiosity to Andrew Jackson.[2] He aimed a pistol at Henry Clay and tried to do the same to Daniel Webster. He had little use for John C. Calhoun, a man he believed united "to the savage ferocity of the frontier man all the insensibility of the Yankee character."[3] Yet this same man established long-lasting friendships with a varied cast that included John Marshall, Albert Gallatin, John Taylor of Caroline, and Francis Scott Key. Historian Henry Adams marveled at the "mystery of affection and faith" Randolph inspired in a host of friends.[4]

He entered Congress at the age of twenty-six and mastered the men of the House as skillfully as he mastered his blooded horses. His legislative accomplishments were the achievements of Jefferson's first term: elimination of internal taxes, reduction of the national debt, financing for the Louisiana Purchase, rollbacks in the size of government, and repeal of the Federalist Judiciary Act.

Almost as quickly, he was alone in opposition. The alpha was the Yazoo land fraud. A corrupt Georgia legislature conveyed the vast tract of Yazoo territory to land speculators. An enraged citizenry tossed out the legislature, revoked the transaction, and reclaimed the land. Innocent and not-so-innocent third-party purchasers appealed to the federal government for—to use a present-day term—a bailout. As Madison crafted a plan to pay the claimants, Randolph saw nothing less than federal usurpation of state sovereignty. His opposition was sure and vicious, and it cracked the Republican alliance.

Yazoo was followed in short order by the failed impeachment trial of Justice Samuel Chase—where Randolph's lack of legal ability ensured defeat—and the secret attempt by Jefferson to purchase Florida. The latter episode completed the break. "The *old* Republican party is already ruined, past redemption," Randolph wrote; "new men and new maxims are the order of the day."[5] He alienated the former and would have no part of the latter. He took his stand, Henry Adams wrote, a "queer figure . . . booted, riding whip in hand, flying about the astonished statesmen, and flinging, one after the other, Mr. Jefferson, Mr. Madison, and dozens of helpless Congressmen headlong into the mire."[6]

Jefferson pronounced him finished. "The example of John Randolph, now the outcast of the world," he wrote, "is a caution to all honest and prudent men to sacrifice a little of self-confidence and to go with their friends although they sometimes think they are going wrong."[7] Randolph would not go along. Not with war against Great Britain, not with increased taxes or tariffs, not with expanding federal power, not with "the Holy Catholic Church of Expediency and Existing Circumstances."[8] Far from being finished, Randolph became the *Tertium Quid*—the "third something" of American politics.

He alternatively alienated and inspired a constituency that refused to discharge him from duty. At the Virginia Constitutional Convention of 1829, he could not "move, no, not even change his position, or even walk across the floor, without being tracked to his stopping place by a thousand eyes."[9] His message there harkened to words he said thirty years earlier as a new member of the House: "Governments are like revolutions: you may put them in motion, but I defy you to control them after they are *in* motion."[10] When his end came—at an old sixty—he uttered a single word cloaked with echoes of his past: "Remorse!"[11]

Contemporaries felt the need to describe him. The words rendered Randolph into a walking adjective. "A flowing gargoyle of vituperation," "pale, meager, ghostly," "grotesque," "a phenomenon amongst men."[12] Like Jeremy

Bentham in his auto-icon, Randolph was on permanent display. He entered the House chamber, spurs jingling, with several of his hounds close about his feet. He wore "a full suit of heavy, drab-colored English broadcloth, the high, rolling color of his surtout coat almost concealing his head, while the shirts hung in voluminous folds about his knee-breeches and white leather tops of boots." His hat might be pulled down to his eyes. The heel of a whip tapped in his hand.[13]

He had "no shape but that he was forked," a "tall, spare, and somewhat emaciated" figure. His "long legs, which instead of diminishing, grow larger as they approach the floor," gave him "the appearance of a sort of pyramid." He seemed to unfold in stages.[14] "When he stood up," one wrote, "you did not know when he was to end."[15] His hands were "as fair and delicate as any girls" but with "fingers which might have served as models for those of the goblin page."[16] Randolph's forefinger alone elicited numerous comments for it was his Excalibur, seemingly blinding and slashing opponents at whom he pointed it.

The disjointed mosaic that formed his body would not long hold the stare of gawkers. For the face that stared back was even more arresting. The skin wore "that special hue into which the soft, roseate complexion of the young woman is often changed by time and exposure"; the black hair, the one tangible indication of his Indian heritage, was parted in the middle, and "softened by intermingled threads of silver gray"; the beardless face, marked "with the lineaments of boyhood," but mocked by wrinkles; and the lips "indigo, indicating days of suffering and nights of tortuous pain."[17] Dominating his face were the eyes. "They seemed to look through you into your very soul," one wrote, and were accentuated with "nimbleness and fire." They "flashed rapidly," "brilliant beyond description," with "marvelous power."[18] They were small and dark, probably hazel colored, but often called black by those on whom he cast his penetrating look. Yet his eyes were but precursor to his voice.

The voice squeaked "like a boy's just before breaking into manhood," an intriguing combination of "resonant shrillness and bewitching melody."[19] To some hearers it was "exquisite vocal music," to others a "clear, sharp, staccato voice that spoke of chastity."[20] It was a voice that caused one wit to conjecture that he was "either by nature, or manual operation, fixed for an Italian singer."[21] More often, it was a voice "clear, ringing, shrill, piercing; still, not harsh nor rasping . . . [but] smooth, melodious, musically charming."

"His manner of speaking is the most forcible I ever witnessed," an

observer wrote, "and his language elegant beyond description."[22] N
Van Buren admired Randolph's ability to "launch imputations by a
shake of his long finger, or a shrug of his shoulders, accompanied by
otherwise commonplace words, which it would require in others a lo
rangue to express."[23] Randolph utilized every weapon in the rhetor
arsenal: taunting wit, black humor, foul invective, brilliant metapho
erary imagery, historical allusions, pungent sarcasm, and debilitatii
rision. "For cool, yet cutting sarcasm, severity of retort, quickness of
the play of fancy, and coruscation of wit," one wrote, "he has scarcel
perior."[24] Eyes blazing, voice piping, Randolph was James 3:6 incarnate
the tongue is a fire, a world of iniquity."

Pain was a constant. "I can no longer *do*," he wrote, "I can only *suffer.*
He endured waves of nausea, blinding headaches, and chronic diarrhea that
made him "wish myself with the devil."[26] He suffered from ailments in his
lungs, kidneys, liver, stomach, and intestines. His body shook with spasms
in his legs, arms, and chest. He complained of lumbago, angina, sciatica,
rheumatism, and "pains almost endless."[27] He was laid low with scarlet fever
and yellow fever. He probably was impotent. He would go for days with insomnia, in turn begetting a paralyzing fatigue. "I have not only descended
from the dignity of human nature," he wrote, "but of animal life and barely
vegetable."[28] He treated himself with calomel, magnesia, and "Swain's quack
medicine," before turning to laudanum, mercury, and morphine.[29] Preemi-
nent among all remedies was the "blue pill"—opium—to which Randolph
turned when "seized with the torments of the damned."[30]

Such exaggerated personality traits prompted questions about his sanity.
Randolph suffered from severe bouts of melancholy, aggravated by his literal
isolation at Roanoke and his figurative isolation in Washington. His emotions grew brittle, spawning forlornness so intense that he wept.[31] To him
were accorded "dark days, when the evil genius predominated" and contrasting days when "no one ever knew better how . . . to evince, in countenance and manner, gentler benevolence of heart."[32] Those around him either
politely lamented his occasional "unhappy state of mind," harshly dismissed
him as "partially deranged and seldom in full possession of his reason,"
or chuckled over the irony that he owned a homestead called "Bizarre."[33]
Whether his fits were drug induced, alcohol related, or signs of bipolar disorder is not known. A cousin's words offer both explanation and conclusion:
Randolph was "a man endowed with two souls."[34]

Modern shorthand might label Randolph a conservative, but he was not an ideologue. The principles he articulated were those of the American Revolution, the agricultural interests he represented, the precedential direction of law, and the traditional values of his fellow Virginians. He was no democrat, believing in limited suffrage lodged firmly in a landed gentry. He was not a nationalist, but the strictest of states' rights advocates. He was a champion of individual liberty, though not of the natural rights espoused by Locke, nor extending to the slaves he held as property. He had a lifelong distrust of centralized power, hence his opposition to entanglements abroad and spendthrift government at home. He was a mix of realist and purist, disdainful of cant, yet displaying a consistency that led Henry Adams to call him "the truest and ablest Republican in Congress, the representative of power and principle . . . a sort of Virginian Saint Michael . . . terrible in his contempt for whatever seemed to him base or untrue."[35]

Such consistency wrought inconsistent relevance during his day. Following his success as Jefferson's legislative leader, Randolph was often a force with which to contend, but, just as often, a force easily overcome. Defeat was his frequent companion as the nation expanded, traditions were eclipsed, and democracy supplanted republicanism. His lot was primarily defensive in a profession where success is judged by initiatives passed, monies appropriated, and laws written. Not even his consistent electoral success can be attributed solely to his principled stands. In Randolph's Virginia, personality, relationships, and family name were often the decisive factors among voters.[36] The roster of public policies enacted over his opposition embraces the early history of the nation: Jefferson's embargo, the declaration of war in 1812, the Bank of the United States, and the Missouri Compromise. "Randolph's party," a contemporary noted, "sings very small this session."[37]

Yet his standing did not prompt opponents to lightly dismiss him or friends to entirely desert him. He commanded attention by passionate advocacy and parliamentary maneuvers. He was both spark of conscience and bane of existence. And while his influence waxed and waned during his life, it grew as years passed. "Like Hamilton," Adam Tate wrote, "Randolph would live on after death in the influence he had on American politics. Hamilton's stamp on the nation was grand and institutional. Randolph's negative and ideological."[38] Thornton Miller classified Randolph's speeches with the "legacy of [Patrick] Henry, the Virginia Resolution of 1798," and the essays of Judge Spencer Roane and John Taylor of Caroline, as creating the

"Virginia Doctrine" that dominated the state's political, judicial, and philosophical life during the nineteenth century.[39] Russell Kirk went a step beyond Miller, judging Randolph no less than "a genius, the prophet of Southern nationalism, and the architect of Southern conservatism."[40] Though Randolph lost many political battles, his is the name that resonates through the ages, while those of many of his victorious opponents have faded into insignificance. Even today, a group of "paleoconservatives" gather annually under the banner of "The John Randolph Club."

One is prompted to ask how such enduring appeal corresponds with such erratic contemporary relevance. The answer lies in Randolph's most famous declaration: "I am an aristocrat. I love liberty, I hate equality."[41]

The aristocracy to which Randolph referred was not a hereditary one based on birth or wealth. It was an aristocracy of cultured and civilized citizens who respected tradition, defended established institutions, and adhered to duty.[42] It was an aristocracy symbolized on the Great Seal of Virginia by the Roman goddess Virtus, a sword in one hand, a spear in the other, with one foot on the dead body of Tyranny. The virtue represented on the seal is the Latin translation of the Greek word *arête*, a word that expressed those characteristics of the self-determinative and self-reliant citizen.[43] Thus it was civic virtue—not equality—that defeated tyranny. Civic virtue required a rejection of the Lockean notion that all men were created equal in favor of the language of the Virginia Declaration of Rights, which declared that all men were "created equally free and independent." By stressing the equality of freedom and the necessity of civic virtue, Randolph sought to prevent what Russell Kirk described as "the only state of life in which anything resembling equality of condition actually prevails: savagery."[44] Randolph believed, as Spencer Roane wrote, that tyranny was the result of uniformity.

Rejection of abstract equality, however, was not sufficient in itself. To Randolph every political issue touched on the nature of the human soul. That soul, he believed, best flourished in a state of liberty. Therefore he viewed his role as liberty's advocate. Year after year, in spite of political trends or transient opportunities, Randolph sought to serve but one client: liberty. He sought to save that client by all means and expedients, and at all hazards and costs. He regarded not the alarm, the torments, or the destruction. That he did so reckless of the consequences, though it often involved his country in confusion, is the reason many contemporaries dismissed of the best lands along the James, Appomattox, Staunton, and Roanoke rivers.[6] From these holdings would emerge the estates central in the life of John Randolph: Matoax, where he would spend his youth; Bizarre, where he came of age; and Roanoke, the name he linked to his own.

Little is known of John Randolph Sr. He was a gentleman planter and happily married to Frances Bland, the daughter of another prestigious Virginia family.[7] The couple had two sons before the birth of John: Richard, born March 9, 1770, and Theodorick, born January 22, 1771.[8] The family settled at Matoax and led the life their pedigree predestined. At the outbreak of the American Revolution, John Randolph Sr. took a patriot stand. He sold forty slaves to buy powder to resupply the Williamsburg magazine pillaged by the British, and he scouted routes to a frontier outpost near Canada. His community standing would have cast him in a leadership role in the coming revolution, but Randolph was denied the opportunity to add luster to the family name. He died of unknown causes at the age of thirty-three on October 28, 1775.[9] Two-year-old John, "too young to be sensible of my loss," would know his father only through anecdote.[10] John Randolph Sr. did take one action that served as a harbinger to the life of his namesake son. He expanded the family motto to include the words *Fari quae sentias.* "Speak what you think."[11]

Frances Bland Randolph found herself a twenty-three-year-old widow with means. Her husband's will granted her a life interest in the Matoax estate, twenty-four slaves, house servants, and livestock.[12] The 40,000 acres at Matoax, Bizarre, and Roanoke were divided between Richard, Theodorick, and John. Additionally, the will provided that the Randolph boys "be educated in the best manner without regard to expense . . . even to the last shilling."[13] Thus the family was as well situated as circumstances could expect. Frances was young, "the object of general admiration and pursuit," and reasonably could expect not to remain long in "unhappy widowhood."[14]

John Randolph's "earliest and tenderest recollections" were associated with his birthplace, Cawsons. The home of his grandfather, Theodorick Bland, Cawsons was a "noble mansion" and "the seat of plenty and cheerfulness."[15] Here young "Jack" found himself the family favorite—the "pin basket of the whole house"—and grew into a "talkative" boy with a "mercurial temperament." Family lore recounts that the four-year-old Randolph "swooned away in a fit of passion" and was restored "with difficulty."[16] He also displayed the first of many life-long physical ailments: a thin, fine-textured skin. As he described it, "There is no accounting for difference of skins in different animals, human or brute. Mine I believe to be more tender than many infants of a month old. Indeed I have remarked in myself from my earliest recollection a delicacy or effeminacy of complexion but for a spice of the devil in my temper would have consigned me to the distaff or the needle."[17]

"Jack Randle"—as the local farmers dubbed him—was a precocious lad with a "fondness for athletic sports" who delighted in the "noble trees and beautiful shrubs" of Matoax. The woods were places of adventure where he set traps and "felt my heart beat as I approached with anxiety for the fate of my adventure." There were silent groves, places of solitude, where he would "ruminate, chewing the cud of sweet and bitter fancies."[18] He took note of the surrounding countryside "inhabited by a race of planters of English descent," their "spacious and costly" mansions, and the "taste and elegance" of society. "[B]etter-bred men," he wrote, "were not to be found in the British dominions."[19]

This parochial life was flavored with a dash of the international when William Randolph's ships departed for England, carrying the bounty of his estates. "The departure of a London trader," Randolph recalled, "was an affair of no small consequence to the community." The entire household—family and slaves—would place their orders and then eagerly await "the joyful signal of [the ships' return] in James River." That momentous occasion, he remembered, "was celebrated as a jubilee."[20] "I would prefer dwelling in the mansion where I had passed my infancy," Randolph later wrote, "to the possession of a palace."[21]

It is difficult to precisely limn the young Randolph. Contemporary accounts are few, and Randolph's recollections are often colored by illness and bitterness or nostalgia and wistfulness. Biographers have complicated the process. Henry Adams, repaying in spades the wrath heaped by Randolph upon both presidents Adams, wrote that Randolph was as "perverse in childhood as in manhood."[22] Sympathetic biographers tend to anticipate the adult in the child, creating a Randolph of Roanoke in miniature. These baseless portrayals leave Randolph's youth cloaked in anecdote. What can be accurately discerned in the historical twilight are the forces of culture, society, and tradition that impacted the young man.

Matoax—indeed all the land holdings—was such an influence. The land was central to the Randolph family's status and authority. The land produced the tobacco, wheat, and other crops that formed the basis of wealth.

The land established the great estates and utilized the slave labor that sustained the family's power. The land nurtured the landed gentry, which the Randolphs believed preserved the Commonwealth of Virginia.[23] The land instilled in its owners a genteel sense of self-veneration, balanced with knowledge of their vulnerability to natural elements. The land was permanent; all else was transitory. Riding through the fields at Roanoke in 1781, Frances told her eight-year-old son: "Johnny, all this land belongs to you and your brother Theodorick. It is your father's inheritance. When you get to be a man you must not sell your land. It is the first step to ruin for a boy to part with his father's home. . . . Keep your land and your land will keep you."[24] The lesson took. Randolph would later write that he would not "exchange the feeling of independence that warms me as I range the hills and plains for all in the gift of the President or the People."[25]

"My mother once expressed a wish to me," Randolph wrote, "that I might one day or other be as great a speaker as Jerman Baker or Edmund Randolph. That gave a bent to my disposition."[26] The wishes of Frances Randolph always gave her son's inclinations a decisive "bent." "I never met with any human being," he wrote, "that inspired such strong emotion of reverence and admiration."[27] It was perhaps natural that the widowed mother and youngest son would form a particularly close bond. Randolph "shared [his] mother's widowed bed and was the nestling of her bosom." She alone seemed able to calm his volatile temperament.[28] Together they read the moralistic tales of William Hogarth and *The Expedition of Humphry Clinker*.[29] Frances taught Randolph to dance, "relish Shakespeare," and adhere to religious practices. "Every night after I was undressed and in the morning before I rose," he remembered, "I kneeled down in the bed, putting up my little hands, repeated after my mother the Lord's Prayer and 'The Belief.'"[30] Noticeably, there is no account of serious discipline being meted out by the "eminently cheerful" mother.

Frances aspired for her son "to be something more than a mere country squire" and cultivated the connections necessary to achieve that goal. "After a day of unremitting household drudgery," Randolph recalled, Frances would "order her carriage and spend half the night at assembly in the neighboring market town."[31] She kept a close watch on the family's finances, maintaining "clear accounts and money (not a small sum) in hand."[32] Years later, Randolph would call his mother "the best judge of character that I ever met with."[33] Frances held together the family during three years of widowhood, earning the lifelong respect of her son. To her he owed "all that is valuable" in "mind and character." Pathos and truth mingled in his comment that "only one human being ever knew me. *She* only knew me."[34]

Randolph's instruction also included the code of conduct expected of his station. "Place us where you will," he wrote in 1806, "along with our rights there must coexist correlative duties—and the more exalted the station, the more arduous are these last."[35] The primary duty was to possess "the character of the *real* gentleman." Such character "consists not of plate and equipage and rich living . . . but in *truth,* courtesy, bravery, generosity, and learning."[36] Life "was not given us to be spent in dreams and reverie, but for active useful exertion."[37] Such effort was necessary not only to honor family tradition but also to maintain it through generations. "Men are like nations," Randolph wrote in 1821. "One founds a family, the other an empire—both destined, sooner or later, to decay. This is the way in which ability manifests itself. . . . I have no quarrel with such as are content with their original obscurity . . . but I cannot respect them. He who contentedly eats the bread of idleness and dependence is beneath contempt."[38]

By Randolph's fifth birthday, in June 1778, the conversations among the adults centered on the trials of Washington's army and the promise of independence so recently declared. Anxious days were the lot of adults; Randolph's days were those of a carefree boy. He tussled with his brother Theodorick over the fate of a kitten and endured being "inoculated with [his] whole family." He demonstrated a flair for the dramatic by impersonating characters in a game called "Ladies and Gentlemen."[39] He continued to delight in the hunting, fishing, and trapping in the fields and streams of Matoax, merrily singing ballads taught to him by a "mullato servant girl."[40]

Suddenly, Randolph's salad days ended. On September 23, 1778, Frances Randolph married St. George Tucker. "From that day," Randolph wrote, "there was a change in my situation."[41]

St. George Tucker was born in the British colony of Bermuda on July 10, 1752, and immigrated to Virginia in 1770. He studied law at the College of William & Mary, was admitted to the bar in 1775, and established his practice in Williamsburg. At the outbreak of the American Revolution, Tucker ran arms through the British blockade. He distinguished himself as a colonel in the Chesterfield militia and with service at Guilford Courthouse and the siege at Yorktown. He was appointed a judge of the General Court of Virginia, beginning a tenure on the bench that included service on the Virginia Court of Appeals from 1804 to 1811 and as United States district judge for Virginia from 1813 to 1827. He succeeded George Wythe as professor of law at William & Mary and served with James Madison and Edmund Randolph as Virginia commissioners to the Annapolis Convention. In 1803, he published a five-volume study of Blackstone's *Commentaries*, the first major treatise on American law, and "View of the Constitution of the United States," the first extended commentary on the newly ratified constitution.[42] These achievements, however, lay in his future when he first noticed Frances Randolph. She was twenty-five and "the most beautiful, sprightly, and attractive woman of her age."[43] Tucker abandoned a self-imposed vow "never to marry a widow" and initiated a courtship that swept to marriage.[44] There was to be a new master at Matoax, and the precocious and temperamental Randolph had acquired a stepfather.

If Randolph is believed, "the first blow [he] ever received" was from Tucker's hand. The traumatic event occurred "as soon as the festivities of the wedding had ceased," and the slap heralded the arrival of a "most intolerable tyranny."[45] Tucker's "austere rule" was characterized by "the sneer of skepticism . . . habitual profanity . . . [and] infidel books."[46] The Randolph brothers found themselves confined to their bedrooms "even early in the Forenoon . . . [and] dared not appear at a window unless by stealth." Vigorous protests were offered, but the boys "found the folly of offering them and submitted in silence." Randolph concluded that the dashing attorney-privateer possessed an unsurpassed ability "for making everybody and everything around him unhappy."[47]

Or so the adult John Randolph recalled. Contemporary evidence suggests that he and his stepfather had a cordial, often affectionate, relationship. In letters dating from his youth to his early years in Congress, Randolph repeatedly expressed the "liveliest affection" for Tucker. "My much beloved Father," he wrote at the age of twenty-three, "let me once more express my undiminished respect and affectionate esteem for you, who has proven the unaltered friend of my infancy; who has watched over my youth; and to whose more than paternal care and tenderncy [sic] I owe every acquisition I enjoy." He sought Tucker's views on politics, law, and finances, and professed that he "ever gloried in addressing you by the venerable name of father and friend."[48]

The break between the two men apparently concerned Tucker's management of the estate of John Randolph Sr.[49] Regardless of whether there was any substance to the alleged mismanagement, Randolph began in 1810 to recall more "harshness and severity" than "pride and delight" in his

relationship with Tucker. Therefore it is difficult to determine the exact nature of their relationship during the years they shared at Matoax. What is
beyond the vagaries of memory is that in 1778 the future judge began to impose discipline on boys unaccustomed to such treatment, and Randolph responded by "(acquiring) a temper not to brook tamely [his] unreasonable
exactions."[50] Conflict between the two strong personalities perhaps was inevitable.

In one of his earliest letters, Randolph thanks his stepfather for a book
and pleads "we want a tutor very much."[51] The spirited, precocious boy was
developing into an ardent student. At the age of ten, he "devoured" the
works of Orlando and followed that work with an impressive list of classics.

> One of the first books I ever read was Voltaire's *Charles XII;* about the
> same time, 1780–1, I read the *Spectator;* and used to steal away to the
> closet containing them. The letters from his correspondents were my fa-
> vorites. I read *Humphrey Clinker,* also; that is, Win's and Tabby's letters,
> with great delight, for I could spell, at that age, pretty correctly. Rey-
> nard, the fox, came next I think; then Tales of the Genii and Arabian
> Nights. This last, and Shakespeare were my idols. I had read them with
> *Don Quixote, Gil Blas,* Quintus Curtius, Plutarch, Pope's *Homer, Robin-
> son Crusoe, Gulliver, Tom Jones, Orlando Furioso,* and Thomson's *Sea-
> sons,* before I was eleven years of age; also, Goldsmith's Roman History,
> 2 vols. 8 vo., and an old history of Braddock's war.[52]

The days at Matoax were filled with "Shakespeare, and Milton, and Chaucer, and Spenser, and Plutarch," "Ovid's *Metamorphoses* . . . [and] Pope's
Rape," and "Addison, Young, Thomson, Gay, Goldsmith, Gray, Collins, Sheridan, Cowper, Byron, [and] Aesop."[53] Randolph later would disparage his education as "unfit for the performance of my functions as a citizen," but his
youthful reading supplied him with a seemingly quenchless reserve of literary allusions, scathing ripostes, and sparkling analogies which he employed
throughout his career.[54] A bookstore owner noticed Randolph browsing the
stacks and observed what immersion in the classics had wrought. He saw a
boy "animated and flushed with the brightest beams of intellect."[55]

"On the 6th day of July, in the year sixty-five," went the lyrics of a favorite
song of the seven-year-old Randolph, "at two in the evening, did our forces
arrive; When the French and the Indians in ambush did lay, and there was
great slaughter of our forces that day."[56] The ballad that captured Randolph's

fancy was about the defeat of British General William Braddock during the French and Indian War. In January 1781, residents of central Virginia rightly wondered if they were about to witness another such slaughter. Benedict Arnold—patriot turned traitor turned British general—sailed up the James River, seized Richmond, and destroyed munitions and grain intended for the Continental Army. He then turned south toward Petersburg. Matoax lay directly in his path. St. George Tucker sent urgent word to Frances to flee to the west. Frances received the news in bed, where she had five days earlier given birth to a son, her second child by Tucker.[57] In her weakened condition, she nevertheless organized the removal of the family and as many personal effects as possible. "I always thought that women possess more passive courage than we [men] do," Randolph would write. "I have seen instances of it in my . . . mother, during the last war, that were heroic."[58] A flurry of activity swirled around Randolph as valuables were thrown in trunks, wagons loaded, and children and slaves gathered together. In the midst of the hurried preparation, he saw his mother stuffing "my deceased father's most valuable papers into a pillow case." He watched as his mother put a "steel hilted dagger" into her stays. Their eyes met. "My son," Frances said, "your mother shall never be insulted."[59] Randolph was swept up and placed on a horse for the escape west. The destination was Bizarre.

Overlooking the Appomattox River, Bizarre was a handsome frame structure "with two brick chimneys and two rooms and four rooms without for servants" situated on an eighteen-hundred-acre estate producing May wheat and tobacco. The prosperous plantation would grow to include a "smoke-house, ice-house, pigeon-house, veal-house, and wood-house" and would be for years an aristocratic outpost in this sparsely settled region of Virginia.[60] Subsequent events in Randolph's life would make the estate's name seem prophetic, but on this winter's night in 1781, Bizarre was a welcome sight to Frances Tucker and her household. Tucker joined his family en route and supervised their settlement at Bizarre. He departed as quickly as he arrived, leaving with hurried goodbyes to join Lafayette's command outside of Richmond. For Randolph, the flight from Arnold was a defining event in his life. He had been a part of history. He had faced the real alternatives of liberty or death. He had been a part—no matter how small—of the revolutionary effort. "The impression," he later said, "is indelible on my memory."[61] From that evening forward, the American Revolution marked him, and its principles became his lodestar. Opinionated views soon followed. "I think you are a very fine officer," he wrote Tucker, "and will be able to make the militia fight, for if they do not now I don't think they ever will be collected after running away."[62]

During his sojourn at Bizarre, Randolph made the thirty-mile trip south and saw for the first time the "savage solitude" of Roanoke. The eight thousand acres of meadows and pastures displayed "[e]very variety of tint from the deepest green to the brightest gold and scarlet and the most sober russet."[63] Randolph rode across the fields and streams, becoming so accomplished a rider that locals commented he had been foaled, not born.[64] It was here that Frances admonished her son to "keep your land." As colonial and British forces clashed across Virginia and the Carolinas, the land kept Frances and her boys.

St. George Tucker suffered a bayonet wound during the fighting around Guilford Court House, North Carolina, in March 1781. Recovering quickly, he was promoted to the rank of lieutenant colonel and distinguished himself at Yorktown. The war did not completely divert his attention. He was troubled by his wife's report that the boys "are grown quit idle and troublesome," and by his own fear that they were being spoiled under their mother's easy hand.[65] Accordingly, Tucker directed that the boys be enrolled in Walker Maury's Grammar School. The school served as a preparatory school for William & Mary, with a curriculum focused on instruction in Latin, Greek, and English, and "bore the reputation of being one of the best in the South."[66] The headmaster, Walker Maury, attended college with Tucker, and shared with him an aptitude for applying discipline to unruly boys. He would be a teacher, Tucker wrote, "equally directed to improve their morals and their understandings as their manners."[67]

The Randolph boys, Maury reported to Tucker, "are orderly and governable, and possess good capacities and are assisted by as much, or perhaps more, application than is common in boys of their age." He wrote that the boys were in "a perfect state of health" and "that the mountain air has had a happy affect on little Jack's constitution." Maury concluded the satisfactory report with the comment that he was "much attached" to the boys.[68]

Again, Randolph's recollections differ. His complaints form a bill of indictment that omits no element of discontent. The school house was "sordid [and] squalid." His schoolmates, "with the exception of one or two gentlemen's sons," were "vulgar, brutal, savage" and "lost no opportunity to do us an ill turn." The curriculum offered no maps of Virginia, no "chronological tables," and only "as much Latin as sufficient to furnish out a bold translation of the ordinary school books." Randolph reserved his most contemptuous invective for the school master. Walker Maury was "the most petulant and malignant wretch in creation," "the most peevish and ill-tempered of pedagogues," who "tyrannized and tortured" his students by "cruel punishment . . . unattended by any the slightest good." So complete was his revulsion at every level with Maury and his school that Randolph, his vituperative censure spent, cursed the very ground. "The red mud," he spat out, "I to this day remember." At Maury's school, he wrote, "my very heart died within me."[69]

Randolph's accounts of his school days, one writer aptly concluded, "read like Dickens."[70] The disciplinary tactics associated with the pedagogy of the day might have justified Randolph's scathing recollections, but no contemporary evidence exists to support his characterization of his classmates or curriculum. Most likely, his extensive reading placed him ahead of the other students, thus breeding an intellectual boredom that spawned contempt. One comment offers insight. "You may judge what I was made to endure," Randolph wrote after listing his criticisms, characterizing himself, almost as an afterthought, "the most thin-skinned sensitive little creature in the universe."[71] Randolph's reaction to Maury—as with that to Tucker—may have been shaped as much by his thin-skinned temperament as by any action of the stern taskmaster.

In the winter of 1783, Maury moved his school to Williamsburg, Virginia. Randolph hoped to be granted a reprieve based on this shift in locale, but he and his brothers made the move as well. The school was located "in the old capitol . . . where Henry spoke and Independence was declared" and consisted of more than a hundred students divided into four classes.[72] Randolph was now being "flogged regularly" but continued to shine academically.[73] He mastered Greek and committed the "Westminster grammar to memory" while walking around "the base of Lord Bottetourt's statue." During his first term in Williamsburg, Randolph met "a shy boy" with "spiral white locks" named Littleton Waller Tazewell with whom he began a lifelong friendship. The two boys established a bond as they worked through "Sallust and Virgil . . . Greek and French languages and the elements of Geometry."[74] Randolph altered the description of Helena and Hermia in *A Midsummer Night's Dream* to describe the two friends: "Both on one bench without a cushion / Both reading of one lesson / Both in one Sallust—Both in one key."[75]

Randolph's long-hoped-for relief from the "tyranny, hardly bearable of

Maury" came at last in early 1784 when he departed for Bermuda to visit the extended Tucker family. The origin of this trip is unclear. Randolph wrote that "the state of my health induced my mother" to send him south, there to be joined by the complete family "twelve months later." The trip might also have been an attempt to counter the youth's emerging rebellious nature. By this time, he had "acquired a temper not to brook tamely [Tucker's or Maury's] unreasonable exactions."[76] Whatever the motivation for the trip, Randolph received the news with joy. He exchanged Sallusts with Littleton Tazewell and fled Maury's school. He arrived in Bermuda in July 1784.

Randolph's recollections of his months in Bermuda are conspicuously positive. He stayed at "old Mr. Tucker's house"—the residence of Colonel Henry Tucker, father of St. George Tucker—and delighted in the "good country gentleman's library." To his already impressive reading list, he added works of Chatterton, Rowley, Young, and Gay.[77] He found his tutor, Mr. Ewing, to be "a very worthy man" with "great abilities." Randolph's sole complaint was that Ewing offered "no Greek class and would not take the trouble of teaching a single boy."[78] He was treated with "innumerable kindnesses" by family and friends "too numerous to particularize," and spent "hours every day in swimming." He often "sat for half a day on a cliff watching the rutted face of the Atlantic or the coming storm." He likened his sentiments to those of a poet. "In all Lord Byron's descriptions of the ocean," he wrote, "I recognize my own feelings." Randolph's sixteen months in Bermuda was a blissful time "of essential service to me in many respects."[79]

Upon his return from Bermuda, and approaching his thirteenth birthday, Randolph was enrolled again in Maury's school. There he renewed the erratic theme of academic distinction marked by undisciplined conduct. He wrote his mother that he had "left off Latin and devoted myself entirely to Greek and French," had finished Virgil, and eagerly awaited "the long expected time . . . when I shall begin Horace."[80] This scholastic talent contrasted with an inability to endure even the slightest offense. He engaged in a "violent quarrel" with classmates about "whether I should burn a candle in my room or not." He and Theodorick took a disliking to the dorm steward, precipitating several altercations. Maury responded with "cruel and infamous treatment."[81] The breakdown of this increasingly untenable situation came in late 1786 when the boys left Maury's school under unexplained circumstances.

Randolph enjoyed a few months at home, but in March 1787 he and Theodorick found themselves bound for Princeton. No explanation of this selection has survived, but Princeton's reputation for theological broad-mindedness and tolerance of religious dissent mirrored Tucker's personal beliefs. The boys were placed in the grammar school "although we were further advanced than any of the Freshmen and most of the Sophomores."[82] That complaint aside, Randolph was initially pleased with Princeton. "I like Dr. Witherspoon better than any old Gentleman I ever saw," he wrote of John Witherspoon, president of Princeton and signer of the Declaration of Independence. "He is more like a father to us than a master."[83] His contentment increased when Richard Randolph joined his brothers during the summer. The surroundings may have satisfied, but Randolph believed he was "ten times a better scholar than the master," and began to view the school as a "subterranean abode of noise and misrule."[84] He participated in an elocution contest and was "conscious of my superiority over my competitors in delivery" and "despised the award and the umpires in the bottom of my heart." The grammar school, he noted, provided him with habits "by no means propitious to study."[85] His complaints achieved the desired effect. In September 1787, after just six months in the grammar school, Randolph was transferred to Princeton College.

"When we get into college," fourteen-year-old Randolph wrote Tucker, "I shall study very hard, not only to be the best scholar in the class, but to give you and Mama all the pleasure in my power." Parental approval was not his sole motivation. "[Our] class was examined," he wrote to his mother, "and I obtained a premium for which I expect the watch you promised me."[86] This letter reached Frances late in her eighth pregnancy. In December, Tucker advised Randolph of the glad tiding that Frances had given birth to a girl. The letter also contained a somewhat ominous directive. "Do not leave Princeton," Tucker wrote, "till you hear from me again."[87] Ignoring that request, Randolph headed to New York, where he and Theodorick planned to "spend the little money we had hoarded for that purpose." While there, the boys received another letter. It was a summons from Frances to come "to her dying bedside." On January 1, 1788, the boys set out for Virginia.[88]

Randolph knew nothing of his mother's illness, but must have realized the physical toll Frances had endured in bearing eight children in eighteen years. He could do nothing as he was jostled mile after mile but pray for the woman who "knew the delicacy of his frame, the tenderness of his heart, the irritability of his temper."[89] He and his brothers arrived at their mother's bedside on January 8, 1788. The attending physician's prescription of brandy and hot water "in which had been boiled rosemary or some other aromatic herb" conceded the hopelessness of the cause.[90] The death struggle lasted ten more days.[91] On January 18, 1788, Frances died at the age of thirty-six. Randolph was devastated. It seemed, he wrote, "unnatural and shocking" that the "sun rose and set [and] the order of nature went on."[92] Frances was buried at Matoax beside the grave of John Randolph Sr. Her epitaph aptly captured Randolph's sentiments: "When shall we cease to mourn for Frances Bland Tucker?"[93]

Randolph spent four mournful months wandering among neighboring estates along the Appomattox and visiting Littleton Tazewell in Williamsburg.[94] "I would be very glad my Dear Papa," he wrote to Tucker during these aimless days, "if you would . . . let me know to where I am to go. . . . I must confess to you that I do not think Princeton is the place."[95] He had been "shut up in the Grammar school [for six months] without being allowed to learn anything and almost deafened with noise." Tucker proposed that Randolph enroll at Columbia College in New York, likely due to the fact that Randolph's uncles, Thomas Tudor Tucker and Theodorick Bland, resided there and might be able to monitor the unruly youth.[96] Joining Randolph would be Theodorick and a slave named Syphax. "All I know of [Columbia]," Randolph tepidly replied, "is that their classes are the same as those in Princeton."[97] His attitude improved when he learned that Richard would join his brothers after attending the Virginia Ratification Convention. Richard was nineteen and, as Randolph ever remembered him, "the most manly youth and most elegant gentleman I ever saw . . . regular, studious, above low company of any sort."[98] Randolph's devotion was admirable, but misplaced. Richard possessed "passions which [he] had never resolution to govern or resist."[99] He had wandered from William & Mary, to Princeton, and now to Columbia without obtaining a degree, squandering his tuition money along the way. To add further distraction, he had fallen in love with a distant cousin, seventeen-year-old Judith Randolph. At Columbia, Richard's mind would not be on studies. Under these less-than-auspicious circumstances, Randolph's education continued its erratic course.

New York in June 1788 swirled with political activity. Nine of the thirteen states had ratified the proposed Constitution of the United States. This was a sufficient number for the compact to go into effect, but New York and Virginia—the two largest and most critical states to the fledgling union—had yet to ratify. Rumors and debate filled New York City as the deliberations of the two state conventions stretched from spring into summer. In Virginia, Patrick Henry opposed ratification, denouncing the "specious imaginary balances, [the] rope-dancing, chain-rattling ridiculous ideal checks and contrivances." In New York, Alexander Hamilton supported ratification, touting the "strength and stability in the organization of our government and vigor in its operations."[100] Randolph was an eager and engaged observer. "The words *party, Tory, anti* and *federalist*," he wrote, "compose the greatest part of the conversation of this place." His agrarian heritage led him to embrace Antifederalist arguments that the proposed Constitution was too radical a change in customary political forms, a means for an all-powerful central government, and detrimental to local institutions, beliefs, and practices. As Randolph's later career would confirm, he was "an antifederalist when hardly breeched."[101]

Virginia ratified the Constitution on June 25, 1788. New York followed on July 26. The new government was established and would sit in New York City. Though opposed to ratification, Randolph joined in "a very grand procession . . . down Broadway thro' Wall Street . . . to the Federal Green." There, he and more than five thousand people dined on two roasted oxen. "[It] put me in mind," Randolph wrote, "of the great preparations which were made in Don Quixote for the wedding of Camacho." He noted that "there was not a single Drunken Man or fight to be seen." The festivities were capped off when "a party of *Federalists,* as they call themselves . . . went to the Governor's where they gave three hisses and beat the rogue's march around the house."[102]

"[B]urning with the thirst of knowledge," Randolph "set seriously to work" at Columbia, reading Livy, Xenophon, Cicero's *De Officiis,* and Demosthenes' *Orations.*[103] He found algebra "very dry," reported that he "mastered the Eaton grammar," and participated in oral examinations. "Brother T and myself are to mount the Rostrum," he wrote to Tucker, "but I believe my speech will be a little longer than that of a student at Edinburgh who, being forced to speak, told the audience '*Vir sapit qui pauca loquition.*'"[104] He was "constantly reading" and wrote that he never went to bed before midnight. Among the faculty, Randolph particularly admired Cochrane, a humanities professor whom he judged "a most accomplished scholar." He wrote that he "amazed" his teacher with "the rapidity of my progress." When Cochrane accepted a position at the College of Nova Scotia, Randolph called his resignation "next to the loss of my mother and my being sent to Walker Maury's school . . . the greatest misfortune of my life."[105] Cochrane's departure seemed to generate renewed discontent. "I am very anxious to go Home, never to return," Randolph wrote to Tucker. "I believe my dear sir, that a class is the greatest drawback in the world. You must do everything which the class does and nothing else."[106]

This latest manifestation of Randolph's "violent distaste for formal schooling" indicates that his reactions to Princeton and Maury's School went beyond mere dislike of locale, curriculum, or professors. Possessed of a vigorous intellect, Randolph did not find stimulation in colonial colleges.[107] "I think I could read more to a better purpose in my own room," he wrote to Tucker, "than to sit an hour to hear my classmates." Ten days after writing this letter, he sounded a similar complaint. "Here I have no one to whom I can make observations on the authors I am reading," he wrote, "and who may instruct me in any particulars." Tucker was not moved. Randolph stayed put, but petulantly turned to reading "only the trash of the circulating library."[108]

Lack of academic stimulation, though, may have been only part of the reason for Randolph's attitude. Shortly after his arrival at Columbia, he received a letter from Tucker laying out unpleasant facts about the status of his late father's estate. John Randolph Sr. had endorsed notes of one of his brothers to English creditors. The brother defaulted, interest accrued, and soon all Randolph property had been mortgaged.[109] "There now seems to be a moral certainty," Tucker wrote, "that your patrimony will all go to satisfy . . . debt from your Papa." The consequences of such an action, he continued, "must be obvious to you—your sole dependence must be on your own personal abilities and exertions."[110] Randolph's already pronounced sensitivity regarding financial matters worsened as he processed the news contained in Tucker's letter. He wrote that his expenses "have been enormous and by far greater than our estate . . . can bear." He hoped to be able to "shun the rock of prodigality" and not be reduced "to poverty . . . to despair and all the horrors attending it." Tucker's financial decision, however, rendered his supplies "so scanty . . . that [he] became necessitous [and] of course unhappy." Physical ailments followed shortly, accompanied by "great uneasiness," and fear of being robbed of what little he had.[111] Lack of money, discontentment with school, and actual or perceived ailments formed a toxic combination with Randolph's volatile temperament. He summed up his condition to a friend: "Sovereign is misery."[112]

His brothers were no help. Richard left Columbia to pursue Judith. Theodorick, "undistinguished and somewhat slow-thinking, boisterous and rowdy, largely unmanageable," became the source of another problem.[113] He was "devoted to pleasure and fun" and "of all things in the world, he detested most a book." The Randolph apartment took on the atmosphere of a fraternity house. "Often have they forced the door of my study," Randolph wrote, "and tossed the books over the floor; sometimes out of the window."[114] Initially protesting, Randolph found himself falling "into the habits and way of life of [his] unfortunate brother." Their reputation spread. "You have been told things," Randolph wrote Tucker, "to the prejudice of Brother T and myself which are as false as those who told you them."[115] In what must have been a particularly stinging rebuke, Tucker wrote that Randolph would not be conducting himself in such fashion if his mother were alive. He warned the boys to "[c]heck every emotion of passion or disgust and avoid every possible subject of altercation or disagreement."[116] Randolph promised "to act up to the advice," but in subsequent letters he twice defended himself against charges of laziness, denied a report of Theodorick's intoxication, and threatened that he might become "a votary of the Billiard Table and the Faro Bank."[117] Explanations of incidents were often accompanied by contrite admissions. "I did not keep that check on my tongue which is so necessary to preserve," he wrote in explaining one altercation. "I have observed that Petulance of Temper of which you speak and endeavor to break myself of it."[118] Still the antics continued. When not carousing with Theodorick, Randolph was skating on a "flooded Manhattan meadow" or visiting "a thousand different places." He wrote a friend that he was "jaded with riding" and had developed a "very great tremor in my hands occasioned by too violent exercise."[119] Soon began the familiar chant to leave Columbia. "I am here under no control," he wrote to Tucker, "and can follow any inclination I chose without the least curb on my actions."[120] The request was denied.

Randolph found respite in political activity. He frequently dined with many members of the new Congress. Some brought news of home. "The last thing that I heard of you," Randolph wrote to Tucker, "was from Mr. [James] Madison who told me that he saw you fifteen days before his departure."[121] Randolph was in the gallery—"when I ought to have been at school"—when the first session of the first United States Congress convened on April 8, 1789. He "spent every day . . . attending its sittings" listening to the debates between Ames and Madison.[122] On April 30, he witnessed "the coronation (such in fact it was)" as George Washington was inaugurated first president of the United States.[123] His letters were peppered with political commentary. "The Senate has become worse every day," he wrote in August 1789. "They want to have ten dollars a day and the Representatives six only . . . because the *Senate* represented the *Sovereignty of the People* and [the House] the *People themselves.* The fallacy of which assertion was soon discovered . . . [in that] the people were certainly more powerful than their servants."[124] He judged Senate opposition to "allowing the militia arms" as nothing more than their fear "that the citizens will stop their full career of tyranny and oppression."[125] Randolph would long remember those days watching the nascent government take form. "The Constitution," he later said, "was in its chrysalis state. I saw what Washington did not see; but two other men in Virginia saw—George Mason and Patrick Henry—the poison under its wings."[126]

Randolph's letters showed signs of future partisan bite in several rhetorical jabs he took at John Adams. The vice-president, he wrote in August 1789, was "continually filling the papers with encomiums on titles and other such nonsense."[127] The next month he disgustedly reported that "Mr. V.P. says no man can be a sensible man without understanding Latin or French." He was delighted when a senator challenged Adams's statement by asking "what he thought of General Washington."[128] Randolph's anti-Adams bias was supplemented when his brother "was spurned by the coachman of the vice-president for coming too near the arms blazoned on the scutcheon of the vice-regal carriage."[129] Whether this incident actually occurred, Randolph would need little motivation in future years to smite the administration of John Adams "hip and thigh."[130]

Unsuccessful at persuading Tucker to allow him to leave Columbia, Randolph altered his request and asked to study law under George Wythe. "I can attain a great more knowledge (and at much less expense) in Williamsburg than in New York," he argued, "nor would I quit William and Mary until I have made myself master of that profession which I am determined to pursue." Whether moved by Randolph's desire to follow in his profession, or simply worn down by persistent complaining, Tucker relented. Randolph came home to Virginia in spring 1790.[131] In addition, his wish to study law was granted—although not precisely as he requested. He would not study in Williamsburg under George Wythe, but in Philadelphia under his cousin, Edmund Randolph, the attorney general of the United States.

It was to be another new start in another new city for the seventeen-year-old Randolph. "Today a man is blest with honors, riches, and happiness," he wrote shortly before embarking on his legal studies; "tomorrow's sun beholds him o'erwhelmed with poverty, despair, and everlasting woe."[132] In such a mindset, John Randolph arrived in Philadelphia in September 1790.

2

Macbeth Hath Murdered Sleep

But none beheld with clearer eye
The plague-spot o'er her spreading
None heard more sure the steps of Doom
Along her future treading.

The honor of serving as the nation's first attorney general was diminished ever so slightly by its meager salary of nineteen hundred dollars. "With every frugality, almost bordering on meanness," Edmund Randolph fumed, "I cannot live upon it as it now stands."[1] Thus the attorney general took in three students: John Randolph, Lawrence Washington—the president's nephew—and Joseph Bryan. But official duties intruded on this private venture, and the attorney general could manage to instruct Randolph barely "once a fortnight." The curriculum was similarly irregular. "[Hume's *Treatise of Human Nature*] was the first [book] he put into my hands," Randolph wrote, "telling me that he . . . wished me to go through a course of metaphysical reasoning." Hume was followed by "Shakespeare . . . Beattie on Truth . . . Kames' *Elements of Criticism*, and . . . Gillies' *History of Greece*." Listing these titles on a book flyleaf, Randolph scrawled at the bottom *"Risum teneatis?"*—"can you restrain your laughter?"[2]

Before Randolph got to "the first book of Blackstone," this latest scholastic endeavor was spiraling in the direction of previous ventures. He struck up a friendship with Joseph Bryan, a "bluff, hearty, affectionate, choleric, vehement" boy, who apparently held legal studies in similarly low regard.[3] Before long, Randolph and Bryan had "abandoned a profession for which neither of us had been qualified by regular education, and commenced men of pleasure, plunging into the gayety that fills the mouth with blasphemy."[4]

Randolph's lifestyle in Philadelphia carried a high price tag. "I shall be obliged," he wrote Tucker in October 1790, "to expend more money this quarter than the next by a great deal . . . to fix myself comfortably."[5]

Randolph explained that the expenditures were necessary to purchase winter provisions, but, in fact, substantial debt was the cost driver. He would buy, on credit, "any bauble" that caught his fancy, only to immediately regret the purchase. "Many a nights' sleep has been broken by sad reflection," he wrote, "on the difficulty into which I had plunged myself, and in devising means of extrication. At the approach of my creditor, I shrunk, and I *looked* no doubt as meanly as I *felt*."[6]

Randolph soon admitted his folly. "This I hope, my dear son," Tucker wrote in a letter enclosing $268, "will be the last demand of the kind you will ever have to pay and I rely on your promise that it shall." Randolph rejoiced in the "inexpressible satisfaction of being free from debt" and pledged that his "expenditures from this date until the same time twelve months shall not exceed four hundred dollars."[7] Other dalliances were not so easily dispatched.

"The ladies of Philadelphia are fair and alluring," Randolph wrote in 1811 to his cousin, "and your time of life is most propitious to their power over your heart."[8] His advice was rooted in experience. "You well know my sentiments on a certain subject," he wrote in February 1791 to Henry Rutledge, "a pin for existence without her—but I will drop a subject which never fails to demand the tribute of a sigh."[9] The next month, he raised the same subject in cryptic words. "My sentiments," he wrote, "are still the same on *a certain subject* and ever will remain so."[10] By summer, his emotions were sufficiently recovered for him to counsel Rutledge to "let a second mistress light up another flame and put out this."[11] In the meantime, his friend Joseph Bryan was preparing to marry "a woman as beautiful as the morning who was in the best society in Philadelphia" when Randolph intervened. "I saved him from marriage, when under age, with a woman . . . whose mother kept a boarding house and knew her true character. One hour more would have consigned my friend to the arms of infamy. I rescued him at the hazard of my life; for I am satisfied that he would have cut my throat, if I had not established her falsehood to him. She married that very day the object of her real attachment."[12]

"To me," Randolph concluded, "Mr. Bryan rendered a service not precisely of the same but somewhat analogous nature of which some day or other I will give you the strange history." No letter survives in which Randolph describes the somewhat analogous situation. Thus the tantalizing hint has become the subject of speculation, suggesting to some "an entanglement, if not indeed a marriage, in Philadelphia."[13] Old Virginia lore holds that Randolph was discovered in a compromising situation with a woman named Hester Hargrave, daughter of an Irish washerwoman, and married her to save himself from disgrace. Hester subsequently returned to Ireland without having granted a divorce to Randolph, thus binding him to her for life.[14] Accordingly, Randolph's bachelorhood was grounded not on impotency or irascibility, but in an undisclosed secret marriage. Intrigue aside, no evidence exists to support this tale. Randolph never mentioned any name like "Hester Hargrave" in any one of his thousands of surviving letters and, most telling, none of his legion of political enemies ever hinted at such an affair. Perhaps the service Joseph Bryan provided his friend was to save him from the clutches of Hargrave or another woman with like designs. What is clear from these yeasty days is that Randolph's attention was not on the study of law.

"After having lived a life of dissipation for the last three months," Randolph wrote in February 1791, "I soon found that ignorance and vice were the unerring attendants of what is dignified by the appellation of Pleasure; but which is the surest road to infamy and guilt." His intemperate behavior was catching up to him. "It is impossible," he wrote, "to conceive in what manner a life of debauchery destroys the finer feelings of the mind, and repels those virtuous emotions which alone . . . render us superior to the brutes of creation."[15] Warning words came from Virginia. "I beg you would not neglect yourself," Tucker wrote, "or run the hazard of a disorder which I fear is in some degree hereditary fixing itself upon you as it has on your unfortunate brother [Theodorick]."[16] As Randolph sought to check himself from complete recklessness, his thoughts turned to religion. "[A] man, I should think," he wrote to Tucker, "derives more consolation and real happiness from a firm belief in a national Religion than from any other source in life."[17] He pursued the same topic with Henry Rutledge. "By religion, I do not mean the peculiar principles of any sect in the world," he wrote, "but those sentiments which sensible and good men entertain for the Author of the Universe, and those actions which are an undeniable evidence of those gratitudes for the blessings which they enjoy thro his means."[18]

Thoughts on religion and politics held his interest; the study of law did not. "I do not see Mr. [Edmund] R[andolph] once a fortnight," he complained to Tucker, "I am therefore to read and make my own comments which I could do as well in the wilds of Kentucky as in the desert of Philadelphia."

The law was, at best, a mere means to acquire "a sufficiency to support me genteelly in my native country."[19] He was done with this latest academic farce. In early 1792, Randolph returned to Virginia.

The traumatic events of John Randolph's life to this point had been either of his own making or the consequences of his brittle temperament. But the year 1792 would be his *annus horribilis*, filled with troublesome events, none of which were his making. On February 14, Theodorick Randolph died at the age of twenty-one. During the year prior to his death, "he was reduced to a mere skeleton . . . unable to walk . . . his bones worked through his skin." Randolph blamed the years at Columbia, during which Theodorick "had undermined his constitution and destroyed his health forever."[20] In reality, Theodorick's death could have been brought on by any one of the numerous diseases that plagued eighteenth-century America, but no definitive answer survives. Whatever the cause, Theodorick was gone—a life wasted in idle pursuits.

In June, Randolph found himself the victim of one of the more virulent of plagues. Traveling through Richmond, he was struck down with scarlet fever. A family friend, Henry Lee, wrote that he found Randolph "at Anderson's tavern in an airy room much afflicted with the scarlet fever and sore throat." Lee checked again the next day and reported to St. George Tucker that "the crisis of the disorder is passed."[21]

Randolph's diary offers no details of this illness, noting only: "attacked with scarlet fever and lay ill at Anderson's Tavern."[22] By July, he was sufficiently well to travel to Williamsburg to meet the "young, beautiful, amiable and rich" new wife of St. George Tucker.[23] Given Randolph's trait of minutely detailing his physical ailments, this paucity of information leads one to believe that the scarlet fever attack had no lasting impact. Nevertheless, Randolph's bout with scarlet fever has been repeatedly cited as the primary source of his many physical problems. The disease, one wrote, "left him without the palpable signs of manhood . . . [and] from this time on Randolph was probably unable to father natural children." Another writer concluded the "physical peculiarities that emerged . . . in 1792 . . . left him beardless, emaciated, and with a peculiarly shrill, high-pitched voice."[24] Randolph's later description of the impact of the fever piques interest. "So few charms had life for me," he wrote, "so strong was the disgust that I had taken to the world that I was indifferent to the issue of my disease."[25]

The attack of scarlet fever may have aggravated Randolph's numerous maladies, but it was not the source of his arrested physical development. The culprit there was most likely Klinefelter syndrome, a condition caused by an additional X chromosome in males.[26] The phenotypic features of Klinefelter syndrome mirror Randolph's distinguishing physical characteristics: a tall, slender body with long legs and shorter torso, decreased facial hair, infertility, and psychosocial or behavioral problems.[27] A precise conclusion eludes due to the various and peculiar ailments from which Randolph suffered from his earliest days, yet the one constant—a striking physical appearance distinguished by a beardless face and a high-pitched voice—strongly suggests an endocrine imbalance, and Klinefelter syndrome offers a compelling explanation. What seems certain is that the tortures Randolph endured during his sixty years were not the result of a single attack of scarlet fever.[28]

Analysis of Randolph's physical condition necessarily leads to a discussion of his impotence. Dr. Francis West conducted a postmortem examination of Randolph and recorded that the "scrotum was scarcely at all developed" with only a right testicle "the size of a small bean."[29] Dr. West and his colleague, Dr. Joseph Parrish, concluded that Randolph "must have been destitute of the powers of virility."[30] Randolph's impotency was an open secret during his life. "My apathy is not natural, but superinduced," Randolph wrote in one of the many oblique references to this condition. "There *was* a volcano under my ice, but it is burnt out."[31] His condition prompted occasional insults and snickers, but no contemporary aspersions were cast on his overall masculinity.[32] Only in modern studies are found the terms "androgyny" or "ambiguous sexuality."[33] Jefferson biographer Dumas Malone's conclusion that Randolph's "excesses of arrogant belligerency" were an "over-compensation for his lack of virility" dismisses the reams of letters, speeches, and facts that illuminate the causes of Randolph's political and personal actions.[34] For his part, Randolph kept his affliction in proper perspective. It did not prevent him from pursuing his one great romance, seven years after the scarlet fever attack, nor did it lessen his lifelong desire for female companionship and his own family. "If matrimony has its cares," he wrote, "celibacy has no pleasure. . . . [A] man must have a bosom friend, and children around him, to cherish and support the dreariness of old age."[35]

Following his visit to Williamsburg, Randolph traveled to Bizarre, where his brother Richard had settled with his wife, Judith. The two cousins had ignored the objections of the family and married on Christmas Day, 1789. Richard, twenty-two, had chosen the life of a gentleman farmer, in part because his aimless educational wanderings had provided him with no career. Judith, two years younger than her husband, gave birth to a son, St. George

Randolph, in the spring of 1791. About that time, Judith's sixteen-year-old sister, Ann Cary Randolph, moved in with the couple. Ann, known as Nancy, soon became the object of Theodorick's ardent attention. At some point in 1791, Theodorick told Randolph that he was engaged to marry Nancy. Theodorick's subsequent death in February 1792 left Nancy "in low spirits." When Randolph arrived at Bizarre, he was warned to avoid mention of his late brother. He apparently forgot the admonition and "once named him to her and she burst into tears." Other than that one instance, the visit passed without incident, though Randolph thought Nancy's "pallid and emaciated appearance . . . something of a greenish blue under her eyes" indicated that "she labored under obstruction." Randolph departed Bizarre in September, noting "the most perfect harmony subsisted in the family."[36]

The perfect harmony observed by Randolph was in fact disguised chords of dissonance. Nancy was pregnant, possibly by Theodorick, possibly by Richard. Judith, expecting her second child, was suspicious of her husband, jealous of her sister, and worried about her first-born who, it would soon be discovered, was a deaf mute. It was only a matter of time before talk—disturbing, scandalous talk—began to spread that Richard paid too much attention to Nancy.

On September 30, Randolph joined Richard, Judith, and Nancy on a visit to Glenlyvar, the home of Mary and Randolph Harrison.[37] Nancy wore a "closed great [coat] buttoned round her" and "complained of being very unwell." She made her apologies as soon as possible and retired to bed. Judith and Mrs. Harrison checked on her later in the evening and administered "essence of peppermint." The Harrisons and Randolphs bade their goodnights shortly thereafter. Randolph slept elsewhere that night, perhaps at Carter Page's nearby home, or at a local tavern.[38]

The silent night at Glenlyvar was shattered by piercing screams. Mrs. Harrison investigated and was told that Nancy was ill and in need of laudanum. Soon calm descended, and Mrs. Harrison returned to her bedroom. Sleep was again frustrated as heavy footsteps were heard traipsing up and down the stairs. The movement of servants was noticed, hushed whispers heard, furtive shadows cast. Mr. Harrison assumed a physician had been summoned. Soon the house was quiet. Only cursory comments were made by the Randolphs about the unsettling events. Nancy had suffered a "hysteric fit," they told their hosts. The Harrisons "entertained no unfavorable suspicion."[39]

In subsequent days, word spread from the slave quarters to the master's house that a newborn baby was found dead on a pile of shingles a few yards distant from the mansion. There were bloodstains in the room where Nancy spent the night, and the Harrisons now recalled a "curious odor."[40] The story spread through the social strata of Randolph peers, seemingly gaining in horrific detail upon each telling. Nancy had miscarried or delivered a still-born child or delivered a healthy child that had been murdered by her hand, or by the hand of the father, the adulterous Richard Randolph.

John Randolph professed to be unaware of these events. He received "the first intelligence of what was alleged to have happened at Glenlyvar" while in route to Williamsburg.[41] His reaction to the story is unrecorded. He might have dismissed it as idle gossip or refused to credit a story generated by slaves. He might have already known the truth. That he continued to Williamsburg—where he was to enroll at William & Mary—shows he either gave the story little credence or was a maintaining a public façade of normalcy.[42] In the meantime, Richard's reputation plummeted and the atmosphere at Bizarre worsened. Richard was faced with finding a way to silence the "horrid and malicious lie" or leaving the Commonwealth.[43] On April 17, 1793, Richard placed an open letter in the *Virginia Gazette* announcing that he would appear at Cumberland Court and "answer in the due course of law, *any charge of crime which any person or persons whatsoever shall then and there think proper to allege against me.*" He challenged any person to step forward and "state, with *precision* and *clearness* the *facts* which they lay to my charge and the *evidence* whether *direct* or *circumstantial* by which I am to be proved guilty."[44]

The Virginia establishment was leaning against Richard. "I see guilt in but one person," Thomas Jefferson wrote to his daughter Patsy, "and not in her." Martha Jefferson "Patsy" Randolph found herself involved in the affair by virtue of her marriage to Nancy's brother. She now recalled a conversation with Nancy about the medicinal use of Gum Guiacum. That medication was generally used to treat colic, but it was known to induce abortion.[45] When Richard appeared at Cumberland Court House on the appointed day, he was charged with "feloniously murdering a child said to be borne of Nancy Randolph."

Facing charges of incest and murder, Richard sent a dispatch to Patrick Henry, the one Virginian whose reputation and legal abilities could instantly stay the flow of vilification. Legend has it that the two men haggled over Henry's fee, but Richard was in no position to bargain. As if retaining Henry were not enough, Richard hired John Marshall—a mere seven years distant from becoming chief justice of the United States Supreme Court—as co-counsel. *The Commonwealth v. Richard Randolph* was set for hearing on April 29, 1793.[46]

The Richard Randolph hearing presented all the sensational elements of a lurid drama: lust and betrayal, incest and murder, lies and deception, all occurring within a privileged class accustomed to living by its own rules. The courtroom was filled to overflowing. It is unclear which witnesses gave testimony in person and which had their depositions entered into the record.[47] However it was presented, the testimony did not disappoint.

Carter Page, Richard's uncle and former aide to Lafayette, knew of "no criminal conversation" between Richard and Nancy but had "seen them kissing."[48] Patsy Jefferson Randolph recounted her story about Gum Guiacum and stated she "did suspect that Miss Nancy was pregnant."[49] Randolph Harrison had "observed imprudent familiarities" but suspected nothing "until information was given by a negro-woman, that she had miscarried."[50] Mrs. Harrison repeated the story told her by one of her slaves—that Nancy had miscarried—but professed not to believe it.[51] Witness after witness dismissed the incest story as preposterous, but still the condemning words rolled out: "too fond of each other," "fondness for each other," "kissing," and "suspicious of a birth or an abortion." Judith Randolph's testimony was the trial's decisive moment. It was as if everyone knew the truth, but the betrayed wife had the right to declare the official truth. Judith testified that she saw nothing, effectively ending the trial.[52]

John Randolph was called among the final witnesses. He repeated that Theodorick had told him "while in Philadelphia that he was engaged to Miss Nancy." He recounted the story of his recent stay at Bizarre, during which time he "frequently lounged on the bed both with [Nancy] and [Judith] and never suspected her of being pregnant." He observed no change in Nancy following the visit to Glenlyvar other than "that her complexion was somewhat clearer than before."[53]

No slaves from Glenlyvar were allowed to testify.

Richard was found "not guilty of the felony wherewith he stands charged." No incest had occurred, the empaneled gentry stated; no life had been snuffed out. His peers may have absolved Richard of guilt, but no afterglow of innocence surrounded him as he left the courthouse. Richard and Nancy, perhaps Judith, knew the truth of the matter, and it was not the truth established by the verdict. A child had been born and, whether stillborn or murdered, had been dumped in the field behind Glenlyvar. Nancy later would state that Theodorick was the father, but her confession was made during a bitter exchange with Randolph, with Richard long dead. Randolph joined his brother and the two sisters for what must have been a surreal trip to Bizarre. His curt diary entry teems with portent: "The trial. Return. Quarrels of the women."[54]

Randolph's political beliefs became pronounced during his time in Williamsburg. His agrarian background, antifederalism, and distrust of the tendencies of centralized government brought him naturally into Jefferson's newly formed Republicans. Increasingly bold in expressing his views, Randolph apparently did so with such vigor in a debate that classmate Robert Taylor challenged him to a duel. Though fighting a duel meant expulsion from William & Mary, the two met in a field near Williamsburg and took their appropriate places. Both got off first shots, and both missed. Not wishing to announce the matter satisfied, Randolph's second shot hit Taylor in the posterior. At that point, the two decided they had done enough and "reconciled on the spot."[55] Randolph was again out of school—not that he wanted to remain longer in Williamsburg. "I have found my conduct and character during my residence in that place," he wrote to Tucker, "canvassed in so ungenerous and malicious a manner, that were it not the residence of yourself and your beloved family, I never would set foot in it again."[56]

Randolph's republicanism had pulled him into a duel; now it was pulling him into a distant field of battle. Like most Jeffersonians, Randolph was a strong supporter of the revolutionaries in France.[57] In May 1793, one month shy of his twentieth birthday, he asked Tucker to allow him "to go immediately to France and to enter the Army of the Republic." He begged to be allowed to "*serve* the noblest cause in the world" as opposed to leading the life of "a miserable attorney who stoops to a thousand petty villainies in order to gain the sum of fifteen shillings." He assured Tucker that he had "not one spark of a lawyer in me, except it be contention; and that had much better be exercised against enemies than friends."[58]

The blockade-running Tucker was no stranger to adventure, but he rejected the plea out of hand. Randolph, suffering from yellow fever, did not put up a fight. He traveled back to Philadelphia "to while away the time of my minority" while purporting to study law.[59]

Randolph turned to the two things that aroused his interest: politics and riotous living. He "slashed a crimson streak across Philadelphia . . . drank more than was good for him" and generally acted the "hearty young hellion."[60] This time he did avoid incurring debt. "I have known the sweets of that situation too well," he wrote, "again to plunge into the same gulph of slavery, of extreme misery."[61] He was again a regular attendee in the gallery of the House of Representatives. He feared the interests of the South were not being well served by "men who offer themselves as candidates who cannot punctually attend." He fumed at this dereliction of duty. "There is *no senator* from Maryland and but one from Georgia," he wrote in January 1794. "Thus are the interests of the Southern States basely betrayed by the indolence of some and the villainy of others." When Albert Gallatin, newly elected senator from Pennsylvania, was denied his seat based upon his disputed citizenship status, Randolph smelled a Federalist rat. "Altho' he came here in 1780," he fumed, "took up arms in our defense, bought lands and settled, yet . . . he was declared not qualified according to the Constitution."[62] He asked Tucker for his constitutional analysis of the issue and lamented the loss of Gallatin's "abilities and principles."[63] Randolph's righteous indignation was prescient. He would ever display a highly developed sense of justice, a suspicion of Federalists, and adherence to strict construction of the Constitution.

On June 2, 1794, Randolph attained majority age. He left Philadelphia and ended all pretext of formal schooling. He settled at Bizarre, where the uneasy alliance of Richard, Judith, and Nancy held tenuous sway. He "rode from one racefield to another," became a master horseman and hunter, and "visited from place to place among friends." His remained a life of restless aimlessness. "You inquire after my plans," he wrote a friend, "I have none . . . I exist in an obscurity from which I never shall emerge."[64] At night, he paced the halls of Bizarre, chillingly exclaiming "Macbeth hath murdered sleep," or saddled his horse and took nocturnal rides around the estate. He was living "the life of a mere lounger," bored with "society . . . conversations and company."[65] He traveled to Charleston, South Carolina, and Savannah, Georgia, to take in the races. From that trip emerges the earliest surviving description of Randolph. A bookstore owner recalled "a tall, gawky-looking flaxen-haired stripling, apparently of the age from 16 to 18, with a complexion of a good parchment color, beardless chin, and as much assumed self-confidence as any two-footed animal I ever saw. This was John Randolph."[66]

"[D]issipation, races, public dinners, [and] balls" occupied most of Randolph's time, but his thoughts were never far from politics. His letters were filled with strident republicanism, terms native to the French Revolution, and concerns about Federalist rule: "Never was the sway of one man [Washington] more perfect in any country, than that of the president is in this—the proof is before us—where the personal influence of *one* man be-comes sufficiently great to force a people who glory in their Liberty, into measures the most grating to their feelings and inimical to their interests and freedom, *there* Tyranny commences. . . . the president has riveted the chains of his country."[67]

National events stirred him. The Treaty of Paris of 1783 ended the Amer-ican War for Independence but left many issues unresolved. England still occupied frontier forts in the Northwest Territory and frequently incited Indians along the border. Embroiled in war with France, England widened its attacks on neutral ships. This policy resulted in the seizure of more than 250 American ships and the impressment of American sailors. A commer-cial war—perhaps an actual war—loomed. President Washington reacted by recommending defensive measures to Congress and dispatching Chief Justice John Jay to London to attempt a negotiated settlement. The resulting Treaty of 1795—"Jay's Treaty"—was probably the best result that could have been secured by the young nation. The British agreed to relinquish their military posts on the frontier, and vessels under seventy tons would be al-lowed access to West Indies markets; the United States agreed to arbitration of British claims for debts incurred prior to the Revolution. England did not agree to recognize the neutral rights of American ships, compensate slave-holders for slaves carried off by the British, or stop agitating the Indians. The issue of impressment was ignored.[68]

Jay's Treaty, historian James Sharp writes, "divided the country like no other issue in the history of the young republic."[69] Republicans viewed Jay's Treaty as evidence of a burgeoning alliance between the United States and Great Britain. Thomas Jefferson called it an "infamous act" and "noth-ing more than a treaty of alliance between England [and] the Anglomen of this country against the legislature [and] people of the United States."[70] The French Directory drew the same conclusion and increased its harassment of American ships.[71] The treaty pushed Randolph further into the Republi-can Party. He put his views on display at a dinner in January 1795, when he offered the toast: "George Washington, may he be damned if he signs Jay's Treaty."[72]

It was during this season in search of himself, Randolph later recalled, that his religious skepticism overwhelmed the teachings of his mother and he became, briefly, "a deist, and by consequence an atheist."[73] He developed a "prejudice in favor of Mahomedanism . . . [and] rejoiced in all its triumphs over the cross."[74] He adopted the French calendar, dated letters "19 Floreal" and "6 Messidor," and referred to longtime friends as "Citizen." When challenged on a political point by a neighbor, Randolph engaged in a "very irksome" debate, but "did not drop it until I had repeated to him every invidious reproach which he had in my presence cast upon *the French*."[75] His rhetoric took on a decidedly French accent when he wrote that Federalist leaders should be "brought to the block: this is the only atonement which can be made by them for their political sins."[76]

In May 1796, Randolph was taken abed with a "bilious fever." Richard sat with his brother until the illness passed, then returned to Bizarre.[77] Randolph followed within a few days. He had traveled but a few miles when a message met him: Richard Randolph was dead.[78] The culprit was an "inflammatory fever" which rapidly increased in virulence.[79] When Richard slipped into a delirium, Nancy dashed off a letter to St. George Tucker, hoping it would reach Randolph as well. "Our poor dear Richard is on the brink of the grave," she wrote, "Jack, come or it will be too late."[80] The note never reached Randolph.

Stunned and devastated, Randolph spurred his horse onward, arriving at Bizarre shortly after Richard's funeral. He was told "an emetic" had caused Richard's death, but he could hardly deal with the information. "I have nobody to unburthen myself to," he wrote to Tucker. "In silence, are all my sorrows and, in the solitude of the night, indulged. . . . I am stupefied. . . . I go to bed but cannot sleep."[81]

Richard Randolph, like Theodorick, was a prodigal son. At best, he had squandered the advantages of wealth and privilege; at worst, he had brought scandal and disrepute to the family. Even in death, he left a mixed message. His will freed his slaves, but his excessive debts kept them in bondage for several more years.[82]

John Randolph, twenty-three years old, was now manager of his patrimonial estates, responsible for Judith, her sons—St. George, a deaf-mute, and Tudor, destined to become a consumptive—and her sister Nancy. Though master of Bizarre, he had a reputation as a radical Republican and an unchecked wild spirit, not much different from his two deceased brothers. Curious fate had presented Randolph with large opportunity. No one knew how he would respond.

Randolph's immediate concern was economic. "My father's whole estate was under mortgage for debt," he wrote, and "[Richard] left considerable debts of his own." The topping on his financial woes was a judgment in favor of the Hanburys, the estate's primary British creditor.[83] Randolph blamed his uncle Theodorick Bland for "maladministration" but wasted little time with recriminations. Breaking for the only time with his mother's admonition never to sell land, Randolph sold Matoax for three thousand pounds sterling. He then implemented savings wherever he could find them. "I actually lived in a cabin covered with *pegged* shingles," he wrote, "because I had not one dollar to buy nails." He experimented with farming techniques and systematically applied management principles.[84] He took "no receipts on loose paper," had all his transactions witnessed, copied his bills so he could "at a glance see the cost of any article or brand of expense." He formed "no intimacies with . . . neighbors under a seven year acquaintance" and adapted his "supplies judiciously to their intended end."[85]

His patiently practiced forbearance produced results. Randolph paid all the debts of his father and brother within three years. Once out of debt, he turned his zeal to purchasing land and expanding his holdings.[86] He completely reversed the fortunes of his estate. It was an unexpected outcome. "I sometimes reflect with astonishment," Randolph wrote to St. George Tucker, "on the vast fund of hilarity which I once possessed, flown never, I fear, to return. I sometimes look back on my past life and think that I have been in a dream."[87] Well he might have thought, for the rowdy youth had become a man of standing. His peers and neighbors took note.

It was during these years of recovery that Randolph courted the woman he "loved better than my own soul or Him who created it."[88] Maria Ward was born in 1784 at Winterpock, an estate not far from Matoax. Her father, Benjamin Ward, died before she was born, so Maria viewed her mother's second husband, General Everard Meade, as father. The Meade family lived at the Hermitage in Amelia County, some forty miles from Bizarre. It was there that Randolph visited his friend Hodijah "Dije" Meade, son of General Meade.[89] During these trips, he became acquainted with Maria, eleven years his junior. A letter of Maria Ward's granddaughter tells that Randolph advised Maria "what to read and sometimes read with her. It followed, of course, they both fell desperately in love, and were engaged for many long years."[90]

It is not likely that Randolph was engaged "for many long years" to a girl just entering her teens, but his name was "scratched with a diamond on one of the window panes at The Hermitage," and his courtship of Maria was an event.[91] Slaves at the Hermitage recalled Randolph "riding the finest horse you ever saw . . . [with] his pack o'hounds along" and that he "just flung the money 'mongst us by the handful."[92]

One such visit in 1799 began like all the rest. Randolph, twenty-six, and Maria, fifteen, took a walk in the garden. A calm conversation changed quickly into a strong exchange and, within moments, Maria retreated to the house and Randolph stormed to his horse "as if in a frenzy." Not taking the time to loose the reins of his mount from the post, he pulled a knife and slashed them. He galloped away—his engagement with Maria ended.

What transpired in the garden is unknown. Randolph's first biographer, Hugh Garland, implies that Randolph's impotency—his "special sorrow"— prompted the breakup.[93] Biographer William Bruce rejects that theory and concludes "that the marriage never took place because rumors of the affair in which Randolph had become involved in Philadelphia . . . came to the ears of Maria Ward and her mother."[94] Both explanations might hold truth, or the cause may have been no more than a young girl deciding she had confused infatuation with love. Maria did not have to rely on rumor or physical impairment to have pause with regard to the Randolph family. "No one now living knows, I believe, why the engagement was broken," Martha Archer wrote in 1878; "both were miserable ever after." That was not true for Maria Ward, who married Peyton Randolph, son of Attorney General Edmund Randolph, in 1806, but it was more true than not for the master of Bizarre. "[T]he love of an amiable and sensible woman," Randolph would write about Maria, "one who loves with heart and not with her head out of romances and plays. That I once had."[95]

In March 1797, John Adams assumed both the presidency and deteriorating relations with France. Seeking a settlement, Adams sent a diplomatic mission to Paris, but the delegation was met with a demand for a large cash bribe in exchange for a meeting with French foreign minister Talleyrand. The insulted delegation returned home. President Adams released a report of the incident, using the terms X, Y, and Z instead of the names of the respective French agents. The "XYZ Affair" ignited a firestorm of anti-French sentiment and sparked the undeclared "Quasi-War" with France.

Jefferson was convinced that the XYZ Affair was being blown out of proportion—bribery was not an unusual coin of diplomatic exchange—and was another Federalist attempt to drive the United States into an alliance with England. More ominous to Republicans were the actions of the Federalists to consolidate power under the cover of international crisis.[96] At the height of the Quasi-War, the Federalist Congress passed and President Adams signed the Alien Act, authorizing the president to deport aliens "dangerous to the peace and safety of the United States" during peacetime, and the

Sedition Act, declaring that any treasonable activity, including the publication of "any false, scandalous and malicious writing," was punishable by fine and imprisonment.[97]

Federalists asserted that the acts protected the nation from alien citizens of enemy powers and prevented seditious attacks on the central government. Republicans viewed the acts as unconstitutional infringements on speech and a step toward the tyranny they suspected was at the heart of Federalist policy. Randolph proposed establishing an armory dedicated specifically to opposing administration policy.[98] Jefferson preferred firing rhetorical guns and so drafted the Kentucky Resolution, asserting the right of a state to nullify federal acts contrary to the Constitution. The Kentucky state legislature adopted the resolution on November 16, 1798. Virginia followed suit, adopting its own resolution, drafted by James Madison, on December 3, 1798.[99]

Randolph was a persistent, articulate, and aggressive advocate for Republican policies during these tumultuous days. Given his standing, it was logical that local leaders would take notice. In the fall of 1798, State Senator Creed Taylor approached Randolph with the idea that he stand for Congress. Randolph expressed the proper reluctance expected of a potential candidate, but he did not dismiss the matter out of hand. "I am now as well satisfied, as I was when you first made to me the proposal of permitting my friends to declare my willingness to serve my fellow-citizens in the House of Representatives," he wrote; "that it is an office to which I can not rationally entertain the *smallest pretensions*."[100] It was all Taylor needed to launch a campaign.

George Washington took a different view of affairs from that of Jefferson and Randolph. He supported the Alien and Sedition Acts as measures advancing national security and unity, and dismissed Republicans as merely "opposing every measure that is calculated for defense and self preservation." He was disturbed about Virginia's role in challenging federal actions. "Everything dear and valuable to us," he wrote, "is assailed." Washington decided to attempt once again to alter the course of human events. His first step was to turn to the only man with a reputation that approached his own.[101]

"It would be a waste of time," Washington wrote to Patrick Henry on January 15, 1799, "to attempt to bring to the view of a person of your observation and discernment, the endeavors of a certain party among us . . . [and] what must be the inevitable consequences, of such policy, if it cannot be arrested." The Republican Party, he wrote, hung "upon the wheels of government as a dead weight," favored "the nefarious views of another Nation," endangered America's neutrality, and "systematically and pertinaciously pursued" measures "which must eventually dissolve the union or produce coercion."

Henry's character, Washington wrote, "would be a bulwark against such dangerous sentiments . . . a rallying point for the timid, and an attraction of the wavering." He asked Henry to become a candidate in the next election for either Congress or the Virginia General Assembly. "I conceive it of immense importance at this crisis," Washington concluded, "that you should be there."[102] Though Henry judged himself "too old and infirm ever again to undertake public concerns," Washington's letter had the desired effect. He announced he would seek election to the Virginia House of Delegates. He would attend Court Day in Charlotte County in March and there address his fellow citizens.[103]

From the small farms and the large estates, from the country stores and wayside inns, the people of Southside Virginia came to see their hero. The dominant political sentiment of the area tended to favor Republicanism, but popular sentiment embraced Henry. Here was King George III's greatest foe, the herald of "Liberty or Death," making a dramatic—and possibly final— appeal to his countrymen. Hundreds of Virginians crowded into the village surrounding Charlotte Courthouse. Emotions ran so high that a Baptist minister felt compelled to admonish a group of admirers that "Mr. Henry is not a god." His rebuke was lost in the cheers as Henry stood once more before the people.[104] He was pale, slightly stooped, clearly ill. But his voice, initially "slightly cracked and tremulous," soon achieved the familiar resonance as his well chosen words came forth. Only the sounds of nature competed with Henry for the attention of the rapt, adoring audience.[105]

The actions of the Virginia legislature in response to the Alien and Sedition Acts, Henry said, had "planted thorns upon his pillow." Such actions— taken without proper authority—"would probably produce civil war." Virginians would find themselves fighting an army commanded, no doubt, by George Washington. "Where is the citizen of America," he asked, "who will dare to lift his hand against the father of his country?" Henry conceded that he had opposed the ratification of the Constitution, with its "unlimited power over the purse and sword consigned to the general government," but "he had been overruled, and it was now necessary to submit to the constitutional exercise of that power." This prudent course, he argued, would not leave citizens helpless. "If am I asked what is to be done when a people feel themselves intolerably oppressed, my answer is ready: overturn the government. But do not, I beseech you, carry matters to this length without provocation."[106]

Henry left the stage and retired to an adjourning tavern. The crowd waited to see who would respond for the Republicans. Randolph moved to the front. It is tempting to read Randolph's later characteristics into this first public appearance. One imagines the blazing eyes, the skeletal forefinger sweeping and thrusting, and the slashing invective confounding the opposition. But no account exists of what Randolph said or how he said it that March day.[107] Tradition holds that he spoke for three hours; humbly conceding the greatness of Patrick Henry, not directly challenging Washington, but effectively asserting the Republican view of individual liberty, limited government, and states' rights. Randolph left no record of the encounter, other than to acknowledge that in taking on Henry he faced "fearful odds."[108]

The voters responded by electing Patrick Henry to the Virginia General Assembly and John Randolph to the United States House of Representatives. Henry died three months later, on June 6, 1799, having never taken his seat. Six months following, in December 1799, John Randolph entered Congress.

3

Ask My Constituents

While others hailed in distant skies
Our eagle's dusky pinion,
He only saw the mountain bird
Stoop o'er his Old Dominion!

Randolph approached the Speaker's dais on the opening day of the Sixth Congress to take his oath of office. Speaker Theodore Sedgwick, a Federalist from Massachusetts, glared at the "tall, gawky-looking flaxen-haired stripling," no doubt wondering if this was the stuff of which republican revolutions were made. Feigning solemnity, Sedgwick or the Clerk of the House—history does not record which one—asked if the twenty-six-year-old Randolph was old enough to serve in Congress. The twitter of bemused chuckles that followed the impertinent inquiry hushed as Randolph's response ricocheted around the chamber.

"Ask my constituents," he snapped.[1] The impact of Randolph's response to the barely concealed insult was galvanic. To Republicans spoiling for a fight, it was the opening salvo, a scintillating sign of things to come. To Federalists it was *lèse majéste*.

House Republicans picked a proposal to increase the standing army as the first issue on which they would engage the Federalists. John Nicholas of Virginia introduced a resolution opposing the creation of twelve new regiments of infantry and six troops of dragoons.[2] Adoption of this proposal, he submitted, would cut government spending and eliminate the danger to liberty posed by a standing army in peacetime. Representative John Marshall, soon-to-be chief justice of the Supreme Court, scoffed at the notion that America was at peace. "We are, in fact, at war with France, though it is not declared in form," he said. "What security then is there that no disposition will exist to invade us?" Budget cuts could be found elsewhere, he argued, but the savings "would bear no proportion to the immense waste of blood, as well as treasure, which it might occasion us."[3] Representative James Bayard of Delaware perceived several threats to the polity lurking within the Republican proposal. The measure, he fumed, was part of "a system which had for its object the debilitation and degradation of the General Government." Republicans, he charged, wanted congressmen to "forget your country, abjure your religion, suppress the impulses of nature, and maintain the equality of vice and virtue."[4]

Federalist after Federalist catalogued the calamities of Jacobin republicanism: disdain of tradition, contempt for religion, and the equality of the guillotine. Randolph listened for three days. He then took the floor.

He started slowly. He "did not flatter himself with the hope of throwing much new light upon the subject." He praised his friend Marshall, whose "ingenious researches and logical deductions have often commanded my admiration," but—his shrill voice rising—as "he has been unable to produce any arguments of weight upon the subject, I shall take it for granted that none can be adduced." The issue, Randolph asserted, was not economy in government. The standing army was unconstitutional. "The spirit of that instrument and the genius of a free people," he argued, "are equally hostile to this dangerous institution." Even if a standing army could pass constitutional muster, he continued, this concentration of power was a greater threat than the distant French to a free society. "A people who mean to continue free must be prepared to meet danger in person," he said, "not to rely upon the fallacious protection of mercenary armies." The question, he judged, is "simply, whether we will consent to the reduction of an expensive establishment, hostile to our liberties—which cannot be brought to act against the enemy, and which, even in the case of invasion, would make but a paltry part of our defense—and appropriate any saving of the public expenditure to objects of real utility. . . . When citizen and soldier shall be synonymous terms, then will you be safe."[5]

And, Randolph caustically asked, what of this army? Americans, he said, "feel a just indignation at the sight of loungers, who live upon the public, who consume the fruits of their honest industry." Members shifted in their seats, wondering what would flow next from the boy with the high-pitched voice. "They put no confidence, sir, in the protection of a handful of ragamuffins."[6]

Republicans had picked this fight, but Randolph's vigorous rhetoric took them aback. Apparently some members advised Randolph that an explanation, if not an apology, for the terms "mercenary," "loungers," and "ragamuffins" might be in order. Randolph's reaction to these entreaties is not recorded, but the next day he offered his version of an apology. He expressed regret at using the term "ragamuffin," but still rejected the notion that the "liberties and independence" of the people should be entrusted to the protection of "men the most abject and worthless of the community."[7]

It was not a very good clarification, but most Republicans viewed the matter honorably concluded. "J. Randolph has spoken twice with infinite applause, on two successive days," Thomas Jefferson wrote, "tho' . . . he used a word, *ragamuffins*, in speaking of the common soldiery, on the first day. He took it back of his own accord very handsomely the next day."[8] Federalists harrumphed.

The night of his second speech, Randolph and several colleagues attended the Chestnut Street Theatre to see performances of *The Stranger* and *Blue Beard*.[9] Randolph was seated in a box with Congressmen Gabriel Christie, Joseph H. Nicholson, Nathaniel Macon, and New York Lieutenant Governor Stephen Van Rensselaer. At some point during *Blue Beard*, two marines, Captain James McKnight and Lieutenant Michael Reynolds, noticed Randolph's presence. The two soldiers began an animated conversation, interspersed with glances toward Randolph. At that moment on the stage, as if choreographed with the drama that was developing in the audience, "a number of men, with a drum, pikes, etc., appeared."

"I think," McKnight called out, "our ragamuffins would make a better appearance than those men." Randolph did not react, but he heard the dialogue between McKnight and Reynolds and concluded the intent was "to insult me personally." The chatter below continued, with other spectators making the connection between the soldiers' repartee and the congressman in the box. "He doesn't hear you," someone said to the marines, "go closer." Needing little prompting, McKnight and Reynolds moved into the rear of Randolph's box and continued their review of *Blue Beard*.

"What do you think of those ragamuffins?" McKnight asked. "Those ragamuffins are not Pennsylvania, they are black Virginia ragamuffins." Van Rensselaer leaned over to Macon and stated the obvious: "These men intend to insult Mr. Randolph." Still, the target of the spleen showed no reaction. The marines decided to escalate everyone's discomfort level. Reynolds noticed a slight space between Randolph and the partition wall. He pushed forward, stood on the seat, and "dropped with such violence" as to jostle Randolph. McKnight remained in the back of the box and continued his soliloquy. When Reynolds rose, McKnight moved forward and flopped in

the space beside Randolph. Finally, the play ended. The congressmen surrounded Randolph, determined to escort him quickly from the theater.
McKnight reached out and gave the cape of Randolph's coat "a sudden and
violent pull."

"Who was that," Randolph cried out, "that jerked my coat?" McKnight
said nothing. Randolph repeated the question, this time adding that the perpetrator was "a damned puppy." Again no one admitted to the deed. Randolph left the box, surrounded by his friends and followed by McKnight
and Reynolds. As they entered the narrow stairwell, the marines pushed in
hard in an effort to send Randolph tumbling down the steps. They underes-
timated the strength of the hefty Joseph Nicholson, who "[resisted] the pressure" and held back the shoving marines. Randolph's party emerged from
the theater into the winter night. McKnight and Reynolds followed for a
distance down Chestnut Street, maintaining their menacing chatter, until
they tired of the shenanigans and turned down a side street. Thus the high-
wrought evening ended without serious incident. Randolph remained calm
throughout, and his shaken associates breathed a collective sigh of relief,
convinced the matter was destined to be forgotten. Little did they know
their colleague.

Nicholson and Macon may have viewed the "Playhouse Incident" as
merely two marines behaving boisterously, but Randolph viewed it differently. It was not a personal attack; it was an attack by an entrenched interest—the military establishment—on the independence of the legislature.
Randolph had dared to advocate a reduction in the military and, unable to
contend with him in the field of argument, military operatives had sought
to insult, intimidate, and injure him. He was not alone in this view. "It
would seem," Thomas Jefferson wrote, "as if the army themselves were to
hew down whoever shall propose to reduce them."[10] Randolph would not exchange gibes with soldiers in a playhouse, but he would not let the matter
fade with the fall of the curtain.

"For words of a general nature uttered on the floor of this House . . .
in my official capacity," Randolph wrote to President Adams, "I have been
grossly and publicly insulted by two officers." He sketched the facts, provided the names of witnesses, and reminded the president it was within his
"province to provide" a remedy. "It is enough for me to state," he concluded,
"that the independence of the Legislature has been attacked, the majesty of
the people, of which you are the principal representative, insulted, and your
authority contemned."[11]

The letter bristled with French-accented republicanism. Randolph dated it the "24th [year] of Independence," asserted that he addressed the president "in the plain language of man," and signed it as "your fellow citizen." Thus a letter about insulting language was widely viewed as insulting to the president. "This stripling comes full to the brim with his own conceit and all Virginia democracy," Abigail Adams fumed. "He chatters away like a magpie."[12]

The president forwarded the letter to the House. He pointedly mentioned that he would offer no "comments on its matter or style." Since the incident related "to the privileges of the House," it should be investigated there, he dismissingly concluded, "if anywhere."[13] Federalists chortled over their good fortune. Randolph had shown republicanism in its unadorned radical state, marked by immature behavior, irresponsible conduct, and disrespect of institutions and officials. Representative John Kittera moved the matter be referred to a select committee for investigation. Immediately, Randolph was on his feet. If he had believed the House "could have remedied the abuse," he would have brought the matter before his colleagues. It was his belief, however, that the Congress had no jurisdiction. It was the duty of "the Commander-in-Chief . . . to restrain men under his command from giving personal abuse and insult." House Federalists were in no mood to consider procedural or constitutional niceties. The "Playhouse Incident" was referred to a Federalist-dominated committee.

The committee held no public hearings, opting instead to accept statements and affidavits from the parties. All confirmed Randolph's recital of the facts, though McKnight and Reynolds denied knowing that Randolph was in attendance. Neither of them explained the remarkable coincidence of their word choice, box selection, and stairwell conduct. McKnight, no doubt sensing he would be protected by the committee, hurled one final insult, stating that, for Randolph's "youthful appearance and dress, I had no idea of his being a member of the House of Representatives."[14]

The committee found "that sufficient cause does not appear for the interference of the House on the ground of a breach of privilege." It conceded that "a series of circumstances . . . appeared to Mr. Randolph, and others present, to evince premeditated insult," but found the acts had been "satisfactorily explained" or were "of a nature too equivocal to justify reprehension and punishment." The House took the better part of five days debating the report, focusing primarily on whether Randolph had departed "from the usual forms of decorum observed in official communications."

The Federalists delighted in the spectacle, waxing at great length about the impropriety of the representative from Virginia. Randolph's behavior, James Bayard said, defied the "approved usages of time [and] the precedents of our forefathers" and was "an innovation which promised no good and destroyed what had been found beneficial."[15] Samuel Sewell condemned the "kind of comparison of equality in the mode of address always decorous in itself, and which ought not to be used from an inferior to a superior officer of the Government."[16] Republicans offered a spirited defense, but the matter was beginning to appear silly. "I wish to ask the House what we are about," William Shepard said. "I think we are debating on a matter of very little consequence indeed."[17] Randolph was unapologetic. "I entertain no doubt upon the issue," he said. "But in the unshaken conviction of the propriety of my procedure, and in the approbation of my constituents, whose honor and whose interests it will ever be my object to maintain, I can have no cause of personal regret."[18] The House adopted a resolution expressing "a respectful sense of regard which the President of the United States has shown to its rights and privileges" and took no other action.

Randolph was amused by the umbrage taken regarding his language. "Although I do not deal in bows and humble servants and all that trash," he wrote to Nicholson, "yet I have some of the milk of human kindness in my composition."[19] When the secretaries of war and navy requested information about the incident, Randolph treated the request with mocking contempt. "Our little Mars and his brother of the ocean," he wrote, "made a formal application to me for information relative to the misconduct of the gallant heroes who protect our poor carcasses from being made into soup maigre to feast the cannibal directory."[20] Nor did Thomas Jefferson detect any significant damage. Randolph, he wrote, "has conducted himself with great propriety, and I have no doubt will come out with increase of reputation."[21]

The impact of the Playhouse Incident upon Randolph's reputation depended on which side of the aisle the question was put. What the episode displayed to all was Randolph's independent spirit, somewhat prickly disposition, and supreme self-confidence. "I should as soon therefore think of going to Sir Isaac Newton to inquire whether the sun illuminates this earth," he wrote to his sister-in-law, "as to inquire of Senaca or Hutchinson what were my duties as a man. . . . I examine with care and a desire to form a correct opinion every argument which is suggested by my own mind, or that of another, upon every subject with which I am familiar. But to me the opinions of Thomas Jefferson and Thomas Fool are of equal value. . . . I should certainly give to those of the former a very thorough investigation, but if in the search of my judgment, they were as naught, I should not allow them the more . . . weight on account of their origin. . . . I *am* a citizen of the republic of Reason."[22]

Randolph was conspicuous in several other debates during the final weeks of the session. On April 9, 1800, he delivered what he later judged to be the "best speech that I ever made."[23] The topic was the ceding of jurisdiction by Connecticut of territory west of Pennsylvania, land known as the western reserve of Connecticut. The *Annals of Congress* made no record of the speech, noting only that Randolph spoke against the resolution.[24] The first session of the Sixth Congress adjourned on May 14, 1800. "Tired as I am with the scene," Randolph wrote to Joseph Nicholson, "yet I cannot feel a little depressed at the idea of a separation from so many good fellows with whom an uninterrupted interchange of good offices has passed for more than [five] months."[25] Randolph would not long suffer pangs of separation. The political blood-sport that was the presidential election of 1800 was fully joined.

Republican and Federalist partisans, convinced the nation stood on the brink of either anarchy or monarchy, flayed without restraint at the two presidential contenders. Thomas Jefferson was a sham patriot, an atheist enamored with French philosophy, and a libertine who bedded his female slaves. John Adams was a closet monarchist, vainglorious and pompous, and a traitor to the principles of the American Revolution. The election of 1800 was only the second contested presidential election in the young republic's history, but the apocalyptic rhetoric made it seem a struggle for the nation's survival.

"The intelligence which we hear from your quarter is very inauspicious," Randolph wrote to Nicholson. "It is confidently asserted that Maryland will follow the example of Massachusetts and take effectual measures to deprive Jefferson of even a single vote."[26] Randolph's watch for Federalist intrigue was not idle paranoia. In Pennsylvania, Federalists introduced legislation establishing a Grand Committee that would prevent some electoral votes (primarily those cast for Jefferson) from being counted. The bill failed, but a similar maneuver was attempted in Maryland. "[T]he magic wand of the governor of Maryland," Randolph wrote, "may cause the whole of this delightful vision to vanish and may conjure up in its room the most gloomy and terrible apparition."[27] Randolph corresponded with Republicans in

South Carolina, North Carolina, and Georgia, admonishing that "neither fraud nor force shall impose Mr. Adams upon the people against their consent."[28] As to his own state, Randolph was satisfied that "our good people of Virginia are more unanimous and firm than ever."[29] After riding through his district and visiting with his fellow freeholders, he buoyantly proclaimed "that the downfall of federalism is at hand."[30]

Preparing to depart for the new capital city of Washington, Randolph asked Nicholson to use his "good offices" to procure "a comfortable asylum in that terrible and dreary wilderness."[31] In exchange, Randolph promised to "furnish a pair of good horses and a couple of excellent servants towards the establishment" and a gig to "very commodiously transport us both." Hearing nothing from Nicholson on the subject, Randolph expanded his offer to include "Madeira wine of the very first quality."[32]

Well might Randolph be concerned. The nascent capital of the United States offered few creature comforts. It was a town attempting to spring fully grown from the swampy woods. One wing of the Capitol was complete, and from that point one could gaze down Pennsylvania Avenue—not really an avenue but a virtually impassable swath of mud cut through the underbrush—and make out the president's mansion. Spaced erratically along the fairway were fifteen or so crudely built boarding houses. Flanking the mansion—not yet the "White House"—was the square brick Treasury building and the combined offices of State and War. Wherever one walked, there was always the putrid whiff of swamp, the dangerous bite of the mosquito, and the annoying muddy ruts of roadways. It was, Randolph wrote, a town of "bad accommodations, worse roads, extravagant bills, yea, and even of drunken society."[33] Only when one reached the brick and stone homes of Georgetown, which sat on higher ground, did the area take on the look of a proper city. It was there that Randolph found housing. For twenty-eight dollars a week, he received two rooms at the McLaughlin House, a private table, board for his servants, and livery for three horses.

The outcome of the presidential election was still in doubt when the second session of the Sixth Congress convened on November 17, 1800. The race seemed to hinge upon a few states, but, with the slowness and inaccuracy of reports, even that assessment was not certain. Randolph seized upon every scrap of intelligence. "S[outh] Carolina has voted unanimously for Jefferson and Burr," he wrote on December 16. "Our Tories begin to give themselves airs in expectation of a *tie*."[34] The next day he reported that "Georgia has followed the example of S. Carolina. . . . [T]is *hoped* that Maryland, Jersey, and

Vermont will vote for Jefferson."[35] This information was enough for the *National Intelligencer* to declare Jefferson elected.[36] Confirmation of the electoral votes came slowly, but as December ended, it became apparent that John Adams had been defeated. What was not apparent—surprisingly, stunningly so—was whether Thomas Jefferson had been elected.

When the electoral votes were counted, Jefferson found himself tied at seventy-three votes with his running mate, Aaron Burr of New York. There was a definite understanding that Jefferson was standing for the presidency and Burr for the vice-presidency, but Republican electors had voted for both men and not distinguished between the offices. The defeated Federalists saw an eleventh-hour opportunity to deny Jefferson. "Mr. Burr's good fortune," John Adams wrote, "surpasses all ordinary rules, and exceeds that of Bonaparte."[37] The election—uncertain for the past year and uncertain still—would be decided in the House of Representatives.

Randolph shared the angst of his fellow Republicans at this unexpected turn of events. "If we suffer ourselves to be bullied by the aristocrats," he wrote, "they will defeat the election." He scoffed at a Federalist suggestion that "we must pass a law designating the person who shall exercise presidential powers . . . since there can be no elective one."[38] He even went so far to warn Federalists that "if they chose to defeat the election and to jeopardize the union . . . [t]hey might take upon themselves the responsibility of the measure. That however dear the union was to us, it was cherished as the means, not the end, of national happiness."[39] Though frustrated and distressed by Federalist maneuvers to maintain power, Randolph also was uneasy about Republicans dividing themselves into Jefferson and Burr camps. To Randolph, the individual holding the office was less important than the application of Republican principles. "I need not say how much *I* would prefer J. to B.," he wrote to Joseph Nicholson, "but . . . [if] our salvation depends on a *single* man, 'tis not worth our attention."[40]

Nicholson was taken aback by the scent of disloyalty in Randolph's letter and so advised him by return post. Randolph sought to reassure Nicholson, but his answer was fraught with portent. "The loss even of *one* man of mind may be, will be felt, perhaps severely, to any cause," he wrote; "but it is my clear conviction that if every man who is now, or ever has been, in publick employment were to die, in one night the affairs of the U.S., however embarrassed for the time, would be immediately restored, perhaps improved; and that the people would continue to govern themselves as they now do, according to their sovereign will and pleasure."[41] It was the answer of an independent man dedicated to fundamental change.

There was still a doubt whether Republicanism of any stripe would control the executive branch. The matter was placed before the House of Representatives on February 11, 1801. Each of the sixteen states would cast one vote; nine states constituted a majority. House members crowded into a small room just off the Senate chamber to choose the third president of the United States. Randolph cast his vote for Jefferson and posted letters to James Monroe and St. George Tucker advising them of the balloting:

> Seven times we have balloted—eight states for J—six for Burr—two, Maryland and Vermont divided. . . .
>
> We have balloted ten times. The result (with some variety in the majorities of the respective states) uniformly the same.
>
> It is now three in the morning. We have balloted 22 times & the result has been invariably the same—I see no prospect of an election. What are their motives I will not pretend to define.
>
> All firm—No election in my opinion. 28 Ballots. I have not slept for 32 hours.[42]

The Republicans were holding strong, thwarting all Federalist intrigue. On February 14, Randolph wrote to Tucker that balloting had gone on for thirty-one hours with no result.[43] The increasingly irrelevant Alexander Hamilton tried to dictate strategy to his Federalist colleagues, but it was Representative James Bayard who broke the deadlock. Bayard sought assurances that Jefferson would strengthen the Navy and look kindly upon reappointment of a close friend. Jefferson's acceptance of the deal was conveyed to Bayard, who then cast a blank vote on the 36th ballot.[44] That gave Jefferson a majority in Delaware. South Carolina followed suit. Jefferson had ten states and the presidency. "Thus," Randolph wrote to James Monroe, "ends this strange business."[45]

Randolph returned to Bizarre, riding high on a crest of partisan approbation. "The sentiments which you have been pleased to express concerning my political conduct," he wrote to Monroe, "are reciprocated on my part."[46] Randolph would certainly be a part of the House leadership when Congress convened the following December, and he believed his party stood at a unique moment in history. "The present alone is at our disposal," he wrote, "on the use to which it is applied depends the whole of what is estimable or amiable in human character."[47] He worried still about Republicans who viewed electoral success as the primary end of their efforts. "[In] this quarter, we think that the great work is only begun," he wrote to Nicholson, "and that without a *substantial reform* we shall have little reason to congratulate ourselves on the mere change of men."[48] He saw the lure of power, of office, of station, threatening to destroy all that was to be gained. Republicans had "scarcely . . . chanted *Te deum*" before their "political intercourse began to stagnate."[49] He fretted that Republicans would "prefer the loaves and fishes of the hour to the glory of regenerating their country, of restoring to our manners and our language the nervous tone of independence."[50]

Thus uneasiness coexisted with confidence as Randolph set out for Washington in the winter of 1801. It was as if he anticipated a great retreat from the success so recently obtained. Preparing himself, he prepared others. "Be assured," he wrote to Nicholson, "that my light shall not be hidden under a bushel."[51]

4

Master of the House

All parties feared him: each in turn
Beheld its schemes disjointed,
As right or left his fatal glance
And spectral finger pointed.

What would they do—these radical Republicans—now that they commanded a majority in Congress? Fear-mongering Federalists painted them as reckless demagogues enslaved to the whims of the people, disdainful of tradition, and purveyors of extreme French egalitarianism. They believed, one Federalist huffed, "that the *vox populi* is *vox dei*."[1] They would systematically enact their agenda, Representative James Bayard said, pausing at each step to "feel the public pulse." Then as "the fever increases . . . the moment of delirium will be seized to finish the great work of destruction."[2] The pikes of the French Revolution would be seen in the streets of Washington.

President Jefferson attempted to allay the fears of his defeated foes. "We are all republicans," he asserted in his Inaugural Address, "we are all federalists." His party's assumption of power signaled neither the dissolution of the Union nor the emasculation of the government. The will of the majority would prevail, Jefferson said, but "that will, to be rightful, must be reasonable" and protect the equal rights of the minority. As always with Jefferson, there was subtlety. He did not capitalize "republicans" or "federalists" in his text, thereby rendering the distinction a philosophical one, rather than a partisan one. Still, the moderate tone of the address went well toward achieving the desired effect. Bayard judged it "in political substance better than [the Federalists] expected; and not answerable to the expectations of the Partizans of the other side."[3]

The "Partizans," though, did have a clearly defined agenda. Republicans were determined, Randolph wrote, "to pay the debt off, to repeal the internal taxes, to retrench every unnecessary expense, military, naval, and civil,

[and] to enforce economy."[4] Jefferson's first message to Congress echoed this agenda. "There is reasonable ground of confidence," he wrote, "that we may now safely dispense with all the internal taxes . . . pay the interest on the public debts, and to discharge the principals in shorter periods," and enact "a salutary reduction . . . in our habitual expenditures." He challenged Congress to rein in spending and reduce the size and scope of the "too complicated [and] too expensive" government. Finally, Jefferson called for reform and reduction in the standing military and the federal judiciary.[5] Jefferson's reform agenda met with Randolph's "hearty approbation."[6]

Republicans enjoyed a numerically comfortable majority of sixty-eight members to thirty-eight Federalists in the House of Representatives. The count was a tighter eighteen to fourteen in the Senate. When the House convened, Nathaniel Macon, a Revolutionary War veteran, antifederalist legislator, and "foremost public man of North Carolina" was elected Speaker.[7] Henry Adams described Macon as an "ideal Southern Republican, independent, unambitious, free from intrigue, true to his convictions," but added that the Speaker was "on his knees to [Randolph] as before an Apollo."[8] William Branch Giles, a senior member and Jefferson ally, assumed the role of House majority leader. Randolph, six months shy of his twenty-ninth birthday, was named chairman of the Ways & Means Committee, effectively becoming House majority whip.[9] This job proved not so simple a task, even with superior numbers. "The character of the present congress," he wrote to Tucker, "altho it is republican in the general, or rather let me say hostile to the late administration, is by no means *marked*." Randolph found the majority to be "somewhat unwieldy" and bemoaned a "want of concert [and] even of discordance of opinion."[10]

"We are," Randolph wrote shortly before the start of Congress, "for a change of important principles."[11] He began that change on December 29, 1801, with a resolution "to reduce the military establishment of the United States." He followed this resolution with measures "to inquire whether any, and what, reductions can be made in the civil expenses of the Government of the United States," and "to inquire whether any, and what, alterations should be made in the Judicial Establishment of the United States." While these resolutions began their journey through the committee process, Randolph's Ways & Means Committee prepared legislation abolishing internal taxes and paying the national debt. Turning his attention to the federal budget, Randolph warned his colleagues that "he was unwilling to expend the public money, except in cases of absolute necessity."[12]

He seemed involved with everything. He was chairman of the committee to select the printer of House proceedings—a plum patronage appointment—and, in concert with Macon and Giles, set the calendar for consideration of legislation.[13] This latter duty required him to precisely factor "the absence of several members of great weight . . . the augmentation of new members not yet fully acquainted with the forms of business, and . . . the unusual mass of information presented to the House."[14] Creating a majority vote for each measure was a daunting task. Party loyalty was blurred by regional interests, and republican ideology was subordinated to pragmatism or politics. "Parties here," Randolph wrote, "consist of the old Federalists courting popularity . . . the same kind of characters, Republicanized, and lukewarm Republicans, who, added to the former, will perhaps constitute a bare majority of the House." He estimated about fifty members were "Republicans who hold the same principles now that they professed under adverse fortune."[15] By the time the Seventh Congress was one month old, Randolph was referring to the House as "the temple of confusion." His solution was to seize leadership of the disparate Republican elements "with a hand so heavy that William Pitt might have envied him."[16]

How did Randolph at twenty-nine, with his boyish looks and piping voice, command an assembly of accomplished statesmen, experienced politicians, and veteran legislators? His authority was based in his chairmanship of the Ways & Means Committee, but that position was not enough in itself to move all men. Part of his power was based in relationships. He was a favorite of Speaker Macon—with whom he shared lodgings—and was friends with Joseph Nicholson, the second ranking Republican on Ways & Means, and Majority Leader Giles.[17] This quartet managed every aspect of House activities.[18] "Mr. Giles and Mr. Randolph," Federalist Representative Manasseh Cutler wrote, "have much more openly avowed the plans of government under the new order of things than was expected."[19] Additionally, Randolph enjoyed "free communications of facts and opinions" with Albert Gallatin, secretary of the treasury and architect of Jefferson's economic package.

Randolph's relationship with Thomas Jefferson was more complex. The two men were distant cousins, but each man's style and temperament bore scant resemblance to that displayed by his kinsman. Jefferson would write that Randolph was "in the confidence [and] views of the administration" and, along with Nicholson, enjoyed "communications . . . [and] influence . . . almost solely."[20] The relationship, however, was never close. At times

Jefferson disclosed matters to Randolph; at other times "mutual delicacy" prevented a full exchange of views.[21] Whether or not the men were on intimate terms during these heady days of the Seventh Congress, Randolph was advocating administration measures and stood in alliance with the president. Thus his actions were cloaked with perceived—if not always actual—presidential favor.[22]

Apart from personal relationships, Randolph's command of the facts and figures associated with major legislative initiatives made him a valuable ally and a feared adversary. "If the gentleman had examined attentively this provision," he instructed an exasperated opponent during one debate, "he would have found it . . . copied almost verbatim from former acts." Representative Samuel Smith expressed "astonishment" that Randolph was "able off-hand to answer so effectively the objections that have been raised."[23] Randolph's mastery of the House Rules and procedures allowed him to deftly deflect Federalist parliamentary maneuvers. On one occasion, sorting through several Federalist motions to postpone debate, he asked "which of their various and contradictory reasons they mean to vote for a postponement—reasons so irreconcilable that if one is correct, the others must be false."[24]

Above all, Randolph's authority in the House was a product of his assertive personality. His "natural quickness of mind and faculty for ready speaking," Henry Adams wrote, "gave him a prominence in a body of men so little marked by ability as was the Seventh Congress."[25] It was a style that alternatively provoked fear or instilled confidence in friend and foe. "Mr. R[andolph]'s popular eloquence," Jefferson wrote, "gave him such advantages as to place him unrivalled as the leader of the house; and, altho' not conciliatory to those whom he led, principles of duty and patriotism induced many of them to swallow the humiliations he subjected them to."[26] Randolph realized that the success of Republican measures would require the lash—not of the whip he clutched in one hand as he spoke—but that of his mordant tongue and searing intellect. Senator William Plumer was the first to describe a sight destined to be legend in the House.

> Mr. Randolph goes to the House booted and spurred, with his whip in his hand, in imitation, it is said, of members of the British Parliament. He is a very slight man but of the common stature. At a little distance, he does not appear older than you are; but, upon a nearer approach, you perceive his wrinkles and grey hairs. He is, I believe, about thirty. He is

a descendant in the right line from the celebrated Indian Princess, Pocahontas. The Federalists ridicule and affect to despise him; but a despised
foe often proves a dangerous enemy. His talents are certainly far above
mediocrity. As a popular speaker, he is not inferior to any man in the
House. I admire his ingenuity and address; but I dislike his politics.[27]

The centerpiece of the Republican economic program was the repeal of
internal taxes. The administration's legislation eliminated taxes on "stills
and domestic distilled spirits, on refined sugars, licenses to retailers, sales
at auction, carriages for the conveyance of persons, and stamped vellum,
parchment, and paper."[28] The Federalists sought to sway public opinion by
introducing their own tax-reduction package. In reality, it was a reduction
on duties that primarily affected the shipping interests of Federalist-dominated New England. This effort went nowhere. Their next bill was more attractive: eliminating the duties on sugar, tea, and coffee. Federalists argued
that this tax cut would reduce the cost of these products and benefit the
poor. "There is not a hut or log-house in this extensive country," John Rutledge of South Carolina asserted, "where these articles are not used." The
Republican proposal, Federalists argued in terms not unfamiliar today, was
a tax cut for the rich. It was a clever move, casting the Federalists as champi-
ons of the downtrodden. Randolph would have none of it. "If revenue should
be found sufficient to extinguish the national debt . . . pay the expenses of
Government, repeal the internal taxes, and yet leave a surplus," he said, "I
will be happy to join gentlemen in making reductions on their imposts."[29]
He then taunted the newly discovered Federalist populism. "The gentleman
has lately taken up the cause of the poor—a cause with which he is just becoming acquainted." The Federalist tax measure was defeated.

Passage of the Republican bill appeared inevitable, so the Federalists
filled the *Annals of Congress* with lengthy speeches about Republican mismanagement of government. "This puts me in the mind of the boy who
pelted stones at the frog," Representative Benjamin Huger mockingly intoned, "and who, when called upon to say why he did so cruel a thing, said it
is a very pleasant thing to me. No doubt it is a very pleasant thing . . . to get
rid of this tax."[30] Randolph tossed back Huger's stones. "There is no species
of taxation so oppressive, whatever its amount," he said, "as that which compels the individual taxed to retrench his personal freedom, that calls upon
him to pay a specific sum, and compels him to pay, no matter what his ability is." And he pointed out that when the Federalists "enjoyed the power, the

idea of reducing the public burdens never entered into their minds; at any rate we heard nothing of it if it did."[31] The bill repealing internal taxes passed the House by a vote of 61 to 24.

The Public Debt bill, constructed by Gallatin and carried by Randolph, addressed the twin Republican goals of paying off the debt and reducing government expenditures. In 1801, the national debt stood at $112 million. The Republican proposal appropriated the sum of $7.3 million annually to be applied "until the whole of the present debt . . . shall be reimbursed and redeemed." The appropriation would be managed by commissioners of the "sinking fund" and would retire the debt within sixteen years. The additional benefit of the bill was that a yearly outlay of $7.3 million toward debt service in an annual budget totaling $9.5 million would leave only $2 million to fund the government. Less money meant less government, a point Randolph made during the floor debate. "A great effect of this appropriation," he said, "will be to insure an economical disbursement of the public money, which will be sufficient for every purpose of Government. . . . I regard this bill as involving a principle more important than any which has been adopted by Government, or which is likely to be adopted for several years."[32]

Randolph managed the Debt bill through three days of debate, tangling with Federalists James Bayard and Roger Griswold. Knowing he had the votes to pass the bill, he treated Federalist opposition with a bemused disdain. "I am sorry to be so unintelligible to the gentleman," he said to Griswold, "but when the laws of the United States are so unintelligible to that gentleman . . . doubtless drawn with perspicuity, and some of them drawn by himself, how can one individual member expect to be understood?"[33] The Public Debt bill passed the House by a vote of 55 to 19. The master of Bizarre was becoming the master of the House.

Republican legislative initiatives flowed virtually unabated. The standing military was reduced, a system to collect delinquent taxes was established, a naturalization act passed, and House representation was apportioned in wake of the Second Census. Randolph's disciplined leadership had tightened up an unwieldy majority. "We show, on this occasion, as I trust we shall on all occasions," he said on the House floor, "that . . . we advance the same principles now, when in possession of power, that we did when we had scarcely any prospect of getting into power."[34] And it was the subject of power that was the central issue in the most significant Republican reform: the repeal of the Judiciary Act of 1801.

Prior to 1801, a justice of the United States Supreme Court performed dual roles. He sat with the other five justices to hear cases on appeal, and he tried cases individually as a trial judge at the circuit court level. This latter responsibility was known as "circuit riding" and forced a justice to endure travel across inadequate roads in oppressive weather to distant courthouses. This unique arrangement often resulted in a justice hearing the same case on appeal that he had decided in trial court. The situation cried out for reform. The Federalist Congress responded by passing the Judiciary Act of 1801, which ended circuit riding and expanded federal jurisdiction in certain matters.

Had the Judiciary Act done no more, it would have produced little controversy, but it reduced the membership of the Supreme Court from six to five justices and created sixteen new circuit court judgeships. The timing of its passage—February 13, 1801, in the waning days of Federalist control of Congress and in the wake of Jefferson's victory—tainted the act with a decidedly partisan scent. John Adams had but twenty days remaining in his term, but he had no intention of leaving the appointment of new judges to his successor. Republicans cried foul at this court-packing and fostered the image of President Adams working late into the night making "midnight appointments." Republicans had long viewed the judicial branch as a seedbed of tyranny. Now this shameless power grab would create a haven for anti-Jefferson judges to harass, thwart, and denude the will of the people. Federalists increasingly viewed the judicial branch as the last redoubt of protection against radical republican reform. Both sides, then, reduced the issue of judicial reform to a power struggle with the most serious consequences for the republic.

The Republican Judiciary bill restored "circuit riding," but lightened the burden on the justices by excluding Kentucky, Tennessee, and Maine from the system and reducing the size of the remaining circuits. The bill's central feature, though, was the repeal of the Act of 1801 and abolishment of the sixteen new judgeships. Federalists knew what was at stake and launched an attack on the bill along several fronts. The Constitution, they argued, provided but one means for removing a federal judge: impeachment for misconduct, not elimination of the judge's position. They recounted the problems of circuit riding and submitted that the Act of 1801 was a genuine reform necessary for an efficient court system.[35] Finally, they assailed the Republican measure as imported French radicalism. "A spirit which has rode in the whirlwind and directed the storm . . . which has swept before it every vestige of law, religion, morality, and rational government," Representative

Archibald Henderson said, "it made its appearance within these walls, clothed in a gigantic body, impatient for action. . . . Have you a judiciary system . . . matured by the wisdom of your ablest and best men? It must be destroyed."[36]

Invective flew about the chamber for thirteen days. The Republicans, it was argued, were animated by the "vengeance of an irritated majority" and would relegate the United States to the "melancholy catalogue of fallen Republics."[37] They were a deranged party of demagogues "influenced by motives which it does not acknowledge even to itself."[38] In words that must have been particularly grating to Randolph, Representative Thomas Morris quoted extensively from the writings of St. George Tucker on the topic of judicial independence.[39] Republicans repeatedly cried order as they heard themselves accused of destroying the Constitution, severing the Union, and any number of other crimes. Roger Griswold, who three years earlier had assaulted Representative Matthew Lyon with a cane and fireplace tongs, picked another fight by saying the Republicans intended "to pervert [the Constitution's] meaning; to make it a nose of wax, to turn it in every direction."[40]

James Bayard delivered the primary speech of the Federalist effort. Holding the floor for two days, he asserted that Republican policies would "reduce the Army to a shadow . . . give the Navy to the worms. . . . [T]he revenue shall depend upon the winds and waves; the judges shall be made our creatures."[41] These steps were but precursors to "children crying for bread, and gray hairs sinking in sorrow to the grave."[42] Federal judges, he argued, have life tenure and serve for good behavior. The Constitution gave no support to the "feudal argument" that "the judges are the President's judges." Again the specter of the French Revolution was raised as Bayard warned that Republican actions had but one consequence for the people: "the gallows." Finally, he concluded, "The meditated blow is mortal, and from the moment it is struck, we may bid a final adieu to the Constitution."[43]

Randolph had remained relatively quiet during the debate, but he alone could answer Bayard's rhetorical flourishes and historical analogies. It was the supreme moment of the battle over the Judiciary. Randolph stood and clutched his whip.

He reminded his colleagues that it was a "long catalogue of unpopular acts which have deprived [the Federalists] of the public confidence." He would not "peremptorily deny" that their self-proclaimed motivation in reforming the Judiciary was to "nobly [sacrifice] their political existence on the altar of the general welfare . . . at the shrine of patriotism," but, he smirked, "in this age of infidelity, I may be permitted to doubt."[44] The bill was constitutional, Randolph argued, because "it aims not at the displacing one set of men, from whom you differ in political opinion, with a view to introduce others, but at the general good by abolishing useless offices." Far from abusing power, the bill set right the disgrace of the midnight appointments. That was the act of "a desperate faction, finding themselves about to be dismissed from the confidence of their country," intending to "pervert the power of erecting courts, [and] to provide to an extent for their adherents and themselves."[45] Federalist "usurpation and ambition," not radical Republicans, had brought the nation to this moment.[46]

Randolph spoke at length about the use and concentration of power, but not just the fleeting power of rival parties. He addressed the potential power of unchecked judicial review. Two years before John Marshall crafted the concept in *Marbury v. Madison*, Randolph warned of its dangers. Had federal judges the authority, Randolph asked, to declare laws unconstitutional? "Here is a new power, of a dangerous and uncontrollable nature," he said; "The decision of a Constitutional question must rest somewhere. Shall it be confided to men immediately responsible to the people, or to those who are irresponsible?"[47]

How, Randolph asked, would judicial supremacy protect the liberty of the citizen? What if a future Congress enacted an unconstitutional law that was subsequently upheld by the federal courts? "Suppose," he asked, expanding on the theme, "your reliance had been altogether on this broken staff, and not on the elective principle. . . . [W]here is your remedy?" He let the question hang in the chamber. Then he answered that the appeal lay with "the nation, to whom alone, and not a few privileged individuals, it belongs to decide, in the resort, on the Constitution."[48]

This thought seemed far-fetched when Randolph uttered it, yet it anticipated the emergence of an unchecked judiciary. Less than twenty years later, John Marshall would fulfill Randolph's prophecy with his sweeping opinion in *McCulloch v. Maryland*. In one case, Marshall would expand federal power to include acts not enumerated in the Constitution, establish the inferior status of the states in relation to the Union, and place the Supreme Court as the ultimate arbiter of constitutional issues.[49]

"A Government entrenched beyond the reach of public opinion," Randolph concluded, "had for ages been accumulating one abuse upon another . . . [until] the nation was compelled to seek refuge in a recurrence to revolutionary principles." This was such a moment. The measure would not destroy the Constitution. It would be, he asserted, "the deathblow to the pretension of rendering the Judiciary a hospital for decayed politicians; to prevent the State courts from being engulfed by those of the Union; to destroy the monstrous ambition of arrogating to this House the right of evading all the prohibitions of the Constitution, and holding the nation at bay."[50]

The debate lasted another seven days before all arguments were exhausted. Bayard attempted four amendments and two postponements before Randolph forced a vote. The Judiciary Act of 1802—repealing the act of 1801, abolishing the newly created judgeships—was adopted fifty-nine to thirty-two.

"The Legislature rises this day," Jefferson wrote. "They have carried into execution steadily almost all the propositions submitted to them in my message at the opening of the session."[51] For Randolph, the first session of the Seventh Congress would ever be the shinning hour of republicanism, that rarest instance when principles became policy. "We sailed on for some time," he said years later, "in the full tide of successful experiment, unobstructed by squalls or adverse gales. . . . At that time, sir, all was prosperity and joy."[52] Randolph was, Henry Adams conceded, "a more important man in May, 1802, when he rode home to Bizarre, than in the previous autumn when he left it. Congress had done good work under his direction."[53]

Randolph stopped in Richmond to revive his spirits by indulging his favorite pastime: horse racing. "Desdemona, that jewel which thousands were sacrificed to obtain," he reported about a certain steed, "is now of as little worth as her biped namesake, after the frantic Moor had wrecked his jealous fury on her fair form."[54] Reaching Bizarre on May 8, Randolph learned that the "repeal of the judiciary and the taxes are equally popular here and throughout the state, except as to a *very* few republicans who think the former unconstitutional."[55] He noted that the Federalists were enjoying some resurgence—"the party begins to look as well as talk big"—but he did not "think the danger urgent." For the most part, Randolph passed a somewhat peaceful summer, managing his plantations and writing letters to friends and colleagues. He contended with an oppressive Virginia climate, "enough to shatter any carcass less than that of a Mammoth," and with the uneasy relationship of sisters Judith and Nancy, which hung over the house as heavily as did the humidity.[56] A degree of solace came, as usual, on horseback. He crossed the countryside, talking with constituents, inspecting his holdings, and planning how to stave off a Federalist counterattack in the coming session. "You may . . . rely," he wrote to Nicholson, "upon my entire, altho feeble, cooperation in defeating the schemes of any man, or set of men, who shall presume to make the best interests of themselves a subject of dirty traffick for their eventual aggrandizement."[57]

Upon arriving in Washington in December 1803, Randolph assumed the role of House majority leader in wake of the ill health of William Giles.[58] A month into the session, William Plumer wrote that Randolph, "a pale, meager, ghostly man, has more popular and effective talents than any other member of the party."[59] Following the history and histrionics of the first session of the Seventh Congress, the second session was decidedly more subdued. International affairs drove the agenda. In October 1802, Spain's King Charles IV transferred the Louisiana territory to France. The Spanish agent in New Orleans promptly revoked American access to the ports—effectively closing navigation of the Mississippi River. Jefferson had long harbored the hope of obtaining New Orleans from the Spanish, but now the acquisition became a national necessity. The president knew he must prevent Napoleon from establishing a presence on the continent. He directed Secretary of State James Madison and Ambassador to France Robert Livingston to seek a diplomatic settlement. Randolph brought the matter to the attention of the House on December 17, expressing the view that "it behooved the whole United States to cherish and protect" the free navigation of the Mississippi. He suspected that the Federalists would exploit the situation for partisan advantage. "They have more than one object in this," he wrote to James Monroe. "To embarrass the adm[inistration] with a foreign war, thereby creating a great expense, at the same time that the revenue is materially diminished, is the primary object; for they well know that the success of the present men and measures is almost reduced to a mere question of finance."[60]

Two days after this letter, the Federalists began to beat the war drum. Randolph defended the administration by documenting the prudent steps taken by President Jefferson and reading into the record a lengthy defense drafted by Monroe. He then pointed his forefinger at Roger Griswold and hurled Federalist accusations of "Jacobinism and disorganization" back across the chamber. Federalists, he growled, were "sickening at the sight of the public prosperity" and thus sought "war, confusion, and a consequent derangement of our finances" to achieve public favor."[61] One week later the

Congress authorized $2 million for the purchase of New Orleans. Randolph had provided Jefferson with the necessary means to exercise his options regarding the nation's expansion.

For the second time in as many years, Randolph returned to Bizarre in triumph. He had been "the most active member of the House," Henry Adams wrote, "all financial business came under his charge, while much that was not financial depended on his approval; in short, he with his friend Nicholson and the Speaker controlled legislation."[62] On his thirtieth birthday, June 3, 1803, Randolph—brilliant and eccentric, confident and arrogant—stood alongside Jefferson, Madison, and Monroe as Virginia's most prominent statesmen. He was easily re-elected to the House.

Randolph's summer at Bizarre got off on a wrong foot, literally, when one of his mounts threw him and he suffered a dislocated shoulder. His good spirits helped him through "two more days of hell," and he even jokingly conceded to his sister that he might have a tendency toward hypochondria. But, he quickly added, if that were true, why did he "suffer from pains almost endless?"[63] His bantering tone continued in a series of letters regarding the consolidation of Republican gains. "I think you wise men at the seat of government have much to answer for in respect to the temper prevailing around you," he wrote to Albert Gallatin. "By their fruit ye know them."[64] He told Nicholson to "quit the vile practice of eating and drinking, reduce yourself to the standard of activity (about my size)" in order to train newly elected Republicans.[65] And always he watched the Federalists. "The humiliation of this country is their triumph," he wrote to James Monroe, "her honor and prosperity their defeat."[66]

Word arrived in July that Monroe and Livingston had signed a treaty whereby the Untied States would acquire from France the entire Louisiana Territory. Exceeding their authority, the ministers negotiated terms providing for a purchase price of $15 million with ratification within six months of the signing date of April 30, 1803. Time to act was short. Jefferson immediately released the treaty and called Congress into session for October 17. While approval of the treaty rested with the Senate, Randolph would bear responsibility for securing the purchase price and explaining how the government could acquire territory absent a specific grant of such authority in the Constitution.[67]

Randolph introduced a resolution "that provision ought to be made for carrying into effect the treaty."[68] For the next week, he held the floor virtually alone, delivering three major addresses and responding to Federalist feints and thrusts. If the House was satisfied with the terms of the treaty, he argued, "let us pass the laws necessary for carrying it into effect."[69] Roger Griswold answered Randolph's decidedly Hamiltonian stance by questioning the constitutionality of the treaty. "If it be constitutionally made and ratified?!" Randolph snapped back, smarting ever so slightly at being called on an apparent contradiction. "Really, sir, this is the age of ingenious distinction. Unfortunately, I am too dull to comprehend how a treaty can be constitutionally ratified which is not constitutionally made."[70]

"This may be logic in some schools," Randolph concluded, "but surely it does not deserve, in this House, so respectable an epithet."[71] Still, a purist such as Randolph must have recognized the anti-republicanism of his position. Expansion necessarily led to centralization of power; new states, with no history of exercising sovereignty, would look favorably on an activist federal government. "To subdivide the state," he had written earlier that year, "and thereby to bring their governments into contempt has long been the favorite idea of federalism. They know that to reduce the large states to impotence is the first great step to consolidation—is to take off the principal check on the unconstitutional tendency of the general government."[72] Likewise, a nation extending across so vast a territory would spark nationalism distinctly hostile to states' rights, a fact borne out in less than ten years when new western states championed federally funded internal improvements. Monroe had exceeded his authority, Jefferson was hedging on the principle of strict construction, and Congress was being asked to ratify a *fait accompli.* Any one of these actions by a Federalist administration would have sparked Republican backlash—with Randolph in the lead. Yet in this instance, Randolph held his tongue and served his president, though not without a warning. "The constitutionality," he wrote to Jefferson, "is the theme of opposition."[73] The president considered submitting a constitutional amendment, but refrained from doing so due to the tight time frame for approval.[74] Thus it fell to Randolph to present an argument consistent with Republican principles and the Constitution.

The practice in operation at the time of ratification, he argued on October 25, 1803, was to allow the states to "rightfully acquire territory in their allied capacity." How much more, he asked, "is the existing Government competent to make an acquisition?"[75] Reminding the Federalists of their war-talk the prior January when the port of New Orleans was closed,

Randolph made the obvious point: "Can a nation acquire by force that which she cannot acquire by treaty?"[76] Jefferson had chosen "political right" as opposed to "physical power" to obtain the territory. "If the navigation of the Mississippi alone was of sufficient importance to justify war," he said, "surely the possession of every drop of water which runs into it . . . would be acknowledged as inestimably valuable."[77]

The enabling legislation passed the House and reached the president's desk on October 31. Randolph had loyally carried out another of Jefferson's bold initiatives, one he believed was "destined to form a new era in our annals."[78] The Federalists, beaten again, viewed Randolph with disdain. "The manner in which he exercised his authority today," Senator William Plumer wrote, "was very disgusting. . . . Profuse in censuring the *motives* of his opponents—artful in evading their arguments, and peremptory in demanding the vote—sitting on his seat insolently and frequently exclaiming *I hope this motion will not prevail*—or when it suited his views, *I hope this will be adopted.*"[79]

Disdain of Randolph was not limited to Federalists. On November 25, Virginia Representative John Wayles Eppes—President Jefferson's son-in-law—introduced a resolution instructing Randolph's Ways & Means Committee to inquire "what reduction may be made in the expenses" of the government. Randolph, mildly annoyed, opposed the motion with the observation that his committee already monitored expenditures. Eppes pressed the matter, commenting that if the committee possessed the authority "they had either omitted or neglected to discharge it." Randolph, now slightly more animated, cut to the chase, demanding that if Eppes's motivation was censure, "let the gentleman bring forward a fair and open resolution of censure, and not aim at producing this effect in a side way."[80] Eppes's resolution was voted down, but not before Randolph declared he would speak his mind on issues before the House "without reference to the quarter from which it shall proceed." That comment was viewed by many as a veiled reference to Jefferson, who, it was assumed, occupied the same quarter as his son-in-law. As that view gained currency, Randolph rushed to assure the president that "[certain] expressions of mine, used in debate on Friday last, having been interpreted by some as conveying an allusion to the executive, I have no hesitation most explicitly to disavow every intention of such a nature."[81]

Jefferson responded that his son-in-law spoke for himself and Randolph need not offer an explanation of his remarks. "I see too many proofs of the imperfection of human reason," the president wrote, "to entertain wonder or intolerance at any differences of opinion on any subject."[82] The incident would merit little note did it not appear in retrospect to be the first hint of a coming break between Randolph and the man whose cause he had so long championed.

5

An Evil Daily Magnifying

He held his slaves: yet kept the while
His reverence for the Human;
In the dark vassals of his will
He saw but Man and Woman!

No hunter of God's outraged poor
His Roanoke valley entered;
No trader of souls of men
Across his threshold ventured.

Amid the flurry of the historic seventh session, Randolph presented a routine committee report regarding the Indiana Territory. The report responded to a letter from William Henry Harrison, president of the Indiana Territory Convention (and future president of the United States), requesting that slavery—barred in the territory by the Northwest Ordinance—be allowed for a ten-year period. Harrison argued that a labor shortage required a suspension of the ban, but he was also concerned that slaveholders were settling in Kentucky, not Indiana, due to the ban.[1] The request was referred to a committee chaired by Randolph. The committee reported that it was "inexpedient to suspend" the ban on slavery, but went beyond a simple denial of Harrison's request. The committee members, the report continued, "deem it highly dangerous and inexpedient to impair a provision wisely calculated to promote the happiness and prosperity of the Northwestern country, and to give strength and security to that extensive frontier." The "salutary operation of this sagacious and benevolent restraint" of slavery would provide the citizens of Indiana with "ample remuneration for a temporary privation of labor and of emigration."[2]

It is unknown if Randolph drafted the report, but he commanded a majority on the committee and could direct the report as he saw fit.[3] Therefore it is curious that a slaveholder representing slaveholders would assert the authority of the federal government to preserve the free labor status of the

Northwest Territory—curious, but not surprising. Randolph's views about slavery were a complex mixture of realism, religion, culture, and custom.[4] His views reflect the conflict, identified by Lacy Ford in his study of slavery and the South, between slavery and "republican ideals, which treasured liberty and despised dependence."[5]

"[We] must concern ourselves with what is," Randolph told Josiah Quincy, "and slavery exists."[6] That comment concedes that slavery existed, in part, because Randolph was one of its most vigorous defenders against any actual or perceived attack, deeming it "a question of life and death" for the South.[7] Yet this same man confided to Quincy that the "curse of slavery . . . an evil daily magnifying, great as it already is, embitters many a moment of the Virginia landholder who is not duller than the clod beneath his feet."[8] Randolph was a persistent opponent of the slave trade, considered emancipation to be a viable option, never bought or sold slaves, and repeatedly condemned the institution.[9] Like Joseph Nicholson, he supported manumission, but stopped short of abolition.[10] He was, by all accounts, a humane master.[11] When Randolph's 383 slaves were manumitted, only seven bore any "fleshmarks," and none of these had been caused by physical abuse.[12] Many times, Randolph articulated the conflict Ford identified—often combining condemnation and defense of slavery in the same sentence. "I have often bewailed the lot that made me their keeper," he wrote in 1818. "I now bow with submission to the decree of Him who has called me to this state and pray to be enabled to discharge the duties of it."[13]

In his youth, Randolph read the anti-slavery essay of British abolitionist Thomas Clarkson. The "impression made on my mind by the dissertation," he wrote, "sunk deep."[14] He asserted that, from the time he read the pamphlet, "all my feelings and instincts were in opposition to slavery in every shape; to the subjugation of one man's will to that of another."[15] It is not surprising that Randolph would be drawn to Clarkson's essay, which bristled with eloquent appeals to "reason, justice, nature, the principles of law and government, the whole doctrine, in short, of natural religion, and the revealed voice of God."[16] Randolph no doubt heard echoes of his own principles when he read: "With respect to the *loss of liberty*, it is evident that men bear nothing worse . . . and that they have shewn, by many and memorable instances, that even death is to be preferred."[17] Yet the impact of Clarkson was diluted, Randolph wrote, "by pleasure, or business," by custom and culture.[18] "I read myself into this madness, as I have read myself into some agricultural improvements," he said, figuratively shaking off Clarkson's influence, "but, as with these last I worked myself out of them, so also I worked myself out of it."[19]

Yet a dash of Clarkson's spirit can be seen in Randolph's reaction to Gabriel's slave rebellion. During the summer of 1800, a literate and physically imposing slave named Gabriel organized a far-reaching slave revolt.[20] His plan called for taking Governor James Monroe hostage, while simultaneously forming alliances with poor whites and Indians. Gabriel found startling success recruiting slaves for this far-fetched plan. His reach extended from Richmond, south to Petersburg, east to Norfolk, west to Albemarle—virtually to the doorstep of Bizarre.[21] The revolt was undone by rain and the loose lips of several conspirators. Sixty-five slaves were put on trial; twenty-six—including Gabriel—were hanged. Randolph expressed relief that the revolt was quelled, but saw similarities between the revolutions he championed and the actions of Gabriel and his followers. "The accused," he wrote, "have exhibited a spirit, which, if it becomes general, must deluge the southern country in blood. They manifested a sense of their rights, and contempt of danger and a thirst for revenge which portend the most unhappy consequences."[22] Randolph knew the spirit of liberty when he saw it.[23]

Randolph also reflected the "evangelical Christianity" that challenged the morality of holding slaves.[24] "I tremble," he wrote, "for the dreadful retribution which this horrid thirst for African blood . . . may bring upon us."[25] Randolph's "conscience and the Bible" produced the "conviction that the evils of emancipation (they are great and serious) are in their nature temporary and that they are incident to every great change in human condition." Worse consequences, he judged, "followed the reformation in England."[26]

In addition to the influence of republican ideals and Christianity, Randolph exhibited a benevolent spirit in his words and actions regarding slavery. In so doing, he demonstrated the rare characteristics identified by Lacy Ford as "the paternalistic ideal." Essential to that ideal was that "slaves must be recognized as human beings, regardless of their alleged inferiority."[27] While Randolph always maintained himself as master, he recognized the humanity of his slaves and treated them accordingly. "My best friends," he wrote "are a few faithful slaves. . . . [They] are a loyal and for their opportunity good people."[28] He repeated this refrain in numerous letters, even at one point referring to his "family of more than two hundred mouths looking up to me for food."[29] While he often warned other slaveholders about uprisings, he apparently entertained no thought of his own safety. "I sleep with windows open to the floor, my doors are never fastened, seldom shut," he wrote. "I might be robbed or knocked on the head any night of the week . . . but I lie down without apprehension & awake in safety."[30] He even favorably compared slaves to many of his fellow freeholders. "I need not tell you that from the time I entered Virginia I found . . . everything mean, dirty and disgraceful and out at elbows," he wrote. "The negroes alone are cheerful, docile, and obliging & I verily think the most respectable."[31]

Paternalism required that "the day-to-day governance of a slave population should be conducted similarly to how male household heads governed their white families, that is, with a combination of fairness and firmness, a balance of affection and discipline."[32] Randolph made certain that his "negroes are attended to in sickness and in health, their comfort promoted as far as practicable, and their labor abridged by being judiciously directed as well by mechanical contrivances."[33] He recognized that he needed to "extort from the laboring portion of my slaves as much profit as will support them and their families in sickness and in health, in infancy and when past labor" while at the same time making "a fair rent for my land and profit on my stock." He conceded that to accomplish that balance "without severity to the slaves or pinching them in necessaries of life" was "an arduous problem."[34] At times, Randolph met this obligation with sentiments as perverse as the institution itself. "I received last evening, by your servant Billy," he wrote to a neighbor, "your letter . . . requesting me to sell his wife to you."

> The woman is extremely infirm, labouring under an uncommon and incurable disease . . . besides some other affliction which has prevented and will forever prevent her being a mother. Her personal services are of little worth, but her trustworthiness renders her to *me* of great value, as you will readily conceive from my peculiar situation and frequent absence from home. This however ought not—and should not enhance her price to you in case she may wish to leave me. The connection between her and Billy was formed very much against my wishes, foreseeing the very case which has come to pass. . . . Since I began this note I learn from her mother (for Nancy is very ill) that, upon consulting her, she declares that she has no wish to be sold.[35]

The nineteenth-century slaveholder believed he must exercise stewardship, most often expressed "in a Christian form."[36] Randolph's stewardship was demonstrated primarily in his humane treatment of his slaves, but he often contemplated their fate. "But one subject presses hard upon me, among my worldly concerns," he wrote to his brother. "It is the making of suitable provision for my slaves . . . at my death."[37] He worried about the "cruel fate to which our laws would consign them" once he was gone.[38] He refrained from selling parts of his estate because of "the fate to which my poor, miserable slaves would, in that event, be exposed."[39] Additionally, Randolph did not buy or sell any slaves, attempted to keep families together, and provided freedom and land in his will. During his life, he settled for treating his slaves like "the Catholic negroes of Maryland who are like the Irish Peasant implicitly guided by the Priest."[40] At Roanoke, Randolph was the priest.

Finally, "paternalism required the paternalist to show some larger scope of humanitarian concern . . . in the acceptance of a broader social responsibility for making slave society work humanely as well as profitably."[41] In this regard Randolph was particularly attentive to actions taken by Virginia and by sister states. He denounced South Carolina for reinstituting its slave trade. "To her indelible disgrace," he wrote, "she has legalized this abomination. All her rice, indigo, and cotton is to be converted into slaves. The labor of the miserable negro is to procure fresh companions of his wretchedness. . . . It behooves Virginia, in my opinion, to look to the consequences."[42]

Randolph frequently condemned the Virginia legislature for its failure to take any constructive steps toward betterment of slave conditions or gradual emancipation. "To rouse the stupidity and apathy of the Virginia Assembly," he wrote in 1811, "will, I fear, be a hopeless task." He believed it would take slave uprisings, "the blaze of their houses and the shrieks of their wives and children" to force policy initiatives.[43] His stepfather, St. George Tucker, had proposed in 1797 a plan for emancipation, and his distant cousin, George Tucker, had introduced a similar plan in 1800. No comments from Randolph on either plan have survived, but he surely knew of them, and later condemned the legislature's failure "to devise some plan for arresting an evil, which hitherto they have suffered to increase upon us, with the most astonishing supineness."[44]

Ford concludes that "virtually no slaveholder succeeded in fulfilling the paternalistic ideal, and probably few tried with a high degree of consistency."[45] Randolph's record demonstrates that he came very close on both accounts.

Randolph's public positions, however, did not reflect his private attitudes. To his credit, his republican, states' rights, strict constructionist philosophy was not crafted as a defense of slavery. Both Randolph and John Taylor of Caroline, Adam Tate writes, "primarily used states' rights to oppose political centralization."[46] Randolph applied to slavery the same views he applied to a host of issues throughout his political life. The unpleasant, but nevertheless true, fact is that the Constitution protected slavery. To Randolph, federal efforts to limit or diminish the institution were no different from other efforts to tamper with the words of the Constitution. In a short time, however, defense of states' rights, tradition, and the Constitution came to equate with the defense of slavery.[47] Once that position was reached, Randolph was forced to conclude, his nobler traits aside, that one "will find no instance in history where two distinct races have occupied the soil except in the relation of master and slave."[48]

Randolph saw nothing in the abolitionist movement except concealed attempts by northern mercantile interests to subjugate the South into an agricultural colony. "These Yankees have almost reconciled me to negro slavery," he wrote. "They have produced a revulsion even on my mind, what then must the effect be on those who had no scruples on the subject. I am persuaded that the cause of humanity to these unfortunates has been put back a century, certainly a generation, by the unprincipled conduct of ambitious men, availing themselves of a good as well as of a fanatical spirit in the nation."[49]

Randolph's lifetime of conflicting public and private sentiments were summarized in a speech he delivered on March 2, 1826. Slavery had to be addressed, he said, because time was running short. It was "a thing which cannot be hid—it is not dry rot that you can cover with the carpet, until the house tumbles about your ears. You might as well try to hide a volcano, in full operation—it cannot be hid—it is a cancer in your face."[50]

Randolph saw danger on all sides—in the South living with an increasingly unstable system, and in the North's radical abolitionism. Serious men should take the matter seriously. "It must not be tampered with by quacks," he snapped, "who never saw the disease or the patient."[51] The radicalism of abolition societies boded ill for the very people they proposed to champion. "When men are furiously and fanatically fond of any object of any set of opinions whatever," he warned, "they will sacrifice to that fanatical attachment their own property, their own peace, their own lives. . . . Fanaticism, political or religious, has no stopping place short of Heaven—or of Hell."[52]

Randolph counseled prudence. "From my childhood," he said, "all my feelings and instincts were in opposition to slavery in every shape; to the subjugation of one man's will to that of another," but reform had to come constitutionally and at its own pace.[53] "If they would only be content to let

the man alone . . . he will, maybe, get well; or at best, he can but die a natural death—probably an easy one. But, no sir, the politico-religious Quack
. . . will hear nothing but his nostrum. All is to be forced—nothing can be
trusted to time, or to nature." Slavery, Randolph believed, would fall under
its own weight. "It has run its course in the Northern States; it is beginning
to run its course in Maryland. The natural death of slavery is the unprofit-
ableness of its most expensive labor. It is also beginning in the meadow and
grain country of Virginia."[54]

Randolph moved to an axiomatic conclusion. "The moment this labor of
the slave ceases to be profitable to the master," he predicted, "if the slave will
not run away from the master, the master *will* run away from the slave."[55]
He warned his colleagues that "a statesman, never losing sight of principles,
is to be guided by circumstances; and, judging contrary to the exigencies of
the moment, he may ruin his country forever."[56]

Randolph's remarks amounted to an invitation for the North to treat on
the issue, but within the Constitution. By the time he uttered these words,
though, circumstances had probably outrun reasoned discussion, just as
circumstances had never been quite right for Randolph to take any action to
set slavery toward ultimate eradication. Randolph could do little more than
lament the "great danger . . . that has increased, is increasing, and *must* be
diminished, or it must come to its regular catastrophe."[57]

6

Yazoo Men

Sworn foe of Cant, he smote it down
With trenchant wit unsparing,
And, mocking, rent with ruthless hand
The robe Pretence was wearing.

Republican desire to reform—or control—the federal judiciary was not satiated with passage of the Judiciary Act of 1801. The Federalists, Jefferson wrote, had "retired into the judiciary as a stronghold. There the remains of federalism are to be preserved and fed from the treasury, and from that battery all the works of republicanism are to be beaten down and erased."[1] His words were hardly spoken when the Federalist battery fired a significant blast. In early 1803, Chief Justice John Marshall, speaking for a unanimous court in *Marbury v. Madison,* announced: "It is emphatically the province and duty of the judicial department to say what the law is."[2] By the stroke of his quill, Marshall laid the groundwork upon which future courts would establish the supremacy of the judicial branch—the very danger about which Randolph had spoken during the repeal of the Judiciary Act.[3] Though Marshall had restricted judicial review to only those cases in which Congress had unconstitutionally meddled with the Court, Jefferson saw the decision as creating "a despotic branch."[4]

Republicans scrambled for a response. The Constitution offered little guidance. Article III, Section 1, stated that judges "shall hold their offices during good behavior." This undefined phrase implied life tenure for appointees, which reduced Republican options to little more than a judicial death watch. "[How] are vacancies to be obtained?" Jefferson had written two months into his term. "Those by deaths are few; by resignation none. Can any other mode than that of removal be proposed?"[5] The obvious option was the largely undefined process of impeachment, but who would be the test case? Marshall, by virtue of his general character and conduct, had carefully placed himself beyond the reach of impeachment. Associate Justice Samuel Chase was less sure-footed.

Arrogant, short-tempered, harsh, and imposing, Justice Chase seemed "to move perpetually with a mob at his heels."[6] His patriotic credentials were impeccable: early, passionate supporter of liberty; friend of George Washington; signer of the Declaration of Independence. Appointed to the Supreme Court in 1796 by Washington, Chase established himself as a capable, but partisan, Federalist judge. His open support of John Adams during the 1800 campaign caused Republicans to view him as the most obnoxious symbol of judicial misconduct. Chase made the Republican case much easier during several high-profile cases. The first involved John Fries, a Pennsylvanian charged with treason in regard to the Whisky Rebellion of 1794. Fries had been convicted but had won a new trial, at which Justice Chase was to preside. On the trial day, Chase handed his written opinion to the clerk before hearing testimony or argument from counsel. Fries's stunned attorneys watched their client convicted and condemned to death without having argued the case.[7]

Chase followed this case with one involving James Callender—the most infamous scandal-mongering propandist of the day. In 1797, Callender had broken the story on Alexander Hamilton's adulterous affair with Maria Reynolds, landed a job with the pro-Jefferson *Richmond Examiner,* and published a scathing personal attack on President Adams titled *The Prospect Before Us.* Judged even by the immoderate standards of the day, Callender's language in the pamphlet was shockingly provocative. Chase decided to call Callender to task. He issued a warrant for Callender's arrest, set an immediate trial date, bullied the defense attorneys, and refused to dismiss a juror who admitted his prejudice. Callender was convicted at what was little more than a show trial.[8] Chase's circuit riding took him next to Newcastle, Delaware, where he tried to initiate a Callender-like trial against another Republican newspaper editor. Even sympathetic Federalist prosecutors could find nothing objectionable in the defendant's paper.[9] Finally, charging a Baltimore grand jury in May 1803, Chase left little of his view of Republicans to the imagination: "The independence of the national judiciary is already shaken to its foundation, and the virtue of the people alone can restore it. . . . [O]ur republican constitution will sink into a mobocracy, the worst of all possible governments. . . . [T]he modern doctrines by our late reformers, that all men, in a state of society, are entitled to enjoy equal liberty and equal rights, have brought this mighty mischief upon us; and I fear that it will rapidly progress, until peace and order, freedom and property, shall be destroyed."[10]

"You must have heard of the extraordinary charge of Chase to the grand jury at Baltimore," Jefferson wrote to Joseph Nicholson. "Ought this sedition and official attack on the principles of our Constitution, and on the proceedings of a State, to go unpunished?" Having condemned Chase's conduct and encouraged a response, Jefferson then invited himself out of the controversy. "I ask these questions for your consideration. For myself, it is better that I should not interfere."[11]

The president knew there could be but one response: impeachment. Nicholson agreed but declined to assume principal management of the case. He was being touted as Chase's replacement on the court and did not wish to be viewed as the driving force hastening the justice's departure. Speaker Macon agreed that Nicholson's discretion was necessary in this case and so assigned the management of the impeachment to Randolph.[12]

On January 5, 1804, Randolph told the House that Chase "has been found wanting in his duty to himself and his country" and asked for a formal inquiry. "[Let] us throw aside these leading-strings and crutches of precedent," Randolph told his colleagues, "and march with a firm step to the object before us."[13] In quick order, a House committee reported on March 12 that Chase should be impeached. The House adopted the recommendation by a vote of 73 to 32. Randolph presented seven articles of impeachment on the day before Congress adjourned. The first two articles charged Chase with misconduct in the Fries trial. The third, fourth, and fifth articles dealt with Chase's "manifest injustice, partiality, and intemperance" in the Callander trial. The sixth article raised the impropriety of Chase's conduct during the trial in Newcastle, Delaware. The seventh and most serious charge addressed the political harangue Chase delivered to the Baltimore grand jury. The vote on the articles was scheduled for November.[14] Randolph had reignited the war with the federal judiciary and had every reason to believe that he was acting on the direct wishes of the president. If the past was prologue, Chase's removal would be handled with dispatch.

Randolph had one more item to put on Congress's agenda. In January 1795, the Georgia legislature directed the governor to transfer more than thirty-five million acres to four land companies at a cost of one and a half cents per acre. The vast tract of fertile land—known as the Yazoo land, after one of its major rivers—consisted of the territory between the western boundary of Georgia and the Mississippi River. The land giveaway was stunning in itself, but amazement turned to outrage when it was discovered that every member of the legislature who voted for the transfer had been bribed with shares in the Yazoo land companies.[15]

The state of Georgia erupted in righteous indignation. Legislators were burned in effigy, localities passed resolutions of condemnation, and newspapers published scathing denunciations. It was reported that a state senator, "to avoid being tied to a sapling and whipped, fled to South Carolina, whither he was followed and killed by some of his constituents."[16] United States Senator James Jackson resigned his seat and returned home to lead an "Anti-Yazoo" party. In 1796, the citizens of Georgia elected a completely new legislature—throwing out every corrupt legislator.[17] The new legislature promptly rescinded the land transfer, nullified the enabling legislation, and ordered all records of the nefarious deed expunged from public record. The enrolled law conveying the lands was publicly burned in a ceremony on the state capitol grounds, the spark ignited by reflecting the sun's rays through a glass.[18] The hand of God, it was said, was alone sufficient to purge the state of this great sin.

Nonetheless, as the hated law burned on the lawn of the state capitol, the Yazoo land companies were busily selling shares of the real estate to innocent third-party purchasers. And—God and Georgia notwithstanding—the Constitution of the United States prohibited impairment of contracts. So the question was presented: Who owned the land? The state of Georgia by rescinding the corrupt transfer? Or the numerous purchasers who bought land from state established land companies? Opinions varied—Alexander Hamilton weighed in on behalf of the purchasers—so a federal commission was established to clear the cloud from the Yazoo land titles. The United States was represented by the three highest-ranking members of the Jefferson cabinet: Secretary of State James Madison, Secretary of Treasury Albert Gallatin, and Attorney General Levi Lincoln. In April 1802, the commission proposed that Georgia cede the Yazoo territory to the United States for $1,250,000 and a reserve of five million acres to satisfy other claimants. Thus the innocent purchases would be refunded in cash or land, the disputed lands would be territory of the United States, and the corrupt land companies and former legislators were left to the mercy of local prosecutors.[19] The recommendations were presented to Congress on February 7, 1804, for what was expected to be perfunctory review and speedy approval. The commission, however, had failed to anticipate one contingency. A coiled whip awaited the Yazoo proposal.

The issues presented themselves with startling clarity to Randolph. The citizens of Georgia had the sovereign authority to repeal the corrupt and illegal actions of its legislature without interference from the federal government. That was the essence of state sovereignty. The right of contract did not extend to corrupt actions. That was the essence of public ethics. The central government had no authority to meddle in economic matters. That was the essence of private property rights. The executive branch of government had no business placing expediency above principle. That was the essence of tyranny. The Yazoo matter was all corruption, intrigue, cunning, and manipulation—the old foes of republicanism.[20] Randolph had seen the skull beneath the skin of Federalism. Now he saw it again in the combination of Republicans and speculators he dubbed "Yazoo men."

Randolph countered the Yazoo proposal with his own resolution "barring any claims derived under any act of the State of Georgia passed in the year 1795, in relation to lands ceded to the United States."[21] This resolution, the *Annals of Congress* recorded, prompted "a long and interesting debate . . . on the circumstances attending the Yazoo speculation."[22] The unreported debate was apparently more than just interesting. Senator Plumer wrote that Randolph engaged in insufferable "insolence and abuse" in a heated exchange with Congressman Willis Alston of North Carolina.[23] The two men had not cooled off by that evening, when they found themselves seated at the same dining-room table at Miss Shields's boarding house. Dinner repartee between the two men turned into cutting comments. Alston "ventured rather indirectly to contradict this political giant in some matter of fact," Massachusetts Representative Manasseh Cutler wrote. "Johnny told him he should not permit himself to be contradicted by any man without satisfaction, and especially from such a man as he was."[24] With that, Randolph threw a glass of wine in Alston's face. Alston answered by hurling a glass decanter at Randolph's head.[25] From that point, the story takes on divers accounts. Randolph was said to have broken a glass or a decanter over Alston's head, or thrown a bottle of gin at him. Another account reports that the two men broke much glassware, but "the blood of the grape was all that was shed."[26] Alston sent a challenge, but Randolph refused to receive it, promising "instant death" to anyone who attempted to deliver it.[27] A local judge intervened before the matter escalated, directing both men to keep the peace.[28]

Randolph was under no similar order to keep peace on the House floor. On February 18, he withdrew his earlier resolution and presented two more.

It was his duty, he said, "to place the subject in such a point of light that every eye, however dim, might distinctly see its true merits." The resolutions asserted that the Georgia legislature was "at no time, invested with the power of alienating" the Yazoo lands, that the "gross and palpable corruption" had been declared "null and void" by "the good people of Georgia," and that no part of "the five millions of acres . . . shall be appropriated to quiet or compensate any claims derived under any act, or pretended act, of the State of Georgia" passed during 1795.[29] The language was unequivocal, but it was still not clear to Republicans how far Randolph would press his point.

On March 7, 1804, Randolph rose to oppose the administration, the president, and his own party. "The sovereignty of the States," he began, "has ever been the cardinal principle of my political opinions." The proposed Yazoo settlement was nothing less than "federal usurpation" of the will of the citizens of Georgia. But more than that, "gentlemen not only annihilate this act, without a scruple . . . they denounce as subversive the rights of Georgia, and with them, of every state in the Union."[30]

"If they pass the bill in question," he warned, "they do an act which whole ages of political penance will never atone." Republicans squirmed uneasily as the purple passages Randolph normally reserved for Federalists were directed at them. "Some men," Randolph lilted, "have a smooth, oily, insinuating address; they can make you a proposition ruinous to yourself or to your country, with a face couched in smiles."[31] He viewed with a jaundiced eye the partnership of Alexander Hamilton and James Madison. "Persons of every political description are marshaled in support of these claims," he sneered; "we have to contend against the bear of the arctic and the lion of the torrid zone."[32] Randolph gave the House a promise of things to come. "This is one of the cases which, once being engaged in, I can never desert or relinquish, till I shall have exercised every energy of mind and faculty of body I possess, in refuting so nefarious a project."[33] When he finished, the House adjourned without acting on the Yazoo recommendation.

The Yazoo issue created an unsettled feeling. "[Randolph's] manners," Senator Plumer wrote, "are far from conciliating. Many of the party dislike him and on trifling measures they quarrel with him, but on all measures that are really important to the party they unite with him. He is *necessary* to them—they know it—he knows it—and they dare not discard him."[34] Some Republicans began to murmur, in earshot of Federalists, that they hated their "assuming, very arrogant" leader.[35]

Randolph detected no animosity. "When I cross the Potomac," he wrote to Gallatin, "I leave behind me all the scraps, shreds, and patches of politics which I collect during the session, and put on the plain homespun, or, as we say, the 'Virginia cloth' of a planter, which is clean, whole and comfortable, even if it be lonely."[36] Even with the Chase impeachment and Yazoo settlement hanging over his summer break, Randolph passed the months at Bizarre in relatively good spirits and in health "somewhat better than it was, although far from good."[37] He was shocked to hear the news that Aaron Burr had killed Alexander Hamilton in a duel, but saw no elevated principles in the dispute. Hamilton, he judged, had been injured "in a point which he, of all men in the world, could least brook—his vanity."[38]

In October, Randolph traveled to Fredericksburg to take in the races, a final respite before Congress convened in November. He recorded no thoughts about Chase or Yazoo, but he provided a friend with his an assessment of the national political scene: "We have acquired a comfortable stock of reputation and seem determined to live on our principal, as long as it lasts. . . . In all nature I know nothing to which the assembled wisdom and virtue of our land can be assimilated, but a fowl, whose head has just been wrung off by a remorseless cook and whose peaceful yet awkward contortions excites, at once, our pity and our laughter. In this way we flutter about, now tumbling into the water, now into the fire, to the amusement of the idle, the scandal of the grave, and the emolument of news-printers."[39]

The second session of the Eighth Congress convened on November 5, 1804. "The number of eminent men now there is indeed very great," Randolph's half-brother Henry St. George Tucker wrote. "It appeared to me that I saw every one I ever heard of."[40] Young Tucker was not far off in his observation; the city was filled with dominating personalities. There was Aaron Burr, indicted by two states for murder, to preside over the Chase trial if the House voted impeachment; Chief Justice John Marshall, a rough-hewn, hail-fellow-well-met, warily eyeing the Republican trajectory; James Madison, uncommitted in the Chase matter, more concerned with the fate of the Yazoo settlement he drafted; John Quincy Adams, independent and churlish, patriotic and vain, one of only nine Federalist Senators; and Justice Samuel Chase, red-faced, white-haired, subdued, surely not the bellicose judge portrayed in the articles of impeachment. Above the fray was the most dominating personality of them all: President Thomas Jefferson, weeks shy of an overwhelming re-election by an Electoral College vote of 162 to 14.

It was his note to Nicholson that started the Republicans down the road to impeachment. But now the president turned mute as the furies he had unleashed and encouraged took their turbulent course.

Almost a month passed before Randolph introduced the topic on everyone's mind: the articles of impeachment of Justice Chase. In very businesslike fashion, the House added an additional count regarding the Callender case and adopted all eight articles on November 30, 1804.[41] Randolph was appointed a House manager to conduct the trial in the Senate, along with Nicholson, Caesar Rodney of Delaware, Peter Early of Georgia, George Washington Campbell of Tennessee, Christopher Clark of Virginia, and John Boyle of Kentucky. The matter was sent to the Senate on December 7. The Federalists were convinced that conviction was certain. "Our public, I engage, will be as tame as Mr. Randolph can desire," wrote Fisher Ames. "You may broil Judge Chase and eat him."[42] John Quincy Adams glumly concluded that "the whole branch of the Supreme Court [is] to be swept away. . . . And in the present state of things I am convinced it is as easy for Mr. Randolph and Mr. Giles to do this as to say it."[43]

Federalist pessimism had some basis in reality. The Senate was comprised of thirty-four senators, twenty-five of whom were Republican. Twenty-three votes were needed on any one article to convict Chase and remove him from office. The Republicans had shown remarkable unity in advancing their program since 1801—much of the success directly attributable to Randolph. The federal judiciary remained the last barrier to a complete and successful revolution. Surely the numerically superior Republicans, again under Randolph's direction, would not falter in taking this last step.

That step, though, was slightly more difficult than Adams predicted. Randolph had made the case more challenging by drafting eight articles instead of concentrating on the clearly improper instruction to the Baltimore grand jury. He had constructed a complex web of legal issues ranging from corrupt motives to bad manners. The Senate would be forced to sort through all of these issues, while simultaneously determining if the constitutional benchmark of "good behavior" was breached by the high standard of crimes and misdemeanors or by the less imposing standard of any act dangerous to the public liberty, and whether any standard at all justified removing Chase. And as always, Randolph fretted about Republican unity. "In truth," he wrote to James Monroe, "after deducting from our number those who are influenced by local or *personal* views, we cease to be a majority, at least I fear so—and the federalists are on the watch to foment every discontent which breaks forth."[44]

Assisting Randolph was William Giles, his former House colleague, now senator from Virginia and juror in the upcoming trial. One December afternoon, the two men found themselves seated in front of a fireplace in the company of Senators John Quincy Adams and Israel Smith and took the opportunity to present their theory of impeachment. "[If] the Judges of the Supreme Court should dare, *as they had done,* to declare an act of Congress unconstitutional," Adams recounted their appeal in his diary, "it was the undoubted right of the House of Representatives to remove them." Impeachment, the Republicans contended, "was nothing more than a declaration by Congress to this effect: You hold dangerous opinions, and if you are suffered to carry them into effect you will work the destruction of the nation."[45]

Adams sat tight-lipped and skeptical, before excusing himself with the curt comment that he "could not assent to [that] definition of the term impeachment."[46] Giles "labored with excessive earnestness" to persuade Smith, but the fireside chat ended with no thawing in the hardening positions of the contending sides.

Preparation for the Chase trial so occupied Randolph that he spoke in the House only four times during the month of December. "I am as lonesome and solitary as a monk," he wrote, "or rather a hermit."[47] Illness struck in the form of a "severe attack on my stomach and bowels, of a bilious nature" and by mid-January Randolph commented that his "health of late is very infirm."[48] Still he labored on. "The Yazoo claim," he wrote to St. George Tucker, "[and] the impeachment are all at this time on my shoulders and crush me to the earth."[49] It was in such a state of mind and health that Randolph delivered a speech on the Yazoo issue that would define him for years to come.

Everyone in the House chamber knew Randolph opposed paying any sums to Yazoo land purchasers or speculators. So it was no surprise when he took the floor on January 29, 1805, to oppose another attempt to settle the claims.[50] What was not expected was "a tirade such as the House had never yet heard."[51] For two days, Randolph subjected the House, his party, and the commissioners to the verbal equivalent of being drawn and quartered.

Suffering from "personal indisposition" and "the pressure of other important business," Randolph wasted no time with oratorical flourishes or parliamentary niceties. He reached straight for a blunt instrument. He condemned the majority for forcing a "public plunder." Their desire to adopt the recommendation was surely "to effect some evil purpose, acting on previous pledge[s] to each other" to attain the nefarious object. He huffed at the so-called innocent third-party purchasers. When the act was passed in 1795, he said, "it caused a sensation scarcely less violent than that produced by the passage of the stamp act or the shutting up of the port of Boston." Only those "guilty of gross and willful prevarication" could have been ignorant of "that act of stupendous villainy."[52]

In this instance, Randolph spoke from experience. He had been visiting Joseph Bryan in Georgia in 1796 and witnessed the tumult over the land fraud. He could not conceive that any citizen paying the slightest attention to public affairs would not have received substantial warning that some prudence was necessary when purchasing Yazoo lands. He reminded the House that George Washington had reported the events in Georgia to the Congress in February 1795. This act alone, he declared, was "ample notice to the whole world."[53] Yet the speculators would not stay their hand nor purchasers their appetite. "Goaded by avarice, they buy only to sell, and sell only to buy," he exclaimed. "The retail trade of fraud and imposture yields too small and slow a profit to gratify their cupidity. They buy and sell corruption in the gross, and a few millions, more or less, is hardly felt in the account."[54] Had the Congress, he asked, descended to such "moral and political depravity," he asked, to side with the "swindlers of 1795?"[55] No, he asserted, not where principles were involved. "[The] contact, being laid in corruption and fraud, was null and void, *ab initio*, he argued; "since, the original grant being obtained by bribery and fraud, no right could vest under it." Such an issue "bid defiance to palliatives, and it is only from the knife, or the actual cautery, that you can expect relief. There is no cure short of extirpation. Attorneys and judges do not decide the fate of empires."[56]

Randolph condemned Gideon Granger, postmaster general of the United States, and a land speculator, for lobbying on behalf of the New England–Mississippi Company in favor of the settlement. He suspected Granger was swapping "snug appointments and fat contracts" in exchange for support.[57] The sordidness of the episode troubled Randolph almost as much as the departure from principle. It was the hated Federalist Party that sanctioned corruption, not the reform-minded Republicans. Since taking his seat in the

House in 1799, he had struggled against that "monster generated by fraud, nursed in corruption, that in grim silence awaits his prey . . . the spirit of Federalism!"[58] Now his fellow Republicans were "the unblushing advocates of unblushing corruption," tossing a sop to "this Cerberus of corruption, this many-headed dog of hell." If the Yazoo Bill passed, Randolph pledged he would never again comment on "the crimes and follies" of Federalist administrations. "I should disdain to prate about the petty larcenies of our predecessors," he concluded, "after having given my sanction to this atrocious public robbery."[59]

The House adjourned, its members beaten and angered by the lash of Randolph's words. "I must either acknowledge," Erastus Root of New York fumed, "that I have been bribed, that I am base and corrupt, or . . . that I have leagued in sentiment with the [Federalists]."[60] Senator Plumer provided a similar review. Randolph's speeches, he wrote, "were too personal, his allusions to brothel-houses and pig stys too coarse and vulgar, his arraigning the motives of members, charging them with peculation, bribery and corruption were insufferable."[61]

Randolph's stand, hyperbole aside, was consistent with traditional Republican principles.[62] The Yazoo affair *was* thoroughly tainted with corruption. Perhaps not the corruption Randolph saw as Gideon Granger roamed the halls, or which he perceived in the Madison-crafted resolution, but in the initial act of the Georgia legislature which had subsequently been overturned by the people. Now the people's decision was threatened by the central government. Such an action trespassed on the fundamental principles of state sovereignty, federalism, and integrity in government. "Of what consequence," Randolph asked, "is it that a man smiles in your face, holds out his hand and declares himself the advocate of those political principles to which you are also attached, when you see him acting with your adversaries upon other principles, which the voice of the nation has put down, which I did hope were buried never to rise again in this section of the globe?[63] There were two persons going into a shop, Randolph said; "[One] of them stole a piece of goods and handed it to the other to conceal under his cloak. When challenged with the theft, he who stole it said he had it not, and he who had it said he did not take it. 'Gentlemen,' replied the honest tradesman, 'what you say may all be very true, but, at the same time, I know that between you I am robbed.' And such precisely is our case. But I hope, sir, we shall not permit the parties, whether original grantees who took it, or subsequent purchasers who have it, to make off with the public property."[64] The Congress had refused to fund other less corrupt and more worthy cases, Randolph argued, such as relief for families of Revolutionary War soldiers. But now, the Congress was acting in such a way as to remind him of the London charity for prostitutes that turned away a poor innocent girl until she went out and qualified herself. "With equal discretion," he said, "the directors of the Committee of Claims suffer nothing to find support in their asylum but what is tainted with corruption and stamped with fraud. Give it these properties and they will give it equity."[65]

Randolph shamed or persuaded enough of his colleagues to back off for the moment. "His party, as well as the rest," Congressman Cutler wrote, "had an intolerable whipping. . . . Most of them are known to be in favor of the claims, but whether it was fear of Randolph or some other fear that drove them from their seats is uncertain."[66] It was an unexpected defeat for the administration, made more stunning because it came at the hands of its most stalwart defender. Randolph left his wearied colleagues with a warning: "In whatever shape the subject may be again brought before the House, it will be my duty, and that of my friends, to manifest the same firm spirit of resistance, and to suffer no opportunity to pass of defeating a measure so fraught with mischief."[67] The pro-Jefferson Richmond *Enquirer* hailed Randolph's actions: "If ever there was a statesman, who triumphed over the disadvantages of youth; who inflexibly pursued 'the right instead of the expedient'; who dared to set his face against the imposing opinion of the three ablest men of his own party and the principal officers of the government; who with an equal mind braved danger and corruption; who arrested the progress of one of the greatest speculations that ever originated in fraud, and was disseminating corruption; that man is John Randolph."[68]

Randolph would thwart passage of the Yazoo settlement at every subsequent session until the issue was finally settled by the United States Supreme Court in 1810 in the case of *Fletcher v. Peck.* It would then take another four years—and Randolph's temporary absence from the House in 1814—before the House would pass the commission's recommendations.

Jefferson was nonplussed. He had been slightly wary of his cousin but now confessed that he "did not know what course to pursue with Mr. Randolph." The president complained that Randolph would not consult with him or with his friends, but "regardless of them all, pursues his own course."[69] According to Madison biographer Irving Brant, Randolph's "disruptive influence" posed a "visible hazard" to Madison.[70] So the secretary of state, not desiring to strengthen Randolph's hand, took no position on Chase's impeachment.[71]

With Jefferson demurring, Madison mum, and Randolph unpredictable, it was hardly an auspicious time to launch the supreme Republican effort against the Federalist judicial enclave.

7
The Tertium Quid

The pathos which from rival eyes
Unwilling tears could summon,
The stinging taunt, the fiery burst
Of hatred scarcely human!

It seemed all official Washington packed into the Senate chamber for the trial of Justice Samuel Chase. Republican House members who brought the charges sat alongside sullen Federalists anticipating another defeat. Intrigued cabinet officers sat next to intently interested Supreme Court justices. The benches and tables were covered in crimson cloth; the visiting ladies were covered in high fashion. "The most perfect order and silence is preserved thru the house," Henry St. George Tucker wrote, "notwithstanding the great crowds."[1]

Glittering as impressively as the gold braid of the visiting foreign ministers was Chase's defense team. It consisted of Joseph Hopkinson, a rising star of the Philadelphia bar; Philip Barton Key, a London-trained attorney and brother of Francis Scott Key; Robert Goodloe Harper, a former representative from South Carolina and former senator from Maryland; and Charles Lee, former attorney general of the United States. The lead defense counsel was Luther Martin, attorney general of Maryland, the most tenacious trial lawyer of his day, and a man who "knew more law drunk than the managers did sober."[2] Chase's attorneys and the House managers sat in chairs and at tables covered with blue cloth bordering the center aisle. Surveying it all was the presiding officer, a man under as much legal scrutiny as Justice Chase: Vice-President Aaron Burr. With high drama and high stakes, the trial was called to order on February 4, 1805.

Justice Chase unfurled an aggressive defense. Where facts cleared him, they were assiduously detailed. Where the law was in his favor, it was expounded upon at length. Where the articles were vague, they were exposed and dismissed. Where Chase's rulings were affirmed by other judges—as was the case in six of the eight articles—the rulings were pointedly exhibited. Law, facts, and precedent mingled with the not-so-subtle insinuation that politics, not the Constitution, was driving the prosecution. Countering the Republican theory of impeachment, Chase's attorneys articulated a high standard. Judges could be removed "only for treason, bribery, and corruption, or other high crime or misdemeanor." There must be "some act done or omitted, in violation of some law forbidding or commanding it." Each article, they argued, failed to meet that standard. Chase's opinion in the Fries case was grounded in precedent, "and surely he need not urge to this honorable Court, the correctness, the importance, and the absolute necessity of adhering to principles of law once established."[3] He denied bias in Callender's case and dismissed as "altogether erroneous" the allegations regarding his conduct in Newcastle.[4] His comments to the Baltimore grand jury were but "an argument, the force of which as a patriot he might feel, and which as a free man he had a right to advance."[5] Defiance was mixed with humility, brilliance with the debility of age, partisanship with patriotism. Chase concluded by appealing his case to "his Omnipotent Judge . . . for the rectitude and purity of his conduct as to all the matters of which he is this day accused."[6]

The rhetorical talents that so well served John Randolph on the floor of the House, that delighted the freeholders of Southside Virginia, and that animated the revolutionary reforms of the Seventh Congress, were ill suited for a legal proceeding. Impeachment by the House of Representatives was a political process, but the Constitution had transformed the Senate chamber into a courtroom, the senators into jurors. Randolph made no corresponding adjustment to his deportment. There before him sat Justice Chase, the personification of the final Federalist stronghold Republicans meant to overcome. Clutching the articles of impeachment instead of his whip, Randolph knew but one way to proceed: head-on, at daggers drawn.

On February 9, Randolph opened the case for the prosecution. He complained of the "severe pressure of disease" and, remarkably, that the prosecution had been allotted little time to consider Chase's statement. He would proceed, however, because he stood "on impregnable ground."[7] For the following hour and a half, Randolph became tangled in the legal traps he had unwittingly laid out in the multiple count articles.[8] At no point did he clearly articulate the managers' theory of impeachment, namely, that impeachment and removal constituted the only remedy for misuse of power by federal judges.[9] Instead, Randolph challenged the senators to infer criminal intent, to "figure to yourselves a spectacle more horrible," and to recall Chase's "rude and contemptuous expressions . . . vexatious interruptions . . . [and] indecent solicitude." He finished by promising that the prosecution would "bring forward in proof, such a specimen of judicial tyranny, as, I trust in God, will never be again exhibited in our country."[10]

"Randolph made his speech," Representative Manassah Cutler wrote. "Nothing great." William Plumer concurred, calling it "the most feeble, the most incorrect, that I ever heard him make."[11] The Richmond *Enquirer* called Randolph's efforts a "triumphant success," but felt the need to remind its readers "that Mr. Randolph is no professional lawyer; that he never read over Judge Chase's plea . . . that he spoke without a note before him; and that his spirits and health had been worn down by excessive exertion and bodily disease."[12]

For two weeks, the contending sides wrangled. The Senate heard from forty-nine witnesses—eighteen for the prosecution, thirty-one for the defense. The testimony provided no advantage for either side. "Mr. Randolph," Senator Plumer wrote, "has a tedious circuitous method of asking questions." The tedium worsened as the questions centered on procedure, personalities, and proprieties. "Gravity himself could not keep his countenance at the nauseating littleness which were resorted to for proof of atrocious criminality," John Quincy Adams wrote to his father, John Adams, "and indignation melted into ridicule at the puerile perseverance with which *nothings* were accumulated with the hope of making *something* by this multitude."[13]

One of the more intriguing moments occurred when Chief Justice John Marshall took the witness stand on behalf of the defense. Knowing that if the Republicans succeeded in removing Chase, he and his Federalist colleagues might be next on the impeachment list, Marshall gingerly sparred with Randolph.[14] "Did you observe any thing unusual," Randolph asked, "in the conduct on the part of the counsel towards the court, or the court towards the counsel, and what?" "There were several circumstances that took place on that trial," Marshall responded, "on the part both of the bar and the bench which do not always occur in trials. I would probably be better able to answer the question if it were made more determinate."

Randolph tried another route. "[Is] it the practice in courts," he asked, "when counsel objects to the legality of an opinion given by the court, to hear arguments of counsel against such opinion?" Marshall again danced around the question. "There is . . . no positive rule on this subject, and the course pursued by the court will depend upon circumstances." Vice-President Burr interrupted and asked Marshall if he recalled "whether the conduct of the judge on this trial was tyrannical, overbearing, and oppressive?"

"I will state the facts," Marshall replied. "The counsel . . . persisted in arguing the question of the constitutionality of the sedition law, in which they were constantly repressed by Judge Chase. . . . If this is not considered tyrannical, oppressive, and overbearing, I know nothing that was so."[15]

"The Chief Justice," Plumer disappointingly noted, "really discovered too much caution, too much fear, too much cunning. He ought to have been more bold, frank, and explicit than he was."[16] Plumer's beleaguered Federalists colleagues did not share his pessimism. Marshall's discreet responses, the performance of Chase's attorneys, and the lackluster testimony made conviction suddenly seem less certain.[17] Two senators, feeling particularly bold, ventured to comment about Randolph's "calumny." Hearing of the insult, Randolph sought out the senators and exacted a denial before he issued a duel challenge. Nor was this Randolph's only contact with the jurors. In what today would meet all the requisites of jury tampering, Randolph held frequent discussions with Senator Giles just off the Senate floor during court sessions. "Not very consistent with my idea of impartial justice," John Quincy Adams snapped.[18] Emotionally and intellectually exhausted, Randolph was not making sound decisions. Then, on the eve of the trial's conclusion, he was, he wrote, "seized with all the torments of the damned" and "was compelled to have recourse to Dr. T who gave me an opiate." He complained of a fever and pain "which flies, like lightning, from my head to the stomach, bowels, hands."[19]

Closing arguments began on February 20 and were staggered between the opposing sides. "Stupefied . . . with opium and want of rest," Randolph continued to direct strategy, writing instructions from his sickbed. "Do all you can to stop [Campbell's] mouth and bring out Clark," he wrote to Nicholson. "[I] would wish him to bear particularly on the [fifth and sixth] articles."[20] Campbell performed better than Randolph's pessimistic assessment. It was not necessary, he told the senators, "that the offense should be an indictable one, to render it subject to impeachment, but that the officer has abused the trust reposed in him and endangered the liberties of the people." Campbell hammered away at Chase's behavior. His conduct, he argued, is "the strongest possible evidence of corrupt motives, of partiality, and a determined design to overleap all formal rules of proceeding, to oppress the unfortunate defendant." The summations of Campbell, Early, and Clark provided the Senate with two paths to conviction: Chase's partisan conduct was detrimental to the system of justice; or Chase's partiality was a misdemeanor.[21] These arguments put the prosecution in as strong a position as it had occupied in some time. It was only temporary.

"We appear," Joseph Hopkinson said, "for an ancient and infirm man, whose better days have been worn out in the service of that country which now degrades him."[22] He moved immediately to Chase's strongest argument: that a judge could be impeached and removed from office for only an indictable offense.[23] Removal from office was a drastic constitutional step and should not be based "on the mere caprice or opinion of any ten, twenty, or one hundred men. . . . It must unquestionably be for some offense, either of omission or commission, against some statute of the United States or . . . of a particular State, or against the provision of the common law."[24] What law, Hopkinson asked, had Chase violated? Whom had he offended? "The House of Representatives," he incredulously answered his own question. "And is he impeached for this?"[25]

Hopkinson knew his audience. The United States Senate prided itself on being a deliberative body, one not stirred by gusts of passion. Hopkinson appealed to that sentiment. He wanted to make the senators view themselves as possessing the same traits of independence, firmness, and stability possessed by judges. He reminded the Senate of the deaths of Seneca and Socrates. "An independent and firm Judiciary, protected and protecting by the laws," he speculated, "would have snatched the one from the fury of a despot, and preserved the other from the madness of a people."[26] Or, he might have said, an independent and firm Senate.

Hopkinson's argument, Plumer wrote, was "luminous . . . logical, [and] strongly fortified by legal authorities." Key and Lee took the Senate through a review of each article before yielding to the senior member of the defense team. Luther Martin rose on Saturday, February 23. He looked and acted every inch the Federal Bulldog.[27] The ravages of drink and riotous living were etched in his countenance, as was his contempt for Thomas Jefferson and the radicals who had brought the Republic to such a point. He reminded senators that he had been with Washington, Hamilton, and Madison in Philadelphia during those hot months when the Constitution was drafted. Having been present at the creation, he could offer a first-hand analysis of the impeachment provision. He repeated the argument that impeachment lay only with indictable offenses, but he raised the bar even higher. Not every indictable offense was an impeachable offense. Would the Senate re-move a judge who, in a moment of anger, hit a litigant or an attorney? That would be an indictable offense, certainly, but impeachable? "I am ready to go further," Martin stated; "the crimes ought to be such as relate to his of-fice, or which tend to cover the person who committed them with turpitude and infamy."[28] Running circles around the Republican case, Martin looked askance at leaving "judges, and all your other officers, at the mercy of the prevailing party."[29]

The veteran lawyer took a dim view of attorneys unable to take a tough talking from a judge. Chase may have used the word "damned," Martin de-clared, but he could not "apprehend it will be considered *very* offensive. . . . [W]e say indiscriminately a very good or a damned good bottle of wine, a damned good dinner, or a damned clever fellow."[30] In other words, attor-neys—and Congressmen—needed to grow up. "If, sir, judges are to be cen-sured for possessing legal talents, for being correctly acquainted with the law in criminal cases, and for not suffering themselves to be insulted, and the public time wasted," Martin drolly scoffed; "I pray you let not . . . gentle-men of legal talents and abilities be degraded by placing them on the bench. . . . But let us go to the corn-fields, to the tobacco plantations and there . . . find men enough possessed of what seems to be thought the first requisite of a judge: a total ignorance of the law!"[31]

Martin had turned in a masterful performance.[32] If it did not in itself save Chase, it was indicative of the professional and polished performance consistently displayed by the defense team. It fell to Nicholson to rally the House's case. Far from being a political attack on the independence of the judiciary, he argued, this impeachment would secure that very indepen-dence, and not that of the judiciary alone, but of the entire government and the people. "If our laws are not faithfully administered; if the holy sanctu-ary of our courts is to be invaded by party feeling," he said, "we may indeed boast that we live in a land of freedom, but the boast will be vain and illu-sory."[33]

Nicholson's point had merit. Why was the Republican attempt to im-peach any more partisan than Chase's political charge to the Baltimore grand jury? Was the threat of removal of a federal judge more dangerous to the public liberty than an abrupt predetermined sentence of death to a litigant? Was there not more to be feared from unchecked judicial author-ity than from the Senate exercising a clearly delegated constitutional duty? The case at bar concerned Justice Chase, but its implications were of lasting import. Caesar Rodney spoke strongly to this point: "Give any human being judicial power for life . . . you may call him a judge or justice, no matter what is the appellation, and you transform him into a despot, regardless of all law, but his own sovereign will and pleasure."[34] The court adjourned following Rodney's summation. The next day, February 27, Randolph would conclude the case against Justice Chase.

"On the morning when it was expected my brother would begin," Henry Tucker wrote to his father, "the house was more crowded than ever. Every one seemed anxious to get to the Senate chamber lest they should not get a seat. This indeed was the case with myself, as every place was occupied before I got in. During his argument every attention seemed to be fixed, and tho between almost every sentence he was compelled to swallow some wine and water or to take a part of an orange, yet the interest was completely kept up."[35] Tucker's comments about Randolph's performance were overtly succinct: "What shall I say to you of him. You know him."

Randolph's three-hour speech did nothing to help the case at bar or his own place in history. It was, Manasseh Cutler recorded in his diary, "an outrageous, infuriated declamation which might have done honor to Marat or Robespierre."[36] His most sympathetic biographer concedes "it added little or nothing to the reputation which he had acquired during the Sixth and Seventh Congress." His harshest biographer wrote that Randolph "flung himself like a child on the ground, crushed by the consciousness that his mind could not follow out a fixed train of thought."[37] Henry Tucker was again more sympathetic, writing that he did not "regard this argument as the greatest proof of his ability." John Quincy Adams spared no feeling. Randolph's speech, he wrote, had "as little relation to the subject-matter as possible." It lacked "order, connection, or argument" and consisted "altogether of the most hackneyed commonplaces of popular declamation, mingled up with panegyrics and invectives upon persons, with a few well expressed ideas, a few striking figures, much distortion of face and contortion of body, tears, groans, and sobs, with occasional pauses for recollection, and continual complaints of having lost his notes."[38]

How to explain such a performance? Randolph was ill, as his letters and those of Adams and Henry Tucker confirm, and his physical, emotional, and nervous state was hardly sturdy enough to support his efforts.[39] It is possible that he was under the influence of opium. If, as Tucker described, Randolph was drinking a wine mixture between almost every sentence in a speech of over three hours, he could have become intoxicated during the course of his remarks. That he was ill prepared was manifest. He had displayed amateurish legal talents during the trial, and this lack of legal acumen could not long be disguised by political rhetoric.[40] Any one of these factors might have combined with his belief that principles were adrift among lesser men to produce a speech more akin to logorrhea.

· Randolph took ownership of the entire process with his first words. The prosecution, he said, was "instituted at my own motion" and the "indictment drawn by my own hand." The "strongest body of evidence that perhaps was ever adduced" supported the "sum and substance" that Chase had "demeaned himself amiss—partially, unfaithfully, unjustly, corruptly."[41]

Things quickly deteriorated from that fairly cogent beginning. Justice Chase was a "great culprit," "a man whose violent temper and arbitrary disposition perpetually drives him into acts of tyranny," "haughty, violent, imperious," "an unrighteous judge thirsting for . . . blood," "too far gone in political gangrene," and displaying "the sullen pervasiveness of guilt, half ashamed . . . trembling . . . now soothing, now threatening."[42] Chase's position "that impeachment and indictable are convertible terms is almost too absurd for argument."[43] The defense's precedents hailed from the "Star Chamber . . . the tribunals of Henry VIII . . . the tools and parasites of the house of Stuart." Randolph guffawed that he could not "suppose [Luther Martin] serious."[44] He taunted "the jester of the sovereign people, a jester at your laws and Constitution."[45]

Randolph plied the jury with excuses for his own erratic performance. He was ill, he told the senators, he had missed much of counsel's argument, and he had lost his notes.[46] Still he would persevere, he asserted, for he had "studied at the feet of far different Gamaliels" than had Martin and Hopkinson. One after the other he illuminated the "succession of crimes each treading on the heel, galling the kibe of the other—so connected in time, and place, and circumstance . . . as to leave no shadow of doubt as to guilt."[47] He bemoaned that "the great principles for which our forefathers contended" would be "frittered away by technical sophistry."[48]

"We have performed our duty," Randolph told the Senate. "We have bound the criminal and dragged him to your altar." As he spoke these words, his voice broke and he began to weep.[49] "It remains for you to say whether he shall again become the scourge of an exasperated people, or whether he shall stand as a landmark and a beacon to the present generation, and a warning to the future." As spectators gazed in discomfort, Randolph choked out his final words. "In the name of the nation, I demand at your hands the award of justice and of law."[50]

"Mr. Randolph certainly was *correct*," Plumer wrote, "when he said his argument would be *desultory*, if by argument he meant what he *uttered*. The word *argument* I think inapplicable to this performance. It is too dignified for such a *feeble* thing."[51]

"Is Samuel Chase, Esquire, guilty or not guilty of a high crime or misdemeanor in the Article of Impeachment just read?" So spoke Aaron Burr following the reading of each article. None of the eight articles received the required two-thirds vote. Only three received majority votes. Article eight—from the start the strongest of the charges—received the highest total of votes: nineteen. "There not being a constitutional majority on any one article," Burr announced, "it becomes my duty to pronounce that Samuel Chase, Esquire, is acquitted on the Articles of Impeachment exhibited against him by the House of Representatives." The trial was ended.

It was a stunning defeat for the Republicans, the first significant setback since their assumption of power. The defeat was not an orphan, but most pointed at Randolph's inept management as the reason for Chase's acquittal. None of the managers, however, articulated a clear reason why the Senate should take this step.[52] They were poorly prepared, and their partisanship wore thin with even a Republican Senate. Also, it did not go unnoticed that Jefferson adopted a sphinxlike silence and Madison seemed to delight in Randolph's misfortunes.[53] As the trial went on, it became easier to separate the prosecution of Chase from the goals of the Republican majority. Once freed from that stricture, the Senate needed to be presented with compelling reasons to remove Chase. That did not happen.[54]

Randolph stormed out of the Senate chamber, Nicholson close on his heels. In turn they took to the floor of the House. Randolph introduced a constitutional amendment providing for the removal of federal judges by a vote of Congress. Nicholson followed with an amendment authorizing state legislatures to recall senators. The amendments were made, John Quincy Adams scoffed, "just at the pungent moment of disappointment."[55] But the fight—like the trial—was ended. So too was the chance for any serious check on the exercise of power by the federal judiciary. Congress adjourned the next day.

Before leaving for Bizarre, Randolph dropped a farewell note to his friend Joseph Nicholson, seemingly attributing his performance at the Chase trial to an unidentified malady known to only his intimate friends: "By *you*, I would be understood. Whether the herd of mankind comprehend me or not I care not. Yourself, the speaker [Macon] and [Joseph] Bryan are of all the world alone acquainted with my *real* situation. On that subject I have only to ask that you preserve the same reserve I have done. Do not misunderstand me, my good friend. I do not doubt your honor or discretion—far from it. But, on this subject, I am perhaps foolishly fastidious."[56]

The countryside of Virginia seemed to revive Randolph's spirits and health. Domestic matters, often vexing, were generally favorable. He noted he could receive no more than seven dollars per hundred-weight for tobacco, but the Roanoke plantation still produced a record crop. "This I calculate," he wrote to fellow planter David Parish, "will make me a return of from $20,000 to $25,000."[57] He was on his horse within a week of arriving home, setting off on a 120-mile cross-country ride. In spite of "exposure without sufficient defense to the late severe change of weather" during the ride, he wrote, "I daily gain strength."[58] He purchased a new gig—a light, two-wheeled, one-horse carriage—and "determined to break his large black horse to it."[59] The horse did not take to the situation and ran wild, forcing Randolph to leap from the gig as the horse descended down a steep hill. Randolph and the horse escaped unharmed, but the new gig was destroyed. Shortly after that incident, Randolph heard "dreadful accounts of the health of his negroes" at Roanoke. Suspecting mistreatment as the slaves began "dying like sheep," he mounted the same big horse and tore off at full speed from Bizarre. Randolph left no account of what he discovered about the condition of his slaves, but would comment that the "Master's presence is the only check (and that insufficient) upon the malpractices of the overseers and of the negroes too, poor creatures."[60]

At a Fourth of July celebration in Petersburg, near Randolph's birthplace at Cawsons, a collection of Republicans gathered to toast the day. One reveler offered a toast to Randolph, saying: "What he doth, he doth in honor, led by the impartial conduct of his soul."[61] While Randolph's reputation with his colleagues in Washington was deteriorating, it remained strong with his constituency. "[The] *good people* have again deputed me to serve them," he wrote to Nicholson, "and, by the blessing of God, so I will, at least as faithfully as Mr. Chase, of pious memory."[62] The Yazoo issue and the Chase acquittal, Randolph wrote, "are making a devilish noise here." His fellow freeholders were irritated at the acquittal, "but *disgusted deeply* at the attempt made to pour wine and oil into his wounds out of the public stores."[63]

Though Randolph fretted that his enemies had "the press entirely under their control" and that he was "denounced as a Jacobin republican," his re-election to the House was never in doubt.[64]

What was in doubt, at least in his mind, was the state of Republican principles.[65] "Never did the times require more union and decision among the real friends of freedom," he wrote to Nicholson, but "[everything] and everybody seem to be jumbled out of place, except a few men who are steeped in supine indifference, whilst meddling fools and designing knaves are governing the country under the auspices of their names."[66] He likened Jefferson and Madison (though not by name) to "whimsicals" who "advocated the leading measures of their party until they were nearly ripe for execution, when they hung back, condemned the step after it was taken, and on most occasions affected a glorious neutrality."[67] Jefferson had hung back during the Chase trial, and this lack of backbone did not bode well for the future. Randolph feared that "the whole force of the adversaries of the man and . . . of his *principles* will be bent to take advantage of the easy credulity of his temper, and thus arm themselves with power to set both at defiance as soon as their schemes are ripe for execution."[68] Randolph viewed the secretary of state as a Federalist sympathizer cloaked in Republican home-spun, a cunning manipulator, and an unprincipled master of double-talk. "Mr. M[adison]'s administration (for his election is looked upon as settled)," he wrote, "is not to be subjected to the scrutiny and strictures of such an antagonist as I am supposed to be. Whether I shall be able to withstand this decree of destiny, time alone can shew."[69] The alliance of Madison intriguers, Yazoo men, and Republicans who "have plunged into the Charybdis of federalism" filled Randolph with despair. "I *do not* like the aspect of affairs," he wrote to Nicholson. He confided to Albert Gallatin that if "Monroe would succeed [Jefferson], my regret would be very much diminished."[70]

The long-playing saga of sisters Judith and Nancy at Bizarre came to an end a short time after Randolph returned from Washington. What prompted the act, so long simmering, is not certain. Randolph wrote that he discovered Nancy's "intimacy with one of the slaves" and her "epistles to this Othello." Nancy contended that Randolph suspected her of murdering Richard Randolph, and so evicted her.[71] The confrontation occurred when Nancy returned with Judith's son Tudor from a stay in Staunton.

"Nancy," Randolph said abruptly, "when do you leave this house?"[72] According to Nancy's recollection, Randolph added: "The sooner the better, for you take as many liberties as if you were in a tavern." Randolph recorded no reaction to his demand; Nancy recalled that she replied: "I will go as soon as I can." Bitterness and personal agendas make recollections of the incident unreliable. The only certain fact is that Nancy Randolph left Bizarre in 1805 at the request of John Randolph. It was the latest event in a story not yet ended.

Another saga awaited in Washington. Like his predecessors, Thomas Jefferson found himself embroiled in issues stemming from European wars. England and France were locked in the latest of their seemingly interminable struggles, and the United States found itself subjected to naval harassment by both powers. As American vessels were seized and sailors impressed into British servitude, the Senate called on the president to send a special mission to England in an effort to resolve the contending issues. The idea occurred to Representative Christopher Clark that Randolph should be appointed special commissioner to Great Britain. "The superlative talents of Mr. Randolph," Clark said, "the great services he had rendered his country, the ardor and inflexible integrity of his mind . . . all combined to point him out as the (most proper) person for the station."[73] Clark collected "subscribers to a paper to that effect" and presented the matter to the president.[74] Jefferson deftly turned aside the request, commenting that there "existed but little hope of terminating the dispute by negotiation" and, in any event, James Monroe, the minister to England, could handle the matter. "The subject of Mr. Randolph's appointment," the Richmond *Enquirer* reported, "was then entirely dropped."

Randolph knew nothing of Clark's efforts on his behalf, nor had he sought any foreign appointment.[75] "If I did not know you so well," he said to Clark upon reaching Washington, "I should suppose you were sent to me by the executive, to buy off my opposition, which they fancy must take place from the course they pursue."[76] Randolph affected indifference over the matter, but political scuttlebutt perpetuated the story that Jefferson had rejected him.

Rumors about Randolph's status as House leader aggravated the perceived slight. The word at boardinghouse dinner tables was that the administration wanted Barnabas Bidwell of Massachusetts to replace Randolph.[77] Jefferson did nothing to dispel the notion, but he realized that, to get rid of Randolph, he would have to acquiesce in the removal of Speaker Macon. Jefferson's golden silence was never more resounding than when administration allies nominated Joseph Varnum for Speaker. It took three ballots, but Macon prevailed, "to his great joy and the annoyance of the friends of the Administration."[78] The Speaker promptly named Randolph chairman of Ways & Means. The anti-Randolph maneuver had failed, and this time, unlike the mission to England, Jefferson's fingerprints were all over it.

Randolph was in a sour mood when he dined with Anthony Merry, the British minister to the United States, in the wake of events in the House. Merry asked if Randolph would join in a post-dinner game of cards. "No, sir," Randolph snapped, "I do not know a king from a queen, or a *king from a knave*."[79] His mood had not improved when Bidwell stood to deliver his first speech in the House. Josiah Quincy watched Randolph, "dressed in his usual morning costume—his skeleton legs cased in tight-fitting leather breeches and top-boots, with a blue riding coat, and the thick buckskin gloves from which he was never parted, and a heavily loaded riding-whip in his hand," briefly listen before walking "slowly out of the House, striking the handle of his whip emphatically upon the palm of his left hand, and regarding poor Bidwell as he passed him with a look of insolent contempt."[80]

On December 3, 1805, Jefferson sent to Congress the first message of his second term. "[The] nations of Europe are in commotion," the president wrote, "and arming against each other." He catalogued the "piratical acts" of the combatants and mocked the "new principles . . . interloped into the law of nations, founded neither in justice nor the usage of acknowledgement of nations."[81] Spanish actions at the Florida border had forced him "to give orders to our troops on that frontier to be in readiness to protect our citizens, and repel by arms any similar aggression in the future." The president proposed strengthening the militia and constructing more ships to respond to "these injuries from some of the belligerent powers."[82]

Three days later, Jefferson sent a confidential message to Congress. He recounted the failures of diplomatic efforts to resolve the differences with Spain, mentioned that France might arbitrate a settlement as to the Florida boundary, and, in contrast to the belligerent tone of his Annual Message, assured Congress that war was not necessary. "But the course to be pursued," he wrote in typical Jefferson vagueness, "will require the command of means which it belongs to Congress exclusively to yield or deny. . . . To their wisdom then I look for the course I am to pursue."[83] The president confided to Barnabas Bidwell and Albert Gallatin that he wanted Congress to pass a set of resolutions recounting Spanish offenses and outlining American policy and responses. Following adoption of the resolutions, Congress would secretly appropriate $2 million to purchase Florida. None of these specific action items was listed in the confidential message. The House referred the message to a select committee, whose chairman—surely to Jefferson's chagrin—was John Randolph.

Randolph convened the committee on December 7. Bidwell promptly introduced a resolution authorizing an appropriation for the purchase of Florida. Randolph dismissed the motion out of hand. "There was not a syllable [in the president's message] about the purchase of the Floridas," he said, "or an appropriation of money for foreign negotiations . . . not a word in it to induce us to believe that Spain was willing to make the sale."[84] Randolph adjourned the committee and requested a meeting with the president. Not knowing precisely what to expect, Jefferson advised Gallatin that everything "had better be suspended till that is over."[85]

The two Virginians affected cordiality, but by now it was clear that their relationship was well nigh over. Randolph told the president that his committee had been charged with reviewing the confidential message and recommending appropriate steps. He pledged his cooperation and willingness to craft any policy the president desired, so far, he added, as his principles would permit. Jefferson responded that he wanted $2 million to purchase Florida. Randolph replied he would never support such an action. The president had not asked for such an appropriation, he said, in either his Annual Message or his confidential message. To attempt to make the Congress initiate the policy and appropriate the money was to shift the responsibility of the executive to the legislature. Moreover, Randolph continued—growing more animated—the president had admitted that negotiations with Spain had failed. How then could this project be viewed as anything other than paying extortion money? What would be the reaction of Great Britain? Could the United States ever again negotiate with foreign powers from a position of strength? Jefferson listened passively as Randolph rattled off his reasons for opposing the purchase. The president expressed his disagreement, and the meeting ended.[86] "The *great man,*" Senator Plumer said of Jefferson, "cannot render Randolph subservient to all his views."[87]

Randolph's next meeting, with Secretary of State James Madison, was destined to be similarly unproductive. Randolph viewed Madison as the chief Yazoo man, a pseudo-Federalist, and the man behind the Florida intrigue. Madison had long avoided contact with Randolph and made no attempt "to hide his amusement" at the outcome of the Chase trial.[88] The meeting was brief. Randolph recalled that Madison told him "that France was the great obstacle to the compromise of Spanish difficulties; that France would not permit Spain to come to any accommodation with the United States, because France wanted money, and that we must give her money."[89]

It is doubtful that Madison spoke to an avowed enemy in such terms regarding such a complex issue. But Randolph had accurately assessed the shadowy relationship between Spain and France. The Spanish regime was a mask for France, and the $2 million for Florida would end up in Napoleon's coffers. If Randolph's course of action was not determined before his visit to Madison, it was firmly in place as he left the secretary's office. "All the objections I originally had to the procedure," he would say, "were aggravated to the highest possible degree."[90] He added disingenuously that his "confidence in the principles of [Madison] . . . died, never to live again." To Randolph, the entire episode reeked of the spirit of Federalism, of government by intrigue, of yet another step away from Republican principles. It was Yazoo again—this time in the distant, mysterious Floridas.

At the height of the controversy, Randolph left Washington for Baltimore to visit his deaf-mute nephew, St. George Randolph, who was embarking for England for specialized education.[91] James Monroe would act as guardian to the young boy in London, a courtesy Randolph would ever remember. Randolph remained in Baltimore for six days, returning to the capitol on December 21. The committee had been unable to meet during his absence, and excitement "waxed high" upon his return.[92] Randolph was wearing full riding regalia as he approached the committee room. He was greeted by Secretary of Treasury Albert Gallatin, his one remaining friend in the administration.

Gallatin showed him a document titled "Provision for the Purchase of Florida." Randolph, removing his riding gloves, icily replied that he would not vote a shilling for such an endeavor. Gallatin backtracked. He was not recommending the purchase, he assured his friend, only a plan to accomplish it should the committee so desire. No, Randolph snapped, that was not the purpose of the document. It was yet another disingenuous move by a president who said one thing in public and another in private. This was the Chase trial writ large. Jefferson and Madison were guarding their reputations, he fumed, while erecting a policy masquerade in which the Congress was to play a deceitful role. Pausing to gather his thoughts, Randolph told Gallatin that he was willing to acquire Florida through open and honorable means, but that this process filled him with disgust. He would not, he snarled, deliver the public purse to the first cutthroat that rattled a saber.[93] Gallatin stood mute, a crumpled proposal in his hand. Randolph stalked off to the committee meeting.

Upon calling the committee to order, Randolph was confronted again with Gallatin's proposed funding plan. Barnabas Bidwell moved adoption of a $2 million appropriation for the purchase of Florida. Randolph smirked, and Bidwell's motion did not receive a second. The committee directed Randolph to prepare a report on the protection of America's frontier borders. The simmering internal feud between Randolph and Jefferson was publicly exploding. Henry Adams—who hated both men—could scarce conceal his delight in recounting "the queer figure of Randolph, booted, riding-whip in hand, flying about among the astonished statesmen, and flinging, one after the other, Mr. Jefferson, Mr. Madison, and dozens of helpless congressmen headlong into the mire."[94]

Randolph's "bowels [were] torn all to pieces," but he set promptly to work on the committee report. Notwithstanding his antipathy towards Madison, he seemed open to some compromise that could resolve the matter with integrity. "If *you* persist in voting the money," he wrote to Nicholson, "the committee will alter its report."[95] Receiving no guidance from his friend, Randolph drafted a report that condemned "the hostile spirit manifested by the Court of Madrid" and the "piratical depredations upon our fair commerce," but declared that "peace must always be desirable, so long as it is compatible with the honor and interest of the community."[96] The report cast opposition to the Florida Purchase in terms economic—the debt of the United States was judged too high to justify such an outlay—and diplomatic—the "rich harvest of neutrality" and unsettled state of the world supported a negotiated settlement.[97] Randolph drafted an accompanying resolution directing the president to raise troops "sufficient to protect the southern frontiers of the United States from Spanish inroad and insult, and to chastise the same." The report was submitted to the House on January 3, 1806. Randolph chose that same day to confirm his split with the Republican Party in a letter to George Hay. Randolph knew Hay would pass only his views to the president—who trusted Hay—and to Monroe, Hay's soon-to-be father-in-law. "The administration," Randolph wrote, "may do what it pleases. It favors federal principles, and, with the exception of a few great rival characters, federal men. Attack it upon this ground, and you are denounced for federalism: are told by those, who agree with you in condemning the same

measures, that you are ruining the republican party, that we must keep together, etc. The *old* republican party is already ruined, past redemption, new
men and new maxims are the order of the day."[98]

The debate on Florida took place in secret. Senator Timothy Pickering
wrote that Randolph offered "determined opposition—sarcastic reproaches
on its advocates, and of strains of eloquence never before heard from him in
that House."[99] Representative Thomas Thompson wrote to Daniel Webster
that Randolph was "a most able, industrious [and] persevering advocate" of
national honor, but that "his eloquence and exertions will be unavailing."[100]
Henry Adams again mingled condemnation with begrudging respect in describing Randolph during the Florida debate as springing "suddenly, violently, straight at the face of his opponent . . . with astonishing quickness
and persistence . . . violent gesticulation and . . . vituperation in well-chosen
language and with sparkling illustration."[101]

Forrest McDonald writes that Randolph's efforts forced Jefferson to
"[crack] the party whip" and put "all his prestige behind the measure."[102] In
the end, the House rejected Randolph's report and resolution by a vote of 72
to 53. Bidwell's resolution authorizing the appropriation of $2 million was
passed by a vote of 77 to 54. With these two votes, Randolph's leadership of
the House Republicans effectively ended. "The example of John Randolph,"
Jefferson would smugly write, "is a caution to all honest and prudent men to
sacrifice a little of self-confidence and to go with their friends although they
may sometimes think they are going wrong."[103]

Randolph had prophesied this betrayal of principles. Yet foreknowledge
did not make the desertion easier to bear. "I am tired," he wrote to Caesar Rodney, "of setting up idols for the mere honor of being sacrificed upon
their altars—of assisting unworthy men to mount the topmost round of
the ladder of ambition, merely to have my head broken when they kick it
from under them." This latest beguilement left him particularly bitter. "Tis
time for Republicans and Republicanism to make a stand against Patriots
(or rather wolves in sheep's clothing) who are secretly acted upon and supported by the federal party (Yazoo!) who they also support."[104]

Chief among the "unworthy men" was James Madison. It was Madison,
he wrote in another letter to Rodney, "who has given the bias to our affairs from their true bearing and direction to Federalism or anything-or-
nothing-ism."[105] Should Madison become president, "for which he is strain-
ing every nerve, supported by all the apostates of our party, the Feds, and a
few good but misguided men," Randolph concluded, "we are gone forever."

He brooded over the fallen statesmen roundabout him and his sentiments slipped into letters to his ward, Theodore Dudley. *"Virtue,"* he wrote on January 31, 1806, "is *essential* to *great excellence* in *laudable pursuits.*"[106] And again on February 15: "Lay down this as a principle, that Truth is to the other virtues what vital air is to the human system."[107]

Toward the end of February, Randolph had his last meeting with Thomas Jefferson. Randolph asked when Monroe would return from England. Jefferson answered that he was leaving that matter to his successor. Knowing the president meant Madison, Randolph responded that Monroe would follow Jefferson as president.[108] Perhaps it was fitting that their last meeting ended on a disagreement about the future of Republicanism.

Randolph was alone in the House. He was no longer a Republican—as he distinguished that designation. Nor could he be a Federalist, even as he found himself a fellow-traveler in opposition. He had at long last become a party unto himself, a republican purist who would sacrifice no principle for political success or collegial acceptance. He was the "third something" of American politics—a *Tertium Quid.*

8

Mystery of Affection and Faith

And over all Romance and Song
A classic beauty throwing,
And laurelled Clio at his side
Her storied pages showing.

The leaders of the respective Republican party factions seemed undisturbed by the split. Thomas Jefferson exhibited characteristic calmness. "Republicanism," he wrote to William Duane, editor of the Philadelphia *Aurora*, was "as solidly embodied on all essential points, as you ever saw it on any occasion."[1] He was more sardonic with regard to his former advocate. Randolph, he wrote to James Monroe, was on track to "a state of as perfect obscurity as if his name had never been known."[2] He conceded that the break was dramatic, but judged that Randolph's "sudden defection . . . could not but produce a momentary astonishment, and even dismay; but for a moment only."[3] The president was confident that Randolph's influence was at an end.

Randolph appeared similarly serene. While events cascaded about him, he took time to sit for a portrait by Gilbert Stuart. Wearing a dark blue coat with a velvet collar and a light gray vest, he appears much younger than his thirty-three years. His slightly blushing cheeks, brown eyes, and dark hair with light auburn streaks prompted one observer to describe the work as "a portrait of Mr. Randolph when twelve years of age."[4] Henry Adams wrote that the portrait presented Randolph as "open, candid, sweet in expression, full of warmth, sympathy, and genius . . . [expressing] all his higher instincts" and displaying "the mystery of affection and faith he inspired in his friends."[5] Stuart's painting shows no hint of the strife in which Randolph was involved during the sitting, perhaps because he displayed none. "I can find no cause for regret," he wrote about this time, "that I have encountered the hostility of the unprincipled and base, or have been deserted by the timorous or the slothful."[6] He was content, he wrote in another letter, "to let my public conduct speak for itself."[7]

Randolph did not have to wait long for another opportunity to let his conduct speak. Reacting to continued British assaults against American shipping, Representative Andrew Gregg of Pennsylvania introduced a resolution prohibiting the importation of all products grown or manufactured in Great Britain.[8] Randolph immediately prepared to join the fray. "I hope," he wrote to Nicholson, "your throat will be in order for Gregg's Resolution."[9] In opposing the resolution, Randolph saw the opportunity to reaffirm Republican principles, outline the Quid terms of engagement with the administration, and fire the first salvo at the nascent presidential campaign of James Madison. Randolph's speech of March 5, 1806, would launch "his long public career of opposition."[10]

He started by addressing the policy impact. The ban on imports, he argued, advanced the mercantile interests of the northeastern states at the expense of the agricultural south. "[If] this great agricultural nation is to be governed by Salem and Boston, New York and Philadelphia, Baltimore and Norfolk and Charleston," he said, "let gentleman come out and say so."[11] This was the mercantile-agrarian argument that would increasingly dominate congressional debates in the years leading to the War Between the States. But Randolph went beyond the mere economic argument. The trade being created by the European situation was war-profit trading. It was not the shipping of American produce in exchange for foreign products. It was a carrying trade that would disappear as soon as the conflict ended. Was such a venture worth risking peace or violating American neutrality? This was just the type of morally ambiguous policy that led to consolidation of power. "That we must give the President power to call forth the resources of the nation," Randolph argued, "that is, to filch the last shilling from our pockets—to drain the last drop of blood from our veins. I am against giving this power to any man, be he who he may. The American people must either withhold this power, or resign their liberties. There is no other alternative."[12]

Above all, the restraint of trade was unconstitutional. "I fear if you go into a foreign war, for a circuitous, unfair carrying trade," he said, "you will come out without your Constitution. . . . We shall be told that our Government is too free; or, as they would say, weak and inefficient. Much virtue, sir, in terms!"[13]

This economic declaration of war, Randolph argued, would by necessity place the United States in alliance with Napoleon. "The iron scepter of the ocean," he warned, "will pass into his hand who wears the iron crown of the land."[14] Aware that his past support of France might be raised against him, Randolph was quick to distinguish "republican France" from the nation under the tyrant's heel. "Gentleman talk of 1793," he scoffed. "They might as well go back to the Trojan War."[15]

Finally, Randolph poked through the façade that Gregg's resolution was a purely commercial measure. It was, he said, a prelude to war. "[These] incipient war measures," he said, "in their commencement breathe nothing but peace, though they plunge at last into war." He scoffed at those who had "not got beyond the horn-book of politics," but were foolishly rushing America into needless conflict. Such men, he said, deserve "a straight waistcoat, a dark room, water gruel, and depletion."[16]

Perhaps if Randolph had stopped at this point, he might have carried the day. His argument was persuasive both to southerners and to those concerned with the nation's commercial future.[17] But Randolph had more to say. He poured forth "the gall of his heart . . . without measure" directly at the administration in general and James Madison in particular.[18] It was at once both a decree of divorce and a declaration of war. "I speak of back-stairs influence—of men who bring messages to this House, which, although they do not appear on the Journals, govern its decisions. . . . They may give winks and nods, and pretend to be wise, but they dare not come out and tell the nation what they have done. . . . I voted against all such under the administration of John Adams, and I will continue to do so under that of Thomas Jefferson."[19]

Federalists delighted in hearing Randolph tell "wholesome and important, tho unpleasant and unpalatable" truths. "It is painful, no doubt," Samuel Taggart wrote, "to have the mask torn off, and Randolph is doing it with no gentle hand."[20] Madison exercised a "left-handed, invisible, irresponsible influence," Randolph told the House, "which defies the touch, but pervades and decides everything."[21] He held aloft a pamphlet authored by Madison in defense of America's neutral rights and exclaimed, "Oh, that mine enemy would write a book!" He punctuated his abuse of Madison by contemptuously tossing the pamphlet to the floor.[22] Randolph "took a very wide range indeed," Colonel Benjamin Tallmadge wrote to Representative Manasseh Cutler, "and pelted the Secretary of State severely."[23]

Finally, Randolph turned toward his colleagues on the Republican side of the House. There no longer existed any common ground of party, requirement of loyalty, or discipline of chain of command to shield them from his verbal darts. "Well, sir," he said, turning to, and on, his colleagues,

> What have you done? You have had resolutions laid upon your table, gone to some expense of printing and stationary—mere pen, ink, and paper, that's all. Like true political quacks, you deal only in handbills and nostrums. Sir, I blush to see the record of our proceedings; they resemble nothing but the advertisements of patent medicines. Here you have "the worm-destroying lozenges" . . . [and] "Sloan's vegetable specific," an infallible remedy for all nervous disorders and vertigoes of brain-sick politicians. . . . Your mouth is hermetically sealed. Your honor has received a wound which must not take air. . . . It seems that your sensibility is entirely confined to extremities. You may be pulled by the nose and ears, and never feel it, but let your strong box be attacked and you are all nerve—"Let us go to war!"[24]

The affairs of the nation had been entrusted not to "reasonable men," Randolph concluded, but "to Tom, Dick, and Harry, to the refuse of the retail trade of politics."[25]

It was another provocative performance. Randolph had shown that his ability to take up the cudgels of the House was undiminished by his new status as minority man within a majority party. "His language is very appropriate and forcible," Senator Plumer wrote. "It was the most bitter, severe and eloquent philippic I ever heard. . . . There will appear in the newspaper the substance of it, but not its spirit and highly finished eloquence, elegance, and well turned periods. The stenographer cannot relate them."[26] Representative Thomas Thompson also believed the speech would lose its force in translation. "Randolph has made a violent attack upon the President," he wrote to Daniel Webster, "and treated Madison's host with ineffable contempt. . . . If it appears on paper as he delivered it, the impression it will make on the public mind must be great."[27] Words of encouragement came from an old friend. "You have become, it seems, anti-ministerialist," Joseph Bryan wrote. "I cannot help thinking you have acted a manly part and one that eventually will do you honor."[28] The Richmond *Enquirer* continued to walk a tightrope between the warring Republicans. Randolph's speech, it reported, was from "the mind of one of our ablest politicians." The paper went on to warn "our republican friends that it is a duty . . . not to prejudge or too hastily condemn him."[29]

Randolph gave a second speech on the resolution and was followed by several other Quids.[30] It became apparent that Gregg's resolution lacked sufficient support to pass the House.[31] Joseph Nicholson introduced a milder resolution, drafted by the administration, which prohibited importation of only those goods that the United States could supply with its own industry. Nicholson's resolution passed 87 to 35, with 9 Republicans joining all the Federalists in opposition. Not wishing to oppose his friend, Randolph left the chamber without voting.

Ignoring the fact that Randolph had single-handedly derailed Gregg's resolution, Jefferson hailed the vote as a victory. "I have never seen a H[ouse] of Representatives more solidly united in doing what they believed to be the best for the public interest," he wrote to James Monroe. He announced his verdict on Randolph in one sentence: "There can be no better proof than the fact that so eminent a leader should at once and almost unanimously be abandoned."[32]

Jefferson may have considered him abandoned, but Randolph's long historical view taught him that alliances could shift, particularly during presidential campaigns. Randolph's candidate for 1808 was James Monroe. The choice was somewhat obvious—Monroe was the only Republican prominent enough to mount a serious challenge to Madison—but it was also a strategic selection. Monroe was a more dynamic personality than Madison, had disagreed with Jefferson's secret message to Congress regarding Florida, and was disappointed that his advice regarding Anglo-American policy had been generally rejected.[33] Randolph enjoyed a cordial relationship with Monroe, who had been acting as guardian in London for St. George Randolph. The combination of these auspicious circumstances, Randolph suspected, might be enough to compel Monroe to enter the race.

Randolph began to prod Monroe toward a presidential run. "There is no longer a doubt," he wrote, "but the principles of our administration have been materially changed."[34] He assured Monroe that the Old Republicans were united in their support of him for president and "will never consent" to "raise Mr. M[adiso]n to the Presidency." A month later, he detailed the "decided division" within the party, advised that Speaker Macon and Joseph Nicholson were in league with him, and warned Monroe "against a compromitment of yourself to men in whom you cannot wholly confide."[35] He praised Monroe's "wisdom and . . . character" and condemned Madison's "cold and insidious moderation." He expressed the determination of the Old Republicans "not to have a Yazoo President . . . nor one who has mixed in the intrigues of the last three or four years at Washington."[36]

Randolph left aside no argument to persuade Monroe, even casting unsubstantiated aspersions at what he dubbed Madison's "unfortunate matrimonial connection." Jefferson learned of Randolph's efforts and rushed to hold Monroe in line. "You must not commit yourself to him," Jefferson wrote. He warned that an alliance with Randolph would leave Monroe "embarrassed with such a *soi-disant* friend."[37] He advised that Monroe's "great body of . . . friends are among the firmest adherents to the administration" and predicted that Randolph would likely become a Federalist.[38] Monroe refused to declare himself a candidate, but confided to Randolph that "circumstances have occur'd during my service abroad which were calculated to hurt my feelings . . . which may produce a change in the future relations between some of them and myself."[39] That was enough to nurture Randolph's hopes that Monroe might yet consent to challenge "the weak, feeble and pusillanimous" Madison.[40]

According to Henry Adams, Randolph controlled the House for the remainder of the session "by audacity and energy of will."[41] In a series of speeches, he "kept the field of argument alone against the whole host of his guards or brethren, and even silenced their batteries."[42] Calls of "order" echoed through the House as Randolph taunted, ridiculed, and lashed the administration. On March 13, 1806, Randolph waved one of his goblin-like fingers and confirmed the existence of the "third something" of American politics. "There is another question relative to what is generally called *quiddism*," he said. "I am willing to meet gentlemen on that ground. If we belong to the third party, be it so."[43]

Later that month, Randolph again stopped action on the Yazoo compromise. "This bill may be called the Omega . . . but, with me, it is the Alpha; it is the head of the divisions among the Republican party; it is the secret and covert cause of the whole."[44] Republicans found themselves "bruised and sore, mortified, angry and ridiculous" as Randolph mocked their arguments as "so excessively light that they at once vanished in thin air."[45] The Richmond *Enquirer* congratulated "our country upon the rejection of the Yazoo bill" and praised Randolph as "the man, to whose zeal, intrepidity, and genius, we . . . owe the expiring convulsion of this monster."[46]

Day after day, as the Washington winter began to thaw, Randolph employed extemporaneous eloquence to call out the "gentlemen . . . fond of sheltering themselves behind great names."[47] His exasperated colleagues tried to give as good as they got, calling Randolph "a maniac . . . accidently broke out of his cell" and a "petted, vindictive school-boy."[48] Randolph was unmoved. "I found that I might co-operate [with the administration] or be an honest man," he told the House on April 7, 1806. "I have therefore opposed, and will oppose them."[49]

Having again halted the Yazoo settlement, Randolph disrupted the administration's plans to purchase Florida. Congress had appropriated funds for the purchase of Florida from the customs duties on salt. On April 14, Randolph introduced a resolution repealing the salt duty.[50] It was a cunning move. He knew public opposition to the salt duty was significant, and that congressmen would oppose his resolution at their peril. He knew also that repeal would force the administration to scramble for funds. Randolph's political acumen proved on target. Before the year was out, President Jefferson yielded to public pressure and requested the repeal of the salt duty. Florida would be purchased, if at all, with money from the Mediterranean Fund.[51] The "abandoned" Quid had forced another tax reduction and again diverted a best-laid plan of the administration.

During one of his numerous attacks on Madison, Randolph declared that, if the secretary of state's nefarious influence was ever fully disclosed, it "would fix a stain upon some men in the Government and high office, which all the waters in the ocean would not wash out."[52] Congressman John Jackson, brother-in-law of Dolley Madison, leapt to his feet to defend Madison against a charge "destitute of truth and foundation."[53] During the course of his speech, he referred to Randolph as "my colleague." From across the chamber came the high-pitched voice. "I am not the gentleman's colleague."

"Very well . . . John Randolph," Jackson began, but was immediately called to order by the Speaker for referring to a member by name. Flustered, Jackson responded: "Sir, I know of no more appropriate appellation unless it is the descendant of Powhatan."[54] It appeared for a moment that a challenge was imminent, but Randolph had toyed enough with Jackson and let the matter drop.

Things went further with Congressman Thomas Mann Randolph, husband of President Jefferson's daughter Martha. Thomas Randolph's congressional career was singularly undistinguished. He labored under the burden of a close proximity to power without the acquisition of any.[55] This may have contributed to a violent temper and abusive nature. Perhaps he was spoiling for a fight or seeking an opportunity to become an administration spokesman when he suddenly sprang into action during a House debate on April 21, 1806. Congressmen Willis Alston, William Findley, and David Williams were engaged in a vigorous debate over the Mediterranean Fund, the source that would fund the Florida Purchase. The debate, commencing after a dinner recess, featured sharp words and repeated calls of order, the *Annals of Congress* noted, "by a number of gentlemen, and among others by Mr. T. M. Randolph."[56] Several strong remarks piqued the interest of John Randolph and, appearing mildly amused at the passionate debate, he expressed the hope that "no honorable gentleman, who has heretofore kept the noiseless tenor of his way, because we have adjourned for half an hour, has permitted his passions to indulge in an asperity not shown on any former occasion." He trusted that "whatever contumely or hostility may have been manifested during the earlier period of the session, we would have thrown off in the last moments of it."[57]

By Randolph's mordant standard, his remarks were mild, almost tongue-in-check, and though directed at no one in particular, they most likely applied to Findley, who appeared slightly inebriated following dinner.[58] Yet Thomas Mann Randolph convinced himself that the word "contumely" and the phrase "noiseless tenor of his way" were directed at him. The man who rarely spoke unleashed a voluble earful. He conceded that he had "not made much noise this session," but that John Randolph had "made more than has been useful." He challenged Randolph's patriotism and judged him "bankrupt forever as a popular statesman . . . without compass or rudder, tossed on the surges of his passion." He then leveled a not-so-subtle threat. "I have always thought, and always shall think, that lead and even steel make very proper ingredients in serious quarrels, and I shall never be unwilling, when honor requires, to mix either or both."[59]

Stunned members turned toward John Randolph in anticipation of a certain response by word or whip. His seat was empty. He had removed himself to a remote room of the Capitol from whence he dispatched Congressman James Garnett to confront the president's son-in-law.[60] Garnett asked if the remarks were directed at Randolph. Thomas Randolph admitted the obvious. Garnett coolly replied that John Randolph would expect "to meet him either that night (which he preferred) or in the morning."[61]

Duel negotiations began in earnest between agents of the two Randolphs. At this point, several members told Thomas Randolph that the words to which he took offense were clearly not directed at him.[62] The hot-tempered Randolph decided at that moment to break off duel discussions. He returned to the House floor, admitted his mistake, acknowledged his improper "severe and harsh language," and apologized for his "disrespect" to the House. Garnett reported the matter to John Randolph who, no doubt, allowed himself a mischievous grin and announced he was satisfied. "Thus," the Richmond *Enquirer* reported, "the business terminated."[63] So too did the first session of the Ninth Congress.

Randolph was in high spirits upon his return to Bizarre. "I found my family well," he wrote, "and my plantation in better order than (under *existing circumstances*) I expected."[64] He recorded a good crop of may wheat, "more tobacco than ever," and "corn enough."[65] He amused himself "very pleasantly in shooting" and wrote to Nicholson that he "shot eight partridges and a hare . . . at twelve shots, so that you see I improve."[66] Though his health was uneven, he took "strong exercise" and was on his horse "after an early breakfast until four o'clock (sometimes five)."[67] His perspective seemed to improve when away from Washington and his letters from the summer and fall of 1806 reflect a general contentment. "[As] long as the right of property and of personal liberty remains untouched (and how long that will be is more than I can tell)," he wrote a friend, "I may make a shift to crawl thro' this world with the rest."[68]

Politically, he was still in favor with his fellow freeholders. "Those whom I saw there and all of whom I heard (with one exception only)," he wrote after spending a day at Charlotte Courthouse, "approved the course which we have taken."[69] Rumors that he might be challenged in the next election dissipated as no opposition materialized.[70] He spent several days in Richmond, during which time he discussed the national political scene with Thomas Ritchie, editor of the Richmond *Enquirer*. Randolph sensed he might have found a Quid ally. "If I am not much mistaken," he wrote after the meeting, "his new faith is already shaken to the very foundation."[71] It is true that Ritchie was an admirer, but he had no intention of breaking with the president.[72] He privately viewed Randolph "as lacking the tempering influences of experience requisite in a statesman" and began to distance the *Enquirer* from the Quids.[73]

Randolph faced more immediate problems with two other Republican newspapers. The Philadelphia *Aurora* and the *National Intelligencer* revived the Thomas Randolph affair and took issue as to which man first backed down. Again showing a lack of judgment, Thomas Randolph began to equivocate about his apology. Though John Randolph wrote that he had had "enough of this," he warned he would not "yield a bloodless victory to my enemies."[74] For a time it appeared that duel discussions would again commence, but James Garnett clarified the record in a letter to the Richmond *Enquirer*.[75] Meanwhile, Thomas Jefferson undertook to dissuade his son-in-law from forcing the matter. "How different is the stake which you two would bring into the field," he wrote, comparing the worth of the sensitive young man to that of John Randolph. "On his side, unentangled in the affections of the world, a single life, of no value to himself or others. On yours, yourself, a wife, and a family of children, all depending for all their happiness and protection in this world on you alone."[76]

Jefferson's cruel assessment of Randolph—"a single life, of no value to himself or others"—was no doubt cast in such fashion to dissuade Thomas Randolph from pursuing a duel. However, it also reflected the president's attitude toward the man who had called him on principle, divided the party, and vexed his administration. If he had known of Randolph's next planned salvo, Jefferson might have encouraged his son-in-law to take a shot at the Old Quid.

"I have this day commenced my long projected work," Randolph wrote to Garnett on June 19, 1806. The work, written over the pseudonym "Decius," was a defense of his actions during the Florida debate.[77] "I want nothing," he wrote to Nicholson, "but justice to be done to my motives, which I know to have been upright, and I am content."[78] The "Decius" letter recounted the events surrounding Jefferson's annual message, the secret message, and the intrigue inherent in the escapade. Randolph wrote that "facts have been misstated, opinion misrepresented—much truth suppressed and more falsehood suggested." These actions, he asserted, were those of a power-hungry party that had "erected a political idol on whose altars he, who dared to mention its infallibility, must prepare to bleed."[79] Randolph argued that the Quids had no choice but to act as they did, even against such odds.[80]

Randolph repeated his argument that he was willing to "acquire [Florida] honorably" but would "never consent to proceed in this way . . . as if [Congress] had no character to lose." Secrecy and intrigue had marked this policy from the start, he wrote, and the Congress could not "dwindle into a mere chamber for enregistering ministerial edicts." Randolph lost none of his effectiveness as a speaker when he turned to the written word. "All I can say," Joseph Bryan wrote after reading the article, "is you have a confounded way of writing and speaking broad-out, you can't learn to call black blue and yellow white."[81]

The president was at Monticello when he read the Decius letter. Though he "eschewed profanity," Jefferson uncorked a tirade about Randolph's "bold and unauthorized assertions."[82] Though Randolph was criticizing "back-stairs' influence," Jefferson fumed, he "never spoke of this while he and Mr. Nicholson enjoyed it almost solely."[83] The president outlined several corrections of fact, which the *Enquirer* published. Additionally, the paper printed a response penned by Barnabas Bidwell, and expressed "decided dissent" with the Decius letter.[84] Meanwhile, Jefferson turned his attention to seeking out congressional candidates to drive Randolph from the Ways & Means Committee. "There was never a time," the president wrote, "when the services of those who possess talents, integrity, firmness, and sound judgment were more wanted in Congress."[85] Jefferson wanted to be rid of this man.

Randolph prepared for the upcoming session of Congress with his usual flurry of letters to friends and colleagues. "Have you heard the latest scandal of the day?" he wrote to Joseph Nicholson, who had left Congress to become a Maryland judge. "It is said, and believed too, that the P[resident] and John Walker have had an interview . . . [and] peace has been restored between the august parties and established on the most durable basis."[86] Randolph's impish delight in passing on this morsel of gossip was based on the longstanding rumor that Jefferson, at the age of twenty-five, had made advances to Mrs. Walker.[87] If Jefferson was meeting with Mr. Walker, might that not signal that the chief executive had new worries about the old story? That the meeting supposedly took place at the home of the secretary of state was alone sufficient to trigger intrigue. Madison was never far from Randolph's mind. "Depend upon it," he wrote in another letter to Nicholson; "a very large majority of us are decidedly opposed to Madison's pretensions, and if the other states leave it to Virginia, he never will be president."[88] Condemning Madison's "cold and insidious moderation," Randolph continued to urge James Monroe to be active, prudent, and available.[89]

In other letters written during that summer, however, Randolph seemed to have resolved himself to the zeitgeist of the polity. "If my countrymen are determined to forge their own chains," he wrote, "whilst I will resist them to the utmost of my ability, I shall not break my heart about it, should they succeed."[90] He expected nothing from the Republican Party except "the rule of federalism, christened over again, and swaddled in the garb of moderation."[91] Still, as he prepared to again leave Bizarre for Washington, he believed that never "had the cause of free government more to fear than now."[92]

Joseph Bryan shared Randolph's frustration. Yet he sought to restrain the behavior of his friend. "I greatly wish you to remember what I have often told you, that with a little complaisance you may do anything. . . . By god, with a little management, without too visibly altering your manners, you may place your foot upon the neck of any man you please, the president alone excepted."

"You are a colossus," Bryan concluded, "but the Colossus at Rhodes was blown down by *wind*."[93]

9

House Cynosure

Bard, Sage, and Tribune! in himself
All moods of mind contrasting,
The tenderest wail of human woe,
The scorn like lightning blasting.

As soon as the gavel dropped to begin the second session of the Ninth Congress, a move was made against Randolph.[1] Willis Alston proposed that membership on standing committees be determined by House vote, not by appointment by the Speaker.[2] The underlying presumption of Alston's motion was clear: Randolph would not sit on Ways & Means if the membership voted. Alston got his vote, but Speaker Macon held enough of his allies in line to survive this challenge to his power by a narrow vote of forty-two to forty-four. The referendum on Randolph failed—just barely.

Macon proceeded to make committee appointments, but he stopped short at Ways & Means. Randolph was not in his seat. Macon could not appoint an absent member to a committee and was left with no alternative than to fill Randolph's spot with another.[3] "[Such] was my sense of duty," Macon wrote, "that I could not act otherwise."[4] The Speaker's remorse—and any corresponding delight among administration forces—was short-lived. Randolph soon arrived, and the "mystery of affection and faith he inspired in his friends" was promptly manifested. James Garnett withdrew from the Ways & Means Committee, creating a vacancy that the Speaker filled with Randolph. The new chairman of Ways & Means, Joseph Clay, promptly stepped aside, and the committee reinstated Randolph as chairman.[5] Jefferson's allies had failed, but everyone recognized that it had been a very near thing. Randolph recorded no comment regarding the machinations to remove him from his sole remaining position of authority, but he did skip the traditional courtesy call paid on the president by members of Congress.[6]

Randolph may have been an Ishmael within the Republican caucus, but his views seemed to still animate policy. In his message to Congress, Jefferson endorsed two of Randolph's positions: repeal of the salt duty and suspension of the non-importation act.[7] Randolph allowed himself a fleck of self-satisfaction as he watched his colleagues squirm at this de facto endorsement of his positions. "They remind me of a practice which I have heard of in military punishments," he wrote, "to give the offender a bullet to chew on to enable him to bear the pain and keep from crying out. They chewed the bullet with a vengeance."[8] Several Republicans began to adjust their behavior toward their former leader. "The temper of the house at present," Randolph noted, "seems less intolerant and violent than at the last session."[9] He found that he was being treated with "the greatest apparent cordiality" and heard that "[the] higher powers are in the same goodly temper."[10] Talk began to percolate of a truce between the administration and the Quids, but Randolph would take cordiality only so far. "It is reported," he wrote, "that I have made overtures to the reigning powers on my behalf and that of the minority, to forgive and forget the past. . . . Nothing can be farther from the truth. So much for that."[11]

Lest there be any mistaking his sentiments toward reconciliation, Randolph reminded the House "that to suspend [the non-importation act's] operation is to acknowledge the impolicy of having originally passed it."[12] He made it clear that repealing one tax was not enough to soothe fundamental differences. "I hope to see the time," he said, "when all the taxes of the General Government shall be repealed, except a small ad valorem duty of five per cent."[13] Finally, Randolph reminded his colleagues that they had pointed "the finger of scorn" at him, called him "mad-dog," and accused him of "political defection." Did they now expect him to remain silent when "all measures for which this denunciation was made" were adopted? "No, sir," he said, "I cannot take a retrospect of the past without feeling a degree of conscious pride that my aid was not given, that I had no hand in the acts of commission or omission that have brought us to this deplorable state of things."[14] If there was to be any reconciliation, it would have to come from the Yazoo men and the prodigal Republicans. For his part, Randolph would continue "to be true to those principles which I have constantly maintained and, God willing, ever will maintain so long as I have a seat on this floor, or have life."[15]

Compared with the hurly-burly of the previous session, the second session of the Ninth Congress was palpably calmer. Randolph regularly participated in debates, but only a proposal to temporarily suspend the Writ of Habeas Corpus in certain cases stirred him to match his past eloquence. "It has been truly said," he warned the House, "that no man becomes perfectly wicked at once; and it may be affirmed, with equal truth, that a nation is never enslaved at once."[16] The bill was overwhelmingly defeated. He was equally succinct during a debate over a bill regarding slave importation. The bill prohibited "the importation of slaves into any port or place within the jurisdiction of the United States" after January 1, 1808.[17] Randolph had long opposed the slave trade, and so spoke little on the merits of the bill, but when a provision was proposed forbidding the transportation of currently owned slaves within the United States, he again asserted that constitutional property rights—even in human beings—were paramount. Additionally he warned that the bill "might be made the pretext of universal emancipation," and further that, "if ever the time of disunion between the states should arrive, the line of severance will be between the slaveholding and the non-slaveholding states."[18]

At times during 1806, disunion seemed more than just a prediction. On November 27, 1806, President Jefferson issued a proclamation stating that "sundry persons . . . are conspiring and confederating together to begin a military expedition or enterprise against the dominions of Spain."[19] The phrase "sundry persons" was purposely vague, but everyone in Washington knew it referred to one specific person: Aaron Burr.

The former vice-president had been very active since leaving office. Avatar-like, Burr turned up in Philadelphia, Cincinnati, Nashville, and New Orleans, always drawing a collection of interesting persons.[20] He chatted up British Minister Anthony Merry, charmed the wealthy Harman Blennerhassett of Ohio, and received a hero's welcome during a visit to Andrew Jackson. He was often in the company of the general-in-chief of the United States Army, James Wilkinson, a man already on the payroll—as Agent Number Thirteen—of the Spanish government. Burr may or may not have traced out invasion routes to Mexico, but he seemed to attract a number of adventurers and ne'r-do-wells.[21] To what end these activities were directed has vexed generations of historians. He was either planning a filibuster (a sometimes-legal invasion by a private army) into Spanish territory, or he was conspiring to overthrow the western states and territories, invade Mexico, and become emperor.[22] What is clear is that Jefferson did not assume Burr to be innocent, and so he began to discreetly monitor the situation. In early 1806, a ciphered letter attributed to Burr, but not in his hand, proclaimed that "the gods invite us to glory and fortune." Almost immediately,

General Wilkinson donned his third turncoat and betrayed Burr, writing to Jefferson that "the destruction of the American Union is seriously menaced." Jefferson subsequently issued his proclamation and made brief reference to "this enterprise" in his Message to Congress.[23]

All of Washington sought to ascertain the seriousness of Burr's actions. "I wish it were in my power to give you some authentic information respecting Col. Burr's late movements in the western country," Randolph wrote to James Monroe. "Some gentlemen from that quarter treat the alleged conspiracy as a matter of ridicule, but for a variety of circumstances, above all from the known character of the man, there is much reason to believe it to be real and serious."[24] Impatient that "we have nothing here but rumors . . . which are contradictory and unintelligible," Randolph introduced a resolution calling upon the president to lay before the House any non-confidential information in his possession regarding "any illegal combination of private individuals against the peace and safety" of the United States.[25] Randolph's resolution passed with minor amendments, and Jefferson responded in a Special Message on January 22, 1807. The president stated he had "little . . . as to constitute formal and legal evidence," but declared that Burr's "guilt is placed beyond question."[26]

No one in Washington knew that, four days before the president's message was sent to Congress, Burr had surrendered to authorities in Mississippi. Those tidings were followed by conflicting reports that Burr had jumped bail, been captured, and had again attempted escape. At length he was under guard and headed east. Arriving in Fredericksburg, Virginia, in early March, Burr learned that he was to be transported to Richmond for trial. At the same time, Randolph learned that he too would make the trip to Richmond. He had been summoned for service on the Burr grand jury.

Randolph caught a glimpse of the famous prisoner prior to the start of the trial. "Colonel Burr (*quantum mutates ab illo!*) passed by my door the day before yesterday under a strong guard," he wrote. "His very manner of traveling, altho' under arrest, was characteristic of the man—enveloped in mystery."[27] Burr arrived in Richmond on March 26 and was taken before the presiding judge—Chief Justice John Marshall. Observers could not help but note the irony as one enemy of Jefferson stood for trial before another enemy of Jefferson. Certainly the president took notice, particularly when Marshall issued preliminary rulings favorable to Burr's defense.[28] Writing to Senator William Giles, Jefferson condemned the "tricks of the judges" and accused the Federalists of making Burr's cause their own. He fumed—as he did before he set the Chase trial in motion—that federal judges acted without restraint or constitutional check and were beyond the reach of the people. "Impeachment," he snapped, "is a farce." The president resolved to counter Marshall's partisanship by actively involving himself in the prosecution. All means were justified to convict Burr, a man he likened to "a crooked gun, or other perverted machine, whose aim you could never be sure of."[29]

The courthouse in Richmond proved too small a venue for the crowds that flocked to witness the trial, so the United States Circuit Court for the District of Virginia convened in the chamber of the Virginia House of Delegates. Seated alongside Randolph in the jury box was William Giles, senator from Virginia and Jefferson confidant; Wilson Cary Nicholas, former senator and friend of Jefferson; Littleton Tazewell, Randolph's childhood friend and future governor of Virginia; James Pleasants, another future governor; James Barbour, later to serve as governor, senator, and secretary of war; James Garnett, Randolph's fellow Quid; and Joseph Cabell, who with Jefferson would found the University of Virginia. Burr's defense team consisted of three well-respected attorneys—John Wickham, Benjamin Botts, and John Baker—under the management of Edmund Randolph, former attorney general of the United States. The elder Randolph would manage the defense until the arrival of Burr's chief defense counsel: Luther Martin, the Federalist bulldog who saved Justice Chase. The United States was represented by George Hay, soon to become the son-in-law of James Monroe; William Wirt, future attorney general of the United States; and Alexander MacRae, lieutenant governor of Virginia. Viewing the proceedings from the audience was a lean, hard-looking westerner, with a budding reputation for a quick temper and handy pistols, Andrew Jackson of Tennessee. Another future military hero, Winfield Scott, was in attendance, as was the architect Benjamin Latrobe and author Washington Irving. The room was filled with so many men of distinction that it could have been a portrait by Trumbull. Presiding was Chief Justice John Marshall, who was, Winfield Scott would write, "the master spirit of the scene."[30]

The prospective jurors had a definite Jeffersonian tint, but decades of political skirmishes, scores of personal differences, and multiple divided loyalties made for an unpredictable mix. Burr challenged only Giles and Nicholas, and Marshall dismissed both from service.[31] Randolph rose and asked to be excused. "I have formed," he told the Court, "an opinion concerning the nature and tendency of certain transactions imputed to the gentleman now before me."[32] Marshall denied the request, stating that "a man must not only have formed but declared an opinion in order to excuse him."[33] He then named Randolph foreman of the jury. The grand jury was sworn but promptly excused while the court awaited the arrival of General Wilkinson. Days passed. "I have been detained here near a week by Burr's trial," Randolph wrote to Nicholson. "When it is to end (I might say begin) is more than I can presume to conjecture. To me it is, so far, tedious enough. . . . So much for this troublesome little man."[34]

Wilkinson took his time traveling to Richmond, leaving the town ample time to stir up rumors and intrigue. Randolph, already suspicious of Wilkinson, developed a strong aversion to the man who "may be expected [to arrive] with the Greek Kalends and not before."[35] He disliked the swirling intrigue that was both subject of and result of the trial. "A system of espionage and denunciation has been organized which pervades every quarter," he wrote to Monroe. "Distrust and suspicion generally prevail in the intercourse between man and man. All is constraint, reserve, and mystery."[36]

Wilkinson strode into court on Monday, June 15, 1807, in full dress uniform with ceremonial sword, swelling, Washington Irving wrote, "like a turkey cock."[37] Randolph's shrill voice instantly sliced through the chamber. "Take that man out and disarm him," he said to the marshal. "I will allow no attempt to intimidate the jury."[38] The swordless Wilkinson testified for four days, convincing Randolph much more of his guilt than that of Burr. The general, Randolph wrote, was "the most finished scoundrel that ever lived; a ream of paper would not contain all the proofs."[39] When Wilkinson finished testifying, a juror—probably Randolph, though the record is unclear—moved to indict him for treason.[40] The motion failed by the narrow vote of seven to nine. "The mammoth of iniquity escaped," Randolph fumed. "Not that any man pretended to think him *innocent*. . . . [Wilkinson] is the only man that I ever saw who was from the bark to the very core a villain."[41]

On June 24, the grand jury returned a bill of indictment stating that "Aaron Burr . . . not having the fear of God before his eyes . . . but being moved and seduced by the instigation of the devil . . . unlawfully, falsely, maliciously and traitorously did compass, imagine and intend to raise and levy war, insurrection and rebellion against the said United States." The true bill was signed by John Randolph. Burr, he wrote, "supported himself with great fortitude" as he was led away to jail to await trial.[42] Randolph, however, was not satisfied. "I did not hear a single member of the grand jury," he would recall, "express any other opinion than that which I myself expressed of the moral (not of the legal) guilt of [Wilkinson]."[43] Before the grand jury was dismissed, Randolph attempted again to return an indictment against the general. He asked Burr to produce a letter from Wilkinson responding to the cipher dispatch. It was widely believed that the letter contained sufficient evidence to indict Wilkinson for treason. Randolph conceded that Burr could not be required to produce the letter or appear as a witness, but trusted he would comply as the jury "had not dismissed all suspicion of Wilkinson."[44] Burr refused, asserting that he could not reveal a confidential communication. Lacking the letter, Randolph gave up his case against Wilkinson. Marshall discharged the jury and adjourned court until the trial in August.

Randolph had no doubt about his vote for the bill of indictment, but the entire episode troubled his highly refined ethical sense. The improprieties seemed to build one on another: the president of the United States actively involved in a trial, an avowed enemy of the president presiding over the trial, Federalists attempting to save Burr for political reasons, Republicans seeking to convict Burr for like motives, the Army of the United States commanded by a traitor, and spectators more interested in intrigue than in justice. The trial seemed to be the latest in a series of troubling tawdry events. "My friend, I am standing on the soil of my native country, divested of every right for which my fathers bled," Randolph wrote to Joseph Nicholson. "Politics have usurped the place of law and the scenes of 1798 are again revived. Men now see and hear and feel and think *politically*."[45]

Randolph did not serve on the jury that tried and acquitted Burr, but his involvement in the matter was not quite ended. He frequently commented that he had "taken down verbatim" testimony that satisfied him "that the old army is rotten to the core; that it is not the safe depository of the sword of this nation; that intrigue and corruption had cankered it to the very heart."[46] Fearing for his reputation and his own skin, General Wilkinson in December 1807 challenged Randolph to a duel. Randolph haughtily dismissed him. "In you, sir," he wrote, "I recognize no right to hold me accountable for my public or private opinion of your character. . . . I cannot descend to your level."[47]

While Randolph sat in the grand jury room, the USS *Chesapeake* set sail for the Mediterranean. On board the thirty-eight-gun frigate were four men recently deserted from the British Navy. The *Chesapeake* had scarcely left Cape Henry when it was confronted by the HMS *Leopard*. The British commander demanded that the *Chesapeake* come to in order to be searched.

The American captain James Barron indignantly refused, and the *Leopard* responded with several broadsides into the *Chesapeake.* Three Americans were killed and eighteen wounded. The *Chesapeake* struck its colors and the British boarded and removed the deserters.[48]

"You have seen the capture of the Chesapeake without even a façade of resistance!" Randolph wrote. "Let those who have contributed to bring this disgrace upon our country take shame to themselves. Indignation in my bosom bears down every other sentiment."[49] Randolph gauged the sentiments of his district and heard a clear message. "Congress should have been convened," he reported, "a strict embargo laid, [British Minister David] Erskine sent home, [and] our ministers recalled.[50] Randolph had long opposed war with any European power so long as that stance was consistent with national honor.[51] "[Now] that *the rupture has taken place*," he wrote, "I would act with the most determined spirit against the enemy, for so I consider England at this moment."[52]

The Tenth Congress convened on October 26, 1807. As the members gathered in the chamber, a familiar figure was not in the Speaker's chair. Nathaniel Macon was ill and absent. Administration loyalists saw their best opportunity to at last rid themselves of Randolph. Moving quickly, they elected Joseph Varnum of Massachusetts as Speaker. Varnum began to make committee assignments. The Committee on Elections was named first, followed by Claims, and then Commerce and Manufacturers. Then Varnum began to read the names assigned to the Ways & Means Committee.[53] George Campbell of Tennessee was announced first, indicating the Speaker's preference for chairman. Alston of North Carolina and Eppes of Virginia, two enemies of Randolph, were next called. Smilie of Pennsylvania, Tallmadge of Connecticut, Fisk of Vermont, and Montgomery of Maryland completed the slate.

It was done, at last. Randolph had been dislodged from his seat of power. "Poor Randolph is lost," John Taylor of Caroline wrote, "and his party has vanished."[54] Randolph recorded no comment.

The new House leadership congratulated itself on sacking the head Quid, but one administration leader viewed it differently. "Varnum has, much against my wishes, removed Randolph from the Ways and Means Committee," Albert Gallatin wrote to his wife. "It was improper as it related to the public business, and it will give me additional labor."[55] The additional labor to which the treasury secretary referred was the sorting through of the various commercial responses to Great Britain's attack on the *Chesapeake.*

Options ranged from a mild non-importation act similar to the one adopted in the wake of Gregg's Resolution to a full embargo. None of the options was appealing. The president glumly told Gallatin that there was no good policy, only one "least bad."[56] Ironically, Jefferson could have found support from Randolph. He supported a temporary embargo to secure American shipping in American ports before taking other actions against Britain. John Taylor ventured that Randolph was contradicting himself.[57] Randolph's plan, however, ensured the embargo would be for only a short duration, because it would be followed quickly by a bold military move. Randolph proposed that the United States invade Canada, Nova Scotia, and Jamaica, and hold these territories "as pledges to be retained against a future pacification, until we had obtained ample redress for our wrongs."[58] In addition, Randolph called for increased arming of the militia and the utilization of flying trains of artillery instead of fixed harbor fortifications and gunboats.[59] Now it was John Taylor who found himself in a contradictory stance, calling Randolph's proposal "the most effectual, principled, and grand measure, which has been introduced since the government has been in operation."[60]

In mid-December, word came from Monroe in London that no redress would be made for the *Chesapeake* and that King George had issued a proclamation commanding the Royal Navy to seize British subjects from all neutral vessels. At the same time, France announced that it would detain and stop American vessels to ensure armaments were not bound for England. These actions guaranteed there would be no negotiated settlement. Some type of war—either economic or actual—was now inevitable. Jefferson opted for a total embargo. The Senate adopted the measure immediately; the House debated for two days behind closed doors. On December 19, 1807, the embargo bill passed by a vote of eighty-two to forty-four. Randolph voted against passage.[61]

Randolph distinguished the "peculiar" circumstances that "compelled me to oppose" the permanent embargo, as compared with his "favorite measure," a temporary embargo and military action.[62] He was not alone in this view. "I also think that an embargo for a limited time will at this moment be preferable in itself," Albert Gallatin wrote to the president. "In every point of view . . . I prefer war to permanent embargo."[63] Jefferson was not moved by foe or friend. He signed the embargo into law on December 22, 1807.

As 1808 dawned, James Madison was moving assiduously toward the presidency. "If the friends of Mr. Monroe mean to act in opposition to the intrigues here," Randolph wrote, "it is time they were in motion."[64] On

January 23, the Republican congressional caucus gave Madison eighty-three of eighty-nine votes cast. Monroe received three votes. Randolph and the Quids were among sixty absent Republicans, lending some credence to the notion that the congressional endorsement of Madison was less than complete. Randolph fanned that flame and took the fight to individual state caucuses. "Massachusetts is much divided," he wrote in mid-February. "These are good grounds."[65] Three days after writing this letter, he reported that "Pennsylvania is decidedly opposed to M[adison]."[66] Monroe let it be known that he would allow his friends to promote his candidacy, but that he would do nothing to seek the nomination. At the same time, he broke off social and political contact with Madison.[67] These steps brought a predictable response from the president. "I have ever viewed Mr. Madison and yourself as the principal pillars of my happiness," Jefferson wrote to Monroe. "Were either to be withdrawn, I should consider it as among the greatest calamities which could assail my future peace of mind."[68]

Randolph, like Samson, had no qualms about bringing down a pillar. Along with sixteen House Republicans, he published a letter in the *National Intelligencer* protesting the action of the congressional caucus. The "Protestors' letter," or the "Randolphia rescript," called the caucus "a gross assumption of power" designed to "produce an undue bias" in the presidential race. Randolph wrote that Madison was "unfit to fill the office of President": "We ask for energy, and we are told of his moderation. We ask for talents, and the reply is his unassuming merit. We ask what were his services in the cause of public liberty, and we are directed to the pages of the "Federalist," written in conjunction with Alexander Hamilton. . . . We ask for consistency as a republican, standing forth to stem the torrent of oppression which once threatened to overwhelm the liberties of the country. . . . We ask in vain."[69]

The Quids knew it would take more than rhetoric to defeat the secretary of state. "The Madisonians," former Speaker Macon wrote to Nicholson, "will not lose anything by neglect or indolence." The only chance was if "in their zeal to keep Randolph down [they] make some lukewarm about Madison."[70] The zeal to which Macon referred was on display in Randolph's congressional district, where Madison supporters were actively canvassing for a candidate. Randolph was not surprised. "My only wonder," he wrote, "is that I should have withstood them so long. You know as well as I do how much they have my destruction at heart and what means they possess for accomplishing it—power, patronage, the press, the Yazoo squad, and every villainy and every villain whom I have endeavored to expose and bring to justice."[71]

The Richmond *Enquirer* joined the fray by calling Randolph "too impetuous to take counsel," "devoted to the idle rage of overthrowing others," and "too vain to be led by others."[72] Opposition forces sang: "Thou art a pretty little speaker John / Though some there are who think you've spoke too long / And even call, sweet Sir, your tongue a bell / That ding-dong, dong-ding, tolls away!"[73]

Several candidates considered opposing Randolph. One neighbor declared his candidacy at Prince Edward Court but was treated with such warmth from Randolph supporters that he withdrew.[74] Another indicated he would enter the race, but, Randolph noted, "his wife and seven children were his eight reasons for withdrawing."[75] The Madison forces found they could not dislodge Randolph. "[We] united with others of the District to shut him out," Josiah Jackson wrote to Madison, "but Randolph's eloquency was such that we fell a long way in the minority."[76] By the end of summer, Randolph could write that, as "far as I can learn, I stand well with the mass of the people whom I represent."[77] He was not as optimistic about Monroe's chances, writing that Madison's election "is looked upon as settled."[78] That assessment was overwhelmingly confirmed when Madison's slate of electors crushed the Monroe slate in Virginia by a vote of 14,665 to 3,408. Though he was "deeply suspicious of the result," Randolph tacitly admitted that Madison's election was inevitable. "I feel more interested," he wrote to Nicholson, "about a new double gun that I lately imported than the wretched intrigues which surround me."[79]

Madison was elected president over Federalist Charles Cotesworth Pinckney by an electoral vote of 122 to 47. Randolph's defeat—like Madison's victory and Jefferson's vindication—seemed complete. The president drolly commented that Randolph and Monroe "avoid seeing one another, mutually dissatisfied."[80] Randolph was more charitable toward the soon-to-be former president. "'Tis already becoming fashionable," he wrote, "to speak disrespectfully of Mr. Jefferson, who will soon discover his real friends, when he is out of power. At the caucus . . . one of them *damned him for an old fool* and said all our difficulties were to be ascribed to him. The court now is paid to the *rising* sun."[81] For his part, Randolph would hereafter refer to Jefferson as "St. Thomas of Cantingbury."[82]

The chamber of the House of Representatives, much like the city in which it sat, was a combination of grandeur and blight. The chamber was highlighted by a grand canopy of scarlet and green velvet with sandstone pillars wrapped in crimson. In striking contrast were the stagnant air, pools of tobacco juice, and tattered curtains and carpets. Alternatively hot and humid or cold and damp, it was generally unpleasant. "We sit," Randolph noted, "in Carbonic-acid-gas, and the tallest of us, when erect, cannot get his chin above water."[83] Randolph contributed to the squalor by bringing his hunting dogs to the House floor, but he made a far greater contribution to the splendor of the chamber by the force of his personality. Francis Gilmer, a boy of eight, witnessed Randolph in 1808, and was struck as "antitheses, jests, beautiful conceits, with a striking turn and point of expression, flow from his lips with the same natural ease, and often with singular felicity of application, as regular series of arguments follow each other in the deductions of logical thinkers."[84] Another observer, Edward Hooper, wrote that he saw "a great orator, statesman, scholar and man of genius, the first man in a great assembly of the representation of a great and free people, whose sway has been extensive, and whose influence is still considerable."[85]

Gilmer and Hooper were witnessing the Randolph of legend. Self-consigned to an isolated minority, his constituency reduced to a small band of schismatics and the freeholders of Southside Virginia, Randolph became the cynosure on the House floor. He was at the height of his forensic abilities and intellectual prowess, easily overwhelming men of lesser talents.[86] "[Like] the water snakes in Coleridge's silent ocean," Henry Adams would record, "his every track was a flash of golden fire."[87] His foes sighed with resignation, just as his friends smiled with knowing delight, when Randolph rose in the House and signaled his intentions. "I wish to be distinctly understood," he said;

> I do unequivocally say that I believe the country will never see such another Administration as the last. It had my hearty approbation for one half of its career—as to my opinion of the remainder of it, it has been no secret. The lean kine of Pharaoh devoured the fat kine. . . . [N]ever has there been any Administration which went out of office and left the nation in a state so deplorable and calamitous as the last. . . . Let us not look back, sir; let the evil of the late Administration be buried with it. . . . I shall be willing to cooperate in every measure [of the Madison Administration] . . . which shall be for the public good. . . . [L]et us get the substance, and not be satisfied by the shadow.[88]

And so began a rhetorical tour-de-force. At times splenetic, at times genial, Randolph stultified House members with wit, sarcasm, metaphors, and epithets. Josiah Quincy reported that Randolph even uttered "a disconnected farrago of long words, apropos to nothing in the universe" in order to secure the ear of the House.[89]

He could reduce the most laborious arguments to cogent phrases. A wasteful government agency was "a moth in the public purse," an overreaching bill sought "to cure the corns by cutting off the toes," and ill-conceived ideas appeared "in all the nakedness of infantile imbecility."[90] Flustered members shook their heads, providing Randolph with material for another sally. "Gentlemen shake their heads, sir, and heads of such weight, too, that I despair of shaking them myself."[91] Any member who dared brook a challenge would receive special attention. "I looked at the gentleman from New York at that moment," Randolph said during one debate, slowly building to a devastating riposte, "with the sort of sensation which we feel in beholding a sprightly child meddling with edged tools, every moment expecting . . . that he will cut his fingers."[92] Nor was there safety in numbers. During one debate, three congressmen challenged Randolph, only to hear the words of the Bard hurled back at them. "The little dogs and all," Randolph purred, "Trey, Blanch, and Sweetheart, see they all bark at me."[93] He dismissed one policy proposal as "oscillating, hesitating, temporizing, tampering, [and] patching-up," and a committee report as all "preface, episode, prologue, and epilogue."[94] He dubbed his colleagues Robert Wright and John Rea (pronounced "Ray") as "a Wright always wrong; and a Rea without light"; and the flip-flopping Samuel Dexter, "Mr. Ambi-Dexter."[95]

A member on the receiving end was well advised to use caution in attempting a comeback. Representative Philemon Beecher of Ohio thrice interrupted Randolph with a motion for the previous question. Randolph paused, allowing the members to ready themselves for what would follow. "Mr. Speaker," he began, "In the Netherlands, a man of small capacity, with bits of wood and leather, will, in a few moments, construct a toy that, with the pressure of the finger and thumb, will cry 'Cuckoo! Cuckoo!' With less of ingenuity, and with inferior materials, the people of Ohio have made a toy that will, without much pressure, cry 'Previous Question, Mr. Speaker! Previous Question!'"[96]

"This is an invention," Randolph once said in assessing a maneuver by the majority, "which gentlemen may think works very handsomely in their hands, but let it be recollected that like that pretty invention the guillotine, the instrument may be worked upon themselves hereafter which is worked by them now."[97] Randolph's scattershot barbs caused equal parts pain and delight among his listeners, and even the author occasionally enjoyed them. "I beg pardon of the House," he said, enjoying his own wit, "I could not restrain a smile at the idea."[98] An ill-advised member took issue with Randolph's delight in his own bon mot during "the present crisis of our affairs." Randolph, unsmiling, assured his critic that he was no "empty giggler" but that he "might surely contend with the poet that there are things (and this bill perhaps is one of them) which are more easily cut and dissolved by the sharp sword of ridicule than by serious argument."[99] One exasperated member resorted to a sputtering taunt about Randolph's supposed impotency. "You pride yourself upon an animal faculty," Randolph sneered with contumelious scorn, "in respect to which the negro is your equal and the jackass infinitely your superior."[100]

The evidence strongly suggests that Randolph developed his multiple-hour speeches as he delivered them.[101] "My manner is spontaneous," he wrote, "flowing, like my matter, from the impulse of the moment; and when I do not feel strongly, I cannot speak to any purpose. These fits are independent of my volition."[102] Randolph's description is supported by the absence of any written speeches in the thousands of pages of his surviving documents.

His inspiration came from an unexpected source. "The greatest orator I ever heard," he told Josiah Quincy, "was a woman. She was a slave. She was a mother and her rostrum was the auction block."[103] Randolph stood among the bystanders and heard the mother appeal first for justice, then for mercy. Realizing she was condemned to separation from her children, she indignantly denounced the crowd. "There was eloquence," Randolph recalled. "I have heard no *man* speak like that. It was overpowering."[104]

Henry Adams dubbed the House members of this era a "mass of mediocrities" providing a rare instance in which he and Randolph were in agreement.[105] "Congress was always bad enough," Randolph wrote, "but at present it out-Hollands Holland. . . . [A] more despicable set was never gathered together."[106] He viewed his "low and contemptible" colleagues as so "sapient" that he had "a mind to try my hand upon a new etymology and prove that sapient is derived from *sap*—i.e., sap-skulled."[107] He chafed at being forced to listen "to every possible manifestation of nonsense" and judged the "incapacity of this body" to have "long ceased to be a subject of ridicule."[108]

Yet Randolph was not opposed to the Madison administration for the sake of opposition. "A factious opposition," he wrote, "I should despise as much as a factious support of government."[109] He conceded that Madison's first message to Congress was "more to my taste than Jefferson's productions on the same occasion."[110] "I am not (as you well know)," he wrote, "one of the admirers of the gentleman now at the head of affairs, but if everything goes to the devil, I do not see how he can be blamed for it, in his *Presidential capacity.*"[111] Randolph's speeches and letters during the Madison administration were more than mere criticism. These years saw Randolph speak and write at length on two primary issues: states' rights and individual liberty. "If I were called upon to establish a criterion, an infallible touchstone of the soundness of political principles," he said on the House floor,

> It should be made to consist of nothing so much as a sacred regard for the rights of the States. An enlarged and liberal construction of State rights is, with me, an indispensable requisite . . . If we begin with declaring one law of one State unconstitutional, where are we to stop? We might, we would go on (it is the natural tendency of power never to be satiated as long as there is anything left to devour) until the State Governments, stripped of all authority . . . will be forever abolished, and a great consolidated empire established upon their ruins. I look forward to such an event as the death warrant of the existing Constitution and of the people's liberties. . . . [W]hen [the States] do fall, there is an end of all republican government in the country.[112]

"Asking one of the States to surrender party of her sovereignty," he said, "is like asking a lady to surrender part of her chastity."[113]

The *Annals of Congress*, controlled by the majority, began to heavily edit Randolph's speeches, frequently noting only that he spoke "at considerable length" or "into some length" or an "hour and a half."[114] Republicans paid little attention, dismissing Randolph as driven by frustrated ambition, bitter resentment, mental instability, or a combination of the three. His friends worried. "I am really afraid that our friend R. will injure himself with the nation this way," Nathaniel Macon wrote to Joseph Nicholson. "His talents and honesty cannot be lost without a loss equal to them both, and they cannot be ascertained. But, you know him as well as I do."[115] Albert Gallatin offered a dissenting analysis. "No man," he wrote of Randolph, "is more free of extraneous influences of any kind than he is."[116]

The years of the Madison presidency saw Randolph lay down markers of principle. On individual freedom: "The personal liberty of the citizen is, in principle, as much violated by compelling him to go one hundred miles as five thousand."[117] On constitutional rights: "An armed people must necessarily be a free people. All the parchment in their archives are of less force than a single musket in maintaining the liberties of the citizen."[118] On innovation promoted in the guise of change: "Great changes to be beneficial must be gradual, not forced upon the people. Nature might be coaxed, but she would not be coerced with impunity."[119] In the shadowy, humid House chamber, Randolph anticipated the words a poet would one day write of him: "Bard, Sage, and Tribune! In himself / All moods of mind contrasting."[120]

10

Of Roanoke

Still through each change of fortune strange
Racked erve, and brain all burning,
His loving faith in Mother-land
Knew never shade of turning.

Congress repealed the Embargo Act three days prior to Madison's inauguration. Jefferson's "least bad" policy had nearly destroyed the nation's economy. Exports from New England had dropped by 75 percent, those from
the south by 85 percent. Shipbuilding had declined by two-thirds, and farm
prices plummeted by half.[1] Thirty thousand unemployed sailors wandered
the streets of port cities, drinking, carousing, and cursing Thomas Jefferson. The embargo had not threatened Madison's victory, but it was obvious
that its continuation was not in the best interest of the new administration.

Randolph supported the repeal of "the most fatal measure that ever happened to this country."[2] He grimly noted that the repeal was "defended and
eulogized on positions admitted on all hands to be indisputably true, but
which it was criminal in me to advance three years ago."[3] He hoped the
Congress would not replace it with another measure. "[Let] us, for God's
sake," he pleaded, "sing a requiem to the ashes of the embargo; let not our
successors have to take up the doleful ditty where we left off."[4] He proposed
that merchants should "arm in defense of their lawful trade, against French
decrees, British Orders of Council, and anything else of a similar stamp."[5] If
the armed merchant ship was attacked on the open sea, "you then throw the
onus" on the belligerent nation.

It was not to be that simple. Congress replaced the Embargo Act with
the Non-Intercourse Act, reopening trade with all nations except England
and France. In the event one of those two nations revoked its offending policy, the president was given authority to restore trade with that nation. This
amalgamation of trade and restraint, of carrot and stick, Randolph wrote,

was a "most lame and impotent conclusion."[6] Ill and disgusted, he departed for Bizarre.

Randolph's chronically bad health was at a new low. He was "racked with pain and never for two hours together free from some affection" of his "stomach and bowels."[7] He suffered from "rheumatism and erratic gout" and "a most distressing and obstinate complaint—chronic diarrhea."[8] He was "laid up with sciatic, lumbago, and a defluxion on my head . . . [and] extreme pain [in] my breast."[9] He treated himself with a variety of concoctions, including liberal doses of opium, but worried that there "is nothing left for the medicine to operate upon."[10] Randolph sought relief by hunting partridges, woodcocks, and ploven, but this normally relaxing venture came within a spark of being fatal. Reloading his gun, Randolph poured gunpowder on a still burning charge. The resulting explosion burned his hand, but fortunately did no more. "What so many patriotic personages have, for years, been labouring to accomplish is at last effected, although not precisely in the way they have aimed at," Randolph dryly noted. "I have been blown up."[11]

Though Randolph injected some callous humor into his recounting of this accident, his spirits were as low as his health.[12] "I am alone and out of the world—buried alive," he wrote to James Garnett.[13] He spent night after sleepless night in pain or drug-induced stupor. Many more such nights of agony, he wrote, would "deprive me of my senses."[14] His eccentricities took on a darker hue. "Life is, indeed, for the most part, to me, a burden," he confessed.[15]

His burden was acerbated by the "vexations and vulgar details to which a Southern planter must, in some degree, attend, or encounter certain ruin."[16] In successive seasons, Roanoke endured a drought "so severe . . . [that] the corn was scarcely visible," followed by waves of heavy rain that destroyed the tobacco crop.[17] Wheat prices dropped so low it was cost-prohibitive to send a wagon of goods to the market.[18] "Thank God," Randolph wrote about his business affairs, "I am indifferent or philosophical enough, if you please, not to fret about it."[19] Plantation issues were as irksome as the weather. "I have been involved in a disagreeable dispute with a rascal of an overseer (an Irishman)," he wrote to Garnett, "who threatened to bludgeon me and then swore the peace against me." Normally not one to shy away from a fight, Randolph soothed over the matter when the overseer "performed every freak of indolence . . . that passion aided by detection in guilt and alcohol could prompt."[20]

Business problems were constant. "For my part I think overseers are just

like Statesmen and other men," Randolph wrote. "They have a language official, and conduct personal; one cants about his employer's interest; the
other, about the good of his country. . . . [B]oth encroach, pillage and fleece
with all their might and main."[21] While sorting through his affairs, Randolph discovered he was owed a small sum of money by an unrelated namesake, John "Possum Jack" Randolph, "a man of great strength and . . . a professed bully." Randolph heard that he had "persuaded a poor girl with about
6,000 dollars . . . to marry him," and decided the time was right to collect the
debt.[22] The two men met at Powell's Tavern, and Possum Jack promised to
pay the debt. When he failed to perform as promised, Randolph swore out a
writ against him.[23] At their next meeting, Possum Jack attacked with a knife.
Randolph pulled out his ever-present whip and left "a mark upon him that
he will not soon lose."[24] Bystanders stepped between the battling Randolphs.
"His attack was most cowardly," Randolph wrote, "and, notwithstanding
his pistols loaded with nails and his knife which cut my clothes a little, and
his skill at gouging!!! he got the worse of the affair. My left eye was hurt by
his long nails. I received no other injury."[25]

It was during this time of fluctuating crop prices and rows with local
ruffians that Randolph affixed "of Roanoke" to his name. He had removed
permanently to the secluded homestead in 1810. The only sign of habitation on the grounds, a visitor noted, was a single cabin, "so completely and
closely environed by trees and underwood of original growth that it seemed
to have been taken by the top and let down into the bosom of a dense vir-
gin forest."[26] Randolph would build a second cabin and several out-build-
ings, but those additions would not lessen the overwhelming feeling of isolation that ever characterized Roanoke. It was not residence alone, however,
that prompted Randolph's modified appellation. The term "of Roanoke," he
wrote, was "the designation of John Randolph my father to distinguish him
from J. R. of Williamsburg (Edmund's father), by it he 'did plead and was
pleaded' as lawyers say." In addition to paying tribute to his father, Randolph
found it necessary to distinguish himself from other men of same name
whose signatures were being passed off as his own.[27] Perhaps one reason was
left unstated. Randolph was established on his own property—land he had
kept in obedience to his mother's long-ago admonition—and he alone could
utilize the sobriquet. It was another way to distinguish an already unique
man.

"As to politics," Randolph wrote in August 1809, "I have nothing to say.
Like the sailor who was blown up at a theatre, I am wondering what trick

they'll play next. If some great change be not wrought very soon, I shall be blown up in good earnest."[28] Randolph's analogy seemed apt as Madison's policies toward Great Britain veered from tragic to comic. The president reached an agreement with British Ambassador David Erskine whereby the British government would suspend its Orders-in-Council by June 10, 1809, if Madison suspended non-intercourse against Britain. Madison did so by proclamation on May 20, not knowing that Erskine had exceeded his authority. The British government promptly repudiated the agreement. In response, Madison reinstated non-intercourse with Britain on August 9, further befuddling an already confusing situation. Erskine was recalled and replaced by Sir Francis Jackson. Upon reaching the United States in October, Jackson entered into discussions with Secretary of State Robert Smith, a man whose only qualification for the nation's highest diplomatic post, Randolph wrote, was that he "can spell."[29] The talks produced nothing but discontent. Jackson would not revive the Erskine matter and had no authority to negotiate repeal of the Orders-in-Council. As these issues were the crux of Anglo-American disagreement, there was nothing left to discuss. In November, Madison cut off communication with Jackson and requested his recall. "At present," Randolph wrote, "there appears an utter destitution of wisdom, vigor, or dignity in her councils."[30]

Randolph was not in Washington when Congress convened on November 27. He was laid low with chronic diarrhea, which was his "daily and nightly companion."[31] During his absence, Senator William Giles introduced a resolution denouncing British Minister Jackson and calling upon the nation "to repel such insults and to assert and maintain the rights, the honor, and the interests of the United States."[32] Though more than two-hundred miles distant, Randolph entered the debate by publishing a series of newspaper essays under the pseudonym "Mucius."[33] He extended a surprising compliment to Madison, writing that he found much in administration policy that merited his approbation. He urged Madison to separate himself from the "bankrupt policies" of Thomas Jefferson, and beware of the counsel of Secretary of State Smith. The nation, he asserted, was in no financial condition to wage war against European powers. War would destroy the nation's economy, derange the government, and jeopardize "the whole frame of the constitution."[34] The Mucius letters signaled that Randolph would be a vocal anti-war leader.

While opposing positions solidified, Nathaniel Macon proposed a bill excluding all British and French vessels from American ports, and confining imports from those countries to American ships coming directly from the point of origin. About that time, Randolph arrived in Washington with all the delicacy of a battering ram. He was unable to discern, he said, "anything like design, anything like concert" in administration policy. He pointed out that the "system of smuggling, of illegal trade, the most ruinous to the fair trader, the most injurious to the agricultural interest and destructive to the revenue" that he had predicted was in full force. "I would wish to ask this House," he concluded, "after all that has been said or that can be said on the subject, whether we must not—we may make as many wry faces as we please—go back to that ground (if it be possible to regain it) which we have so childishly and wantonly abandoned?"[35]

Randolph hurled two thunderbolt proposals. First, that the military and naval establishments—"the great drain and sinks of the public Treasury"—be reduced; and, second, that all commercial restrictions—"a toy, a rattle, a bare plaything, to amuse the great children of our political world"—be repealed.[36] War, Randolph scoffed, was not a real threat. "We have, thank God, in the Atlantic," he said, "a fosse wide and deep enough to keep off any immediate danger to our territory. The belligerents of Europe know, as well as we feel, that war is out of the question."[37] Randolph's proposals offered a clear alternative to war and non-intercourse, and effectively killed Macon's bill. Republicans regrouped and introduced new legislation.[38] "Macon's Bill No. 2" restored trade with the warring powers and gave them until March 3, 1811, to revoke their edicts. In the event that one of the powers took positive action, the president would revive the Non-Intercourse Act against the other nation. The on-again, off-again trade policy was on again, at least for one year.

Randolph had been in Washington for only a few weeks, but had displayed, Henry Adams wrote, "more of the qualities, training, and insight of a statesman than were to be found elsewhere among the representatives in the 11th Congress."[39] Joseph Nicholson seized upon Randolph's mildly complimentary words about Madison in *Mucius* as proof that "the two planets, so long in opposition, are once again in conjunction."[40] Others viewed Randolph's obstructionism differently, and long-nursed resentments threatened to explode. During a floor debate that floundered for hours, Randolph, citing his "own unfitness from fatigue," asked the House, "as a favor," to adjourn. The motion carried.[41] As members made their way off the floor, Willis Alston looked in Randolph's direction and growled that "the puppy still [has] respect shown him."[42] Unsure if he was heard, Alston pushed in front of Randolph on the staircase and repeated his comment.[43] A shrill voice pierced through the stairwell: "Alston, if it were worth while, I would cane you. And I believe I will cane you."

Randolph brought down his cane on Alston's head, knocking off his hat and drawing blood. Alston turned and attempted to fight back, but he was on lower steps and could not reach Randolph. Some of the "ruffians who were with him," Randolph wrote, "wrested the cane from behind and put it into his hands." Randolph stared down at Alston and waited for a blow. Alston "dared not use [the cane]" and turned away.[44] Alston sported a bandaged head the next day, and there was no more talk of puppies.[45] Randolph's triumphant diary entry read: "To Washington. Cane Alston."[46]

Having brandished his cane against one adversary, Randolph found himself preparing to draw his dueling pistol against another. He was speaking in his usual discursive manner when Congressman John Wayles Eppes, a son-in-law of Thomas Jefferson, accused Randolph of rambling on merely to delay action on the bill. Randolph responded with force. Later that evening, Congressman Richard M. Johnson delivered a duel challenge from Eppes to Randolph.[47] The next day, Eppes was practicing so demonstratively that "some gentlemen of Congress heard the retort of the pistols at the lodgings on the Jersey avenue near the Capitol."[48] The situation took on comic proportions when General James Wilkinson—Randolph's sworn enemy since the Burr trial—undertook to instruct Eppes in target practice.[49] Wilkinson allegedly boasted that "if they fight, Eppes will kill him."[50] Congressman William Crawford, Randolph's second, began to worry that this duel might actually do more than just satisfy honor. He discussed his concerns with Randolph, whose only comment was that he wanted the meeting "the sooner the better."[51] This heightened Crawford's concern, so he and Richard Johnson crafted mutual explanations that allowed Eppes to withdrew his challenge. "So ends this ridiculous farce," Randolph wrote.[52]

Randolph may have called his latest brush with the code duello a farce, but he was ever ready for the field of honor if the situation required. "For my part," he wrote, "I always thought of dueling that it [is] to be tolerated as a necessary evil (by no means encouraged) and my opinion on that head remains unchanged." Though he pitied the man "who kills his adversary [more] than the party who is killed," he was convinced "all that is worth living for requires that the risk should sometimes be encountered." Perhaps reflecting on the fact that his many duels rarely reached the firing stage, he conceded that in "nine cases out of ten, both parties are decidedly wrong—foolhardy, perhaps; or cowards, at heart, trying to get a name as fighting men." Still, the culture he sought to maintain required the right to defend honor. "But there are cases," he concluded, "where gentlemen must fight . . . and if men must fight . . . there is not, *as in our politics*, a *third* alternative. . . . Abolish dueling and you encourage bullies as well in number as in degree."[53]

Having failed to remove Randolph through one method, John Eppes tried another. He moved into Randolph's district and announced he would challenge him for Congress. Randolph saw the hand of Jefferson in the move. "An emissary from the 'old man of the mountain' has been slyly moving around the country," he wrote. "All the initiated have been busily at work, like moles, under ground and this has been and is their plan of operation, to assail me by every species of calumny and whisper, but, Parthian-like, never to shew their faces, or give battle on fixed ground, moving about from individual to individual, and securing them man by man."[54] He worried about the "virulence of the newspapers" and the "diabolical spirit" exerted against him, but assessed Eppes's chances of victory as "entirely hopeless."[55] His confidence appeared merited when he crushed Eppes in Charlotte County by a vote of 462 to 77.[56] One week later, Eppes edged Randolph in Buckingham 199 to 198. Randolph dismissed the loss due to "a great many bad votes," and subsequently carried Prince Edward by a vote of 250 to 98, and Cumberland, 171 to 140.[57] The ballot had proved no more adept than the bullet in removing Randolph from Congress.

Randolph attributed his "non-attendance in Congress during the last two sessions" and the "exertions . . . made to poison the public mind against me" as accounting for Eppes's showing.[58] "Proteus himself could not assume so many shapes as the Falsehoods which have assailed me from every quarter," he wrote. "A long address of an hour was insufficient for their bare enumeration and denial."[59] His race was indicative, he thought, of the general state of politics. "Every thing now-a-days seems to be connected by the rule of inversion," he wrote, "nothing simple, nothing open, fair or candid; all mystery, plot and indirection. . . . I am tired of politics and sick of politicians."[60]

Absent in Randolph's explanation about the vote against him was an acknowledgement of the growing sentiment favoring war against Great Britain. War fever manifested in the election to Congress of Felix Grundy in Tennessee; William Lowndes, Langdon Cheves, and John C. Calhoun in South Carolina; and Henry Clay in Kentucky. Fully two-thirds of the New

York and Tennessee congressional delegations were new members, as were half of the representatives from Vermont, New Jersey, North Carolina, South Carolina, Georgia, and Kentucky. Forty-five percent of the Twelfth Congress would be freshmen.[61] These Republicans—"war hawks" Randolph would call them—were tired of foreign insults and ineffective responses. They meant to end the commercial standoff with Britain or fight.[62] Randolph had no illusions about the two principal War Hawks: Clay and Calhoun. "They have entered this House with their eye on the Presidency," he said, "and, mark my word, Sir, we shall have war before the end of the session."[63]

Events played into the hands of the War Hawks. Napoleon seized the opportunity provided by Macon's Bill No. 2 to announce that France would honor American shipping rights. This forced Madison to impose non-intercourse with Britain. Napoleon then sequestered American ships in French ports and declared all ports in the French alliance closed to American trade. Madison had been tricked by Napoleon into an anti-British posture, but the War Hawks used the opportunity to fan war sentiment.[64] The young nationalists, sensing that events were turning in their favor, gathered on the eve of the Twelfth Congress to discuss strategy. They would not wait on Madison; they would pass a declaration of war. But they did not view the resolute British, the scheming French, or the vacillating president as their greatest obstacle.

How, one member asked, would they "bridle John Randolph?" The solution presented itself as quickly as the question was posited: by electing a Speaker. But they realized, one nineteenth-century commentator noted, that the new speaker "must be a man who can meet John Randolph on the floor or on the field, for he may have to do both."[65] More discussion ensued until a consensus emerged on one man: Henry Clay.

Henry Clay—"Harry of the West"—was a native Virginian with a winning personality who had migrated to Kentucky to practice law. Possessed of a sharp wit and tongue, he found success in the courts and at the gaming tables. He married well, served in the state legislature, and was sent to the United States Senate at the constitutionally problematic age of twenty-nine. In 1811, he sought election to the House of Representatives for the express purpose of implementing nationalistic policies. His colleagues knew he possessed the gifted mind, the experience, and the tactical skills necessary for legislative success. They knew as well that he had fought a duel in which he allowed his opponent to fire three times at him. This was the man who could carry the Republican program. Moreover, this was the man who could control John Randolph. On the first day of the Twelfth Congress, Clay was elected Speaker of the House.[66]

"A collision," Congressman Jonathan Roberts said, "between [Mr. Clay] and Mr. Randolph was inevitable."[67] Members did not have a long wait. Randolph came into the House, dressed in riding attire, with a favorite dog at his heels. Clay cast a glance and ordered the doorkeeper to remove the animal.[68] In the past, Randolph might have brandished his whip at the doorkeeper and ended the matter. In this instance, he objected by raising a point of order. Clay ruled against him. Randolph appealed in vain to his colleagues, who were delighted to uphold their new Speaker. The dog was removed.

The pace to war quickened. On November 29, 1811, Peter Porter presented the report of the Foreign Relations Committee, stating that the "wrongs" of Great Britain, "so daring in character, and so disgraceful in their execution," required the United States to "tamely and quietly submit, or . . . resist by those means which God has placed within our reach."[69] The report offered a series of resolutions calling for filling the ranks of the military establishment, raising an additional force of 10,000 regular troops and 50,000 volunteers, fitting out and commissioning all navy vessels, and arming American merchant ships.[70] The resolutions were, for all purposes, a declaration of war. The first resolution, filling already authorized ranks, passed by a vote of 117 to 11—Randolph voting against it. On December 9, 1811, Felix Grundy brought forward the second resolution, the authorization to raise an additional 10,000 men. Grundy said he had "no desire to prolong debate," so merely "invited those who were opposed . . . to come forward and state their objections."[71] Randolph accepted the invitation, but not before asking Grundy to explain "for what purpose these additional troops were wanted." Grundy feigned surprise that Randolph would make "any inquiries into the motives or objects of that committee of which he himself was a member" but would articulate the reasons that influenced the committee's recommendations. Randolph put his white-topped boots up on his desk and listened.

"The true question in controversy," Grundy began, "is the right of exporting the productions of our own soil and industry to foreign markets." To this cause, Grundy added the impressment of American sailors, the agitation by Britain of "the savage tribes," and pledges to France arising from the Non-Intercourse Act.[72] "This war, if carried on successfully," he continued, "will have its advantages. We shall drive the British from our Continent . . .

[and] I am willing to receive the Canadians as adopted brethren."[73] Grundy grew more confident by the sentence, perhaps believing he was leaving Randolph with no grounds on which to mount a challenge. But Grundy was new to the House.[74]

When Randolph stood to oppose the rush to war, he knew he could not stay the hand of the War Hawks. "*Unconnected, unconsulted,* and *betrayed,*" he wrote, "I still wage a feeble war against that horde of upstart patriots who are ruining our common country."[75] He knew that the combination of growing nationalism, war fever, and ambition for empire would overwhelm his call for peace. "We are here blind and deaf—but not dumb," he wrote to John Taylor of Caroline. "We talk—Gods! How we do talk! Of Wars and conquest and aggrandizement, and hope as much after the St. Lawrence and the Canadas, as ever . . . the Israelites after the flesh pots of Egypt."[76] He knew that his best political and rhetorical efforts were destined to defeat. "We shall stand," he wrote to James Garnett, "(or rather *fall*) together."[77] He realized that he would be in as small a minority as ever he had been. "[It] requires an unceasing recurrence to the principles and motives, by which I am actuated," he wrote, "to sustain me in the unequal conflict."[78] He knew his position carried a personal price. His long friendship with Joseph Nicholson would fall victim to their differing views on the war.[79] He felt the effects of his sinking health and "a tide of black misanthropy and despair."[80] Yet no consideration would deter him from hurling defiance at the War Hawks and offering his countrymen another option. Such a stand would provide scoffers with more material to judge him nothing more than an irrelevant irritant. But stand he would.

The question, he began his speech of December 10, 1811, was one of peace or war. "A war not of defense, but of conquest, of aggrandizement, of ambition; a war foreign to the interests of this country, to the interests of humanity itself."[81] He professed to not understand how Republicans could advocate such a war. Republicans had long suspected standing armies, even "when the command of the army . . . was reposed in the bosom of the Father of his country." This principle had caused Republicans to be "denounced as the partisans of France" in years past, and now "held up as the advocates of England."[82] But this "firm and undeviating" principle found its basis in a healthy suspicion of the concentration of power. "There is a fatality," he warned, "attending plentitude of power."[83]

Who were these men, he asked, who sought to speak for Republicans? "If we must have an exposition of the doctrines of Republicanism," Randolph smirked at Grundy, "I should receive it from the fathers of the church, and not from the junior apprentices of the law."[84] He pointed at the War Hawks and sneered: "Gallant crusaders in the holy cause of Republicanism! Such Republicanism does indeed mean anything or nothing."[85]

The fear of British agitation of the Indians "was well calculated to excite the feelings of the Western people . . . but it was destitute of any foundation."[86] Indeed, he said, one need look no further than the Congress to find the source of the nation's troubles with the Indians. "Advantage has been taken of the spirit of the Indians," he argued. "Under the ascendency then acquired over them, they had been pent up by subsequent treaties into nooks, straightened in their quarters by a blind cupidity, seeking to extinguish their title to immense wilderness for which (possessing as we do already, more land than we can sell or use) we shall not have occasion for half a century to come. It is our own thirst for territory, our own want of moderation, that has driven these sons of nature to desperation, of which we felt the effects."[87]

Randolph smiled "at the liberality" of Grundy "in giving Canada to New York." Why, he scoffed, he could see the Capitol "in motion towards the falls of Ohio" in some newfangled northern-dominated nation. "Go! March to Canada," he shouted. "You have taken Quebec—have you conquered England?"[88] This was Randolph's strongest ground, and he savored mocking the War Hawks' infatuation with the Great White North. "Really, I cannot conceive of a weaker reason offered in support of a present measure." Then the jest departed his voice. "This war of conquest, a war for the acquisition of territory and subjects," he said, "is to be a new commentary on the doctrine that Republics are destitute of ambition—that they are addicted to peace, wedded to the happiness and safety of the great body of their people. . . . It is a dangerous experiment."[89]

His dark eyes were blazing, his forefinger sweeping to and fro, his boot-encased foot stomping with each point. Calhoun seethed as Randolph systematically punched holes through the War Hawks' argument.[90] "What a silence reigned throughout the House!" an observer noted. "Every one appeared to wait in anxious, almost breathless, expectation, as if to catch the first sound of his voice. . . . You forgot for a moment in listening that he is an enemy to our revered and excellent President."[91]

The government, Randolph pronounced, "was not calculated to wage offensive foreign war—it was instituted for the common defense and the general welfare."[92] He issued a chilling warning to the South. "During the war of the Revolution," he said, "no fear was ever entertained of an insurrection of the slaves." But "doctrines . . . disseminated by peddlers from New England" had wrought a "silent but powerful change . . . upon its composition and temper." Such a change encouraged insurrections and left the South vulnerable to attacks from within. "While talking of taking Canada, some of us are shuddering for our own safety at home," he cautioned. "The night bell never tolled for fire in Richmond that the mother did not hug her infant more closely to her bosom."[93] This was one of the first instances where Randolph specifically linked slaveholding interests to republican principles. In so doing, Adam Tate writes, Randolph "associated his major political enemies, the political centralizers who pushed for war, with abolitionists, New England manufacturers, and wild-eyed French Revolutionists."[94] While this was the practical effect of Randolph's words, it is doubtful he intended such a broad impact. He was merely using every possible argument to garner support for his anti-war position.

Randolph pointed out the cultural and historic ties with the British and condemned any alliance with Napoleon, "who has effaced the title Attila to the 'Scourge of God!'"[95] He warned the House to "count the cost of the enterprise" for "Virginia planters would not be taxed to support a war."[96] As he had done during the debate over the Yazoo claims, the trial of Justice Chase, and the imbroglio over the secret purchase of Florida, Randolph called "upon those professing to be Republicans to make good the promises held out by their Republican predecessors when they came to power—promises which for years afterwards they had honestly, faithfully fulfilled." Do not, he pleaded, take the last step to becoming "infatuated with standing armies, loans, taxes, navies, and war."[97] "What Republicanism," Randolph concluded, "is this?"

Randolph had not quelled the war tocsin, but he had muffled its sure clarion call.[98] Even though they had the votes to pass the resolutions, the War Hawks realized they could not let Randolph's assertions go unchallenged. Someone had to respond. That task was given to Congressman Calhoun. It would be his maiden speech in the House. Calhoun was not yet the cast-iron man captured in Brady's daguerreotypes. He was a thirty-year-old ardent nationalist, lean and tall, with piercing dark eyes. He was restrained, logical, thorough, and cold—seemingly the perfect contrast to Randolph.

Calhoun granted that Randolph correctly judged the committee report to "mean nothing but war or empty menace."[99] He conceded that war "ought never to be resorted to [unless] it is clearly justifiable and necessary," but cited the "character of the injuries received; the failure of . . . peaceful means . . . impressments of our seamen [and] depredation on every branch of our commerce" as ample support for war.[100] Beyond these reasons were the higher causes of "the sense of independence and honor."[101] Such sentiments, Calhoun said, turning to Randolph, were "so imposing as to enforce silence even on the gentleman from Virginia." Whose fault, he continued, was it if the nation was not prepared for war? "Who has been a member for many years past," he scoffed, "and has seen the defenseless state of his country even near home, under his own eyes, without a single endeavor to remedy so serious an evil?" Did Randolph seriously maintain that Americans would not pay taxes to support the war? "If taxes should become necessary," Calhoun indignantly said, "I do not hesitate to say the people will pay cheerfully. It is for their Government and their cause, and would be their interest and duty to pay."[102] The slave-holding Calhoun soothed fears of slave insurrections. "Had we anything to fear from that quarter, which I sincerely disbelieve," he said, "the precise time of the greatest safety is during a war, in which we have no fear of invasion—then the country is most on its guard."[103]

One by one, Calhoun countered the products of Randolph's "fruitful . . . imagination." If the gentleman "really wishes to promote the cause of humanity," he continued, "let his eloquence be addressed to [British Foreign Secretary] Lord Wellesley or [Prime Minister] Mr. Percival and not the American Congress." And he could tell them—just as Calhoun was telling him—"if they persist in such daring insult and injury to a neutral nation . . . it will be bound in honor and interest to resist . . . that the calamity of war will ensure; and that they, in the opinion of wounded humanity, will be answerable for all its devastation and misery."[104] Calhoun yielded the floor.

For a moment there was silence. Then gleeful Republicans erupted in cheers and applause for the young Hercules. Calhoun, the Richmond *Enquirer* reported, was "one of those master spirits, who stamp their name upon the age in which they live."[105] He had "dared touch the untouchable."[106] House Republicans acted as if some demon had been exorcised from their midst, "expressing the almost universal satisfaction of the party that Randolph had at last met his match."[107] Other members, emboldened by Calhoun's example, took to the floor to make similar, but less impressive, speeches. At length, George Troup of Georgia suggested an end to the debate. After all, he said, it was "the great mass of the House . . . against the solitary gentleman from Virginia."[108]

The solitary gentleman responded the next day. "If a writ were to issue against [the Republican Party]," Randolph commented, "it would be impossible for a constable with a search warrant to find it."[109] Knowing that his words had little chance to persuade, Randolph drew on his vast reserve of tactics to delay the majority. "I never saw sharper symptoms of intensive parliamentary war," he wrote, "than at present."[110] Randolph was an expert at these maneuvers and filled the pages of the *Annals of Congress* with time-consuming motions.[111] He introduced a resolution authorizing the president to employ the army in road construction.[112] He hoped to pull a few members away from the War Hawks in common opposition to increased taxes. "[You] will hear the flap of the ominous wings of the Treasury pouncing upon your table," he warned, "with projects of land tax, excise, hearth tax, window tax. Excise not merely on whiskey—that great necessity of life, but upon leather, candles . . . in all the forms of oppression and extortion, so that the habitation of a man will no longer be his castle."[113] Though he seemed to delight in the fight, he anguished over a vision of "the sacking of our towns, savaging of our coasts, and our sons and brothers dying like rotten sheep."[114] Such the folly of the "hot-headed enthusiasts."

The resolution to enlist an additional 10,000 men passed the House by a vote of 110 to 22. The four remaining resolutions passed by similarly lopsided votes. Randolph voted against each one.

Daily, war grew inevitable. Daily, Randolph kept up the fight. "The avenues to the public ear are closed against Truth," he wrote, "and as to Congress, they are and long have been the tools of prejudice, faction and power. It is a hopeless task to address one's self to them. I would as soon undertake a voyage to Constantinople to convert the Mufti to Christianity. . . . I listen to the wisest of them, and to me their talk is as the talk of children."[115] He argued often with Calhoun, the "Yale-College Orator," who "has not been educated in Connecticut for nothing." The South Carolina representative, Randolph wrote, combined "the savage ferocity of the frontier man" with "all the insensibility of the Yankee character," the "cold unfeeling Yankee manner, with the bitter and acrimonious irritability of the South."[116]

Resolutions were passed and taxes raised, but the nation was not quite ready to start fighting. To buy time, Madison requested a sixty-day embargo on shipping. James Monroe, again allied with Madison and serving as secretary of state, testified before the Foreign Relations Committee that the embargo would provide time for preparation.[117] It would be the final step before a declaration of war. "The die is cast," Randolph wrote, "and the ruin of a nation is the chief price paid for bolstering up the consistency of a few of the most weak and worthless individuals in it."[118]

Still, Randolph would not be silent. "Is this the way which the honorable Speaker with so much gallantry has advocated an honorable war?" he asked during the debate on the embargo.[119] "If you mean war," he taunted the War Hawks, "if the spirit of the country is up to it, why have you been spending five months in idle debate?"[120] This was a bold assertion for Randolph, who must have realized that he was the major reason for the five months of debate. Exasperated, Clay called Randolph to order, and the temporary embargo passed. "As usual," Randolph wrote, "I am crucified."[121]

The war would start in June, unless the opposition could stay the hand of the War Hawks. If they could hold on until the spring elections, changed public sentiment might be reflected in the results. Randolph's exchanges with Calhoun grew more pointed, the frustration of the House more palatable. Clay repeatedly attempted to stem Randolph's tirades, lest one of his comments find its mark and hinder the well-oiled war machine. "The damned rascal," President Madison snapped after reading one of Randolph's speeches.[122] Then in May came news that New York and Massachusetts had elected Federalist legislatures, a clear anti-war vote.[123] "Old [Thomas] Sammons," Randolph wrote of his colleague from New York, "returned from the Mohawk river . . . as decided an advocate for peace as he was a partisan of war at the commencement of the Session."[124] Was this the break Randolph had sought? Had the old Quid frustrated another major policy? Clay realized he must once and for all silence John Randolph.

Randolph began another marathon speech on May 29, 1812. He called it his "last effort to rescue the country."[125] The hours passed. He recited the schedule of American shipping vessels, dissected the difference between a Council of Prizes and a Council of Commerce, and denounced the "tools, the minions, sycophants, [and the] partisans of France" in and out of the administration.[126] This would be a war, he said, "unexampled in the history of mankind." He was about to explain why, when a voice came from across the chamber.

"A point of order," Calhoun called out. The question of war, he stated, was not before the House. Therefore Randolph was speaking contrary to the Rules of the House. Randolph shook his head and countered. He was speaking prefatory to a resolution. Calhoun again rose. If that was the case, he said, then the gentleman from Virginia should submit the resolution in writing. Clay nodded. He ruled that a resolution must be submitted in writing prior to debate.[127]

"I then call upon the gentleman to submit his proposition," Calhoun said.

Randolph protested. Clay told him to sit down.

"My proposition," Randolph bellowed, "is that it is not expedient at this time to resort to a war against Great Britain."[128]

Clay repeated himself. The motion must be in writing.

"I appeal," Randolph shot back.

The House sustained Clay's ruling by a vote of 67 to 42. During the vote, Randolph had scrawled out the resolution and handed it to the Clerk. He took the floor again, prepared to resume his speech. Clay would have none of it. He ruled that the House must decide whether it would hear debate on the resolution at that time. Randolph appealed again. The privilege of the floor, he said gravely, "was the last vestige of the liberty of speech enjoyed at the absolute will of the majority." He realized he was in a fight for his parliamentary life, and he called down fire from Heaven on Henry Clay: "It appears to me we have forgotten the old-fashioned liberty. . . . I once had the honor of being under the Federal regime, in what was called the Reign of Terror. I there enjoyed the liberty of speech. I had a right to protest against the acts of the men in power. . . . Has it come to this. . . . After having been fourteen years on this floor, is a man to be told he knows nothing of the rules of the House?"[129]

Clay interrupted again, directing Randolph to confine his remarks to the decision of the Chair. "The right to regulate its proceedings," Clay sniffed, "was a right inherent in every public deliberative body." He put the question to the membership: shall the House hear Randolph's resolution?

"No," the House thundered, by a vote of 72 to 37.

Randolph sat down.[130]

Events proceeded rapidly. Madison presented his War Message on June 1, 1812. Congress declared war on Great Britain on June 17, 1812. Unbeknownst to all was the fact that Great Britain had repealed its Order of Council on June 16. Thus the primary reason for the war no longer existed.

"Take care of yourself," Randolph wrote to John Taylor on the day war was declared. "Every man who will not work quietly in the political harness is to be written, pointed, or *knocked* down. . . . The temper of 1790s was mildness and moderation compared with that of the present day. The reign of horror has begun."[131]

11

An Irreclaimable Heretic

His harshest words of proud rebuke,
His bitterest taunt and scorning,
Fell fire-like on the Northern brow
That bent to him in fawning.

"I have discharged my duty towards you," Randolph wrote to his constituents, "lamely and inadequately, I know, but to the best of my poor ability."[1] Though Randolph believed four out of five of the citizens in his district opposed the war, patriotic fervor was edging into Southside Virginia, bringing on its wings condemnation of his anti-war stance.[2] Locals in a tavern offered toasts calling for Randolph to receive "a suit of Tory uniform, tar and feathers."[3] The Richmond *Enquirer* censured him as "a nuisance and a curse."[4] The political consequence of such discontent was that John Eppes announced he would again challenge Randolph for Congress. Latching onto the patriotism of the moment, Eppes declared his candidacy on July 4, 1812. Randolph scoffed dismissively. Eppes, he said, had entered the race while "under the influence of our American Bacchus, to whom the vine has not yet been dedicated."[5]

Randolph crisscrossed his district for two months. He rode thirty-four miles in a heavy rain to campaign in Prince Edward County. He debated Eppes on at least four occasions.[6] One rapt viewer recalled how Randolph's presence on the stump emptied "the courthouse, every store, and tavern, and peddler's stall, and auctioneer's stand, private residence."[7] One audience stood in the sun for five hours listening to him.[8] He was only thirty-nine years old, but he was a legend to the freeholders from whose ranks he came and to the younger men who all their lives had known but one representative. After his years of service, he said at Charlotte, he would have preferred to ask his constituents for an honorable discharge. But in "the hour of trial and in the day of danger," his sense of duty would not allow it.[9] He then launched into a defense of his position on the war. "These are no ordinary times," he said to the assembled throng. "The state of the world is unexampled; the war of the present day is not like that of our revolution, or any which preceded it, at least in modern times. It is a war against the liberties and the happiness of mankind; it is a war in which the whole human race are the victims, to gratify the pride and lust of power of a single individual. I beseech you, put it to your own bosoms, how far it becomes you as freemen, as Christians, to give your aid and sanction to this impious and bloody war."[10]

Eppes cast himself as an unabashed supporter of the administration. His supporters accused Randolph of being a foreign pensioner and "abounding in British gold."[11] Randolph fired back, indignantly saying that his relationship with the voters had survived "the press, the intrigue of envious and aspiring men, [and] the whole patronage of the Executive government" and would survive this latest smear.[12] Eppes was an interloper, a racehorse imported to run against him. Randolph repeated this line throughout the district, reminding the voters that an opponent should have come from their own stock. "Where are your Daniels, your Bouldins, and your Carringtons," he asked, naming the most prominent families in the area. In Prince Edward, this roll call was met by a snip from Colonel Gideon Spencer, who believed his family should have been included. "And your Spencers," he yelled from the crowd. "Yes, and your Spencers," Randolph replied, pausing for effect, "always excepting you, Colonel." The crowd roared its approval.[13]

"Prince Edward was never more unanimous," Randolph wrote after the raucous rally, "her blood is up . . . it spread like electricity."[14] Yet the strong undercurrent of support for the war persisted. "There is a great sentiment prevailing," Randolph noted, "that this disapprobation should be suppressed to avoid an ill effect abroad." The only war by which his constituents could judge their conduct was the American Revolution, and during that war, Randolph well remembered, "every man not entering heartily into the cause was justly deemed an enemy and often treated as such."[15] The election was turning into a referendum on patriotism, a far more formidable foe than Eppes.

When Randolph arrived in Washington for the second session of the Twelfth Congress, it seemed as if his predictions about the war were coming true. General William Hull had surrendered Detroit to the British without firing a shot, William Eustis had shown himself to be an inept secretary of war, and President Madison muttered that the nation was "in an embarrassing situation."[16] James Monroe disclosed to Randolph that affairs were so unorganized that he was acting as war secretary as well as secretary of state. "Our great folks," Randolph wrote, "are sadly perplexed."[17] Things were in such disarray that Randolph began to refer to Washington as "Babel," and the Capitol as a temple "of confusion of ideas, as well as of Tongues."[18] Ordinarily, Randolph would have taken advantage of the befuddled condition of his opponents to advance his cause, but he was seriously ill with rheumatism, high fever, and "pains in every limb and joint."[19] His few remarks during this session were more subdued. "[The] people of this country," he said, setting the tone for his speeches, "if ever they lose their liberties, will do it by sacrificing some great principle of free government to temporary passions. There are certain great principles, which if they be not held inviolate at all seasons, our liberty is gone. If we give them up, it is perfectly immaterial what is the character of our Sovereign; whether he be King or President, elective or hereditary—it is perfectly immaterial what is his character—we shall be slaves."[20]

To new members, Randolph might have seemed a caricature of himself; to veteran members, a tiresome Johnny-one-note. He confessed to being an "irreclaimable heretic," and that if he was wrong, he had been wrong for fourteen years. He had seen all manner of Machiavellian acts during his years in the House but still expressed shock over Republican "ostentatious contempt" for principle.[21] When he rose to speak on January 13, 1813, he may have intended to speak over the heads of the membership and directly to the voters back home, or he may have thought this might be his last session. For whatever reason, his speech was part benediction and part prognostication.

He was so ill when he rose that the *Annals of Congress* noted he was "apparently under the effects of a serious indisposition."[22] He said he was sickened at the state of the union and wished he could forget the policy decisions that had brought the nation to its present point. But in remembrance there was hope, so he would try again. "The merest reptile," he said, "the worm itself, will turn when trod upon."[23]

He had seen dark days before. He had witnessed the abuses of the Adams administration and had joined the revolution that elected a Republican majority. The acquisition of power was not the animating force of that revolution. Nor was electoral success, nor lust for patronage. The Republican revolution was a revolution of principle. "Is it necessary for me at this time of day," he asked, "to make a declaration of the principles of the Republican party?" He knew it was necessary, for to do so would exhibit how far the party had strayed. "What are they?" he asked.

> Love of peace, hatred of offensive war; jealousy of the State Governments towards the General Government, and of the influence of the Executive Government over the co-ordinate branches of that Government; a dread of standing armies; a loathing of public debt, taxes, and excises; tenderness for the liberty of the citizens; jealousy, Argus-eyed jealousy, of the patronage of the President.[24]

Cloaking non-republican actions under the Republican banner did not sanction the actions. In such cases, members should follow the arc of principle, not the chord of party dictate. "I care not with whom I vote," he said, stating the obvious, "I will be true to my principles."[25]

Once in power, the Republicans "sailed on for some time in the full tide of successful experiment, unobstructed by squalls or adverse gales."[26] Who could contest the truth of that assertion? Jefferson's first term had been remarkably successful, and remarkably consistent with principle. "At that time, sir," Randolph reminded the House, "all was prosperity and joy." Then came Yazoo—"the first cause of the breach"—followed by increased expenditures, expansion of government, and adventurous foreign policy. Randolph grew noticeably weary as he continued, but he asked the House for its "patience, its pardon, and its pity." Calhoun remained still. Randolph continued, providing chapter and verse where what "was then prophesied is now history."[27] The old spark returned to his voice when he turned to the war and its causes. He had repeatedly argued that Britain's Orders-in-Council "constituted no insurmountable obstacle to negotiation," and now the orders had been repealed.[28] Yet the nation still fought. "At this time," he said, "we should have been at peace; we should have been lying secure in that snug safe haven of neutrality."[29]

Randolph spoke infrequently during the remaining six weeks of the session. He spent most of the time in his lodgings in Georgetown "crippled with sciatic."[30] In early March he returned home, "half dead with fatigue," to resume his campaign.[31] He noted that several friends greeted him cordially, while at the same time expressing the hope that he "would support this miserable war."[32] But there was no possibility of his changing his view. He spoke at Prince Edward Courthouse, then stopped to spend the night at Bizarre. Seated in the parlor with his nephew Tudor, he suddenly realized the roof was afire. He moved quickly to extinguish the flames, but the fire raged out of control. In moments the home and most of its contents were "a heap of smoking rubbish."[33] Randolph's book collection was destroyed, as was "twenty years labor in homespun; carpets, curtains, blankets, glass, china."[34] Bizarre was no more.

Randolph was "unable to make the least exertion of body or mind" in wake of the fire. He made no further campaign efforts. "I have to tell you," Randolph wrote to Josiah Quincy on April 19, "that my election is lost."[35] He carried his home county of Charlotte by a decisive vote of 342 to 176, and defeated Eppes in Prince Edward, 303 to 218. Eppes, however, edged him in Cumberland, 206 to 146, and prevailed in a landslide in Buckingham, 509 to 141.[36]

Randolph attributed his defeat to "seven years unremitting calumny of my motives and character." He declared that Eppes "descended to the lowest and most disgraceful means" by "attending day and night meetings in the cabins and hovels of the lowest of the people."[37] These efforts, he believed, persuaded the voters "that I was the *cause* of the war, that the Government wished for peace . . . but that I thwarted them in everything."[38] Administration allies had lost no opportunity "to wreak their puny vengeance" upon him, and he had to stand against "the patronage and influence of both the government, state and federal, without the aid of a single press."[39] Facing such odds, he marveled that "nearly one thousand freeholders should have persisted in refusing to withdraw their confidence from me."[40] He judged Charlotte and Prince Edward to be "remarkable for their good order, morality, and intelligence." Buckingham, the county that gave Eppes his margin of victory, was notable "for riot and ignorance."[41] In a more generous moment, he placed no blame on the voters. "They have gone by such lights as was accessible to them," he concluded.[42] No where did he concede that the principal—if not sole—reason for his defeat was his opposition to the war.

To his friends he affected relief. "I have cause of self-congratulation," he wrote to Francis Scott Key, "at being disenthralled from a servitude at once irksome and degrading."[43] He was glad to be free of "the dominion of such wretches as (with a few exceptions) composed the majority." He did not regret that he would no longer be "under the abject domination of Mr. H[enry] Clay . . . under the discipline and orders of the Calhouns [and] Grundys."[44] He also took satisfaction in having been defeated while standing on principle. "I prefer that my public life should have terminated as it has done rather than by any act of my own," he wrote to James Garnett, "for the same reason that a violent death by the hand of another is preferable to suicide. No man can now reproach me with the desertion of my post in a time of difficulty and danger."[45] Randolph was a private citizen for the first time in fourteen years.

His bravado aside, Randolph's defeat, combined with the isolation of Roanoke, worked like a depressant on his spirits. "It requires an effort," he wrote, "to take an interest in anything."[46] He complained that his life was "barren of incident" and "removed from society and intelligence."[47] He rode twenty miles to retrieve his mail and give himself something to do. "Some sort of employment," he wrote, "is absolutely necessary to keep me from expiring with ennui."[48]

His health was no better. In the months following his defeat, he complained that his "liver is sclerosis and my whole digestive apparatus gone," his heart suffered "the most violent palpitations," and he was "tortured with rheumatism" and gout. "I hardly know myself," he wrote.[49] Ill health plagued his sister-in-law Judith, while his nephew St. George became "unsettled in his intellects . . . a frantic maniac."[50] Small wonder Randolph viewed life as "a curse from which I would willingly escape if I knew where to fly."[51]

Escape was not an idle thought. On more than one occasion, Randolph considered a change in surroundings.[52] This most Virginian of Virginians wrote of moving to Kentucky or the Mississippi Valley, "where corn can be had for sixpence a bushel, and pork for a penny a pound."[53] He expressed no wonder at the wave of emigration from the old colonies to the new frontier. "Were I to follow the dictates of prudence," he wrote to Key, "I should convert my estate into money and more northwardly."[54] He did find some peace of mind in Richmond at the home of Dr. John Brockenbrough. Randolph spent almost six months there in early 1814 "most hospitably entertained by them and by the inhabitants."[55] Dr. Brockenbrough lived in a stately home that would later serve as the White House of the Confederacy. From that house, Randolph could walk a few blocks to the home of Chief Justice John Marshall. The two men had formed a friendship during their service together in Congress and, somewhat surprisingly given their respective philosophies, it survived for more than thirty years. Randolph considered Marshall to be "the first man in Virginia, if not in the Union," and was drawn to his "amiable deportment" and "extraordinary powers of [his] mind."[56] Marshall derived "unaffected pleasure . . . in the friendship of the 'gallant horse who at a flying leap clears both ditch and fence.'"[57] A shared dislike of Thomas Jefferson might have brought the men closer, but, more likely, each man was drawn to the lively spirit of the other.[58]

Randolph also made a sentimental journey to Cawsons, the place of his birth. He took a boat up the Appomattox River, the "sight of the broad bay formed by the junctions of the two rivers" giving "a new impulse to my being." Disembarking, his spirits sank. "The fires of ancient hospitality were long since extinguished and the hearth stone cold," he lamented. "Here was my mother given in marriage, and here was I born—once the seat of plenty and cheerfulness, associated with my earliest and tenderest recollections, now mute and deserted."[59]

Randolph spent much of 1814 reading the works of British statesman Edmund Burke. "It has been an intellectual banquet of the richest rewards," he wrote after reading one volume. "What a man! How like a child and an idiot I feel in comparison with him."[60] It was natural that Randolph would be drawn to Burke, an eloquent defender of ordered liberty, property rights, and tradition. Additionally, Burke had led an unsuccessful impeachment effort against the governor-general of Bengal, similar to Randolph's pursuit of Justice Chase, and had been rejected by his party over his attitude toward the French Revolution. "What a treasure, what a mine of eloquence, sagacity and political wisdom!" Randolph wrote in April 1814. "The rectitude of his feelings is not less conspicuous than the penetration and foresight of his understanding. He is the Newton of political philosophy."[61]

Randolph found in Burke confirmation of his long-established political philosophy. Burke was not, as it has been posited, Randolph's exemplar. Adam Tate writes that Randolph read "Burke's *Reflections on the Revolution in France* in 1806–07, and the book had a strong influence on him."[62] While Randolph most likely did read *Reflections*, he makes no mention of Burke in his surviving letters from 1806–7, while on three occasions during those years he commends the writings of William Pitt.[63] Randolph's only mention of Burke, prior to his numerous comments in 1814, is a single passing remark to James Garnett in 1811.[64] Despite this paucity of evidence, Randolph's first biographer, Hugh Garland, wrote that "the writings of Edmund Burke are the key to the political opinions of John Randolph."[65] This assertion prompted a vigorous response from Beverley Tucker, Randolph's half-brother. "It can be hardly doubted," Tucker wrote, "that he read his letter on the French Revolution . . . and that he was not insensible to its surpassing eloquence. . . . But we very much doubt if he ever became a convert to the views of Burke, until . . . the last four years of Mr. Jefferson's administration."[66] Tucker's contemporary observation confirms what the record shows: Randolph admired Burke, found confirmation in his writings, and came to view him, certainly after 1814, as a significant influence. The record falls short of confirming the assertion of Adam Tate—and, to a lesser extent, Russell Kirk—that "[reading] Burke and finding God . . . shaped [Randolph's] conservatism in the following years."[67]

Indeed, if there was one contemporary who exercised significant influence over Randolph, it was Judge Spencer Roane of the Virginia Court of Appeals. Roane was born to a prominent Tidewater family, studied law under George Wythe, served in the Virginia General Assembly, and began a thirty-three-year tenure on the bench at the age of twenty-seven. His philosophy, like Randolph's, was based on the Revolutionary War experience, the Antifederalist tradition of the 1780s, and the Virginia and Kentucky Resolutions of 1798.[68] Also like Randolph, Roane displayed a stubborn independent streak, was often irascible, and carried on a long running feud with his judicial colleague St. George Tucker. But the two men were most alike in the practical expressions of their principles—Randolph in the legislature, Roane on the bench. Roane did not hesitate to declare overreaching federal statutes to be unconstitutional, to disregard federal dictates, or to challenge consolidation.[69] "I love the honor and, if you please, the glory of my country," Roane wrote in words similar to those employed by Randolph, "but I love its liberty better."[70] Roane engaged John Marshall in a running battle in the pages of the Richmond *Enquirer* over states' rights, limited government, and judicial review. "At the heart of the Marshall-Roane debate," Thornton Miller wrote in his history of Virginia jurisprudence, "were opposite views of America. Roane still saw a league of sovereign states, while Marshall saw a growing nation."[71]

There was no doubt where John Randolph would come down in such a debate—notwithstanding his friendship with Marshall. "I read Mr. Roane's letter with the attention that it deserves," Randolph wrote. "Everything from his pen on the subject of our laws and institutions excites a profound interest."[72] No letters between the two men survive, but Randolph once told Dr. Brockenbrough to tell Roane "that I fulfilled his injunction, and I trust proved myself a zealous, and consistent, and (I wish I could add) *able* defender of states' rights."[73] Randolph was such an admirer he once exclaimed:

"I want to have Spencer Roane for President."[74] It was consistency of principle that drew Randolph to Roane, in the same manner that it drew him to Burke. And even Roane's influence tended to confirm Randolph's established principles rather than inspire new ones. "In [Roane's] day," Timothy Huebner writes in *The Southern Judicial Tradition*, "public officials viewed their world through the lens of the war for independence, and the eighteenth-century idea of the struggle between liberty and power remained in the forefront of their minds."[75] Thus Roane's view from the bench was shaped by the same influences that shaped Randolph. It is no surprise that Randolph was drawn to Roane and Burke—as he was to others during his life—but it should not be asserted that the views of others were anything greater than thoughts which Randolph put into the caldron of his mind and measured always against the liberty interests of free men.

Randolph's wilderness years were marked also by a flurry of more than 180 letters. "I still keep up an intercourse, you see," he wrote to Key, "with the headquarters of good principles."[76] His thoughts ranged wide over numerous topics. With Dr. Brockenbrough, he discussed the theory that "free will and necessity are much the same"; with Key, that no man "believing in the *Old* Testament, can reject the *New*."[77] To Josiah Quincy, he offered his most succinct view of slavery. "The curse of slavery," he wrote, "an evil daily magnifying, great as it already is, embitters many a moment of the Virginia Landholder, who is not duller than the clod beneath his feet."[78] He expressed the view that the union of the states "was the *means* of securing the safety, liberty, and welfare of the confederacy, and not in itself an *end* to which these should be sacrificed." But, he continued, repeating the words Patrick Henry spoke during their long-ago debate at Charlotte Courthouse, "the question of resistance to any established government is always a question of expediency; and the resort ought never to be had to this last appeal, except in cases where there is reasonable prospect of success, and where the grievance does not admit of palliative or temporizing remedies."[79]

"I have washed my hands of politics," Randolph wrote in one letter, but his remarks invariably turned to that subject. He made no attempt to hide his disdain for James Madison. Once he noted that the vacationing president was "taking the air." He followed that observation with the scathing comment that there was "no danger that *his* wife will die of a miscarriage." On another occasion he pronounced "verily, Mr. M[adison]'s little finger is thicker than the loins of Lord North."[80] His contempt for Madison was exceeded by only that which he reserved for back-sliding Republicans.

"Merciful God," he exclaimed in one letter, "I endeavor to forget all that I ever knew of public affairs. Nothing that *man* can do can ever restore the country and the constitution to what they were previous to the first Embargo."[81]

Randolph's pessimism prompted concerns about the nation's direction. "I have lived to feel that there are many things worse than poverty or death, those bugbears that terrify the great children of the world, and sometimes drive them to eternal ruin."[82] He deplored the "artifice and temporary excitement," the "base and puny acts," and the "tricks and Quackery" that propelled the nation into war.[83] He worried that his countrymen were taking less responsibility for their own freedom. "How," he asked, "can you appoint a guardian to a people bent on self-destruction?"[84] But most often he expressed a wary disapproval of the new order that seemed to be sweeping away transcendent values. "The Constitution is changed," he wrote to Josiah Quincy. "It can never get back to what it was. Old age can as soon resume the freshness and agility of youth."[85] Randolph turned over these issues in his mind and expounded on them to his friends. After filling several pages per letter, he would often huff that he wished he had not entered upon the subject. At least until the next letter.

It was during this time of letters that Randolph made his first disparaging comments about St. George Tucker. He had not spoken to his stepfather in some time. Apparently Tucker made an inquiry through a third party regarding the estrangement. Randolph wrote that he would disclose his reasons if Tucker so desired, but he believed ending all contact was the wisest course. "Cold and heartless men may learn to simulate regard or disguise resentment," he wrote. "I can do neither."[86] Three days later he reversed himself and disclosed to Tucker the reasons for the "alienation in my sentiments." At Francis Tucker's death, he wrote, "she left funds in hand and clear accounts. When I took possession of my estate . . . I had not a shilling." What followed, Randolph said, was an avalanche of claims from overseers, blacksmiths, and sheriffs "without a cent to discharge them." He complained that Tucker had failed to sufficiently provide for him while at college. Finally, Randolph levied the most serious charge. He accused Tucker of mismanagement of his father's estate. He recounted a scene in which Tucker demanded that he sign "certain papers which you drew upon your first visit to Bizarre after my brother's death, but you well know that no account or voucher of the receipt and expenditures of my father's estate was at any time ever exhibited to me."[87]

"Nothing," Tucker tersely responded, "could have been more unexpected by me than the contents of your letter just received." He denied Randolph's allegations. In terms he must have employed many times during his legal career, Tucker stated that for those matters "as are founded upon supposed injuries to yourself, you know where and how to seek redress." To the rest of the letter, he concluded, "no reply is necessary."[88] Two years later, the men would find themselves at an event near Richmond. Randolph ignored Tucker. "Oh, Jack!" the old man exclaimed, "I never thought that one of my children would refuse my hand."[89]

The war continued at its uneven pace. American forces failed to make progress in Canada, and Buffalo fell to the British, but Commodore Oliver Perry triumphed in the Battle of Lake Erie, and General William Henry Harrison won the Battle of Thames. This marginal record was enough, Randolph believed, to "add another year to the life of the war."[90] Visiting his half-brother Beverley Tucker, he saw first-hand the accuracy of this prediction. Orders arrived for Tucker's volunteer company to march east and join other units in preparation for a feared British invasion. Tucker's wife screamed in terror as her husband read his orders. "I never witnessed such agony," Randolph wrote of the scene. The "shrieks of his wife" haunted him as he returned to Roanoke. "Would to God," he wrote, "that James Madison could have heard this tribute of his subjects to the wisdom and mercy of his reign."[91]

Randolph's opposition to the war did not prevent him from joining the effort. When the British landed in Maryland and marched on Washington, Randolph sought and received a military commission from the governor of Virginia.[92] He was ordered to scout the lower country of Virginia between the York and James rivers.[93] Randolph spent four days reconnoitering the area, found nothing, and reported to Camp Holly, outside Richmond. "Drunkenness," he wrote in disgust, "prevails to the most shocking degree in the camps."[94] He wondered if it was possible to drive out "the vendors of spirituous liquors" or, alternatively, "bring them to trial and shoot them." With no orders to do anything else, Randolph spent his time "visiting the tombs of my forefathers." By the end of September, he was released from military duty.[95]

As the war continued and the negative economic impact was felt in Virginia, more and more of Randolph's former constituents encouraged him to stand again for office.[96] His friends began to lobby in earnest, but found him resolute against the idea. "On this point, I am fixed," he wrote. "My course has been a short one—but it has been long enough to surfeit me of the whole race of *politicians,* of whom it is my firm belief, that from the time of Ulysses to the present day, there have not been as many righteous, as would have reprieved the sentence of Sodom."[97] He kept up his protests, but refrained from issuing an outright refusal. By fall the efforts of his friends had given an air of certainty to his election.[98] "It is now confidently said," Daniel Webster wrote to a friend, "that [Randolph] will be in the next Congress."[99]

Randolph, however, was not campaigning. He was not even in Virginia. He was on his way to New York where his nephew Tudor, a student at Harvard, was suffering from tuberculosis. Randolph's destination was Morrisania, the home of Gouverneur Morris, signer of the Constitution of the United States, former minister to France, and one of the wealthiest men in the nation. Tudor Randolph had been taken in at Morrisania because his aunt lived there. His aunt was Nancy Randolph, the subject of the long-distant murder and incest trial, alleged paramour of Richard and Theodorick Randolph, who, by incredible chance and circumstance, was now Mrs. Gouverneur Morris.[100] Randolph was headed for a reunion with the woman he had turned out of Bizarre, penniless.

The path that Nancy Randolph took from Bizarre to Morrisania, from abject poverty to abundant supply, had been as circuitous as it had been unforeseeable. Thirty-one years old when Randolph asked her to leave Bizarre, Nancy lived off the good will of friends from Richmond to Rhode Island to Connecticut. No evidence survives to determine how Nancy provided for herself during these wandering years, though Randolph presumed the worst. Reaching New York in 1808, Nancy played a hunch and contacted Morris, whom she had met once in Virginia. Morris visited her in her dilapidated boarding house and hired her to keep his house. Nancy moved into Morrisania in April 1809. Before the year was out, she and Morris married. In February 1813, she gave birth to a son, Gouverneur Morris II. It was as complete a reversal of fortune as any fairytale could guarantee.[101]

Randolph took the familiar trip north, stopping one evening at Port Conway. He was roused at three in the morning to catch the departing stage. Moving about in the dark, he mistook a staircase for a hallway and fell down the stairs. He was "taken up senseless" at the bottom with an injured shoulder, elbow, and ankle.[102] The accident, he wrote, "nearly put an end to my unprosperous life," but he continued the trip.[103] From his coach, he saw the charred remains of Washington D.C. "The walls of the Capitol and Palace are rapidly decomposing," he wrote, "the massy columns of the Hall of the

Representatives . . . not larger than the ordinary poles of which we build to-bacco houses."[104] Passing through Baltimore, he reflected on the situation in which he and Judith found themselves. Anyone comparing their lives to his own would surely "thank God for his manifold mercies."[105] Randolph arrived at Morrisania on Saturday, October 22. Nancy Randolph Morris greeted him at the door. The two embraced.

Randolph found Tudor improving and believed he would recover, "if we can get him to Virginia in his present plight."[106] Randolph had an uneventful dinner at Morrisania, but the reunion with Nancy had sparked memories of Glenlyvar, the scandal, and Richard's death. Taking leave of his hostess, Randolph pulled Nancy close and whispered in her ear: "Remember the past."[107]

Randolph boarded a coach for the trip from Morrisania, in Westchester overlooking the Harlem River, to an inn on Greenwich Street in Manhattan. His mind remained fixated on thoughts of the woman he had just left. Suddenly, he felt himself being tossed about; pain ripped through his knee, his thigh, the back of his neck. His coach had hit a pile of rocks in the street and toppled over. The next day, he had recovered enough of his senses to scrawl a note cataloging his injuries. "I am," he concluded, "a cripple for life."[108] The trip to New York was turning surreal.

Two days later, Randolph received a visit from David Ogden, a nephew of Gouverneur Morris. As the conversation progressed, Randolph found it "not difficult to discern" what Ogden thought of the character of his uncle's wife.[109] Randolph's already low opinion of Nancy Morris rendered him a willing hearer of any scandal-mongering about her. For the next few hours, Ogden obliged. He told Randolph that Morris had sought a character reference about his prospective bride from John Marshall, that Nancy had used Randolph's name to vouch for her chastity, and that she had listed Randolph as one of her suitors, indeed as one who had offered her marriage.[110] Ogden also confided his suspicion that Nancy's child was not the son of Gouverneur Morris, but "the offspring of an illicit amour" with a servant.

Randolph needed no persuading to believe the worst of Nancy Morris. He told Ogden he had never proposed marriage to Nancy and offered his view that Chief Justice Marshall surely had been misled as to her character. If she had lied to Judith and Richard, and lied about him, she must have lied to Morris to trap him into marriage. Randolph wrote to Morris requesting a meeting. The letter was intercepted by Nancy, who responded that her husband was ill and unable to meet. Randolph read into this answer a "watchfulness . . . as if in constant fear and suspicion of being detected."[111] While he contemplated his next step, David Ogden paid a second call. This time he told an even more incredible tale. He said Nancy would kill anyone who attempted to reveal her true character to Morris, and that she had tried to kill him by introducing a "noxious and offensive-smelling" vapor into his bedroom. Randolph had long held the suspicion that Nancy had murdered his brother Richard. Now standing before him was someone who believed she was capable of such an act.

Over the next several days, Randolph pondered what to do. He apparently did not consider that Ogden lost a substantial financial interest when Morris married and became a father.[112] He sought the counsel of two friends who were in the area, Harmanus Bleecker and Captain Stephen Decatur, but apparently did not consider leaving New York and putting this episode behind him.[113] Denied a meeting with Morris, he could do nothing but hobble about his apartment, festering in discontent and distant memories. The only action available to him—as had been the case so often in his life—was to unleash his torment in words.[114] He resolved to write "a letter to Mrs. Morris containing at once a history of her manifold issues and a warning against them." He disingenuously asserted that his purpose was to "to impress upon your mind a sense of your duty towards your Husband, and if possible, to rouse some dormant spark of virtue, if, haply, any such should slumber in your bosom."[115]

The vitriol flowed in a series of sentences that left nothing to interpretation or imagination: "vice and sin," "life of wretchedness," and "habitual and inveterate disregard of truth." He had never proposed marriage, he wrote, calling the story another "falsehood that you may coin to serve a turn." That same conniving spirit caused her to prompt Morris to write John Marshall, a man who "knew no more of your general and subsequent course than the Archbishop of Canterbury." "Cunning and guilt are no match for wisdom and truth," he wrote, "and yet you persevere in your wicked course." Randolph then turned to the source of his misery: the events at Glenlyvar.

Her devotion to little Gouverneur had caused Randolph to recall that her "hands had deprived of life that of which you were delivered in October 1792 at Randolph Harrison's." He offered his version of the affair. She had seduced his dying brother, Theodorick, and then begged Richard Randolph to protect her secret. Richard had gallantly done so, he wrote, "at the hazard of all that man can hold dear—domestic peace, reputation and life! His hand received the burden, bloody from the womb, and already lifeless.

Who stifled its cries? God only knows, and *you!* His hand consigned it to an uncoffined grave. To the prudence of Randolph Harrison, who disqualified himself from giving testimony by refraining from a search under that pile of shingles, some of which were marked with blood—to his cautious conduct it is owing, that my brother did not perish by the side of you, on the same gibbet! And that the foul stain of incest and murder is not indelibly stamped on his name and associated with his offspring."[116]

If Randolph's account is true, his beloved brother Richard, his wronged sister-in-law Judith, and his friend Randolph Harrison had committed perjury, and, unless he had discerned these facts years later, so had he. He ascribes no responsibility to Richard for consigning a newborn child to a pile of shingles; indeed he credits this maneuver as quick thinking that saved the family's reputation and Richard's life. In a paragraph full of victims, the dead child is but an obstacle to overcome.

Accusing Nancy of murder, Randolph in effect implicated her in Richard's death by implying that Gouverneur Morris "must sooner or later unmask you, unless he too die of the 'cramp in his stomach'—you understand me!"[117] Randolph had thrown Nancy out of Bizarre when he discovered her "intimacy with one of the slaves." The letter recounted Nancy's travels, displaying such a detailed knowledge that it hints Randolph may have been keeping tabs on her. When he learned of Tudor's illness and realized he would soon be in her company, he hoped a change of circumstances had wrought a change in Nancy. Instead, he found a "vampyre, that after sucking the best blood of my race, has flitted off to the North and stuck its happy fangs into an infirm old man." His venom spent, there was nothing else to write. "Repent before it is too late," Randolph concluded. "May I hear of that repentance, and never see you more!"

12

Dying, Sir, Dying

Fold softly in thy long embrace
That heart so worn and broken
And cool its pulse of fire beneath
Thy shadows old and oaken.

Randolph took a meandering path home from New York. He lingered in Philadelphia until mid-January. While there, he ended speculation about his political future. "I have been requested in writing by more than one respectable freeholder," he wrote, "to state explicitly whether or not 'if the people choose to elect me, I will serve them.' At all times, I should conceive it my duty so to do."[1] The letter announcing his availability gave notice that his brief retirement had not sanded his flinty disposition. "We shall be divided into two great but very unequal classes," he wrote, "those who pay taxes and those who receive the proceeds of them." He had "stood an eight years' siege against the whole power and patronage of Government and the incessant roar of the artillery of the press" and was ready to do so again. "To fall in such a cause," he concluded, "was no mean glory."[2] Once committed to the race, he was confident of victory. "I have no doubt of success," he wrote, "if I say the word."[3]

While Randolph looked to electoral success, Nancy Morris looked to retaliation. Randolph's incendiary letter had been delivered to Gouverneur Morris, who passed it on to his wife. Morris's mind and heart were reconciled to whatever had happened in Virginia those many years ago, and the letter had not enraged him enough to file suit or issue a duel challenge.[4] Nancy was not as willing as her husband to let the matter drop. She decided to respond to Randolph, with the added touch of sending copies of the correspondence to his political opponents. "It is well that your former constituents should know the creature in whom they put their trust," she wrote. "Virginians, in general, whatever may be their defects, have a high sense of honor."[5] On January 16, 1815, Nancy Morris poured out the spleen of twenty years. "When you entered this home, and when you left it," she wrote, "you took me in your arms, you pressed me to your bosom, you impressed upon my lips a kiss which I received as a token of friendship from a near relation. Did you then believe that you held in your arms, that you pressed to your bosom, that you kissed the lips of a common prostitute, the murderess of her own child and of your brother?" If he did believe it, Nancy told him to "tell this to the world that scorn be at no loss for an object." If he did not believe it, "make out a certificate that 'John Randolph of Roanoke' is a base calumniator."[6]

Nancy asserted again that Randolph had sought to marry her, but she had been repulsed by his "mean selfishness [and] wretched appearance." She was "betrothed to [Theodorick] and considered him as my husband in the presence of God. . . . We should have been married, if Death had not snatched him away." She had confided all this to Richard, who had protected her reputation on his own volition. She was stunned that Randolph would charge his own brother with being an accomplice to infanticide. Indeed, it was her view that of the Randolph brothers, he alone possessed a sufficiently perverted character to commit such a crime. "You," she wrote acidly, "still have the heart of a savage."

Randolph's letter, like his character, she wrote, was replete with "vainglorious boasting," "malicious baseness," and "downright falsehood." She defied him to "substantiate by the testimony of any credible witness a single fact injurious to my reputation." She painted Morris's nephew David Ogden in the darkest of colors, vigorously defended her husband, and recounted in excruciating detail the days of her "forlorn conditions." Page after page, the letter was a full-throated expression of contempt. "Formerly Jack Randolph," she taunted, "now, 'John Randolph of Roanoke' . . . the affectation of greatness must cover you with ridicule." Her conclusion matched Randolph at his acerbic best: "I trust you are by this time convinced that you have clumsily performed the part of 'honest Iago.' Happily for my life, and for my husband's peace, you did not find in him a headlong, rash Othello. For a full and proper description of what you have written and spoken on this occasion, I refer you to the same admirable author. He will tell you it is a tale told by an idiot, full of sound and fury, signifying nothing."[7]

In the same way that Randolph's letter interpreted events in lights favorable to him and his family, Nancy's response was likewise self-serving. She was writing not only to Randolph, but also to a wider audience. She admitted to a relationship with Theodorick, but did not admit being pregnant. She defended Richard against charges of infanticide, but did not detail the events of the night at Glenlyvar. She responded as would anyone accused of committing murder, but offered no explanation of Richard's sudden illness and death. Though she was justified in responding in kind to Randolph's decidedly ungentlemanly language, her descent to his level makes her a less sympathetic character. Finally, she accused Randolph of reviving the scandal for political purposes, but she was the one who made public the correspondence during an election year. Read together, the Randolph/Morris exchange provides little insight into the Glenlyvar incident, Richard's death, or the years the fractured family spent together at Bizarre.

Randolph never received Nancy's letter. He learned of it when copies of it began to spring up across Virginia. "I learn from authority that I cannot discredit," he wrote to former senator Giles, "that you have in your possession, and occasionally show to others, a written letter . . . from Mrs. Gouverneur Morris addressed to me, containing allegations against me of a nature highly injurious."[8] He warned that he would not allow Giles to be a "*vehicle* of calumny" against him, under the pretext that he was merely passing on information. He stated that a duel challenge would swiftly follow should Giles persist in "intermeddling in any manner in my affairs." He was less strident to another who had received a copy. "I only beg you," he wrote, "to suspend any opinion to my disadvantage . . . until you know *all*."[9] He was convinced that Nancy's attempt to influence the election had failed. "She is too well known here," he wrote, "to do any person an injury."[10]

Randolph had an insatiable need to find a perpetrator, scapegoat, or conspiracy to bear responsibility for Richard's disgrace and death. "I know not why I have said so much about this tremendously wicked woman," he wrote to Harmanus Bleecker, "but I cannot help thinking of her as the cause of my poor brother's death; facts have come to my knowledge . . . which strengthen this suspicion. . . . There is the strongest evidence that he died by poison."[11] A year later, in a tortured replay of Richard's demise, Randolph hurled questions at Judith. "My brother reached home on the 5th quite ill, having been taken on the road," he wrote, "The disease terminated on the 14th, nine days. Why was not I sent for [?]" Did Nancy "mix or hand him the medicine?" Did she have "the opportunity for doing the deed?"[12] Time and again, Randolph returned in memory to the unsettling events of Bizarre and Glenlyvar. The scandal, biographer Robert Dawidoff wrote, "was simply too terrible for him to assimilate. In a sense, he never recovered from the shock . . .

never reconciled himself to these events, never completely accepted them. The pain was always fresh."[13]

Normally in times of emotional or physical trauma, Randolph would turn to self-pity or opium, but in this latest season of despair, he turned to the faith he had learned at Frances Randolph's knee. "I have," he wrote to Reverend William Meade, "the most earnest desire for a more perfect faith than I fear I possess." He confessed "time misspent, faculties misemployed, but above all that I have not loved God and my neighbor as we are commanded to do."[14] He made similar inquiries of other friends, but it was from Francis Scott Key that he received "consolation."[15] Key used the opening provided by Randolph's entreaty to call him home to the faith of his fathers. "May you soon, my friend," Key wrote, "experience the most delightful of all sensations, that springs from a well grounded hope of reconciliation with God! You are on the right track. . . . God is leading you."[16]

Randolph carried Key's letter "constantly in my pocket, reading it frequently."[17] He wrote that he had forgiven "all who have done me an injury, as I have asked forgiveness of those whom I may have wronged"—Nancy Morris apparently not qualifying for either category.[18] His letters during the summer of 1815 focus almost exclusively on religious topics, veering from joyful redemption to despondent self-condemnation. "I have grieved unfeignedly for my manifold transgressions," he wrote to Key. "I have thrown myself upon the mercy of my Redeemer, conscious of my own utter inability to conceive one good thought, or do one good act without his gracious aid."[19] Randolph would emerge from this season a practicing, but never fully confidant, Christian.[20]

National events in the fall of 1814 were as unsettled as Randolph's spiritual life. The nation's capital lay in ruin, the army could not fill its ranks, and the government had defaulted on the national debt. The economic downturn that Randolph predicted had bound together the South and New England in shared agony. Southern commodity prices bottomed out, and northern ships rotted in port. Patriotic citizens found themselves trading with the enemy to generate income. Talk of secession began, not in the South, but in the Yankee Northeast. "It is not to be disguised," President Madison told the Congress, "that the situation of our country calls for its greatest efforts."[21] Madison dispatched Henry Clay, Albert Gallatin, and John Quincy Adams to Ghent, in modern-day Belgium, to discuss a settlement with the British. While the nation waited for word from the negotiations,

Andrew Jackson's forces routed the British in the Battle of New Orleans. The news soon reached America that the Treaty of Ghent had been signed two months earlier. The treaty represented peace without victory. The warring powers were returned to pre-war status, and no issues of controversy were definitively resolved. But the people of the United States were willing to accept peace on almost any terms, and Jackson's heroics made the end appear victorious. The Treaty of Ghent was ratified on February 16, 1815.

The restoration of peace restored Randolph to favor with his constituents. It was as if patriotism had required his removal when the war was declared, and now appreciation for his principled stand required his re-election. Nevertheless, the Richmond *Enquirer* mounted a vigorous opposition. Randolph, the paper intoned, "has so great an itch to be *singular* and his understanding is so completely bewitched by his passions, that it would be wonderful if he were to enjoy a *lunatic interval* for more than one moment."[22] He was "a politician without temper; a writer without judgment; a prophet without the least inspiration." The truth, the *Enquirer* editorialized shortly before the election, "is that Mr. Randolph lives in a world of his own creation."[23] The *Enquirer* should have saved the ink.

"I believe you may consider me as doomed to two years servitude and exile," Randolph wrote when Prince Edward county voted 300 to 175 to send him back to Congress.[24] That win was followed by a sweep of Charlotte, Buckingham, and Cumberland. "You will have heard of my re-election," he wrote to Francis Scott Key—who had recently written a poem titled the "Star Spangled Banner"—"an event which has given me no pleasure, except so far as it has been gratifying to my friends."[25] The Richmond *Enquirer* greeted the result with dismay. "Tories, rejoice," the paper commented. "Friends of Great Britain, go, joy with him! . . . The Snarler is again in!"[26]

Randolph returned to the nation's capital in January 1816.[27] Although living in Washington was like "living as in a boarding school, or a monastery," he was able to acquire "better apartments [and a] better bed" than in past years.[28] The delicacies seemed likewise improved. With Key, he dined on *"new laid* eggs, Virginian sausages, fish, fresh and salt, hominy, *good* coffee and *fine* tea."[29] He supplemented his diet with "ten or fifteen gallons . . . [of] fine old peach brandy" procured from a friend.[30] Even while judging the area to be a "region without souls," Randolph found his surroundings to be in "every way more comfortable."[31]

Randolph marked his arrival in the House by hailing his old foes. "I labor under two great misfortunes," he said, casting his dark eyes toward Henry Clay, "one is that I can never understand the honorable Speaker; the other is that he can never understand me."[32] And he devoted much of his first speech to tweaking Calhoun. The phrases rolled delightfully off his tongue as he critiqued the South Carolinian's "infelicity of illustrations" and bouts with "the horrid phantom which had so much alarmed not his imagination but his judgment."[33] The old Quid was back.

Absence had not made Randolph's heart grow fonder of his contemporaries. Republicans, he wrote, were ruled by "restless ambition, local considerations, and private interest," and consisted of "selfish and cowardly beings who sacrificed their friends, their principles, nay even . . . *their party*, at the shrine of sordid ambition."[34] The opposition fared no better. The few remaining Federalists and scattered other members were "destitute of courage, integrity, or talents."[35] He sparred with his old enemies in the press, writing to the editor of the *National Intelligencer* that his speeches were "very much misapprehended and consequently misrepresented" in that publication.[36] He heard that the Richmond *Enquirer* had written that all was peace until he had taken his seat. "It is a *lie*," he snapped, "a word never fit for a gentleman to use except towards a scoundrel whose daily bread is earned by *lying*."[37] In short, Randolph found politics in Washington pretty much as he had left them; and Washington found him similarly constant. "I challenge any man," he wrote shortly after arriving, "to put his finger upon any vote or act of mine that contravenes it, or to show the vote given by me that tends to abridge the rights of the States, the franchises of the citizen, or even to add to his burthens in any shape; of personal service or of contribution to the publick purse."[38]

Most of Randolph's old allies were no longer members, and his "last political friend," Richard Stanford of North Carolina, was taken seriously ill during the session.[39] Randolph sat by his bedside night after night until his "old friend and sometime fellow labourer" died "without a struggle."[40] Stanford's death was the third in a series of close losses that jolted Randolph. First, his nephew Tudor had succumbed to tuberculosis; then his sister-in-law Judith died on March 10, 1816. Randolph awoke one morning with "the impression that she was in the land of spirits." He saw her, he wrote, "looking so mournfully, yet benignantly upon me."[41] The news of her passing followed shortly after this premonition. "I knew her better than anybody else," he wrote. "Her endowments were of the highest order; and it gave me the greatest comfort . . . to learn that she died as every Christian could wish to die.[42] About Judith Randolph, he wrote little more. If memories of the tangled relationships of long-ago days at Bizarre entered his mind as he laid his sister-in-law to rest, he kept them to himself.

Though Randolph wrote that he was "quite rusty as to certain matters which a debater should have always at his fingers' ends," he eagerly threw himself "in the thickest of the fight" on the floor of the House.[43] Some spectators were seeing him in action for the first time. "He is really a most singular and interesting man," Senator Elijah Mills wrote, "regardless entirely of form and ceremony in some things, and punctilious to an extreme in others."[44] Lewis Machen, secretary of the Senate, wrote that Randolph "seizes the attention by the fascination of his manner, communicates his ideas with great clearness, and gives to the subject every grace which an intimate acquaintance with classic literature seldom fails to impart." Machen drew the same conclusion as others: "for cool, yet cutting sarcasm, severity of retort, quickness of reply, the play of fancy, and corruscations of wit, he has scarcely a superior."[45]

Randolph would need all the talents Machen described. The War of 1812 had sparked a new nationalistic spirit that clamored for roads to be built, canals to be dug, bridges to be raised, and industries to be nurtured. The war had created a spirit of destiny and expansion. That spirit found expression in a host of policy initiatives.

Robert Lowndes of South Carolina proposed a revenue program under which the direct taxation levied during the war would be retained, and one-half of the wartime tariff rates would be continued. The funds from these sources would be used for internal improvements, national defense, and industry subsidization. The engine that powered the war would pave the peace. The bill came from the Republican caucus, but it could have been written by the Federalists of 1798. There was never a question that Randolph would set his face against it.

Randolph spoke on at least nine occasions against the Revenue Bill.[46] He argued that the government already possessed the means to gather sufficient operating sums. It was a "moral certainty," he said, "that there is money enough without this tax, to support the Government—not, indeed, to support its extravagance—not to support its *nepotism*—not to support its abuses—but to uphold it . . . as it was under Jefferson and Washington."[47] He anticipated what in later days would be called supply-side economics when he submitted that, "if they who hold the reins of Government would only dispense with over regulation, instead of being obliged to lay new taxes for resources, they would have had a considerable overplus in the Treasury."[48] He warned again of the dangers of a standing army. "Military men are fond of glory," he said, "the constituent elements of which are blood and taxes."[49] He denounced any policy under which the government would pick "the pockets of the hard working cultivator of the soil . . . in order to hire another man to go to work in a shoemaker's shop or to set up a spinning jenny."[50] And, as he had done repeatedly during his first tour of service in the House, he accused his Republican colleagues of deserting their principles and their party. "Here, sir," he said, "we have another proof that the present Government have renounced the true Republican principles of Jefferson's Administration on which they raised themselves to power, and that they have taken up, in their stead, those of John Adams."[51]

But the critical issue to Randolph went beyond high taxes, oppressive tariffs, and profligate government spending. It was the continued consolidation of power in an ever-expanding central government. The policy underlying the Revenue Bill would destroy the balance of authority between the national and state governments. "[There] is in every Government, the form of which is free," he told the House, "a tendency to domination—to ambition." That nearly insatiable desire could be checked only by a vibrant federal system. The question presented, he argued, is "whether or not we are willing to become one great consolidated nation, under one form of law" or "whether the State governments are to be swept away." And state governments, at least that of Virginia, were not based on the dangerous notions of equality that were driving federal policy, but in "those old respectable institutions" such as local governments, churches, schools, and farms. Federal consolidation threatened "their integrity and preservation" and, in so doing, destroyed society. In clinging to traditional society, Randolph said, "I cling to my country. . . . I am not for a policy which must end in the destruction, and speedy destruction, too, of the whole of the State governments."[52]

The Revenue Bill passed, but Randolph's arguments found fertile ground in an unsuspected place. John C. Calhoun pondered the words of his debating opponent, and twenty years later, in an era with much more at risk, would champion Randolph's position.[53]

If the Revenue Bill was akin to past Federalist policies, the next piece of legislation was an exact replica. On January 8, 1816, Calhoun presented legislation to incorporate the Second Bank of the United States. The corner-stone of Alexander Hamilton's mercantile plan, the First Bank of the Untied States had been chartered in 1791 by the Federalist-controlled Congress, but killed in 1811 when Republicans refused to renew its charter. The scatter-shot methods used to fund the War of 1812 had wrought a change in many minds on the notion of a central federal bank.[54] Calhoun's bill called for a bank with capital of thirty-five million dollars, of which one-fifth would be purchased by the federal government in coin, Treasury notes, or govern-ment stock. The bank would be located in Philadelphia, governed by a board of directors, and have an exclusive charter for twenty-one years.[55] It would be the nation's bank—transacting the government's business, holding the public's funds, and issuing legal tender notes. President Madison had op-posed Hamilton's bank but now reversed himself and, along with Clay and the Republican leadership, supported Calhoun's bill.

Randolph—like most men of agriculture—distrusted banks. Southern planters were hard-money men, adverse to borrowing, opposed to pieces of paper masquerading as money, comfortable with only gold and the orderly transactions of an agrarian economy.[56] A national bank would be another source of unchecked, consolidated power. Moreover, Randolph believed a national bank to be unconstitutional—the position taken by Jefferson and Madison in 1791.[57] Congress had no authority to charter a bank, nor could any such authority be derived from the power to lay and collect taxes, or borrow money. Randolph viewed a Bank of the United States as the next logical step in the centralization of power for the federal government.[58] This new bank, he wrote, "out-Hamiltons Alexander Hamilton."[59]

Calhoun argued that the constitutionality had been established by the chartering of the First Bank. He dismissed concerns about concentration of power and threats to liberty by pointing out that banks were insepara-ble from national commerce and industry. He warned that the nation's cur-rency was in disorder, state banks were issuing paper specie, and inflation was an imminent danger. The new nationalism demanded the fiscal order the new bank would provide.

Randolph responded that all the evils identified by Calhoun could be remedied without a national bank. "To pass this bill," he said, "would be like getting rid of the rats by setting fire to the house."[60] The economic con-cerns were "frigidly and rigorously a mere matter of calculation" best solved by other means. The more important issue, he predictably said, involved the danger of the "spirit of expediency, not only in public but private life . . . the spirit which seeks wealth by every path but the plain and regular path of honest industry and honest fame."[61]

Randolph found many of his colleagues shared his view. "Calhoun is trying to sweeten it to our palates," he wrote of a suggested compromise. "The Treasury notes are now going! going! going! gone!"[62] Randolph engaged Calhoun on almost a daily basis, filed amendments, and taunted the "screwed-up, strained, and costive majority."[63] Calling the bank "unconstitutional, inexpedient, and dangerous," he warned his colleagues against creating a privileged order.[64] "If I must have a master," Randolph declared, "let him be one with epaulettes, something that I can fear and respect, something that I can look up to—but not a master with a quill behind his ear."[65] The opposition made such progress that Henry Clay came into the well of the House to rally the Bank forces. The bill chartering the Second Bank of the United States passed the House by a closer-than-expected vote of eighty to seventy-one.

The battles over taxes and the bank took a toll on Randolph. "I never knew what pain was until Saturday," he wrote. "Believing that I had received my death blow, I was anxious that my last words should be heard by the few friends that were around me."[66] He did not detail the nature of this latest attack, but told a friend that he could "barely crawl to the House to give my feeble vote against the Bank."[67] He treated himself with "a nightly dose of magnesia," but if his physical condition showed any improvement, his emotional condition took precedence in misery.[68] His general angst extended to society at large and to himself in particular. "Mankind," he wrote to Richard Randolph, "seems bent upon making one another as miserable as they can during their sojourn on earth and every day adds to my desire to withdraw myself from all commerce with the world. . . . The change may be in me, but I think I discern a most lamentable one in the character of our people."[69] This latest onslaught of illness kept him from actively participating in the presidential election of 1816. "I have little interest in the election," he wrote, despite the fact that his one-time ally, James Monroe, was the leading contender to succeed Madison. Randolph's only passing comment was "wishing that treachery and double dealing may meet their due reward."[70]

Fleeting relief was found in the lands he loved. "The weather for some weeks passed has been so delightful," he wrote in October 1816, "that I have lived in the open air with my gun and dogs." It was his favorite season. "Nothing can surpass the beauty of the forest scenery at this time. Every variety of tint from the deepest green to the brightest gold and scarlet and the most sober russet. I think the tints and hues defy the pencil."[71]

But these moments were increasingly few. "For my part," Randolph wrote, "if there breathes a creature more empty of enjoyment than myself, I sincerely pity him."[72] He returned to Washington for the second session of the Fourteenth Congress, to be greeted by several new members of the Virginia delegation. To those who inquired after his health, Randolph fixed even the most sympathetic of them with a horrific stare and answered with his own benediction: "Dying, Sir, Dying!"[73]

13

The Moral Authority of My Heart

He knew her faults, yet never stooped
His proud and manly feeling
To poor excuses of the wrong
Or meanness of concealing.

John Randolph's diary is comprised mostly of short entries about the weather or travel. He left behind no memoirs, and his colorful public persona has cast a long shadow nearly eclipsing the private man. Yet when his voluminous correspondence is read together, the man behind the eccentricities emerges. This is particularly so in letters Randolph wrote to family members and his several "adopted" sons.

Randolph considered himself the father of Tudor and St. George Randolph, the two sons of his deceased brother Richard. He was also very close to his godson, John Randolph Clay, and to the Bryan boys, John Randolph and Thomas, the two sons of his friend from his Philadelphia days, Joseph Bryan. Perhaps his closest relationship was with Theodore Dudley, his first cousin once removed, who lived at Bizarre and Roanoke for twenty years. Rounding out the family with whom he most corresponded were his sister Fanny Tucker Coalter, and his niece, Elizabeth.

Randolph viewed these relationships seriously. He tutored his nephew Tudor before sending him to local private schools and then to Harvard. There Tudor excelled before his life was cut short by tuberculosis. Harvard awarded his degree posthumously. St. George, a deaf mute, presented a different challenge. Randolph sent him to London and Paris for specialized education, but the boy's tragic circumstances soon overwhelmed him. He was committed to an insane asylum upon his return to the States. Randolph paid for Dudley's education in Virginia and at medical school in Philadelphia and provided room and board for the Bryans. When John Randolph Clay returned to his home in Philadelphia after living at Roanoke while attending school, Randolph reported to Mrs. Clay that the boy "has been taught to obey, promptly, unhesitatingly . . . to rise early and to be temperate in his meats and drink." Young Clay's constitution had "been toughened and hardened by habits of exercise in the open air," Randolph wrote. "Let them not be substituted by warm parlors, a bed chamber with a fire in it, curtains and sedentary habits."[1]

Given Randolph's actions on behalf of his wards, it is not surprising that his letters focus on education. He made recommendations on readings, offered grammatical corrections, and suggested courses of study. "I hope," he wrote to Dudley, "that you will make every exertion to attain a proficiency in Greek, even at the expense of a temporary neglect of your French and Latin. Indeed, the Greek itself would keep alive your knowledge of the last."[2] Randolph viewed a mastery of languages as the foundation of a sound education and repeatedly recommended the study of Greek, Latin, French, Spanish, and German.[3] "Do you read French? he wrote to Elizabeth Coalter. "If not, why not? You are not one day too old to learn that and Italian, and everything else a lady ought to know—even Greek, if you wish to imitate Lady Jane Grey. . . . I want you to be mistress of the Roman mouth and the Tuscan tongue."[4]

"Herodotus, Thucydides, Polybius, and Livy," he wrote to Dudley "should be read, in preference to those who have made books, merely by pillaging these invaluable ancients."[5] To that list he added Ovid, Homer, Hume, and, on numerous occasions, the letters of William Pitt.[6] Additionally he urged an in-depth knowledge of "the reign of Elizabeth . . . of Charles I, the Protectorate, and Charles and James II," to be supplemented by a history of Scotland.[7] "Do not, however," he warned, "permit history to engross your attention to the exclusion of languages."[8]

He peppered the students with questions. "Why does Milton write *steep* Atlantic stream?" he asked Elizabeth. Then answering: "Because poetry is not prose; altho' prose is often poetry, and of the highest order. . . . [P]oetry affects us by exciting images and thoughts in us, as one instrument, thought not struck, responds in unison to another."[9] "Who is the greatest man that you have met in English history?" he wrote to Dudley. "Who is the worst man? The most learned?"[10] When the correspondents ventured replies, they were often met with extensive grammatical critiques.[11] "You must not think me crabbed and censorious when I notice a little bit of false English and false spelling (and the last proves to me that both are the effects of carelessness) in your letter," he wrote to Elizabeth. "You 'have been disapating it.'

Dissipating what? You see at once the whole matter, and that's enough."[12] Finding one of St. George's letters not up to his usual standard, he recommended the youth "endeavor to express your thoughts as plainly as possible. If you would keep a little diary of the weather—and also of occurrences worthy of being noted and send me the sheet weekly I could correct & return it by the post."[13] Substance was as important as style. "You have the art of writing letters," he told Dudley, "without *putting any thing in them*—and of *answering*, without *replying* to your correspondent."[14]

Academic advice was usually followed with moral instruction. "Let me hope," he wrote to St. George, "that your education will be conducted [agreeably] to those immutable principles, which are true in all nations & ages, & which can never fail to aggrandize the people by whom they are respected."[15] The most important of these virtues was truthfulness. Truth "may be truly called the mother of all the rest. . . . [I]t is impossible for a liar to possess one single good quality."[16] Concerned with John Randolph Clay's "propensity to fibbing," he urged Mrs. Clay to "punish it exemplarily" at the slightest sign.[17] "Lay down this as a principle," he extolled Dudley, "that *truth* is to the other virtues, what vital air is to the human system."[18]

To truth was added temperance, fidelity, industry, and duty.[19] Perhaps recalling his own misspent days, Randolph warned against the snares that awaited them. "I know nothing that I am so anxious you should acquire," he wrote to Dudley, "as the faculty of saying *no*. You must calculate on unreasonable requests being preferred to you every day of your life, and must endeavor to *deny* with as much facility as you *acquiesce*."[20] Money was a frequent topic, with Randolph admitting the mistakes he had made in that regard. Debt "begins with the subjugation of the mind, and ends with the enslavement of the body," he wrote to Tudor.[21] "If you have escaped it," he continued, "you have exercised more judgment than I possessed at your age; the want of which cost me many a heartache."[22]

As always with Randolph, there was a greater principle involved. These virtues were noble in themselves, but nothing, he asserted, "can be more respectable than the independence that grows out of self-denial." Exercising these traits in one's personal and business life led to "the cultivation of his mind, or the aid of his fellow-creatures." Thus would one develop "a spirit of the noblest order."[23] While not specifically referencing his political views, Randolph's advice always pointed toward the civic virtue—or "aristocracy"—which he believed was essential to a free society. "Your success depends upon the discovery of no new principle of human affairs," he wrote to William Thompson, a friend from his youth who stayed briefly at Bizarre, "but upon the application of such as are familiar to all. Decision, firmness, independence, which equally scorns to yield our own rights as to detract from those of others, are the only guides to the esteem of the world, or of ourselves. A reliance upon our resources for all things, but especially for relief against that arch-fiend, the *taedium vitae,* can alone guard us against a state of dependence and contempt."[24]

Subtly rejecting notions of abstract equality or entitlement, Randolph repeatedly wrote that one's destiny lay in one's hands.[25] But he was also concerned with the characteristics he saw in the younger generation of Virginians—traits he did not wish his wards to emulate. He found "self-conceit and indifference" flourishing in Virginia "as if it were their native soil."[26] Randolph was witnessing the coming of age of the third generation since the Revolution, boys born to prosperity earned by their fathers and untested by labor or study. Had he been completely candid, he would have acknowledged that both of his beloved brothers had displayed these same vices—as had he before checking himself. Instead he utilized some of his most vigorous language in condemning the traits that "mar all excellence."

> A petulant arrogance, or supine, listless indifference, marks the character of too many of our young men. They early assume airs of manhood; and these premature men remain children for the rest of their lives. Upon the credit of a smattering of Latin, drinking grog, and chewing tobacco, these striplings set up for legislators and statesmen; and seem to deem it derogatory from their manhood to treat age and experience with any degree of deference. They are loud, boisterous, overbearing, and dictatorial: profane in speech, low and obscene in their pleasures. In the tavern, the stable, or the gaming-house, they are at home; but, placed in the society of *real* gentlemen, and men of letters, they are awkward and uneasy: in all situations, they are contemptible.[27]

On the other hand, Randolph believed the women of Virginia "are the best wives in the world and that, generally speaking, they are too good for the grog-drinking beasts to whom they are yoked."[28] Randolph frequently dispensed advice on romance and marriage in his letters. He advised Dudley to seek a "virtuous and amiable woman" who was "good-tempered, healthy (a qualification scarcely thought of now-a-days, all-important as it is), chaste, cleanly, economical, and not an absolute fool." Nor should he "quarrel with a good fortune, if it has produced no ill effect on the possessor—a rare case."[29]

But he warned his cousin that he was "no match for female adroitness and artifice, even if not seconded by wit, some beauty, and *long practice*."[30] He was just as candid when writing to women. "I would rather see you dead than vain or pert," he wrote to his niece Elizabeth:

> Yours is the beauty, not of complexion or feature, but what they cannot supply, of expression and of grace. You have a happy and ready wit; the quickness of your apprehension is uncommon, even in your sex. I hope that you add to it solidity of judgment, or that experience will bestow it. Set a proper value upon yourself for my sake, for you own, and for your dear mother's. I know not how it happens that very clever men are prone to ally themselves to very silly and insipid women, and thus propagate a race of boobies; or that fine women throw themselves away upon coxcombs and doom themselves "to suckle fools and chronicle small beer."[31]

Randolph's comments about women sometimes veered into the paternalism common in that era, but for the most part he gave the same advice and encouragement to his female correspondents as to his male. "Our sex," he wrote to Elizabeth, "has nothing to boast of over yours, while, in a great many others, you are far before us. You are less selfish, capable of stronger and more constant attachments, and less swayed (whatever satirists may say or sing) by wealth or power."[32] He did, on two occasions, warn Elizabeth about her sometimes sarcastic tone, but this reproach was based in his traumatic experiences with Nancy Morris. Her sarcasm, he wrote, "consigned my most amiable and unfortunate brother to a dungeon, and might have dragged him to a gibbet, blasted the fair promise of his youth, and rendered an untimely death but a welcome and happy release from a blighted reputation."[33] That rare rebuke aside, most of Randolph's letters to Fanny and Elizabeth sought to "secure your esteem and so to deport myself to deserve your love."[34] He confessed to Elizabeth that her letters "constitute my almost only resource against the Dark Spirit that persecutes me."[35]

For the most part, the recipients of his letters believed he had much to impart. "A man having such a soul as John Randolph," Thomas Bryan wrote, "has but one face for his friends. . . . I don't know but I feel a kind of reverence and love for that man."[36] John Randolph Bryan—who would further cement the relationship by marrying Elizabeth Coalter—recalled that "he treated me as a son."[37] John Randolph Clay would travel with Randolph to Russia as secretary of legation, beginning a diplomatic career that would see him later serve as minister to Peru. Elizabeth, who would be entangled in the lengthy will dispute following Randolph's death and who thought her uncle a bit mad, wrote that she "admired his talents, loved him from the tie of blood and because he loved me, and pitied him because he was sick and wretched, and sought my sympathy."[38] Randolph knew that his extended family was not blind "to the defects of my character." But his motivation in providing them with extensive advice and counsel was pure. "If I could lay bare the moral anatomy of my heart," he wrote in words applicable in all his letters, "I would not shrink from your inspection of all its workings *towards yourself,* from the moment I first beheld you, up to the present hour."[39]

14

Two Souls

Mirth, sparkling like a diamond shower,
From lips of life-long sadness;
Clear picturing of majestic thought
Upon a ground of madness.

On March 17, 1817, at Prince Edward Courthouse, Randolph announced he would not seek re-election. He told the shocked crowd that he was "incapable of discharging the duties of a representative." He left them with a farewell toast: "The people of this district, when I forget them, may my God forget me."[1]

For most of 1817, Randolph sat by his hearth, shut off from the world. "My present situation," he wrote, "dreary and desolate as it is, is perhaps the best for me at my time of life and with a broken constitution, faculties impaired or obscured by disease and care, a man is at least safe by his own fireside."[2] Only sixteen letters survive from the months March through December of that year, unusual for a man who routinely posted twenty to thirty letters a month.[3] "I live here the life of a Hermit," he wrote, "for near a fortnight past, I have been confined with a wounded leg and in that time have not seen a white face, except my friend Dudley's."[4] As witness to Randolph's behavior at this time, Theodore Dudley described "delirium" marked by "fits of caprice and petulance, following days of the deepest gloom."[5] Randolph, Dudley concluded, was a man "endowed with two souls."[6]

One is forced to speculate about the causes of Randolph's erratic mental condition. Possibly it was the same source as his physical ailments. Social skill defects, anxiety, and depression are known symptoms of Klinefelter syndrome. Likewise, his well-documented drug use could have provided the impetus for a host of mood swings. Opium triggers surges of euphoria, just as laudanum does dysphoria. In addition, Randolph's life was filled with traumatic events sufficient to shatter the emotional equilibrium of most men. If one must render a diagnosis, Randolph's manic and depressive symptoms, manifesting in agitation, insomnia, uneven temper, persistent sadness, and feelings of hopelessness and guilt, suggest a type of bipolar disorder. Whatever the cause, the years 1817 to 1820 would see Randolph frequently lapse into sinister peculiarity, followed by periods of normal behavior.

Randolph rose between three and four in the morning and mounted a favorite horse. There he would sit "ten or fifteen minutes, wishing to go somewhere but not knowing where to ride, for I would escape any where from the incubus that weighs me down, body and soul . . . the intenseness of this wretchedness."[7] He found some peace "in the fields and woods, with belted waist and pointers at my heels." He wrote that he would not "exchange the feeling of independence that warms me as I range the hills and plains for all in the gift of the President and the People."[8] The sounds of nature were a concert, and he delighted in the "doves, summer red-birds, cardinals . . . squirrels and hares" that frequented his lawn.[9]

He wrote little about politics during these two years, but his competing souls did not diminish his political sagacity. "When I speak of my country," he wrote to Francis Key, "I mean the Commonwealth of Virginia."[10] Randolph must have cloaked his wild mood swings from general view, for by the end of 1818 his friends believed him to be enough of his old self to re-elect him to Congress.[11] Again, Randolph did not object. Indeed, he compared his return to public life "to nothing so well as the dawning sun after a dark, tempestuous night."[12]

It was a propitious time for Randolph to return to Washington. With the war ended, patriotism no longer hushed philosophical and ideological differences. Nationalism had reinvigorated the doctrine of states' rights. The Panic of 1819 had brought the Bank of the United States to disrepute. Sectional differences regarding the tariff, slavery, and internal improvements were causing southerners to lament releasing the genie of centralized government. The Republican principles of 1898 were ascendant, and their greatest champion was returning to the arena.

"I find myself very well received here," Randolph wrote upon his arrival in Washington. He noted that only "an old minority man or two and some ultra federalists now become ultra loyalists" were cool to him.[13] These men tended to avoid him, he chuckled, lest their past connection be remembered to their prejudice.[14] Randolph hailed these signs in the political horizon with "some degree of pleasure." Perhaps, he said, the nation was "coming back to the good old times of responsibility and specification."[15]

Randolph celebrated his return with a rollicking night of drinking at a local tavern. He "was in prime Twigg" and put away enough "to last a full-blooded Yankee his lifetime."[16] His good humor, enhanced by imbibed spirits, prompted him to sing an old drinking song: "Back and sides go bare, go bare, hands and feet go cold. So I am lapp'd and soundly capp'd, with jolly good ale and old."[17]

Randolph's next congressional fight sprang from the request of the Missouri Territory for admission into the Union. When the enabling act reached the House, Representative James Tallmadge proposed an amendment prohibiting slavery in Missouri. The South cried foul. Slavery was recognized in the Constitution, but if the Congress could prohibit slavery in Missouri, where it would stay its hand? The Missouri bill passed the House, but failed in the Senate. Circumstances changed further when Maine applied for admission as a state. Henry Clay and others saw an opportunity for a compromise.[18] Missouri would be admitted as a slave state and Maine as a free state. Future controversies in federal territories would be avoided by prohibiting slavery in all states formed north of the thirty-six-degree, thirty-minute latitudinal line, and allowing slavery south of the same line.[19]

The Missouri question kept Randolph awake at night. He believed the issue touched on "every political relation."[20] He feared it would spark a fanaticism toward slavery, with northerners fixated on abolition and southerners determined to protect the institution.[21] He was joined in this sentiment by his adversary, Thomas Jefferson, who wrote that the Missouri issue, "like a fire bell in the night," was "the knell of the union."[22] Randolph sat unusually quiet in the House chamber, listening to the debate "on the principle that a soldier would not ask for a furlough the day before a general engagement."[23] After Representative John Sergeant made a particularly forceful speech in favor of the restriction on slavery, Randolph handed out a rare compliment. "Never speak again," he said, grasping Sergeant's hand. "Never speak again, Sir!"[24]

Randolph's position was forming along familiar precepts. He opposed the compromise, believing Missouri should be admitted—if at all—on its own merits and not as a balance to Maine. The choice of an abstract latitudinal line to determine the slave status of future states was, as Russell Kirk capsulized his argument, "an endeavor to gloss over a terrible problem by the application of a coat of generalities and a superficial reconciliation of interests."[25] Randolph declared that his zeal to suppress the slave trade "was not surpassed by that of any man in the nation," but the federal government could not do "under the plea of means, which it could not under that of ends."[26] As with almost every political issue, the Missouri issue came down to a question of power. Northern interests were trying to subjugate the South. "God has given us the Missouri," Randolph concluded, "and the devil shall not take it from us."[27]

Randolph addressed the Missouri question on February 22, 1820. He reported that he spoke for "more than two hours" to "as attentive an audience as ever listened to a public speaker."[28] Clay, no doubt knowing what was coming, left the Speaker's chair and listened from the rear of the chamber, alternatively pacing and taking snuff.[29] The chamber hushed as Randolph spoke—"you might have heard a pin drop upon the carpet," he noted—but his words have been lost to history. The *Annals of Congress* did not publish Randolph's remarks.[30] Fragments from various sources indicate that Randolph spoke on the constitutionality of the proposal, while dropping hints that the southern delegations might leave the Congress if the compromise was adopted.[31] Randolph's speech, recalled one observer, was "brilliant and beautiful; full of classical learning and allusion."[32] John Quincy Adams left his usual scathing review. "Egotism, Virginian aristocracy, slave-scourging liberty, religion, literature, science, wit, fancy, generous feeling, and malignant passions," he wrote, "constitute a chaos in his mind, from which nothing orderly can ever flow."[33]

At some point during his remarks, Randolph noticed Clay hovering in the rear of the chamber, "sedulously and affectedly" avoiding eye contact. "The rules of this House, sir," Randolph snapped, "require, and properly require, every member when he speaks to address himself respectfully to Mr. Speaker." That rule, he continued, implied the Speaker, in like manner, would listen. As he "found the Chair resolutely bent on not attending to me," he would sit down.[34] Clay headed back toward the Speaker's dais, suddenly finding himself face-to-face with Randolph, who had stepped into the aisle. "Ah, Mr. Speaker," Randolph growled, "I wish you would quit the chair and leave the House. I will follow you to Kentucky, or anywhere else."[35] All eyes were fixed on the two adversaries, both known to defend themselves with canes, whips, or pistols. Clay did not react to the carefully worded insult, and the two men met the next day to discuss the issue. Clay found Randolph "unyielding and uncompromising to the last."[36]

Randolph spoke on February 25, and again, for "more than four hours," on February 26.[37] "The crowd was immense," he wrote. "It would have been . . . affectation to have pretended ignorance that they were assembled to hear me speak."[38] Clay viewed the reaction of the House and worried that the Old Quid was besting him. Randolph's words and acts, he said, were "near shaking the Union to the center and desolating this fair land."[39] The *Annals* maintained its blackout. Randolph was seen but not heard beyond the stuffy House chamber.

His orations were punctuated with the wheezes of a ravaged lung, and his stamina was sapped by debilitating diarrhea.[40] The House chamber was a ripe habitat for disease. "It smells like a badly kept comodite," Randolph wrote, "in addition to ordure and urine . . . stale tobacco smoke . . . a compound of villainous smells."[41] Still, Randolph talked on, delivering his final unreported speech on March 1.[42]

The compromise package seemed doomed, so Clay split the measures into three separate bills—admission of Missouri as a slave state, admission of Maine as a free state, and elimination of slavery in new states north of the 36/30 line—thereby utilizing different voting alliances to pass each one. Randolph watched in disgust as some northern congressmen voted in favor of individual pieces of legislation that they opposed when packaged together. Randolph dubbed them "doughfaces," men "whose conscience, and morality, and religion, extend to thirty-six degrees and thirty minutes north latitude."[43] The artfully packaged compromise passed. "The slaveholding interest," Randolph wrote, "has been sacrificed by southern and western men from slaveholding states, who have wanted to curry favor for very obvious purposes."[44]

Not prepared to give up, Randolph spoke at "considerable length" on March 3, and moved the House to reconsider its vote.[45] Clay was in no mood to hear the motion and ruled that the matter would be considered the next day. By the time Randolph rose on March 4 to renew his motion, Clay had signed the Missouri bill and sent it to the Senate. Randolph appealed to his colleagues, but Clay's slight-of-hand was upheld by a vote of seventy-one to sixty-one.[46] "Notorious as these facts are," Randolph wrote, "so anxious was one side of that House to cover up their defection; such was the anxiety of the other to get Missouri in on any conditions, that this thing was hushed up." Missouri was admitted, he gruffly concluded, "contrary to the Constitution."[47] In this instance, Randolph was uncharacteristically short-sighted. He had resurrected the states' rights argument but had linked it irreparably to the slavery issue. Thus he forever tainted states' rights and virtually eliminated it as a future protection against centralization.[48]

Randolph seemed to have achieved a fragile equilibrium in mind, if not in body, during the Missouri debate.[49] It was not to last. On March 22, Commodore Stephen Decatur, a naval hero of the War of 1812 and a friend of Randolph, was killed in a duel.[50] Randolph reacted violently to Decatur's death, exhibiting anger and vindictiveness toward anyone who crossed his path.[51] He declared he would produce his own pistol and respond to any perceived insult in the same manner dealt his friend.[52] He spoke twice on the House floor, his emotions consuming him, aggravating his already extravagant personality.[53] He proposed that all House members wear black crepe on their left arms, and followed that with a motion that the House adjourn for the funeral. Both motions were rejected by an uncomfortable House.[54] Judge William Leigh, a longtime friend, viewed these actions as proof that Randolph had lost his mind.[55] Randolph continued to make a spectacle of himself at Decatur's funeral. Many viewed him with sympathy, granting grace to a grieving friend. John Quincy Adams would have none of it. He described Randolph at the funeral "first walking, then backing his horse, then calling for his phaeton, and lastly crowding up to the vault, as the coffin was removed into it from the hearse—tricksy humors to make himself conspicuous."[56] Observers turned away, embarrassed or disgusted.

Frenetic activity followed. He dashed off a will, granting freedom to his slaves and expressing regret at ever being an owner. He appeared at a bank in Richmond and asked for red ink to write a check. "I now go for blood," he chillingly told Mr. Anderson, the cashier. Completing the check, he signed his name and added "X, his mark" beside it.[57] Shortly after that curious moment, Mr. Anderson was walking to the bank when he heard Randolph's shrill voice calling his name. Randolph inquired if he knew of any ships leaving for England. Anderson suggested Randolph leave from New York City. The eyes flashed. "Do you think," Randolph said, "I would give my money to those who are ready to make my negroes cut my throat?" Thus rebuked, Anderson recalled that one ship was nearby on the James River and might be of service—the *Henry Clay*. Randolph threw his arms in the air. "The *Henry Clay*?" he exclaimed, "No, sir! I will never step on the planks of a ship of that name!" Anderson hastily bid a good day.[58]

Back among the shades of Roanoke, Randolph was tormented by "strange phantasies."[59] He rejoiced in "the pure wells of English undefiled . . . Chaucer and Dryden," but labored under a melancholy that made "death desirable."[60]

The isolation of Roanoke was both tonic and torment. "You do not overrate the solitariness of the life I lead here," he wrote to Theodore Dudley. "It is dreary beyond conception."[61] He would escape if he could, but concluded he "must remain a prisoner here, probably for the brief remainder of my life."[62] Yet at the moments when he seemed about to succumb to mortal despair, he would hear the "warbling of the birds and the barking of the squirrels around my window" or sit astride "a very gentle saddle horse."[63] Work ethic was his balance wheel. Life "was not given us to be spent in dreams and reverie," he wrote in a period of sound mind, "but for action, useful exertion; exertion that turns to some account to ourselves, or to others—not laborious idleness."[64]

By the end of 1821, Senator Elijah Mills wrote that Randolph was again "what he used to be in his best days; in good spirits, with fine manners and the most fascinating conversation."[65] In Washington, Randolph resided at Dawson's House, where he found himself "better off both with respect to accommodation and society."[66] His housemates might have differed. "At all hours of the night," Senator Thomas Hart Benton wrote, "[he] was accustomed to tap at my door very softly." Benton would invite him in, and Randolph would "sit on the bed and talk with me in the dark."[67] During normal hours, Randolph found himself the guest at the best Washington tables, dining on separate occasions with Chief Justice John Marshall, Treasury Secretary William Crawford, and Senator Martin Van Buren.[68] He even attended a dinner at the White House, during which he thought he observed an "unqualified expression of misery" in the countenance of President Monroe.[69]

Randolph's sympathy for his former colleague-in-arms went only so far. He still blamed the trio of Virginia presidents for the destruction of Republican principles. Jefferson "did much to impair the principles upon which he was brought into power," and Madison "gave them the *coup de grâce*." Both men—and those like them—had reconciled "with the Holy Catholic Church of Expediency and Existing Circumstances." His former friend Monroe "came in upon no principles, and as he brought none with him, so he will carry none away with him."[70]

In the wake of his stand against the Missouri compromise, Randolph found a number of new adherents among his congressional colleagues. "Like the long waists of our mothers," he wrote, "I really believe I am growing, if not generally, at least somewhat, in fashion."[71] He noted that the House was "not yet becoming tired of me" and that he would "take especial care that it does not."[72] Though the familiar aches and pains coursed through his body, Randolph noted that he "was the liveliest man in the whole company; and, like Falstaff, was not only merry myself, but the cause of mirth in others."[73] He was primed for another fight.

The census of 1820 officially reported what thousands of Americans had confirmed with their feet: the population of the United States was shifting to the West. The old colonies were losing population. This demographic change required a change in the composition of the House of Representatives. Either the number of members would have to be increased, or the ratio of representation per member would have to be increased. A consensus developed in favor of the latter course. Several proposals were considered, but the primary Apportionment Bill raised the size of unit per congressman to 1 to 40,000. Under that plan, Virginia would lose at least one congressional seat. Randolph eagerly entered the fray, knowing "there is a moral assurance that the majority is pretty decidedly against me."[74]

Randolph's opposition was founded on several principles. First was his belief that a representative should be close to his constituents and their interests. The larger the population of the district, the less opportunity for that vital contact. This relationship served not only the constituents of the respective district, but also the overall cause of the Republic. "Government," he asserted in the first of six speeches he delivered against the Apportionment Bill, "to be safe and to be free, must consist of representatives having a common interest and a common feeling with the represented. . . . [N]o government extending from the Atlantic to the Pacific can be fit to govern me or those whom I represent."[75]

Randolph favored a maximum ratio of 1 to 38,000 and would let House membership increase "as numerous as the Constitution would permit."[76] In addition to maintaining the proper relation between citizen and representative, this plan would ensure that Virginia did not lose any seats. This underlying reason was never far from the surface of Randolph's opposition to the bill. He could not abide the thought that Virginia's influence might be diminished. "I cannot vote for any number," he said, "which should go to shear one single beam from the State of Virginia."[77] He scorned recently admitted states as ungrateful family members. "The new states," he said, "had never called and found [the old states] wanting in fraternal aid." Now, he glumly concluded, "we are not considered as entitled even to equality in that character."[78]

Randolph was at his oratorical best during the debate, recalling days long past. "Since my first . . . opposition to the Yazoo bill," he wrote, "I have never spoken with such effect upon the House."[79] He gently chided opponents "who seemed to think that He who made the world should have consulted them about it." He expressed the wish that he could "once see a Congress meet and adjourn without passing any law whatsoever." When one member announced he had not been sent to Congress to make himself agreeable, Randolph tendered to the gentleman "his sincere congratulations that he had been able so successfully to attain the purpose which he may have been sent for."[80] Randolph was invigorated by the issue and the debate. "Yesterday I rose at 3, and today at 2 a.m.," he wrote on the day of the final vote. "I cannot sleep. Two bottles of champagne, or a dozen of gas, could not have excited me like this apportionment bill."[81]

Though he was concerned with the ratio figure and with Virginia's declining power, Randolph's opposition was based on his contempt for abstract theories. Enshrining a random number in the law was nothing more than egalitarianism supplanting tradition, mathematical formulas trumping common sense. "It strikes me," he said on the last day of debate, "that we are pursuing theoretical principles, which ought never to have been permitted to find their way into this Government, to lengths from which eventually the most abstract and metaphysical must recoil." This was the faux equality he viewed as the chief enemy of liberty, an equality "subversive even of the principles of our government and of every principle of union."[82]

Randolph had made another good showing, probably his best since the speech against Gregg's Resolution, but it was for another lost cause. The Apportionment Bill, fixing the ratio at 1 to 40,000, was passed by a decisive vote. "We may now cry out 'Ichabod,'" Randolph wrote, "for our glory is departed."[83]

One month later, Randolph boarded the *Amity* headed for New York, from whence he would travel to Liverpool, England, aboard the steamship *Nautilus*. "Thank God," he exclaimed, "that I have lived to behold the land of Shakespeare, of Milton, of my forefathers!"[84] Randolph spent nearly six months in England, and, as always, he was the object of popular stare. "John Randolph is here and has attracted much attention," Washington Irving wrote. "His eccentricity of appearance and manner make him the more current and interesting; for, in high life here, they are always eager after anything strange and peculiar."[85] Irving admitted, however, that Randolph was more than a side-show. There was something in his "manner, the turn of his thoughts and the style of his conversation" that drew Englishmen to him.

He spent time in illustrious company: George Canning, foreign secretary and future prime minister; Lord Castlereagh, Irish politician and representative to the Congress of Vienna; and Sir Robert Peel, future prime minister. He shared the platform with the abolitionist William Wilberforce at a meeting of the African Institution. In his brief remarks, he condemned the "infamous traffic" of slaves and asserted that Virginia "had for half a century affixed a public brand, an indelible stigma upon this traffic, and had put in the claims of the wretched objects of it to the common rights and attributes of humanity."[86] He sat down, *The Times* reported, to loud applause.

Randolph returned from Europe, Senator Thomas Hart Benton observed, "calm, self-possessed, poised, everything right, natural, and proper."[87] Although the usual complaints about health would creep back into his letters, Randolph's spirits were greatly improved by his travels. "My health," he wrote, "has astonishingly improved within the last fortnight."[88] He was back in the saddle, hunting and shooting, and attending local races.[89] The woods around Roanoke, he wrote, displayed "that indescribable loveliness which shames all the vaunted beauties of spring. No pencil could plain the colors that present themselves to my eyes from the window where I am now writing."[90]

Beyond the hues of fall foliage, political storms were gathering. The forces of modernism were crafting a program of high taxation, increased spending, and far-reaching government projects. Like an actor in an annual Greek tragedy, Randolph would again be the prophet warning of the consequences of deviating from first principles.

15

A Fig for the Constitution

Too honest or too proud to feign
A love he never cherished,
Beyond Virginia's border line
His patriotism perished.

Randolph was fifty years old. Twenty-four years had passed since he had snapped "ask my constituents" to Speaker Sedgwick. He had been a representative for all but four of those years and had outlasted or outlived most of his friends and foes. The new order he had so vigorously fought was firmly in place, the old Virginia fading further in memory. He had considered retiring to Roanoke but was pulled by the desire to fight ancient enemies. "We are arrived at that pitch of degeneracy," he wrote, "when the mere lust of power, the retention of place and patronage, can prevail, not only over every consideration of public duty, but stifle the suggestions of personal honor."[1] So he took his seat in the familiar House chamber, his withered face repelling and attracting, his body shrouded in layers of coats and cloaks.

James Monroe's seventh annual message to Congress was an invitation to joust. The president recommended a survey for the construction of a Chesapeake and Ohio canal, a seemingly mild proposal, but the first move in the direction of federally funded internal improvements. Monroe next suggested "a revision of the tariff," which implied an increase. Such a policy would protect domestic—primarily northern—manufacturers, would provide funds for more government works—primarily in the North and West—and would disproportionally affect the pockets of the South. Finally, almost in passing, the president expressed sympathy for the "heroic struggle of the Greeks" in their fight for independence from the Turks.[2]

The president's address contained all the elements of Henry Clay's "American System"—federally funded internal improvements, a higher tariff, and an activist foreign policy. Clay believed his comprehensive policy served two purposes: it would advance the growth and prosperity of the nation, and it would propel him to the presidency. Now that Monroe had presented this package, Clay was "determined to make the session an engine for his advancement."[3] He would use every trick in his well-documented little book to ensure victory, both in Congress and in the coming election. "Clay's eye is on the Presidency," Randolph remarked, "and my eye is on him."[4]

Randolph no longer affected surprise at the zeitgeist of his old party. Clay's "American System" was the bastard offspring of the Yazoo settlement and assorted dalliances with Federalist policies. It was unconstitutional, but that obstacle had never slowed the forces of modernism and consolidation. "The constitution," Randolph wrote, "is always what the majority pleases it shall be. All prohibitions, checks, etc., of mere parchment and ink are gull-traps for that monster the multitude."[5] He viewed the president with bemused disdain. "Poor M!" he wrote. "He has been dreaming for the last twenty years and is at last awake to his true condition."[6] For his part, Monroe had reached the same conclusion about Randolph as had his three predecessors. He was, the president would remark, "a capital hand to pull down, but I am not aware that he has ever exhibited much skill as a builder."[7]

The Greek issue appeared innocuous. The Greeks, long subjected to the rule of the Ottoman Empire, had revolted in 1821. Americans naturally identified with any people seeking freedom, a sentiment Monroe recognized in his message. Following the president's lead, and with Clay's support, Daniel Webster introduced a resolution calling for the appointment of a commissioner to Greece.[8] This act amounted to tacit recognition of the Greek revolutionaries. Randolph immediately dubbed the resolution "quixotism," and suggested the House sleep on the matter.[9] Clay took to the floor. "Has there," he mocked, "been no pillow reflections on such a subject? Is it now that we are for the first time to 'sleep upon it?' I trust not."[10] Randolph sighed. "I have, indeed, learned, from much higher authority than that of the gentleman from Kentucky, that our passions may sometimes instruct our reason."[11] The sparring between Clay and Randolph elevated the seemingly mundane resolution. Henry Dwight of Massachusetts watched the spirited exchange between the long-time antagonists and praised "the magic wand of the eloquence of the gentleman from Virginia, and the honorable Speaker of the House."[12]

Webster's reputation as an unexcelled orator was already well established when he rose on January 19, 1824, before a packed chamber to speak in favor of his resolution. He was not yet the portly bald figure of later years but a vigorous forty-two-year-old with dark eyes that rivaled Randolph's own in intensity. His complexion reminded observers of the sky before an incoming thunderstorm, earning him the nickname "Black Dan." His voice, like that of Randolph, made an indelible impression on listeners, but there the similarity ended. Webster's voice was rich and sonorous, perfect in pitch, phonetically thrilling. Zeus could have sent the Greeks no stronger advocate than the "godlike Daniel."

Webster extolled the virtues of the valiant Greeks and articulated the responsibilities of the United States. "Whenever a nation attempts to obtain its freedom," he said, "our side of that question ought to be known and declared; we are bound to bring, in aid of its decision, that moral force which must ever reside in the opinion of a free and intelligent nation."[13] He would "not stand by and see my fellow man drowning without stretching out a hand to help him." This help need not be military, only "some token of compassionate regard" from the "great Republic of the earth."[14] The world was weighing all forms of government, he said, "let us speak well of what has done well for us. We shall have the thinking world with us."[15]

Randolph was not intimidated. "Webster is like everybody else," he would later say, "except that there is more of him."[16] Randolph began his major speech on the Greek question by quoting Webster's description of the resolution as "almost nothing, a speck in the political horizon." But, he said, "it is from clouds of that portent in the moral and political as well as the natural atmosphere, that storms, the most disastrous in consequences, usually proceed."[17] The resolution represented "a total and fundamental change of the policy pursued by this Government . . . from the foundations of the Republic, to the present day."[18] In words that could be drawn from twenty-first-century headlines, Randolph asked if the nation was "to go on a crusade, in another hemisphere, for the propagation of two objects as dear and delightful to my heart as to that of any gentleman . . . liberty and Religion[?]"[19] If so, he warned, the nation was wandering into an area and among a people about which it understood little. The character of the "Moslems," he warned, "is a peculiar one; they differ from every other race," and the Koran is "a mysterious book . . . which enjoins . . . all good Moslems to propagate its doctrines at the point of the sword."[20] This race and religion had dominated this distant area of the world "before this country was discovered" and their policy was "straight forward . . . they held by the sword."[21] They were a people who "could boast of being the only one of the powers of continental Europe, whose capital had never been insulted by the presence of a foreign military force."[22] These were considerations, Randolph judged, "worthy of attention before we embark in [this] project . . . the consequences of which no human eye can divine."[23]

Taking such action in defense of the Greeks would establish a precedent that would entrap the nation in countless future battles. "Suppose the people of the British colony to the North of us undertake to throw off the yoke," he asked, "are you ready to stake the peace and welfare and the resources of this nation in support of Canada's independence?"[24] This was the logical consequence of taking the side of the Greeks. "The man who cannot pursue the inference," he scoffed, "would not recognize my picture, though, like the Dutchman's painting, was written under it, 'this is the man, that the horse.'"[25]

"Let us adhere to the policy laid down by [George Washington]," Randolph concluded, "the policy of peace, commerce, and honest friendship with all nations, entangling alliances with none; for to entangling alliances we must come, if you once embark on projects such as this."[26] Randolph sat down. It had been an impressive performance. His speech was tightly reasoned, eloquently stated, and free of panegyric. Webster responded with force. When he finished, the chamber was silent. No member wished to follow the two legislative titans. Representative Timothy Fuller remarked that he felt like "Poor King Richard, when 'as in a theatre, the eyes of men / After a well graced actor leaves the stage / are idly bent on him that enters next.'"[27] Randolph had bested Webster. The House took no action on the Greek resolution.

Clay could survive defeat on a minor resolution, but not on federal funding of internal improvements, the indispensable first element of his "American System." It would build roads for manufacturers, and pave his road to the White House. He would leave this bill to no surrogate. He would present the argument, he would square off with Randolph.

Internal improvements, Clay stated, were implied in the Constitution. They were necessary and proper to enumerated powers. How so? The Constitution authorized the establishment of post offices and granted control of interstate commerce to the federal government. Post offices and commerce implied roads, both building and maintaining them. The power to regulate commerce, he continued, for it to have any meaning at all, must imply "authority to foster it, promote it, to bestow on it facilities similar to those which have been conceded to our foreign trade."[28] Clay found "grammatical criticism . . . always unpleasant," but he countered Randolph's definition of terms. The power "to establish post roads being in its nature original and creative, and the Government having adopted the roads . . . the controverted power is expressly granted to Congress, and there is the end of the question."[29]

Randolph did not interrupt Clay. He sat huddled in his numerous coats, his hat pulled down over his eyes. The words were nothing he had not heard before. They were the natural and inescapable consequence of the Yazoo Bill and the Florida Purchase. The Republican principles that held the government in check, once abandoned, could do nothing to halt the Leviathan. He allowed himself a smile, though, as he listened. He judged Clay's speech "the poorest display that I ever saw . . . pitiful, wondrous pitiful."[30]

"I have never been insensible to my numerous failures as a publick speaker," Randolph wrote to James Garnett, shortly before addressing the House; "on the contrary, I believe not one of the audiences have been so deeply impressed with the sense of them as myself."[31] Likewise, he was cognizant of his "more fortunate and happy efforts." When he rose on January 30 to speak against federal funding for internal improvements, Randolph was on the verge of a very happy effort.

Randolph would attempt to respond to the Speaker's argument, he said, "if indeed . . . amid the mass of words in which it was enveloped, [I am] able to find it."[32] Clay had put the House in a "curious predicament," he continued, "precisely the reverse of Moliere's citizen turned gentleman, who discovered, to his great surprise, that he had been talking 'prose' all his life long without knowing it."[33] And it was on this topic of language that Randolph launched his first assault on the bill. "One would suppose," he mused, "that if anything could be considered as settled by precedent in legislation, the meaning of the words of the Constitution must, before this time, have been settled. . . . And yet, we are now gravely debating on what the word 'establish' shall be held to mean!"[34]

It was by such "dexterous exchanging and substituting of words," Randolph asserted, that the liberty of the people would be sapped. This need not be so. Words not written in the Constitution were not to be considered, words in the Constitution were to be strictly construed. Such a word was "commerce." The commerce clause, Randolph asserted, "grew out of the necessity, indispensable and unavoidable, in the circumstances of this country, of some general power, capable of regulating foreign commerce . . . [and] the difficulties which grew out of the conflicting laws of the States."[35] If the Constitution had included an ad valorem tax of 10 percent, he posited, it never would have been ratified. Thus, the Founders intended that Congress should exercise very limited power over the economy. If any other interpretation was applied, Randolph argued, Congress would have the authority to prohibit domestic commerce in the same fashion as Jefferson's embargo had shut down foreign trade.[36]

Randolph's mind turned to "the last words of Patrick Henry . . . now ringing in my ears." During their debate at Charlotte Courthouse, Henry had warned of the potential "unlimited power over the purse and the sword consigned to the General Government."[37] Now, consolidated federal power perched vulture-like over the American body politic, far transcending even Alexander Hamilton.[38] "Let us," Randolph pleaded, "come to the plain, common-sense construction of the Constitution." He presented a concise construction: "the given power will not lie, unless, as in the case of direct taxes, the power is specifically given—and even then the States have a concurrent power."[39]

If another construction was adopted, the "parchment barriers" protecting the liberties of the people and the rights of the states would be ever breached. Randolph listed a string of horribles surely to follow this ill-conceived policy: regulation of commerce within states, restrictions of specific goods, federal jurisdiction of rivers and lakes, federal labor standards, fraud and corruption in government contracts, enactment of sedition laws, and government spending in the millions.[40] "Are gentleman aware," he asked, "of the colossal power they are granting to the General Government?"[41] In the final analysis, this legislation was about power: its source, its extent, its limits, its dangers. He reminded his southern colleagues of their particular vulnerability. "If Congress possesses the power to do what is proposed by this bill," he warned, "they may emancipate every slave in the United States."[42] Any Constitution so malleable, liberties so sophistic, rights so transitory, could not long sustain a confederated republic. In such circumstances, "it is the power of the States to extinguish this Government at a blow."[43]

Clay struck back hard, accusing Randolph of extremism. "Are we to forget the wants of our country," he asked. "Are we to neglect and refuse the redemption of that vast wilderness? . . . I trust not, sir, I hope for better things."[44] Taunting Randolph's background, he boasted that he "was born to no proud patrimonial estate; from my father I inherited only infancy, ignorance, and indigence."[45] From across the chamber came the response. "The gentleman might continue the alliteration," Randolph piped, "and add insolence."[46]

Clay, the snuff-pinching pragmatist, could never understand the ground upon which Randolph operated. "My conscience acquits me entirely of all blame towards that gentleman, throughout all our acquaintances," he wrote of Randolph. "He has ever been the assailant. I have ever been on the defensive."[47] Randolph would have argued the opposite: it was Clay who was ever assaulting established institutions and principles, with Randolph offering solitary defense. This time, the battle went to Clay. The House passed the survey bill by a vote of 115 to 86.

Clay took the lead on the Tariff debate, speaking on March 30, 1824, for more than four hours. "Let us calm our passions," he urged his colleagues. "The sole object of the tariff is to tax the produce of foreign industry, with a view of promoting American industry." It would not unduly burden any man or section because "no man pays . . . by compulsion, but voluntarily." The South's fears were unfounded, its demands unreasonable. "Can it be expected," he asked, "that the interests of the greater part should be made to bend to the condition of the servile part of any population?" Clay spoke, he told the House, for "the cause of the country . . . founded in the interests and affections of the people . . . as native as the granite deeply embosomed in our mountains." That policy, he concluded, would lead the nation "to riches, to greatness, to glory."[48]

Again, Randolph watched Clay and, again, he was not impressed. Clay, he wrote, "made five [sic] speeches, bad, worse, worst, most worst, worserer and worsest."[49] He thought over his strategy. One reason the Internal Improvements Bill passed was that the legislation called for only taking a survey. It was still possible for Congress to act in subsequent years to avoid the calamities Randolph foresaw. The Tariff Bill, however, contained no similar margin for error. It was an immediate increase in rates. Interests only nominally affected by the survey of a northern canal would reel under the blow of an increased tariff. The South had no manufacturers to protect, but grew the cotton, rice, and other agricultural goods that comprised five-sixths of the nation's exports. Randolph knew this vote would be far closer.

He decided to attack the bill with guerilla tactics: circling it, taunting it, probing it for weaknesses. One day he rose to speak, and the members settled in for a lengthy address. "Sufficient for the day is the evil thereof," he said, and no more.[50] A short time later, he stood gazing about the chamber, musing that he "had no particular relish to encounter windmills of any kind, but of all the windmills that ever would appall the imagination of Don

Quixote himself, defend me from windmills that go by water."[51] On April 8, he spoke for less than ten minutes about the effect of the tariff on slavery, and on April 10 he reverted to his old parliamentary tricks and forced votes on specific duties on tea, frying pans, and brown sugar.[52] Tiring of these skirmishes, Louis McLane of Delaware, "appearing to be much irritated," barked that Randolph "had displayed a good head, but he would not accept that gentleman's head, to be obliged to have his heart along with it."[53] McLane sat mute as Randolph replied that he "would not, in return, take that gentleman's heart, good it may be, if obliged to take such a head in the bargain."[54]

All this was but prelude. On April 15, the House prepared to vote on the tariff bill. "I come to the discharge of this task," Randolph began, "not merely with reluctance, but with disquiet; jaded, worn down, abraded."[55] This bill might be a component of what was called an "American system," but it was a purely sectional bill. Not American at all, but "an attempt to reduce the country south of Mason and Dixon's line, and east of the Allegany Mountains, to a state worse than colonial bondage; a state to which the domination of Great Britain was, in my judgment, far preferable."[56] Randolph reduced the issue to one of power. The south produced the goods that generated the tariff duties. The north wanted that money and they had the votes. But more than this, if Congress again blinked at the Constitution, no liberties were safe.[57] "With all the fantastic and preposterous theories about the rights of man," he thundered, "there is nothing but power that can restrain power."[58] He paused. "I do not stop here, sir, to argue about the constitutionality of this bill; I consider the Constitution a dead letter. . . . You may entrench yourself in parchment to the teeth, says Lord Chatham, the sword will find its way to the vitals of the Constitution. I have no faith in parchment, sir; I have no faith in the abracadabra of the Constitution; I have no faith in it. I *have* faith in the power of that Commonwealth of which I am an unworthy son."[59]

He had been coming to this moment for years. He had defended his principles, fought and lost against the powers and principalities of the new order. But always he had relied on the words of the Constitution. Always he had expressed the belief that in that document were the rights of his fellow freeholders secure, even amid misguided policies. But he had seen the hammer blows descending on it, starting with the *Marbury* case, the consolidation of federal power, and continuing in vote after unconstitutional vote on the House floor. He had reached the moment when he saw that the Constitution meant nothing to those casting the votes. He knew its worth in such an era.

"A fig for the Constitution!" he snapped.[60]

Randolph saw excisemen swooping into homes, searching the premises, "even the privacy of female apartments," measuring, gauging, and weighing everything, levying a tax, and telling the hapless owner that "the tax is a voluntary one."[61] He urged prudence and patience before embarking on this policy path. "The devil," he observed, "is bent on mischief, and always in a hurry."[62]

Randolph had been in Congress long enough to learn how to count votes. The division over the tariff was close, but he might have sensed that Clay would achieve this second prong of his system. He warned the House of the consequence of the vote. "[There] is no magic in this word *union*," he said. "Marriage itself is a good thing, but the marriages of Mezentius were not so esteemed. . . . And just such a union will this be, if, by a bare majority in both Houses, this bill shall become a law."[63]

"We shall not give in," he repeated several times. It was Clay and nationalists and reprobate Republicans who were creating the animosity boiling in the House chamber and festering across the nation. These forces were riveting chains upon a free and peaceful people. And if blood was to be spilled, Randolph concluded, it made no difference "whether it be by the British Parliament or the American Congress."[64]

Clay worked the cloakrooms and halls, saloons and gaming tables, to tack down every stray vote. On April 16, the Tariff Bill passed by a vote of 107 to 102. The average rate of duty was 37 percent—twice the rate adopted in 1816. Randolph heard the tally announced and exclaimed: "when Jesus therefore had received the vinegar, He said, 'it is finished,' and He bowed His head and gave up His ghost!"[65]

Randolph's steadfast stand against encroaching federal power resonated across Virginia. His constituents praised him as "the guardian Genius of the Constitution" and a "Master Spirit" of public policy.[66] "May the ability, independence, and eloquence," a Fourth of July toast proclaimed, "with which he opposed the Greek question, the bill proposing necessary surveys for Internal Improvements, and the Tariff, endear him to every lover of peace, every friend of States' Rights, and every advocate of equal policy."[67] In the ever-whirling kaleidoscope of political alliances, Randolph found acceptance in the camps of old enemies. John C. Calhoun, now secretary of war, read Randolph's speeches, and they gave him pause. It was a turning point in his intellectual growth.[68] He turned from "the confidence and certainty of his early public career" to the internal foundry that would shape him into the cast-iron man.[69] Henry Adams judged Randolph's speeches "full of astonishingly clever touches."[70] The most stunning reversal of judgment came from atop a mountain in central Virginia. Thomas Jefferson declared Randolph one of his "companions in sentiment," and listed him with Madison, Monroe, and Macon, "all good men and true, of primitive principles."[71]

If Randolph was aware of these accolades, he made no comment. He had been judged ahead of his time and behind the times. All that was certain was that time was an illusive companion. "I have lived long enough and hope to die a freeholder," he announced to his constituents at session's end. "When I lose that distinction, I shall no longer have any reason to be proud of being your faithful servant."[72] He left Washington as soon as Congress adjourned, boarded the *Nestor*, and set off on his second trip to Europe.

Randolph spent a month in England before crossing the channel to France. "Here, then, am I," he wrote from Paris, "where I ought to have been thirty years ago."[73] Romantic recollections of the French Revolution were all Randolph found appealing in Paris. It was, he wrote, "the filthiest hole, not excepting the worst parts of the old town of Edinboro, that I ever saw *out of Ireland*."[74] He had not seen "anything that by possibility might be mistaken for a gentleman." He soon quit the city for the mountains of Switzerland. There he savored "the sublime scenery of the High Alps, and torrents and waterfalls, and mountains capped with perpetual snow, and fields of ice."[75] Belgium and Germany were on his itinerary before returning to England for the trip home. As was so often the case, disaster loomed. On the way to Liverpool, Randolph's coach overturned. He suffered a broken collarbone and two fractured ribs, "besides other damage."[76] The trip home was agony.

Randolph's swing through Europe had kept him out of the country during most of the presidential election. Calhoun had emerged as a favorite, but stumbled in several early caucuses. He became the consensus choice for vice-president. The remaining field was the political equivalent of an all-star game. There was Secretary of State John Quincy Adams, brilliant, vain, selfless, self-righteous, the architect of much of Monroe's success; Speaker of the House Henry Clay, champion of the "American System," confident, arrogant, witty, dramatic, a gambler at the card table and in the political arena; and Secretary of Treasury William Crawford, less known to posterity but at the time a formidable candidate, experienced, honest, resourceful, the favorite of the Old Republicans. Towering above them all was the people's choice: General Andrew Jackson. The nation's hero for more than a decade, Jackson embodied a new generation of Americans, rollicking men of the land, intrepid tamers of the West, ardent foes of banks, Indians, and intrusive government. The first seriously contested presidential election in more than twenty years promised to be equal parts dignified debate, cockfight, and backroom intrigue.

Randolph supported Crawford. "I look upon him," he wrote, "as the ablest man in our councils. . . . There is a singleness of heart about him, a plain, manly good sense, and a certain fairness of character that wins my regard and esteem. There is no trash in his understanding—no crooked, double dealing in his conduct." In addition to these strengths, Crawford compensated for the weaknesses of the other candidates. He was part of the Monroe Administration, without being John Quincy Adams; more of a Jeffersonian than Clay; and shared many of Jackson's positions, without the scandals that dogged the general. He was well positioned to become the nation's sixth president, but he suffered a series of paralytic strokes that left him mute and nearly blind. He was expected to recover, but that hope was years distant. He was no longer a serious contender. Nevertheless, Crawford finished third with forty-one electoral votes, ahead of Clay's thirty-seven, behind Adams's eighty-five. Andrew Jackson was first in electoral votes—with ninety-nine—and first in the popular vote—more than forty-thousand ahead of the field. First place, though, did not mean victory. As no candidate received a majority of electoral votes, the Constitution directed that the House of Representatives elect the president from the top three finishers. Thus Clay was constitutionally eliminated, even as Crawford was practically eliminated. The contest was between Jackson and Adams. Randolph returned from Europe just in time for the election's climactic scene.

Randolph continued to support Crawford, as did the entire Virginia delegation, along with the states of Delaware, Georgia, and North Carolina. Jackson held seven states—Tennessee, South Carolina, New Jersey, Pennsylvania, Indiana, Alabama, and Mississippi. Adams could count on the six New England states, plus Illinois and Maryland. New York was undecided. A total of thirteen states would be needed to win, so the remaining states of Kentucky, Ohio, Missouri, and Louisiana were critical. And there was the rub. These states were under the influence of Henry Clay. If he could not claim the prize himself, he could virtually select the man who would.

The capital was saturated with rumors. Clay, it was said, was looking for the best bargain, and Adams was eager to make a deal. Jackson supporters were allegedly mustering arms to march on Washington should their hero be denied. Jobs were promised, threats made, money exchanged. "How humiliating to the American character," Jackson wrote, "that its high functionaries should conduct themselves as to become liable to the interpretation of bargain and sale of the constitutional rights of the people!"[77] Actually, no bargain needed to be cut. Clay had no realistic alternative but to support Adams, a man much more politically compatible than Jackson. Still, Clay's reputation for near-blind ambition fueled the assumption that his support would come at a price. Randolph—knowing and disliking both Clay and Adams—reached the same conclusion.[78]

Representatives tramped through a heavy snow to reach the Capitol on election day, February 9, 1825. Clay had announced his support of Adams, despite the fact that the secretary of state had not received a single popular vote in Kentucky. Adams was one state shy of victory. The states caucused and voted. Randolph and Daniel Webster were elected tellers tasked with counting the votes. It was a dramatic moment when the two men returned. Webster's booming baritone announced "thirteen votes for Adams, seven for Jackson, four for Crawford." Randolph's voice, sounding even higher than usual in comparison with the resonant Webster, broke in with a correction. It was thirteen *states* for Adams.[79] Clay declared Adams elected amid a cacophony of cheers and jeers. Randolph's voice was heard above the ruckus: "It was impossible to win the game, gentlemen, the cards were stacked."[80] The enraged Jackson forces agreed, particularly when Adams announced that Clay would serve as secretary of state. What more evidence of a corrupt bargain was needed? Randolph's reaction was sardonic. "I bore some humble part in putting down the dynasty of John the First," he said, "and, by the grace of God, I hope to aid in putting down the dynasty of John the Second."[81]

Randolph had to attend to one more piece of gnawing business before leaving Washington for Roanoke. On February 21, 1825, he dispatched Senator Thomas Hart Benton to deliver a note to Daniel Webster. "I learn from unquestionable authority," Randolph wrote, "that during my late absence from the United States, you have indulged yourself in liberties with my name [aspersing my veracity] which no gentleman can take."[82] He demanded satisfaction, the details of which Benton would handle. Webster read and reread the note, mumbled a few words, and abruptly took leave of Benton.[83]

The genesis of Randolph's challenge went back more than nine months.

Senator Ninian Edwards of Illinois had leveled charges of mismanagement of public funds against William Crawford. Randolph and Webster were named to a committee to investigate the charges. It was a waste of time. Crawford's explanation, Randolph wrote, was "the most triumphant and irresistible answer that ever met the accusations of a base and perjured informer."[84] The rest of the committee agreed, and Webster drafted a report clearing Crawford of any wrongdoing. Before departing for Europe, Randolph wrote an open letter recounting the committee's investigation and implying that he had persuaded the committee to give Crawford an opportunity to respond to Edwards's charges. Webster's recollection differed, and upon Randolph's return from abroad, the two men had a brief exchange on the House floor.[85]

This started tongues wagging, and Randolph, believing his integrity questioned, issued a duel challenge. Webster authorized Benton to tell Randolph that he had "no recollection of having said anything" affecting Randolph's veracity. He meant to state only that Randolph "was under an entire mistake, or misapprehension as to the facts."[86] As occurred in almost every challenge in which Randolph was involved, an explanation was sufficient for settlement. "The matter has terminated to my entire satisfaction," he wrote, "by a formal written disclaimer on his part of any imputation on my veracity in the House or out of it."[87] The two men agreed to keep the matter confidential, and Webster proposed to "leave his card" at Randolph's lodging, certifying peace between the two men.[88]

Randolph's exertions caught up with him upon his return to Roanoke. His health was "wretched in the extreme," and he sensed "those internal motions . . . that convince me that I cannot hold out much longer."[89] He was treating himself with mercury and commented that he had lost his "grasp upon the world."[90] He made his standard biennial threat to leave public service, but his fellow freeholders would hear nothing of it. They overwhelmingly re-elected him to the House. "Two more years, if I live as long, in that bear garden," he groused. Yet on the horizon lurked another strange twist in his public life.

President Adams appointed Virginia Senator James Barbour to serve as secretary of war. The Virginia General Assembly met in December to select the new senator. Randolph's reputation was enjoying a resurgence, and his friends decided to nominate him for the Senate. On the first ballot, he finished second with sixty-three votes, two behind his half-brother, Henry St. George Tucker. Former Senator William Giles finished third with fifty-eight votes. Last place went to John Floyd, with forty votes, and, accordingly, he was dropped from the second ballot. Tucker's vote increased to eighty-seven, Randolph rose to seventy-nine, and Giles received sixty. Giles would be dropped from the third ballot, but before the vote was taken, Tucker announced that he did not wish to compete with his brother and withdrew. The somewhat stunned chamber was left with one candidate. John Randolph was Virginia's new United States Senator.[91]

Congress had already commenced when Randolph was elected. He resigned his House seat and strolled into the ornate Senate chamber on December 26, 1825. He was greeted by his childhood friend, Littleton Tazewell, now senator from Virginia, and Nathaniel Macon, his old ally from the House, now senator from North Carolina. Presiding over the Senate was newly elected Vice-President John C. Calhoun. Any hopes that a change in locale might work a change in Randolph were immediately dispelled.

"Mr. Speaker!" he said to Calhoun. "I mean Mr. President of the Senate and would-be President of the United States, which God in His infinite mercy avert."[92]

16

The Puritan and the Blackleg

His latest thought, his latest breath,
To Freedom's duty giving,
With failing tongue and trembling hand
The dying blest the living.

Martin Van Buren stands in history's hollow, obscured by the regnant figure of Andrew Jackson. When remembered at all, it is usually as the dandified "sweet-sandy whiskers," short in stature and achievement. This was not the Van Buren contemporaries knew in 1825. He was the shrewd senator who had tamed the New York political field and brought William Crawford within a stroke of the presidency. Now while others collected themselves in wake of the 1824 election, Van Buren was looking ahead. He grasped, swifter than other observers, that the next presidential election would not be another four-man free-for-all. It would be a grudge match between Andrew Jackson and John Quincy Adams. Van Buren put his New York machine squarely behind Jackson, but he realized that new alliances would be needed, new tactics required, perhaps even new parties established.[1] The times were particularly harsh and unpleasant, calling for equally harsh and unpleasant men. Across the Senate chamber, Van Buren saw such a man, "a most extraordinary man."[2] Randolph, he wrote, "was a man of extraordinary intelligence, well educated, well informed on most subjects, thoroughly grounded in the history and rationale of the Constitution . . . eloquent in debate and wielding a power of invective superior to that of any man of his day."[3]

Van Buren and Randolph began to spend many afternoons on horseback rides around Washington.[4] "Altho a devoted equestrian," Van Buren wrote, "I fell far short of him who was as much at home on horseback as an Arab." Van Buren was superior, however, in one key characteristic. He was a good listener, a trait Randolph was pleased to accommodate. Randolph, however, was not completely taken in during these "frequent and long rides." Van Buren, he knew, "rowed to his object with muffled oars."[5]

Not that Randolph needed Van Buren's prodding to oppose the Adams administration. "The days of John Adams have come again," he wrote. "It is now exactly twenty-five years since the latter fled like a thief in the night from the Palace—who then believed that the son was ever destined to occupy it?"[6] He called John Quincy Adams "the evil genius of the American House of Stuart" and "the son of the sedition-law president."[7] He confessed that much of his opposition came from "old animosity rankling in my heart, and, coming from a race who are known never to forsake a friend or forgive a foe," he could act no differently. But the new president introduced a program that guaranteed Randolph's ire. Adams called for federal expenditures for a network of roads and canals, regulation of natural resources, aid to education, a naval academy, and higher tariffs. "The consequences of the meretricious alliance between Old Massachusetts and that Bawd, Kentucky," Randolph wrote, referring to Adams and Clay, "begins to unfold itself."[8] From his new perch in the Senate, Randolph pledged not "to compromise with fraud, and falsehood, and villainy, in any shape."[9] This time Randolph was not alone. The Congress was overwhelmingly anti-administration and intent on scrapping the president's domestic program.

Familiar lines began to appear in the *Register of Debates:* Mr. Randolph "addressed the Senate nearly two hours," "opposed the resolution in a speech of three hours," "spoke repeatedly," "warmly opposed," "opposed the motion at considerable length," and "delivered a speech of nearly six hours."[10] Leaning against the railing as he spoke, Randolph would regularly turn to the doorkeeper and say, "Tims, more porter!" He would quickly down a tumbler of foaming liquid and, sufficiently fortified, continue his remarks.[11] "He talks on," Daniel Webster wrote, "for two, four, and sometimes *six* hours at a time, saying whatever occurs to him, on all subjects."[12] He spread papers and journals on the floor about him, and rebuked anyone who tried to tidy up. On one occasion it was reported that he undressed and dressed himself during the course of a speech.[13] The stolid decorum of the Senate had never witnessed such a spectacle. "I think," Senator Elijah Mills wrote, "he is partially deranged and seldom in the full possession of his reason."[14] Frustrated senators took to leaving the floor when Randolph spoke, but his soliloquies continued.[15]

Van Buren, a master political craftsman himself, appreciated "the severity of [Randolph's] invectives, the piquancy of his sarcasms, the piercing intonation of his voice, and his peculiarly expressive gesticulation."[16] He noted that Randolph's speeches were "more and more annoying the Administration and its friends, in and out of the Senate."[17] This fact alone made him a valued ally. "Whatever may have been his shortcomings," Van Buren wrote, "the political doctrine and principles which he advocated were well adapted to the support of a system like ours—indeed those only by which we can hope to uphold it in its integrity."[18] Calhoun, stone-faced and unemotional in the presiding officer's chair, concurred with Van Buren. "A man of remarkable genius," he mused, while making no attempt to restrain Randolph's histrionics. Calhoun's conversion from Randolph foe to admirer— and ultimate successor—was near complete. He judged Randolph to be "highly talented, eloquent, severe, and eccentric . . . uttering wisdom worthy of a Bacon, and wit that would not discredit a Sheridan."[19]

"I am very sorry that this book," Randolph said one day, holding aloft a copy of the Constitution, "is so seldom resorted to. It is like the Bible, in which we keep receipts, deeds, and never look into it except when we happen to want them."[20] As with all his speeches, Randolph made salient points amid his maze of wanderings. Careful listeners on March 2, 1826, heard Randolph again articulate his view of equality and how it applied in a civil body politic. Calhoun listened hard. "Sir, my only objection is that these principles, pushed to their extreme consequences—that all men are born free and equal—I can never assent to, for the best of reasons, because it is not true . . . even though I find it in the Declaration of Independence. . . . [I]f there is an animal on earth to which it does not apply—that is not born free, it is man. He is born in a state of the most abject want, and a state of perfect helplessness and ignorance, which is the foundation of his connubial tie."[21]

Here Randolph echoed Edmund Burke, rejected John Locke, and dissented from Thomas Jefferson. Men were not born equal—that was manifest by differences in birth, wealth, and physical and intellectual capacities. Rights were not abstract, nor could they be obtained at the expense of others. Rights flowed from the civic virtue exercised by free men within society. Such a civil society, stabilized by traditional institutions, secured freedom and checked inordinate passions. Randolph's reasoning was lost on his colleagues, as it has been misunderstood by subsequent generations. Russell Kirk offered the most succinct summary of Randolph's position. "To presume that a mystic 'equality' entitles the mass of mankind to tinker at pleasure with society, to play with it as a toy, to exercise their petty ingenuity upon it," Kirk wrote, "is to reduce mankind to the only state of life in which anything resembling equality of condition actually prevails: savagery."[22]

Randolph found himself increasingly sought out for counsel. "If I were to tell you," he wrote, "one half of the handsome things that were said to my by Tazewell, Macon, [Van Buren] of New York, Mr. V.P., and many others, you would justly think me as vain [as] a coxcomb."[23] Daniel Webster, alternatively frustrated and fascinated, paid social visits to Randolph, as did Thomas Hart Benton and John Marshall.[24] The most intriguing relationship was with Calhoun. Randolph took no small joy in taunting the solemn vice-president, but Calhoun looked beyond the insults and assiduously sought out his old foe. After one debate, he sent for Randolph, questioned him on a legislative matter, and assured him that his views were "strong and important."[25] "The V.P.," Randolph smirked, "has actually made love to me."[26] Randolph even went about mending some fences in his own way. He purchased five hundred dollars' worth of Jefferson lottery tickets—the somewhat sad relief program established by the Virginia legislature for the former president. "I should have voted for that bill if I had been there," Randolph commented.[27]

As always, Randolph's good spirits could vanish in a second. "At times, he is the most entertaining and amusing man alive, with manners the most pleasant and agreeable," Senator Elijah Mills wrote, "and, at other times, he is sour, morose, crabbed, ill-natured and sarcastic, rude in manners, and repulsive to everybody."[28] Watching a procedural vote go against him, Randolph stormed from the chamber, crying out: "I will have no more of this! . . . Good-bye Tazewell! Good-bye Van Buren! They are all against me! They are all against me, Tazewell, in Virginia too!"[29] It was an idle threat; he was going nowhere. A pet project of Henry Clay had seized his interest.

The Panama Congress was assembling to discuss matters of concern to the Americas, and an invitation was extended to the United States. President Adams, at Clay's urging, authorized American participation in the conference.[30] Congressional reaction was swift. Opposition centered on long-standing concerns about entangling alliances with foreign powers. This policy objection was matched by Jacksonian partisans determined to defeat all administration initiatives, and southern angst over American diplomats treating on an equal basis with black envoys. Van Buren skillfully weaved all opposition forces together to delay approval of Adams's ministerial appointments.[31] It fell to Randolph to deliver the rhetorical blast.

Randolph was at his acid-tongued best during his speech of March 30, 1826. Insightful and incoherent, humorous and disconcerting, the speech reads like an account from the Tower of Babel. "It is an infirmity of my nature," he said, "to have an obstinate constitutional preference of *the true* over the *agreeable*."[32] He suggested his opponents "retire to the obscurity that becomes their imbecility, or befits their shame, and they shall never hear from me the language of sarcasm or reproach."[33] He managed to touch briefly on the Panama Congress, condemning it as a useless foreign entanglement—"a Kentucky cuckoo's egg, laid in a Spanish American nest."[34]

The focus of the speech, however, was an unrelenting attack on the Adams administration and its first minister, Henry Clay. The president, he pronounced, "has determined to become the apostle of liberty, of universal liberty, as his father was, about the time of the formation of the Constitution, known to be the apostle of monarchy." He heaped verbal molten lava on Clay. "Since the revolution of 1801, the practice has been settled, that the Secretary of State shall succeed the President," he mused. "It has been the favorite post and position of every bad, ambitious man, whether apostate federalist or apostate republican, who wishes to get into the Presidency . . . *honestly if they may; corruptly if they must*."[35] He reminded his colleagues of the bargain "between the frost of January, and young, blithe, buxom, and blooming May—the eldest daughter of Virginia—young Kentucky—not so young, however, as not to make a prudent match, and sell his charms for their full value."[36]

The first hour passed, then the second, the words clattering and spreading like a box of ball bearings overturned on a marble floor. Then, drawing on the novel *Tom Jones*, Randolph likened Adams and Clay to two unsavory characters in the book. He had been beaten, he said, "defeated, horse, foot, and dragoons—cut up—and clean broke down—by the coalition of Blifil and Black George—by the combination, unheard of till then, of the puritan and the blackleg."[37]

The literary allusion was insulting—Blifil and Black George were rogues of dubious morality—but the term "blackleg" was an epithet smacking of theft and corruption, reserved for only the most vile swindlers and cheats. The implication was clear: the puritan was Adams, the blackleg was Clay. In a career of going too far, Randolph had exceeded himself.[38]

Clay's response was swift. "Your unprovoked attack of my character, in the Senate of the United States, on yesterday," he wrote, "allows me no other alternative than that of demanding personal satisfaction."[39] Though the blackleg comment prompted the challenge, Clay later admitted his reaction had been long simmering due to Randolph's "gross repeated and unprovoked" verbal attacks. He confessed that "the state of Mr. Randolph's mind" gave him pause, but he signed the letter and sent it off.[40]

Randolph disputed the right of "any minister of the Executive Government of the United States to hold him responsible for words spoken in debate," but he accepted the challenge. Thomas Hart Benton, a friend to both men, sought to resolve the controversy. "I heard it all," he said of Randolph's speech, "and, though sharp and cutting . . . the expression 'blackleg and puritan' . . . was merely a sarcasm to strike by antithesis."[41] He begged Randolph to let him offer this explanation to Clay. Randolph refused, partly because he was honor-bound to proceed, partly because he seemed to enjoy the controversy. "I prefer to be killed by Clay," he allegedly remarked, "to any other death."[42] The duel was set for April 8, 1826, at "the first private spot after passing the new toll bridge on the new turnpike road" in Little Falls Bridge, Virginia.[43] Though dueling was illegal in Virginia, Randolph insisted on the location. Only Virginia soil was worthy to receive his blood. More perceptive observers might have discerned the signal Randolph was sending by his choice of venue. As events would show, he would take the field to defend his honor, but he would not violate the law of his home state by firing at Clay.[44]

Randolph spent the night before the duel writing a codicil to his will, dispatching servants to withdraw gold from his various accounts, and drafting a few letters. "Think of me always, at half past 4 p.m.," he wrote to Thomas Bryan, "in case that we shall never meet again."[45] Death was a real possibility, not only because Clay was an expert shot, but because Randolph had decided not to fire at him. "I have determined to receive, without return, Clay's fire," he told his second, General James Hamilton. "Nothing shall induce me to harm a hair of his head."[46] He confided the same resolution to Senator Benton.[47] On the eve of the duel, Benton sought "fresh assurance" of this decision and visited Randolph. He recounted a visit to Clay's home, where he had observed "the unconscious tranquility" of Mrs. Clay and the children. "How different," he softly said, "all that might be the next night." The unasked question hung in the air.

Randolph—normally defensive when he thought his word was being questioned—replied that he would "do nothing to disturb the sleep of the child or the repose of the mother."[48] He handed over a note, directing Benton to take nine pieces of gold, divide it among himself and the two seconds, and "make seals to wear in remembrance of him." Randolph spent the remainder of the evening reading *Paradise Lost.*

The two men arrived at the appointed hour. Benton again attempted mediation, but the men took their places and were handed their guns. Suddenly a shot rang out. Randolph's gun had a hair-trigger and had discharged the moment it had been placed in his hand. Fortunately it was pointed toward the ground. Poor Benton was now more anxious. Would Clay view the hair-trigger as proof that Randolph meant to shoot to kill? Would Randolph change his mind?[49] Clay calmed the scene by shouting, "It was an accident— I saw it—the shot is near his foot."[50]

"Are you ready?" came the call. Then the command in quick cadence: "Fire, one, two, three, stop."

Clay's shot kicked up dust and gravel behind Randolph but did not hit him. Randolph's shot hit a stump behind Clay.[51] Both shots were close, but far off enough to indicate an intent to miss. Benton rushed the field, hoping to end the matter. Clay waved him off. "This is child's play," he said, and reloaded his piece. He fired again, this time a little closer. The bullet passed through one of Randolph's outer cloaks. Randolph raised his pistol and exclaimed: "I do not fire at you, Mr. Clay." He shot into the air, then moved off his mark and advanced toward his opponent.

"Mr. Clay," he said, extending his hand, "you owe me a coat."

"I am glad," Clay responded, taking Randolph's hand, "the debt is no greater."[52]

The "concluding scene," Benton wrote, "was one of joy and congratulation." The two men, each with their honor intact following the spectacle, walked together off the field. "This last incident," Randolph's half-brother wrote, "I am disposed to doubt."[53]

In the still of the night, Randolph was subdued. "I am a fatalist," he wrote shortly after the duel. "I am all but friendless." His thoughts turned to his mother. "Only one human being ever knew me. She only knew me."[54]

As soon as Congress adjourned, Randolph sailed again for Europe. His ship had barely passed the horizon ere talk began of replacing him in the Senate. Reports of his rambling speeches, of spectators looking down "with titters or open laughter," and of his duel with Clay, caused opposition to swell. The Richmond *Enquirer,* reunited with Randolph in opposition to Adams, supported the embattled senator. "Mr. Randolph's zeal and intrepidity have drawn a fiery wasp's nest around his head," the paper asserted. "He has been exhibited in almost every variety of shape to excite detestation or contempt. He has been painted as a madman, as a malignant, as a dotard. In fact, what animadversion has been spared to him?"[55]

The opposition alternatively approached two congressmen, Philip Barbour and John Floyd, to challenge Randolph, but both men refused. They next sought out Governor John Tyler. The future president was coy, expressing his admiration for Randolph's principles, but not rejecting the idea. Between rejections and lukewarm responses, the opposition despaired of ousting Randolph. The Richmond *Enquirer* predicted Randolph would face no opponent.[56]

Randolph had scant intelligence of these machinations. He was visiting The Hague, where "cleanliness . . . becomes a virtue."[57] His sole comment on the Senate race was to note that, "whenever a man is dismissed from the service of [the people of Virginia], it is strong presumptive evidence (*prima facie*) of his unfitness for the place."[58] He was more interested in another more fascinating bit of news. "And so old Mr. Adams is dead," he wrote about the death of the former president, "on the 4th of July, too, just half a century after our Declaration of Independence; and leaving his son on the throne. This is Euthanasia, indeed. They have killed Mr. Jefferson, too, on the same day, but I don't believe it."[59]

Randolph returned to Washington on the eve of the vote. He found administration forces "chuckling at the prospect of my discomfiture."[60] Unlike many of his previous elections, Randolph made no prediction about the outcome. "To pretend indifference," he wrote, "would be the height of affectation and falsehood; but, go how it may, I trust I shall bear myself under success or defeat in a manner that my friends will not disapprove."[61] As the day grew closer, he became characteristically bitter about the process. "Why is it that our system has a uniform tendency to bring forward low and little men, to the exclusion of the more worthy?"[62] One election eve, John Marshall commiserated with his friend. "His manner," Randolph wrote, "said more than his words."[63]

One hundred miles to the south, legislators gathered to determine Randolph's fate. "The Senate of the United States has been the most august and dignified body in the world," Samuel Moore said, "until Mr. Randolph was elected to it."[64] Governor Tyler's name was put forward and the votes cast. The final tally stood Tyler 115, Randolph 110, others 3. Randolph's brief, tempestuous Senate career was ended.

The Richmond *Enquirer* had been both strongest advocate and harshest critic of Randolph over the course of twenty-five years. Now, the paper offered up that it "would have humbly preferred John Randolph to any other man." Randolph "had warred with the coalition at Washington in a manner which had carried dismay into their ranks . . . had defended the ramparts of the constitution with a zeal which never wavered and an eloquence which none could equal." He seemed, the editorial concluded, "in some respects the very man who was called for by the occasion."[65]

"My first impression," Randolph wrote upon learning of the result, "was to resign." His sense of duty, however, prohibited such a course. He would conduct "a calm and dignified submission to the disgrace that has been put upon me."[66] His public actions lived up to his words. Seeing Governor Tyler at the races in Richmond, he greeted him: "And how is your Excellency? And when I say your excellency, I mean *your excellency.*"[67] To a friend inquiring about his spirits, he wrote that "adversity tries the man. He who yields to its shock with unmanly despondency is unworthy of our sympathy, except for his weakness."[68] Privately, however, Randolph lay awake at night, "listening to the rain," pondering a life with few charms.[69]

Vindication came swiftly. Randolph's replacement in the House, George Crump, announced he would not seek re-election and endorsed Randolph. "I have yet some confidence left in mankind," Randolph wrote, "and much in my constituents."[70]

Three months later, he was back in the stuffy House, the "atmosphere of which is visible and palpable—you may take it between your fingers like ill ground meal."[71] The previous year had been a whirlwind personally and politically—"the most miserable of a not very happy life," Randolph wrote—and his ever fragile body was bearing the brunt.[72] His health took its usual ill turns, but each attack seemed to bring him lower than before, and each recovery made up less ground. Nathaniel Macon commented that Randolph was "more thin and poor than you ever saw him. . . . He is almost skeleton."[73] All of Randolph's letters from this period include graphic descriptions of his ailments. "I daily grow worse," he wrote to Dr. Brockenbrough. "My food passes from me unchanged. Liver, lungs, stomach . . . bowels . . . are diseased to the last extent . . . nerves broken, cramps, spasms, vertigo."[74] This current bout of suffering compelled Randolph to turn to "the use of what I have had a horror of all my life—I mean opium."[75] Sporadic use of the "blue pill" gave way to chronic use, prompting a tragic confession: "I live by, if not upon, opium."[76]

Drug haze and physical debility aside, Randolph was what he had been in his first days in the House: the acknowledged leader of the opposition. There was even a begrudging admiration for this ultimate political survivor. For his part, Randolph showed no sign of auld lang syne. "I shall do whatever I think right," he told the House. "I may stand alone. I have been in small minorities . . . and it is very possible I may be in a minority now—but that will make no difference to me. . . . I am for masks off."[77]

John Quincy Adams was forced to limit to his diary any response to Randolph. "The rancor of this man's soul against me is that which sustains his life," he fumed. "The agony of [his] envy and hatred of me, and the hope of effecting my downfall, are [his] chief remaining sources of vitality."[78] The president's private rant aside, Randolph took great pleasure in Andrew Jackson's victory over Adams in the election of 1828. "Such," he wrote, "are the rewards of ambition."[79]

One cold January evening, Randolph left the Capitol and lifted his eyes in the direction of Virginia. He was struck by the sight of the sun "dipping his broad disk among the trees behind those Virginia hills, not allaying his glowing axle in the steep Atlantic stream."[80] A thought entered his mind, suddenly, inadvertently. Was he not "the most foolish of men to be struggling and scuffing here" while the "Book of Nature unraveled" before him? At Roanoke he had at "absolute command all I want, that is attainable . . . the morning ride, my affairs, my horses and dogs."[81] He thought of his childhood, of the fields of Matoax, of the stimulation of all his senses during days long distant. "I am never so easy," he wrote, "as when in a saddle."[82] He dashed off a series of letters to John Skinner, a fellow sportsman and editor of the *American Turf Register and Sporting Magazine,* on the "perfection of independent travelling." He placed an order for some bits, "russet leather," buckles—"no plated stuff for me"—"spring web (English) girths," and "a fine puppy."[83] He confessed that he had "a sudden taste for improving my estate."[84] Nostalgia apparently overwhelmed the alternative feeling of isolation that also marked his time at Roanoke.

He spoke very little during the remainder of the Twentieth Congress. At its conclusion, he sent a note to Dr. Brockenbrough. "Will you have the goodness to cause to be inserted in the next [*Enquirer*] something to the following effect: We are authorized to state that in consequence of ill health, Mr. Randolph declines being a candidate at the ensuing Congressional Election."[85]

17

Remorse

For her as for himself he spake,
When, his gaunt frame upbracing,
He traced with dying hand "Remorse!"
And perished in the tracing.

Randolph walked away from one legislative body and into another one. Against his wishes, he was selected as a delegate to the Virginia Constitutional Convention. "I'll [have] none of it," he snapped as his name was put forward, but ultimately agreed "with unutterable disgust" to "again become a member of a deliberative, i.e., spouting assembly."[1] His reluctance was born of an innate distrust of constitutional conventions, particularly those that came with change on their wings, filled with "political and religious fanatics [raving] about their dogmas."[2]

Complaints aside, Randolph could not have missed this convention. It would in many ways represent a microcosm of all that he had fought for and against in his public life.[3] The Virginia Constitution of 1776 was one of the pillars of Randolph's political philosophy. The handiwork of George Mason, it was to Randolph the perfect expression of ordered liberty. It vested power in the planters of the eastern part of the state. This was done by apportioning legislative representation by counties, not by population. Thus the eastern section—with numerous small counties—exercised political domination over the western part, with its fewer larger counties. As the western section of the state increased in population, calls for a revised apportionment scheme increased as well. The West wanted apportionment based on white population—which would ensure a power shift in its favor within twenty years. The East—Randolph's natural and hereditary constituency—favored the current system of two delegates per county, regardless of population.

Further complicating the matter was the issue of suffrage. Voting in

Virginia was limited to free white males above the age of twenty-one, who owned a hundred acres of unimproved land, or twenty-five acres of land with a house, or an improved lot in a town. These requirements resulted in disfranchisement for 27 percent of the eligible pool of voters in the eastern part of the state, but nearly one-half of the potential voters in the west.[4] In addition, residents of western Virginia held fewer slaves and generally supported internal improvements and increased tariffs. All of these variables prompted the chant for reform. As such, reform's most implacable skeptic had to be present.

The convention assembled in Richmond on October 5, 1829. James Madison, frail and asthmatic, already formulating a compromise between the sections, made his way slowly into the chamber. Representing Loudoun County was another former president: James Monroe, ill and near destitute, in his fifty-first year of public service since taking a Hessian bullet in the shoulder at the Battle of Trenton. Another veteran of the Revolution, and all the political wars in subsequent years, was Chief Justice John Marshall. A robust seventy-five, Marshall was "against a new constitution . . . against any extension of suffrage . . . against a free white basis of representation."[5] These three historical giants were first among equals in a class that included future President John Tyler, four Virginia governors, seven United States senators, eleven judges, and fifteen members of Congress. The roster of delegates read like the roll call of Virginia *pater familias:* Barbour, Campbell, Garnett, Giles, Leigh, Tazewell, and Upshur. But even among such a constellation, the Richmond *Daily Dispatch* editor, Hugh Pleasants, wrote, "the man who commanded the most interest of all . . . to whom every eye was turned, and whose slightest motion was watched with intense anxiety, was John Randolph."[6]

Randolph wore black crepe on his hat and arm in mourning for the old Constitution. Yet those expecting an immediate dramatic display were disappointed. For days, Randolph sat and listened. He could, of course, listen like no other. When an ally spoke, he would demonstratively lean forward, pull down the corner of one ear with his forefinger, and "utter some monosyllable at the same time, expressive of admiration."[7] Opponents received similarly conspicuous notice, as Randolph would lean forward, gaze "as if with wonder and in awe," before losing interest and sinking back into his seat "with a strong expression of contempt on his countenance."[8]

The convention addressed first the issue of apportionment. James Madison introduced a committee report calling for representation in the House of Delegates on the basis of "the white population exclusively." Instantly, Judge John Green moved that the word "exclusively" be struck and replaced by the phrase "and taxation combined." Madison's proposal would grant the western part of the state an equal basis for representation; the Green amendment, while not maintaining the county basis of representation, would nevertheless favor the eastern part of the state due to the higher tax revenue generated from that region.

The gallery filled in anticipation of Randolph speaking to the amendment, but, Pleasants reported, "the oracle continued dumb."[9] The debate went on for several weeks, while Randolph sat with his eyes fixed on a map of Virginia suspended near him.[10] The suspense was frustrating, but no spectator dared leave Richmond, lest he miss Randolph. "We yet hope," the Richmond *Enquirer* editorialized, "to see the Patriarchs and two or three other orators of the convention to come forth and address their countrymen upon this momentous occasion."[11]

On November 14, 1829, Robert Stanard of Spotsylvania delivered a lengthy speech on Green's amendment. When he finished, James Monroe, presiding over the Convention, looked about him and prepared to put the question to a vote. At last, the voice was heard.

"Mr. President!"

"Never," Hugh Pleasants reported, "have we seen two words produce the same effect." The word went forth—Randolph's up! A crowd "poured in like the water of the oceans, when the dyke gives way."[12] Delegate Hugh Grigsby looked into the gallery and lobby and saw it "crowded almost to suffocation."[13] It was the first time in his long career that Randolph would speak in the collected presence of Madison, Monroe, and Marshall. The hall hushed.

"As long as I have had any fixed opinions," Randolph began, "I have been in the habit of considering the Constitution of Virginia, under which I have lived for more than half a century, with all its faults and failings . . . as the very best Constitution; not for Japan, not for China, not for New England, or for Old England, but for this, our ancient Commonwealth of Virginia." He did not, as a matter of principle, oppose changes to the Constitution, but "the grievance must first be clearly specified, and fully proved; it must be vital, or rather, deadly in its effect; its magnitude must be such as will justify prudent and reasonable men in taking the always delicate, often dangerous step, of making innovations in their fundamental law; and the remedy proposed must be reasonable and adequate to the end in view."[14]

The reformers, Randolph argued, had met none of these prerequisites.

Their motive was the spirit of innovation, the pernicious principle "that numbers, and numbers alone, are to regulate all things in political society."[15] Practical problems, he continued, could not be solved by application of such abstract theories, for "changes, even in the ordinary law of the land, do not always operate as the drawer of the bill, or the legislative body, may have anticipated." Then he condensed in two sentences thirty years of standing against the whirl: "Governments are like revolutions. You may put them in motion, but I defy you to control them after they are in motion."[16]

Tradition, heritage, land, and the Constitution formed from those principles had sustained Virginia for half a century. Having deposed one king, the reformers now clamored for another. "King whom?" Randolph asked. "King Numbers."[17] His forefinger stopped on his old foe Madison. The former president briefly returned the gaze, then bowed his head.[18] The western part of the state, Randolph continued, presented "a case of long-continued, and, therefore, of aggravated injustice," but the complaint was nothing but a power grab: "We are numbers, you have property."[19] Those numbers would "oppress, harass, and plunder" at pleasure. He had seen this tactic at the federal level and could not believe that the assembled wisdom in the room was "seriously and soberly" considering "[divorcing] property from power."[20] Again displaying the prescience that marked so many of his speeches, Randolph predicted the result of unchecked will and appetite, something he could describe but not yet name: the welfare state. He had heard a strange notion, he said, that the government was "not only to attend to the great concerns which are its province, but it must step in and ease individuals of their natural and moral obligations." His dismissed this "pernicious notion" with a devastating broadside: "Look at that ragged fellow staggering from the whiskey shop. . . . [W]here are [his] children? Running about, ragged, idle, ignorant, fit candidates for the penitentiary. Why is all this so? Ask the man and he will tell you, "Oh, the Government has undertaken to educate our children for us. . . . My neighbor there, that is so hard at work . . . is taxed to support for mine."[21]

"Good God," an opponent remarked as Randolph spoke, "what an orator."[22]

"I am very willing to lend my aid to any very small and moderate reforms," Randolph concluded, "which I can be made to believe that this our ancient Government requires. But far better would it be that they were never made, and that our Constitution remained unchangeable." Then came the defiant blast against abstract equality: "I would not live under King

Numbers. I would not be his steward—nor make him my task-master. I would obey the principle of self-preservation—a principle we find even in the brute creation—in flying from this mischief."[23]

The wait had been worth it. Randolph's "clear pronunciation, his classical allusions, his brilliant wit (with rather too much of sarcasm, though less than usual), his ingenuity and force of statement," the Richmond *Enquirer* reported, "all contributed to rivet the attention upon this masterly exhibition. He surpassed our own expectations, high as they were."[24]

Randolph's message—change is not reform—resonated. The vote on Green's amendment was a forty-seven-to-forty-seven tie. Monroe broke the tie, voting "no," but the West had been reduced to a "lean, staggering, rickety majority, tumbling from side to side." They would be unable, Randolph said, "to concoct anything which will commend itself to the good sense of the good people of this Commonwealth."[25] From that point forward, Randolph controlled the convention. "It is difficult," Hugh Grigsby wrote, "to explain the influence which he exerted in that body. He inspired terror to a degree that even, at this distance of time, seems inexplicable. He was feared alike by East and West, by friend and foe. The arrows from his quiver, if not dipped in poison, were pointed and barbed, rarely missed the mark, and as seldom failed to make a rankling wound. He seemed to paralyze alike the mind and body of his victim."[26]

Randolph was a living land mine—exploding violently when a delegate took the slightest misstep. The official proceedings note numerous instances of his one-liners interrupting befuddled speakers. "Enter then a *nolle prose- qui*," he piped at one, using a legal term meaning to voluntarily cease prosecution of a case.[27] He spun stories that prompted "loud laughter . . . in the gallery" which "the Chair repeatedly called to order."[28] He delighted in exposing logical inconsistencies. "A little while ago," he said, dissecting an argument, "and the Constitution, in the eyes of that gentleman, was one mass of political deformity, but now . . . [he] has inverted his glass, and has discovered that its features . . . constitute a companion which any man might feel himself happy and honored to live with."[29] He denied accusations of hostility toward one member, before adding "that there has been nothing in the gentleman's career . . . to induce any man, however, humble his condition, to regard him as an object of envy."[30] Turning on another delegate, Randolph wordlessly seized his own cravat and twisted it in mock suffocation. "You saw it palpable," the convention's secretary wrote, "that he intended to say that Virginia was suffering strangulation from the ruffians who were assailing her."[31] Monroe made no attempt to call him to order; Madison sat mute. Randolph's opponents, historian William Gaines wrote, "had at least the gratification that they were abused in good English."[32]

Ultimately a compromise was reached, but not much of one. The apportionment issue was settled by dividing the state into four sections, with each section receiving the same number of representatives. Thus the West gained representation, but the East's authority remained greater than its population. Suffrage was expanded to holders of leases with terms greater than five years and to taxpayers living in towns. The revised constitution was adopted by a vote of fifty-five to forty, with only one delegate from west of the Blue Ridge Mountains supporting it. Randolph voted against it, predicting "that your new Constitution, if it shall be adopted—does not last twenty years."[33] He was right again. Another constitutional convention was convened in 1850.

Randolph's service in the Virginia Constitutional Convention brought heralds of approbation. He "was literally the hero of the convention," Hugh Pleasants wrote. "[He] had but to open his mouth to rivet attention upon him beyond the possibility of diversion."[34] Randolph allowed himself some satisfaction. "It is most gratifying," he wrote, "to be told by yourself and others, in whose sincerity and truth I place the most unbounded reliance, that I have, by the part I took in the convention, advanced myself in the estimation of my country. With politics, I am now done; and it is well to be able to *quit* [a] *winner*."[35] Yet again, his pronouncement was premature.

Shortly before the convention began, Randolph received a letter from President Andrew Jackson offering appointment as minister to Russia. "Among the number of our statesmen from whom the selection might with propriety be made," Jackson wrote, "I do not know one better fitted . . . on the scores of talents and experience in public affairs . . . than yourself."[36] This letter was followed the next day by one from Secretary of State Martin Van Buren. "You are of course the best judge of your own affairs," Van Buren wrote, "but I really cannot see any objection to your acceptance."[37] Randolph pondered the "unexpected . . . [and] unsought" honor for a week and then accepted the appointment.[38] The public announcement was made following the Virginia convention.

Randolph had been called many things in his long and turbulent career. "Diplomatic" was a term rarely used. Even Jackson had been puzzled when Van Buren suggested the appointment. But the "Little Magician" persuaded the president that Randolph's long service to the nation should be acknowledged, that the appointment would please Virginians and a large segment of the Republican Party, and that Randolph would render useful service if he served "under a president with whom he would be very unlikely to quarrel."[39] Finally, Van Buren advised Jackson that relations with Russia were "simple and friendly" and that "little harm would be done if it should turn out that we had made a mistake."[40] With that ambiguous recommendation, Jackson made the appointment.[41] One wonders if Van Buren's unspoken reason was that the Jackson administration might be best served with Randolph out of the country.

Randolph's nomination was unanimously approved by the Senate.[42] He did not immediately proceed to Russia, but asked Jackson if he might spend the winter in the south of Europe. "Let the request be granted," Jackson scrawled across the bottom of Randolph's letter. "Well aware that he will be always at his post when duty calls."[43] Randolph was given a public dinner in Norfolk and set sail aboard the *Concord* on June 28, 1830.[44] Before long, stories began to drift back across the Atlantic that Randolph had been a terror on the trip. The New York *American* reported that he demanded that a pilot "be thrown overboard into the North Sea," had eaten his breakfast from the head of a porter barrel, rather than sit at the Captain's table, had abused the purser, and "damned the Surgeon General."[45] Randolph denied all allegations of misconduct. "The truth is," he wrote to Van Buren, "that I bore my faculties so meekly about me that our worthy captain began to doubt whether I might not be induced to give up the control which the Government had given me over the ship."[46] The journey ended on August 10, 1830, and Randolph set foot on Russian soil. "All here is, as Mr. Jefferson would say, 'the calm of despotism,'" he wrote. "All newspapers seized as soon as a ship arrives, and suppressed."[47]

"Everything here is new," Randolph wrote of St. Petersburg, "strange, outré . . . but the splendour surpasses anything that I have seen at Paris or London."[48] The splendor was offset by "heat, dust, impalpable, pervading every part and pore . . . insects of all nauseous descriptions. . . . This is the land of Pharaoh and his plagues—Egypt, and its ophthalmia and vermin, without its fertility—Holland, without its wealth, improvements, or cleanliness." Still, he concluded, "it is beyond all comparison, the most magnificent city I ever beheld."[49] Randolph took up residence at the Hotel Demouth, furnished himself with "a handsome equipage and four or five fine horses," and prepared to present his credentials.[50] Dressed in "a full suit of the finest cloth that London could afford" and wearing a steel-cap sword, Randolph was presented to Emperor Nicholas I and Empress Alexandra.[51] Even this simple act of protocol produced wild tales. Randolph had developed a limp which caused him to lean slightly forward when walking. The emperor thought Randolph was about to kneel, and indicated that was not necessary. The rumor spread, however, that Randolph "plumped down on his knees before the Empress of Russia."[52] In fact, Randolph and the emperor enjoyed a pleasant conversation in French, after which the empress presented the new minister to the court.[53] Randolph had been advised that Nicholas "would receive me as one gentleman receives another, and such was the fact."[54]

Randolph's primary assignment was to negotiate a commerce and maritime rights treaty. He met with his counterpart, Prince Carl Christoph von Lieven, and presented the American position.[55] While the Russians pondered a response, Randolph called "on every diplomatic character, whether Ambassador, Envoy, or Charge, or even Secretary of Legation, from the highest to the lowest. Not content with sending round my carriage and servants, I called in person and left my cards."[56] From that auspicious beginning, Randolph's ministry went rapidly downhill. He was struck with "ague," dysentery, and "severe personal indisposition."[57] His weakened body gave way to "a highly malignant continued bilious fever . . . [and] acute hepatitis."[58] He wrote a rambling letter to Jackson in which he expressed the "desire to return home in time to take my seat in the next Congress . . . where I may fight under your banner."[59] Having accepted a post he should have declined, Randolph was now forced to abandon it. He departed St. Petersburg for London on September 7. He had been in Russia for twenty-eight days.[60]

Self-preservation, Randolph wrote to Jackson, "has compelled me to anticipate your kind indulgence and to leave St. Petersburg much sooner and more abruptly than I had intended."[61] He hoped to restore his "shattered system" and return to his post in the spring. In the meantime he had left his aide, John Randolph Clay, as chargé d'affaires to continue discussions with the Russians.[62] Jackson was taken aback, but sympathetic. He offered no objection to the obviously untenable situation.

Randolph spent about a year in London, repeatedly promising to return to St. Petersburg, attempting to monitor treaty negotiations, and sinking ever lower.[63] Soon his lungs began to hemorrhage. "I have little else to tell you," he wrote to Clay, "except that I am going home to die."[64] He submitted his resignation to Jackson and left London in September 1831.[65] He was, he wrote, "a mass of disease and misery, disgusting to myself, and no doubt loathsome to others."[66]

Back home, he was again in demand. He delivered a series of speeches across his district on four consecutive Mondays in November 1831. The assembled crowds again marveled at the "clear, ringing, shrill, piercing . . . smooth, melodious" voice.[67] His wit remained trenchant. He commented that the new secretary of state, Edward Livingston, was "a man of splendid abilities, but utterly corrupt. He shines and stinks like a rotten mackerel by moonlight."[68] When his mind was clear, he was still capable of penetrating political commentary. "I look for civil war," he wrote. "You may live to see Winchester [Virginia] and Richmond in two different states. . . . The country is ruined past redemption by political and religious fanatics bidding at the auction of popularity where everything is 'knocked down' to the lowest bidder."[69]

Yet he was too often surfeited with opium or morphine to sustain a rational mien.[70] He spoke wildly of eradicating his servants and swore that he had received a nocturnal visit from Satan.[71] He envisioned diabolical plots against him and wrote a series of rambling letters to Andrew Jackson.[72]

There would be one final battle for Randolph. The Tariff of 1828, with its high rates, had prompted Vice-President Calhoun to pen the *South Carolina Exposition,* in which he outlined the rights of states to nullify certain federal actions.[73] Jackson subsequently championed tariff reform, but when his administration passed a higher tariff, Calhoun moved to open rebellion against Jackson. South Carolina adopted an Ordinance of Nullification, declaring the tariff null and void.

Although a staunch states' rights man, Randolph did not believe in nullification.[74] It was one of those abstract theories for which he had nothing but disdain. He believed that, if a state was part of the union, it was bound to obey the constitutional laws of that nation. He wrote that South Carolina's action had been "imprudent and rash" and hoped that "Jackson's magnanimity" would lead to reconciliation.[75] He wrote to the president that the "infamous conduct of Calhoun and his wretched creatures has damned him and them everlasting in Virginia."[76] Randolph had never accepted Calhoun, despite the latter's steady movement from nationalist to southern partisan. "Calhoun always had a knack of turning young men's heads," Randolph wrote, "but then he was young himself and with a great character for talents and yet greater for stern uncompromising public virtue."[77] He took grim satisfaction as he watched Calhoun back himself into an untenable corner. "Calhoun by this time must be in Hell," he wrote to Jackson. "He has fallen into the very trap that caught and destroyed Clay. He is self-mutilated like the Fanatic that emasculated himself."[78]

Within a fortnight, however, Randolph turned against Jackson. The president, responding to South Carolina's actions, issued a proclamation declaring that nullification was subversion and the states had no right to secede. Thus Jackson trampled not only nullification, but also state sovereignty, federalism, and states' rights. This act was followed by passage of the Force Bill, authorizing military action to support Jackson's proclamation. Randolph cursed "the infamous bill . . . creating a Dictator, a Military Tribune at least."[79] He announced he was ready to be strapped to his horse Radical and take the field against Jackson's army.[80] "I may yet die in harness, with spurs on (as I always desired to do)," he boasted, "instead of sniveling my life away on a bed like a breeding woman."[81]

"I was not born to endure a master," he wrote feverishly; "I could not brook military despotism in Europe, but *at home* it is not be endured. I could not have believed that the people would so soon have shown themselves unfit for free government."[82] He set out for his favorite forum—the local courthouse.

Randolph appeared to be little more than an animated corpse when he appeared at Charlotte Courthouse. The secretary of the meeting recorded that Randolph was in "a state of extreme feebleness," yet he spoke from 11:00 a.m. "until after nightfall."[83] He presented a series of eleven resolutions asserting the sovereignty of Virginia, denouncing "*ultra*-Federalists, *ultra*-bank, *ultra*-internal improvement" men, and condemning both nullification and Jackson's proclamation. Randolph's resolutions were adopted, and he was re-elected to Congress, the latest manifestation of his hold over his fellow freeholders.

Attendance at Buckingham Courthouse, an observer noted, was unusually large. Unable to stand, his mind clouded by drugs and pain, Randolph sat in the judge's chair and delivered a disconnected harangue that had his friends turning away in embarrassment. Then, for a brief moment, as if awakening from a tortured sleep, Randolph saw and spoke clearly. He concisely sketched the crisis facing the nation and concluded "[there] is one man, and one man only, who can save the Union—that man is Henry Clay. I know he has the power, I believe he will be found to have the patriotism and firmness equal to the occasion."[84]

Randolph was carried out of the courthouse. He returned to Roanoke, demanded his bags be packed, and announced he was returning to England. He would there recover or die. His coach pulled away from the secluded homestead, forever memorialized by its linkage to his name, and bounced across central Virginia. At Potomac Creek he boarded a steamship to cross to Alexandria. He was lifted to his berth, "groaning heavily, breathing laboriously."[85] Passengers on the short trip heard the distressed voice exclaim "Oh God, oh Christ!" In Washington, he was carried into the Senate chamber, where Henry Clay was speaking for compromise on the tariff. "Raise me up," Randolph barked, "I want to hear that voice again." Clay learned that his old adversary was nearby. He concluded his remarks and walked over, hand extended.

"Mr. Randolph," he said, "I hope you are better, Sir."

"No, I am a dying man, and I came here expressly to have this audience with you."

The two men shook hands and took final leave of one another.[86] Randolph stayed for one more debate. John C. Calhoun was lashing Daniel Webster on the issue of states' rights. Calhoun was at his best this day, his logic dicing the eloquence of Webster and defying the hubris of Jackson. Randolph had lost no love for the man he called a "thrice double ass," but on this day, he nodded approval as Calhoun championed their shared principles.[87] "Take away that hat," he commanded a spectator seated in front of him. "I want to see Webster die, muscle by muscle."[88]

Randolph's destination was the packet boat *Montezuma* departing from Philadelphia for England. He reached the city "in stupor and pain" on May 20, 1833, but could make it only as far as the City Hotel.[89] He had the mark of death on him. His friends sent for a local physician, Dr. Parrish, who began his examination by asking the usual routine questions.

"Don't ask me that question," Randolph snapped. "I have been sick all my life."

"There are idiosyncrasies," Parrish protested, "in many constitutions."

Randolph would have none of it. "I have been an idiosyncrasy all my life."[90]

Parrish proffered some suggestions, only to be dismissed with a wave of the hand. "I can take opium like a Turk," Randolph said, "and have been in the habitual use of it, in one shape or another, for some time."[91]

Parrish, like so many others, was taken by the personality of the dying man. "I never met with a character," the doctor would recall, "so perfectly original and unique."[92]

Dr. Francis West arrived later in the day and received a typical Randolph greeting: "In a multitude of counsels there is confusion."[93] Randolph sat propped up in bed, a blanket draped around his head like a hood, topped with a stovepipe hat. He held a coach whip in his hand. By now he was "exceedingly emaciated . . . his limbs being reduced to skin and bone."[94] He passed in and out of coherence, tossed and turned, and issued a steady stream of orders to his servant John, the doctors, and the hotel staff.

By May 23, he could hardly breathe. He was unable, Dr. West wrote, "to expectorate the matter accumulated in his lungs, which had risen high in his throat, threatening strangulation." Randolph twice asked his doctors to perform a tracheotomy, and threatened to do it himself when they refused.[95] Perhaps realizing that his long-predicted demise was at hand, Randolph gathered himself to issue one more uncompromising statement.

"I confirm all the directions in my will respecting my slaves, whom I have manumitted and for whom I have made provision," he said, making certain there were sufficient witnesses present. He repeated his order. "I want them to be enforced, particularly in regard to their support." Then grasping the arm of his servant John, he added: "Especially for this man."[96]

He asked John to bring him an old-fashioned, large-sized gold stud stashed among his luggage. The button belonged to his father, and he had it placed on his shirt. The room quieted. Then, breaking the silence, came the shrill voice, clear and vibrant despite the death rattle in his lungs.

"Remorse," he cried out. "Remorse, remorse, remorse." The dark eyes searched the faces of the startled companions. "Let me see the word," he asked. "Get me a dictionary, let me see the word." There was no dictionary in the room, so Dr. Parrish wrote the word "Remorse" on one of Randolph's calling cards. He handed it to the dying man.

"You have no idea what it is," Randolph murmured. "You can form no idea of it whatever." He handed the card to Dr. Parrish. "Put it in your pocket," he directed. "Take care of it. When I am dead, look at it."[97]

The night passed. It was Friday May 24. At 10:30 a.m., Randolph motioned for a pencil and paper. He scrawled a note to Elizabeth and John Randolph Bryan: "Dying. Home. Randolph and Betty, my children, adieu!"[98]

The end came peacefully—somehow unfitting for such a man. He quieted for over an hour; his breathing grew shorter. At 11:45 a.m., Dr. West noticed "a slight contortion of the right half of his face . . . almost simultaneously with a projection of the lower jaw."[99] John Randolph of Roanoke was dead.

Doctors Parrish and West stood and glanced about the room. It was cluttered with trunks, clothes, papers, and bric-a-brac. One card sat on a nearby table, with three neatly printed words, and one handwritten word.

Randolph of Roanoke
Remorse

Epilogue

"I would not die in Washington," Randolph once groused, "be eulogized by men I despise, and buried in the Congressional Burying Ground."[1] For the most part, his wishes were granted. His body was transported to Norfolk by the steamboat *Pocahontas,* then to Richmond on the *Patrick Henry.* A short service, marked by the firing of thirteen guns, preceded the journey to Roanoke. There his friends buried him just a few paces from the front door, under a tall pine. His face was turned westward, at his direction, so he could keep an eternal eye on Henry Clay.[2]

When Congress reconvened, more than a month went by before Randolph's passing was acknowledged. His successor, Thomas T. Bouldin, rose on February 11, 1834, to explain "the reason why Mr. Randolph's death was not here announced." Those words had barely passed Bouldin's lips when he collapsed and died.[3] One is tempted to conclude that Randolph really did not want to be eulogized in Congress.

Randolph's will freed his slaves and granted them extensive land holdings in Ohio. But this will was one of at least three wills and four codicils that came to light upon his death. It took twelve years of hearings and pleadings to sort through the maze of intentions and establish his will of 1821 and the codicil of December 5, 1821, as the true last will and testament.[4] Randolph's slaves at last received their freedom and made their way to land purchased for them by the Randolph estate in Mercer County, Ohio. They were met there with such hostility and threats of violence that they never took possession of the land. Ensuing litigation—which lasted until 1917—resulted in no recovery. Randolph's slaves and their heirs received nothing of the estate willed to them by their master.[5]

In 1879, John Randolph Bryan traveled to Roanoke and supervised the removal of Randolph's remains to Hollywood Cemetery in Richmond.[6] His final place of rest was on the most elevated point overlooking the James River.[7] Locals joshed that the rumblings heard from that quarter were not passing coal trains, but Randolph turning over in his grave at the latest political outrage. The joke elicited knowing laughter, later slight grins, and finally quizzical looks as Randolph's memory faded in the historical twilight.

In the twentieth century, most historians have reduced Randolph to the Jeffersonian era's public enemy.[8] Dumas Malone judged him "a weird figure and an odd character—willful, capricious [and] neurotic," displaying "excesses of arrogant belligerency . . . explained, in terms of modern psychology, as over-compensation for his lack of virility."[9] Madison biographer Irving Brant diagnosed "something akin to madness" in his conduct.[10] A chorus of writers dismissed Randolph's actions, words, and policy positions as "political and personal," "a literal devotion to a petrified version of the Republican creed," resentment of Jefferson's sway, jealousy of Madison's influence, and a host of "eccentricities and temper."[11] He "temperamentally was unfit to lead a majority," one wrote, "[and] in finest fettle in the work of destruction."[12]

In 1941, a graduate student at Duke University proffered a different view. Russell Kirk found Randolph to be "the most interesting and unusual man ever to be a power in the Congress of the United States."[13] Kirk's alternative judgment became the subject of his book *John Randolph of Roanoke: A Study in American Politics.* "Wisely or not," Kirk wrote, "Randolph would not bend before the demands of the hour, as did Jefferson; nor would he alter his convictions, as did Calhoun. . . . [H]e grew more intense in his beliefs and more biting in their expression."[14] Discovering in Randolph a fascinating combination of realism, consistency, and relevance—a "lively mind" in a "radical man"—Kirk resolved to rescue Randolph from the slights of history. "As a pious act," he wrote, introducing his subject, "I summon up John Randolph from among the shades."[15]

Kirk called the man he summoned forth "a genius, the prophet of Southern nationalism and the architect of Southern conservatism."[16] The conservatism that emerged from his life, letters, and speeches was rooted in a "half-indolent distaste for alteration," a dedication to an agricultural society, a "love of local rights" and "assertive individualism," and a sensitivity about slavery.[17] These impulses were quickened by the strong drift of society away from "the tranquil, agricultural, old-fangled life," and confirmed by the belief "that a democratic passion for legislating is a menace to liberty."[18] Kirk viewed Randolph as the critical link between the conservatism of the Founders and that of John C. Calhoun—a comparison only half of which Randolph would have endorsed. But Kirk asserted that Randolph's quality of imagination and Calhoun's stern logic illustrated to subsequent generations that "conservatism is something deeper than mere defense of shares and dividends, something nobler than mere dread of what is new."[19] Adam Tate concurred in large part when he wrote that Randolph helped create "a constellation of ideas that have been classified as southern conservatism."[20] Randolph "transformed the republicanism of the Revolutionary generation and the antifederalists into a modern conservative ideology that was distinctly southern in nature."[21] John Devanny ranked Randolph alongside Thomas Jefferson in fashioning "the views and sentiments of the Republicans into a political and economic program" that "helped prepare the way for the Jacksonian coalition that brought to fruition much of the Republican program."[22] Thus, a growing body of works on antebellum southern conservatism finds it necessary to contend with Randolph's words and example.

Still, the chasm remains wide, with judgments on Randolph ranging from "the most singular great man in American history" (Kirk) to "descended from cloud-cuckoo land" (Jacksonian-era historian Robert Remini).[23] And what did the Sage of Roanoke have to say? "I am content," he wrote in 1806, "to let my public conduct speak for itself."[24] Randolph's conduct has spoken for itself, but in contrasting alliterative words. Does it speak of purity, principle, and passion? Or pride, politics, and personality? Was it patriotism or patronizing? Pedigree or peculiarity? His words and deeds have left history to wonder if he was a dedicated man of principle, a foolish hundred-percenter, or merely an irritant with a political death wish.

Always there is the self-definition: "I am an aristocrat. I love liberty, I hate equality." Yet there were others who shared Randolph's beliefs—John Taylor of Caroline, Nathaniel Macon, Joseph Nicholson—who did not consign themselves to political exile and historical atrophy. So the question plagues and pursues: why did Randolph? Emotion, eccentricity, and passion provide easy answers, but these traits did not drive him away from the political establishment. They were merely the spice that made the separation so spectacular. Opposition to Jefferson, hatred of Madison, disappointment in Monroe were results, not causes. To find the answer, one must look beyond the pyrotechnics and discern the causes of his trajectory from the pattern of his life.

In detailing the desired traits of a president, Randolph listed "1. Integrity, 2. firmness, 3. great political experience, 4. sound judgment and strong common sense, 5. ardent love of country and of its institutions and their spirit, 6. unshaken political consistency in the worst of times, 7. manners (if not courtly) correct."[25] Though attributing these characteristics to a model president, they were the precise traits to which Randolph aspired, and required of others. He cherished the "manly, straight-forward spirit and manner" that characterized free men, just as he abhorred "the rule of inversion; nothing simple, nothing open, fair or candid; all mystery, plot and indirection."[26] "Wisdom, moderation, and firmness" not only lifted individuals from "tame mediocrity," they also formed the failsafe for free government.[27] "Without morals and a due sense of religion," he wrote, "a free government cannot stand; be the *form* of it whatever it may. If I could see something like the old spirit of independence restored amongst us—open, honest, frank expression of opinion concerning public men and public measures too . . . I should have some hope."[28] Having tested these absolutes from farmhouse to courthouse to statehouse, Randolph resolved to ever stand on them.

Private principles produced political positions. "Decision, firmness, independence," he wrote, "which equally scorn to yield our own rights to detract from those of others, are the only guides to the esteem of the world, or of ourselves."[29] To Randolph, every political issue touched on the nature of the human soul. That soul, he believed, best flourished in a state of liberty. Any action—no matter how trivial—that diminished liberty had to be opposed. "There are certain great principles," he said, "which if they be not held inviolate at all seasons, our liberty is gone. If we give them up, it is perfectly immaterial what is the character of our Sovereign . . . we shall be slaves."[30] Politics was the instrument by which these principles were held inviolate. The purpose of public service was not re-election. He did not believe the freeholders of Virginia sent him to Washington to pass bills, gain seniority, or accept half a loaf. His purpose—their purpose—was only to secure freedom. Contending on the plain of such high ideals, victory or defeat—defined in political terms—was never a consideration. "To fall in such a cause," he wrote, "was no mean glory."[31]

Randolph never failed to denounce liberty's foes in any of their forms: tyranny, cant, idolatry, abstract theories, party hacks, placeholders, and the whirl of change. Government attracted these anti-principles, funded them by oppressive taxation, consolidated them in burgeoning agencies, and facilitated them by opportunism and chicanery. There could be no compromise, no "go along to get along" with such forces. "I challenge any man," he dared his contemporaries and the court of history, "to put his finger upon any vote or act of mine that contravenes [the liberty of the citizen] or to show the vote given by me that tends to abridge the rights of the States, the franchises of the citizen, or even to add to his burdens in any shape."[32] There is no need to look. No such act will be found.

Given such devotion to things well established, it should be no surprise that Randolph expressed himself with such force. His speeches from the Yazoo fraud to the Virginia Constitutional Convention were unabashed cries for consistency by a self-appointed advocate for freedom. His language was harsh because he judged the consistent application of republican principles to be essential to freedom and critical to posterity. What was on display on the floor of the House and at the courthouses across Southside Virginia was that rarest of sights: a man disregarding station, fame, and power to stand for principle.

Randolph's stance often limited his effectiveness and relevance during his time. But his stance has found increasing relevance as history has become his unwitting ally. The government bailouts of 2009 are the natural consequence of the Yazoo settlement. Undeclared wars find their source in the adventuresome foreign policy Randolph denounced. The judicial supremacy he predicted now reigns supreme over all levels and branches of government, rendering confirmation hearings into rogue constitutional conventions. The government spending he sought to reduce before it increased to "millions" is now incalculable. Randolph's words still commend themselves to the current debate over the role and limits of government action and individual liberty.

Thus, it was not eccentricity or personal piques or drugs or insanity that placed Randolph in obstinate opposition to freedom-diminishing policies. In the omnipresent struggle in political life between principle and pragmatism, Randolph unhesitatingly and repeatedly chose principle. That this consistency strikes so many as illogical speaks more to the values of subsequent generations than to Randolph's political acumen or sanity. Randolph's words and actions—startling in the nineteenth century, alien in today's political arena—hold a mirror to the conduct of generations of politicians. Likewise, words he wrote near the end of his life seem to demand a response from his political posterity: "I could not have believed that the people would so soon have shown themselves unfit for free government."[33]

Acknowledgments

John Randolph wrote that his life was "not devoid of interest or events, and might be wrought up into [an] engaging narrative." If this book confirms Randolph's opinion, it is due to the support I have received from many persons over the past ten years.

I am indebted to Andrew Burstein, editor of the Louisiana State University Press Southern Biography Series, for his skillful guidance in taking this project from manuscript to publication. Andy shared freely of his unrivaled knowledge of the Jeffersonian era and repeatedly sharpened my focus. I am grateful to MaryKatherine Callaway, director of LSU Press, for accepting this book, to Rand Dotson, southern studies editor, for patiently instructing me at every step during this process, and to Stan Ivester for his enlightening copyediting.

I drew frequently on the knowledge of David Bovenizer, a fellow Virginian with a profound understanding of Randolph, who was always willing to offer his insight. The late James J. Kilpatrick was the first person to encourage me to undertake a study of Randolph.

The Honorable Donald Lemons, justice of the Virginia Supreme Court, offered guidance regarding Randolph's eccentricities and philosophical bearings. The Honorable William C. Mims, justice of the Virginia Supreme Court, read and offered suggestions on several chapters. The Honorable R. Lee Ware, Virginia House of Delegates, shared his interpretation of Randolph's often misunderstood views about equality.

Munsey S. Wheby, M.D., M.A.C.P., professor emeritus, University of

Virginia Medical School, generously agreed to review accounts of Randolph's health and provide a diagnosis. Tim Willis, owner of Roanoke, allowed me to intrude on his working farm to spend a morning walking in Randolph's steps. John Casteen, president of the University of Virginia, provided me with an informative evening among the papers of Thomas Jefferson. John P. Ackerly, Esquire, searched for articles and individuals of interest. Patrick M. McSweeney, Esquire, offered sound counsel throughout the process. John Ware, my former agent, was an early supporter of this project.

Among the courteous and helpful staffs at numerous libraries and archives, I particularly thank E. Lee Shepherd, vice-president for collections, and the staff at the Virginia Historical Society; Margaret Hrabe and the staffs of the Alderman Library and Special Collections Library of the University of Virginia; Glen Smith, Library of Virginia; the staff at the Madison Reading Room of the Library of Congress; the Honorable Stuart Fallen and the Circuit Court Clerk's Office, Charlotte County, Virginia; and James Benton and Aviel Roshwald of Georgetown University. I also thank David Kim for his translations of Randolph's Latin.

Several of my colleagues at the Office of the Attorney General took special interest in my endeavor. I am grateful to the Honorable Richard Barton Campbell, Tom Moncure, Paul Forch, Alison Landry, Peggy Browne, Amy Marschean, Deb Smith, Jane Perkins, Eric Gregory, Dave Irvin, and Carolyn Blaylock.

My longtime friend and college roommate, Brett Leake, was again a faithful companion during all the twists that accompany writing a book. And friends Wanda and Glenn Murray and Charlotte and Craig Markva were loyal supporters of my efforts.

Roy and Linda Hindman provided me with a peaceful retreat in the mountains of western North Carolina, where I wrote several chapters. My parents, Georgia and Edward Johnson, continued their more than fifty years of consistent encouragement. This book is dedicated to Aloma Hindman, my late mother-in-law, who would have conveyed her pride in my efforts by teasing me about my choice of subject.

Amanda, Sarah, and Andrew have grown accustomed to sharing their father with figures from the past. Their willingness to embrace my decision makes this book a family effort. My wife Holly has been my indispensable, understanding, and patient partner. Great is her faithfulness.

It has been my privilege as a biographer to be associated with John

Randolph for more than ten years. I found him as exasperating and endearing, as inspiring and frustrating, as did most of his contemporaries. In my mind's eye, however, he will ever be standing on the House floor—coiled whip in hand, ghastly appearance attracting and repelling, shrill words piercing the conscience of foe and friend—as freedom's greatest advocate, the embodiment of Ephesians 6:13: "Having done all to stand, *stand.*"

Appendix 1
Randolph Genealogy

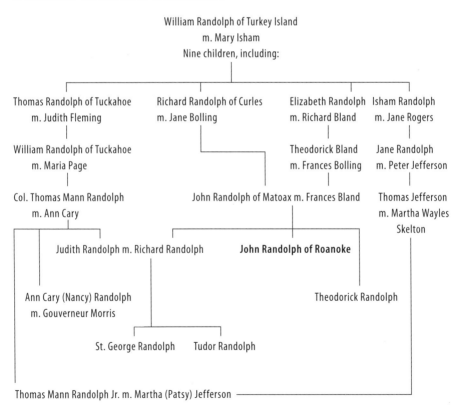

THE LINE OF ST. GEORGE TUCKER

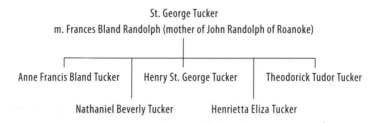

St. George Tucker
m. Frances Bland Randolph (mother of John Randolph of Roanoke)

Anne Francis Bland Tucker   Henry St. George Tucker   Theodorick Tudor Tucker

Nathaniel Beverly Tucker   Henrietta Eliza Tucker

Appendix 2

Randolph's Contemporaries

HARMANUS BLEECKER (1779–1849) served as a Federalist representative from New York from 1811 to 1813. Returning home after one term, he practiced law, served in the state assembly, and was regent of the University of the State of New York. The two men were frequent correspondents, and Randolph turned to Bleecker for counsel during the imbroglio with Nancy Randolph Morris.[1]

JOHN BROCKENBROUGH (1775–1852) was a physician and president of the Bank of Virginia. He met Randolph during the Burr trial, and a close friendship followed. "[Irritable] and sensitive as he was," Brockenbrough wrote of Randolph, "*when alone* he would not only bear with patience, but would invite a full expression of his friend's opinion."[2] The two men corresponded frequently from 1812 to 1833. "Cherish the acquaintance of [Brockenbrough]," Randolph advised Dudley. "He is not as other men are."[3] Brockenbrough's home in Richmond's Court End District—where Randolph often stayed—later served as the White House of the Confederacy.

JOSEPH BRYAN (1773–1812) was Randolph's friend from the rollicking days of studying law in Philadelphia. "Community of tastes and pursuits, very often vicious ones, are the foundation of most youthful friendships," Randolph wrote. "I was most fortunate in two: Rutledge and Bryan."[4] Bryan served in the House of Representatives from Georgia for three sessions before retiring to his estate, "Nonchalance." He kept up a steady correspondence with Randolph until his death in 1812. Randolph acted as godfather to Bryan's two sons.

JOHN RANDOLPH CLAY (1808–1885) was Randolph's godson and spent much of his youth at Roanoke. He served as Randolph's secretary during the ministry to Russia and, following Randolph's resignation, continued in diplomatic service. His posts included: Russia (1830–37), Austria (1838–45), Russia again (1845–47), and Peru (1847–60). His biographer judged Clay to be "America's first career diplomat."[5]

THEODORE DUDLEY was Randolph's first cousin, once removed, and resided with him at Bizarre from 1800 to 1810, and at Roanoke until 1820. Randolph provided for Dudley's education at private schools in Virginia and medical school in Philadelphia. Randolph considered Dudley as a son and relied heavily on his companionship. "I consider myself," he wrote, "under obligations to you that I can never repay."[6] Dudley practiced medicine in Richmond, and in 1834 published *Letters of John Randolph to a Young Relative.*

JAMES MERCER GARNETT (1770–1843) was a member of Congress from Virginia from 1805 to 1809, an original Quid, and one of Randolph's closest friends. In addition to serving with Randolph in Congress, the two men were on the Burr grand jury and fellow delegates to the Virginia Constitutional Convention. They exchanged many letters from 1805 to 1828. Garnett, Randolph wrote, was "one who has been intimately acquainted with all my views, opinions, and conduct from the commencement of the cruel persecution, that savage war on my feelings, my fortune, my fame, and, I might add, my life, that has been waged by the professors of political toleration."[7]

FRANCIS SCOTT KEY (1779–1843), author of "The Star-Spangled Banner" and brother-in-law of Joseph Nicholson, met Randolph while practicing law in Washington. Key was a frequent dinner companion and advised Randolph on many issues. His most significant influence was regarding issues of faith and religion. Randolph said he knew no man "more intrinsically estimable than Frank Key."[8]

JOSEPH H. NICHOLSON (1770–1817) was Randolph's closest congressional ally during the Jefferson administration. He served in Congress from 1799 to 1806 before becoming chief justice of the Sixth Judicial District of Maryland. He and Randolph conferred and corresponded on almost a daily basis until differences about the War of 1812 cooled their friendship.

WILLIAM PLUMER (1759–1850) was a keen observer of the Washington scene during his tenure as United States Senator from New Hampshire. Originally a Federalist, he was later elected governor of New Hampshire as a Jeffersonian Republican. His diary entries and letters frequently painted vivid pictures of Randolph in action.

JOSIAH QUINCY (1772–1864) was vastly different from Randolph in political views and personal demeanor, yet the two men held each other in high regard and exchanged many thoughtful letters. Quincy served in Congress as a Federalist from 1805 to 1813, then returned home to serve as Boston mayor, Massachusetts municipal court judge, and Massachusetts state representative and state senator. He capped off his distinguished career by serving as president of Harvard University from 1829 to 1845.

HENRY M. RUTLEDGE (1775–1844) was another friend of Randolph's youth with whom he maintained a cordial relationship through the years. He once noted that Rutledge was "almost the only friend I have left in the world."[9]

RICHARD STANFORD (1767–1816), "Honest Dick," was a member of the House from North Carolina from 1797 to 1816 and an original Quid. When Stanford passed away, Randolph wrote that he had "lost the last political friend that I had left on the floor of Congress."[10]

CREED TAYLOR (1766–1836) was a member of the Senate of Virginia from 1798 to 1805, the General Court of Virginia from 1805 to 1806, and the High Court of Chancery for the Richmond Division from 1806 to 1831. He recruited Randolph in 1799 to run for Congress.

JOHN TAYLOR OF CAROLINE (1753–1824) was a political theorist, friend of Patrick Henry, several times United States senator, and relentless advocate for states' rights. Randolph admired Taylor's writings on agricultural issues.

LITTLETON WALLER TAZEWELL (1774–1860) served as representative, United States senator, and governor of Virginia. Tazewell met Randolph while the two boys were students at Walker Murray's school, and a life-long friendship ensued.

HENRY ST. GEORGE TUCKER (1780–1848) was Randolph's half-brother and a distinguished Virginian in his own right. Following his graduation from the College of William & Mary, he practiced law and served as a cavalry captain in the War of 1812. He served as a Republican in Congress for four years before joining the Fourth Judicial District of Virginia, followed by the court of appeals. He finished his career as professor of law at the University of Virginia and author of several highly regarded legal treatises. Randolph noted that a visit from his brother was akin to a "sudden flash of lightning [that] makes the succeeding darkness more intense."[11]

Notes

ABBREVIATIONS

Note: The University of Virginia houses originals or copies of Randolph's surviving papers. Letters copied from other institutions, but held at UVA, are noted accordingly.

JRR	John Randolph of Roanoke.
JRR LC	JRR UVA. orig.: Library of Congress.
JRR UVA	John Randolph of Roanoke Papers, University of Virginia (UVA).
JRR VHS	John Randolph of Roanoke Papers, Virginia Historical Society.
JRR LVA	John Randolph of Roanoke Papers, Library of Virginia.
AC	*Annals of Congress,* 6th Congress–18th Congress.
Bruce	William Cabell Bruce, *John Randolph of Roanoke,* 2 vols.
Bryan	Bryan Family Papers, UVA.
CaP	Carmichael Papers, UVA.
DP	Dillon-Polk Papers, University of North Carolina.
Dudley	Theodore Dudley, ed., *Letters of John Randolph to a Young Relative.*
Duke	JRR UVA. orig.: Duke University Library.
Garland	Hugh A. Garland, *The Life of John Randolph of Roanoke,* 2 vols.
HB	Harmanus Bleecker / John Randolph Correspondence, UVA.
HuL	JRR UVA. orig.: Huntington Library Collection.
JMG	James Mercer Garnett / John Randolph Letters, UVA.
JSB VHS	John Stewart Bryan Papers, Virginia Historical Society.
LFP	Loughborough Family Papers, Georgetown University.

MiH   JRR UVA. orig.: Missouri Historical Society Papers.

NYPL   JRR UVA. orig.: New York Public Library.

PaH   JRR UVA. orig.: Pennsylvania Historical Society.

PrU   JRR UVA. orig.: Princeton University.

RMWC   JRR UVA. orig.: Randolph Macon Women's College.

Shorey   Kenneth Shorey, ed. *Letters of John Randolph to John Brockenbrough.*

Taylor   Creed Taylor Papers, UVA.

TC UVA   JRR UVA. orig.: Tucker-Coleman Papers, William & Mary.

TC WM   Tucker-Coleman Papers, College of William & Mary.

TJ LC   Papers of Thomas Jefferson, Library of Congress.

UNC   JRR UVA. orig.: University of North Carolina.

WCB   William C. Bruce Papers, Library of Virginia.

Yale   JRR UVA. orig.: Yale University.

PROLOGUE

1. John Thompson to William Thompson, [1799], Garland 1: 73.

2. JRR to L. W. Tazewell, February 21, 1826, UNC.

3. JRR to James Garnett, February 5, 1812, JMG.

4. Adams, *Randolph,* 160.

5. John Randolph to George Hay, January 3, 1806, JRR UVA.

6. Adams, *Randolph,* 166.

7. Thomas Jefferson to William Duane, April 30, 1811, TJ LC. Jefferson's reference to Randolph as "outcast of the world" was included in his draft but omitted in the letter sent to Duane.

8. JRR to Francis W. Gilmer, July 22, 1821, Bryan.

9. Grigsby, "Sketches," 330.

10. *Proceedings and Debates of the Virginia State Convention of 1829–1830,* 314.

11. "Dr. Francis West's Reminiscences of the Last Moments of the Honorable John Randolph of Roanoke," JRR UVA.

12. Ambler, *Thomas Ritchie,* 35; William Plumer to Nicholas Emery, January 1803, Plumer, *Life of William Plumer,* 248; Rush, *John Randolph at Home and Abroad,* 3; Francis W. Gilmer, *Sketches of American Orators,* Bruce 2: 78.

13. Benjamin Perley Poore, *Reminiscences of Sixty Years in the National Metropolis* 1: 68–69, Shorey, 58–60. See also Adams, *Randolph,* 166. A "surtout coat" is a close-fitting frock coat.

14. Bouldin, *Home Reminiscences,* 47; Catherine Mitchill to Margaret Miller, April 3, 1806, Brant, *Madison* 4: 232–33.

15. Lord John Russell, ed., *Memoirs of Thos. Moore* 1: 415, Bruce 2: 441.

16. Bruce 2: 175; Bouldin, *Home Reminiscences,* 64; Shorey, 60.

17. Bruce 2: 190–95, 441; Bouldin, *Home Reminiscences,* 64; Shorey, 60.

18. Bruce 2: 180, 190–95; Jordan, "Art of Winning Elections," 389, 394.

19. Bruce 2: 184–89; Reminiscences of James M. Whittle, Bouldin, *Home Reminiscences*, 64; *Memoirs of Moore*, Bruce 2: 441; Rev. John S. Kirkpatrick to William C. Bruce, Bruce 2: 195–97.

20. Recollections of William H. Elliott, Bouldin, *Home Reminiscences*, 55; John Augustus Foster, *Diary*, April 2, 1812, Mayo, *Clay*, 477.

21. S. Taggart to Rev. John Taylor, January 13, 1804, Malone, *Jefferson* 4: 444.

22. Kirkpatrick to Bruce, Bruce 2: 190; Samuel C. Jewett to H. A. S. Dearborn, February 5, 1817, Bruce 2: 79.

23. Van Buren, *Autobiography*, 205.

24. *Letters of A. W. Machen*, 44, Bruce 2: 81.

25. JRR to James Garnett, July 19, July 23, 1827, JMG.

26. JRR to James Garnett, January 8, 1812, JMG.

27. JRR to Betty T. Coalter, June 17, 1803, CaP.

28. JRR to Joseph Scott, June 14, 1808, HuL.

29. Randolph refers to his drug use in a host of letters. See JRR to J. H. Nicholson, February 1805, JRR LC ("Stupefied . . . with opium"); JRR to Theodore Dudley, October 29, 1810, Dudley, 73 ("free use of camphor and opium"); JRR to Theodore Dudley, July 21, 1811, Dudley, 93 ("I shall begin . . . to extol calomel as the 'Samson of Medicine!'"); JRR to Theodore Dudley, February 23, 1817, Dudley, 194 ("an ounce of laudanum"); JRR to William J. Barksdale, June 29, 1825, JRR LC ("I am pretty highly charged with mercury"); JRR to James Garnett, February 21, 1826, JMG ("Swain's quack medicine"); JRR to John Brockenbrough, May 30, 1828, Shorey, 106 ("I have derived more relief from [opium] than I could have anticipated"); JRR to John Brockenbrough, 1829, MiH ("I live by, if not upon, opium"); JRR to Andrew Jackson, March 28, 1832, JRR UVA ("dint of morphia").

30. JRR to L. W. Tazewell, April 22, 1826, UNC; JRR to J. H. Nicholson, February 1805, JRR LC.

31. JRR to John Brockenbrough, [1832], Shorey, 139.

32. Dudley, 203.

33. Senator Elijah Mills, March 10, 1826, Bruce 2: 410.

34. Dudley, 204.

35. Adams, *History* 1: 217.

36. Jordan, *Political Leadership in Jefferson's Virginia*, 165–67, 170.

37. Cunningham, *Jeffersonian Republicans in Power*, 88.

38. Tate, *Conservatism and Southern Intellectuals*, 134.

39. Miller, *Juries and Judges*, 96–97.

40. Kirk, *The Conservative Mind*, 151.

41. Notes of Nathan Loughborough, LFP, Part 2, Box 1, Folder 68.

42. Tate, *Conservatism and Southern Intellectuals*, 89–98, 126–30.

43. "The Great Seal of Virginia" in *Code of Virginia* 1 (1950): xi. Though this article is not credited, it was written by Thomas M. Moncure Jr., to whom the author is indebted for sharing his extensive knowledge of the history of the Virginia Declaration of Rights and the Great Seal of the Commonwealth.

44. Kirk, *The Conservative Mind*, 161.

45. Kirk, *Randolph*, 62.

1. KEEP YOUR LAND

1. William Randolph was a nephew of the poet Thomas Randolph and was said to have "possessed something of his poetic genius." Meade, *Churches, Ministers and Families* 1: 139.

2. Wilson and Fiske, *Appleton's Cyclopedia* 5: 174.

3. William Randolph served in the House of Burgesses during the years 1685–99, 1703, 1704–5, and 1710; as attorney general in 1696; and as Speaker of the House of Burgesses in 1698. Tyler, *Encyclopedia of Virginia Biography.*

4. Malone, "John Randolph," 363; Malone, *Jefferson* 1: 12; Bruce 1: 10. "The name [Randolph] was a calling card requiring neither introduction nor apology." Jordan, "Art of Winning Elections," 391. Descendants of William Randolph include Thomas Jefferson, John Marshall, Edmund Randolph, Robert E. Lee, and Thomas Nelson Page. Stanard, "The Randolph Family," 122.

5. Richard Randolph served in the House of Burgesses during the years 1727–40 and 1742–49, and as treasurer of Virginia in 1736–38. Tyler, *Encyclopedia of Virginia Biography.*

6. The seats of the Randolph family on the James River include: Tuckahoe, Dungeness, Chattsworth, Wilton, Varina, Curls, and Bremo. Meade, *Churches, Ministers and Families* 1: 139.

7. Frances Bland's father, Theodorick Bland, was a member of the Virginia House of Burgesses and a successful planter. Her mother, Frances Bolling, likewise came from a prominent family. Hamilton, *Tuckers of Virginia*, 11.

8. A fourth child, Jane, was born on November 10, 1774, but died sixteen days later.

9. The only surviving record touching on the health of John Randolph Sr. comes four years before his death and reads: "I take Mr. R[andolph]'s case to be a bilious remittment, something of the inflammatory kind." Col. Theodorick Bland to Frances Bland Randolph, August 29, 1771, JSB VHS.

10. JRR to Tudor Randolph, December 13, 1813, JRR UVA.

11. JRR to Francis Scott Key, March 2, 1814, Garland 2: 33. The Randolph "arms are described as follows: Gules, a cross fleury, argent, bearing five mullets uiereed, sable. Crest, an antelope erased, holding in the mouth a baton." du Bellet, *Prominent Virginia Families*, 129.

12. Bruce 1: 35. See Parton, *Famous Americans of Recent Time*, 185 ("His father left forty thousand acres of the best land . . . and several hundred slaves to his three boys").

13. Bruce 1: 21.

14. JRR to [St. George Tucker], February 28, 1817, JRR UVA; Garland 1: 3.

15. JRR to Josiah Quincy, March 22, 1814, JRR UVA; JRR to (unknown), February 9, 1832, Bruce 1: 9. See also JRR to Francis Scott Key, March 20, 1814, Garland 1: 2.

16. JRR to Tudor Randolph, December 13, 1813, JRR UVA; JRR to St. George Tucker, June 15, 1788, JRR UVA; St. George Tucker to Theodorick Randolph and JRR, April 11, 1787, Bryan (JRR notation at bottom of letter); Garland 1: 11.

17. JRR to (unknown), January 31, 1826, Garland 1: 11; Bruce 1: 36–37.

18. Bruce 1: 734; JRR to Elizabeth Coalter, March 6, 1824, CaP; JRR to James M. Garnett, February 10, 1823, JRR UVA; JRR to Elizabeth T. Coalter, November 1, 1828, WCB.

19. JRR to Josiah Quincy, July 1, 1814, JRR LC.

20. *The New Mirror* 1: 346, in Bruce 1: 39; Wilson and Fiske, *Appleton's Cyclopedia* 174.

21. JRR to J. H. Nicholson, August 12, 1800, JRR LC.

22. Adams, *Randolph,* 9. Richard Brookhiser likens this biography by Adams—"the brilliant, unstable historian"—about Randolph—"a brilliant, unstable politician"—to "the circle of hell in which the damned gnaw one another." Brookhiser, "America Unabridged," 27.

23. "[No government] can be good," Randolph wrote, "that does not lodge the power in the hands of the substantial landholders of the county." JRR to Thomas Marsh Forman, October 26, 1813, JRR VHS.

24. Garland 1: 18.

25. JRR to Harmanus Bleecker, March 15, 1818, JRR UVA.

26. Garland 1: 23. Jerman Baker was a local attorney. Edmund Randolph was a relative who would serve as governor of Virginia and first attorney general of the United States.

27. JRR to Francis W. Gilmer, March 13, 1824, Bryan.

28. JRR to Tudor Randolph, December 13, 1813, JRR UVA; see also JRR to St. George Tucker, 28 Feb 1817, JRR UVA ("When my mother was yet a widow, the object of general admiration and pursuit, I, the youngest of her children, shared her solitary bed at night").

29. JRR to Elizabeth T. C. Bryan, December 22, 1830, WCB; JRR to Elizabeth T. Coalter, 1825, WCB. William Hogarth was an English painter and critic who produced prints called "modern moral subjects." One such print was *The Four Stages of Cruelty* (1751), a series of pictures displaying acts of criminals. *The Expedition of Humphry Clinker* is a picaresque novel by Tobias Smollett.

30. JRR to Harmanus Bleecker, October 10, 1818, JRR UVA; JRR to Tudor Randolph, December 13, 1813, JRR UVA; JRR to St. George Tucker, February 28, 1817, JRR UVA.

31. JRR to Harmanus Bleecker, October 10, 1818, JRR UVA.

32. Among her responsibilities, Frances Randolph "collected rents from tenants living on her lands, supervised various plantation managers and overseers at work, purchased supplies for the household, and hired white artisans and laborers to perform certain tasks." Hamilton, *Tuckers of Virginia,* 60.

33. JRR to J. R. Bryan, December 28, 1830, *New York Times,* April 20, 1854; JRR to William J. Barksdale, April 16, 1824, JRR LC.

34. JRR to Francis W. Gilmer, March 13, 1824, Bryan; JRR to John Brockenbrough, April 14, 1826, Shorey, 71.

35. JRR to Theodore Dudley, 15 Feb 1806, Dudley, 14.

36. Ibid.

37. JRR to Theodore Dudley, January 8, 1807, June 10, 1821, Dudley, 25, 220.

38. JRR to Theodore Dudley, December 30, 1821, Dudley, 233.

39. JRR to Elizabeth T. C. Bryan, 22 Dec 1830, WCB; JRR memo, ca. May 1796, TC UVA; Garland 1: 13.

40. JRR to Elizabeth T. Coalter, February 20, 1822, Bruce 1: 38.

41. JRR to Tudor Randolph, December 13, 1813, JRR UVA.

42. Wilson, "St. George Tucker," *From Union to Empire,* 70–76; Bauer, *Commentaries on the Constitution;* Tucker, "The Judges Tucker," 789.

43. Garland 1: 4

44. St. George Tucker to Robert Wash, October 2, 1812, TC WM, in Hamilton, *Tuckers of Virginia,* 40.

45. JRR to Tudor Randolph, December 13, 1813, JRR UVA; St. George Tucker to Theodorick Randolph and JRR, April 11, 1787, Bryan (JRR notation at bottom of letter); JRR to St. George Tucker, 28 Feb 1817, JRR UVA.

46. JRR to St. George Tucker, 28 Feb 1817, JRR UVA.

47. St. George Tucker to Theodorick Randolph and JRR, April 11, 1787, Bryan (JRR notation at bottom of letter).

48. JRR to St. George Tucker, January 12, 1796, July 18, 1796, June [24], 1797, May 10, 1799, RMWC; JRR to St. George Tucker, March 1, 1794, HuL; JRR to St. George Tucker, December 26, 1801, MiH; JRR to Anne Frances Coalter, 8 Aug 1791, JRR UVA.

49. Tucker's biographer attributes the break to Tucker's personification of "all the changes Randolph hated in early nineteenth-century Virginia in the decline of extended family loyalties, the abandonment of landed property, and the growth of excessive individuality and greed." Hamilton, *Tuckers of Virginia,* 4.

50. St. George Tucker to Theodorick Randolph and JRR, April 11, 1787, Bryan (JRR notation at bottom of letter); JRR to St. George Tucker, March 25, 1795, RMWC; St. George Tucker to Theodorick Randolph and JRR, June 29, 1788, Bryan; JRR to Tudor Randolph, December 13, 1813, JRR UVA.

51. JRR to St. George Tucker, July 10, 1781, Bruce 1: 47–48.

52. JRR to Theodore Dudley, February 16, 1817, Dudley, 190–91. The books to which Randolph refers are: *The History of Charles XII, King of Sweden* (1731), by Voltaire; *The Spectator* magazine, founded by the English essayist Joseph Addison; *The Expedition of Humphry Clinker* (1771), by Tobias Smollett; the various tales from medieval Europe featuring the adventures of Reynard the Fox; *Gil Blas,* a picaresque novel by Lesage; the *Historiae Alexandri Magni,* by Quintus Curtius Rufus; *Orlando Furioso,* an Italian romantic epic by Ludovico Ariosto; and *The Seasons,* a collection of poems by Scottish playwright James Thomson.

53. JRR to Theodore Dudley, February 16, 1817, Dudley, 190–91.

54. JRR to Richard Kidder Randolph, July 4, 1810, JRR LC; JRR to Theodore Dudley, February 15, 1806, Dudley, 13–16. See also *AC,* 9th Cong., 2nd sess., 420 ("When I was a boy, I recollect to have consulted such chronological tables as I could get access to").

55. Garland 1: 65; Bruce 1: 136.

56. JRR to Theodore Dudley, February 16, 1817, Dudley, 191.

57. Frances had given birth to her first child by Tucker on September 20, 1779, a girl named Anne Frances Bland Tucker. Henry St. George Tucker was born December 29, 1780. She would bear three more children: Theodorick Tudor Tucker, born September 19, 1782; Nathaniel Beverly Tucker, born September 6, 1784; and Henrietta Eliza Tucker, born December 10, 1787.

58. JRR to Henry Rutledge, July 24, 1815, JRR UVA.

59. JRR to Harmanus Bleecker, October 10, 1818, JRR UVA.

60. JRR to James M. Garnett, April 27, 1806, JRR UVA; Bruce 2: 417. The plantation's name could derive from the French word *bizarre* from the Spanish word *bizarre* meaning "gallant" or "brave." The architect Benjamin Latrobe, visiting the plantation in June 1796, wrote that "Bizarre" was "another French name." Carter, *Journals of Latrobe* 1: 142; Crawford, "A House Called Bizarre," E1.

61. *AC*, 12th Cong., 1st sess., 453.

62. JRR to St. George Tucker, July 10, 1781, Bruce 1: 47–48.

63. JRR to Theodore Dudley, February 5, 1813, Dudley, 133; JRR to Harmanus Bleecker, October 27, 1816, JRR UVA.

64. Malone, *Jefferson* 1: 46.

65. Frances Bland Tucker to St. George Tucker, June 4, 1781, TC WM; St. George Tucker to Richard Randolph, Theodorick Randolph, and JRR, July 11, 1781, Bryan.

66. Tyler, "Education in Colonial Virginia, Part II," 6; Johnson, *Randolph of Roanoke*, 45.

67. St. George Tucker to Theodorick Bland, September 21, 1781, Bruce 1: 50.

68. Walker Maury to St. George Tucker, October 6, 1782, TC UVA.

69. JRR to Tudor Randolph, December 13, 1813, JRR UVA; JRR to F. W. Gilmer, July 2, 1825, JRR LC; JRR to St. George Tucker, April 14, 1814, TC UVA; JRR to Theodore Dudley, February 15, 1806, Dudley, 13; JRR to L. W. Tazewell, February 18, 1826, UNC, March 8, 1829, Bruce 1: 60. *AC*, 9th Cong., 2nd sess., 420; 20th Cong., 1st sess., 1130–31.

70. Dawidoff, *Education of Randolph*, 116.

71. JRR to F. W. Gilmer, July 2, 1825, JRR LC.

72. JRR to Tudor Randolph, December 13, 1813, JRR UVA. "The school was regulated most judiciously; and was soon attended by more pupils than any other grammar school. . . . More than one hundred, at one time, were in attendance." Morrison, *Public Education in Virginia*, 112.

73. JRR to Tudor Randolph, December 13, 1813, JRR UVA; Walker Maury to St. George Tucker, September 14, 1786, TC UVA.

74. JRR to Tudor Randolph, December 13, 1813, JRR UVA; JRR to L. W. Tazewell, February 28, 1826, UNC; Bruce 1: 58–59. Littleton Tazewell would serve as governor of Virginia and U.S. senator.

75. JRR to L. W. Tazewell, February 28, 1826, UNC.

76. JRR to Tudor Randolph, December 13, 1813, JRR UVA; Garland 1: 22.

77. These references are to the English poet Thomas Chatterton, who wrote under the pen name "Thomas Rowley," the poet and dramatist John Gay, and the Scottish author Thomas Young.

78. JRR to "my ever dear Jack," April 28, 1789, NYPL; JRR to Tudor Randolph, December 13, 1813, JRR UVA; JRR to St. George Tucker, September 24, 1788, JRR LC; Garland 1: 22.

79. JRR to "Jack," December 6, 1789, NYPL; JRR to "my ever dear Jack," April 28, 1789, NYPL; JRR to Elizabeth T. Coalter, November 1, 1828, WCB; JRR to Tudor Randolph, December 13, 1828, JRR UVA.

80. JRR to Frances B. Tucker, June 20, 1786, TC UVA.

81. Walker Maury to St. George Tucker, September 14, 1786, TC UVA; JRR memo, ca. May 1796, TC UVA.

82. JRR to Tudor Randolph, December 13, 1813, JRR UVA; JRR memo, May 1796, TC UVA.

83. JRR to St. George Tucker, April 22, [1787], TC UVA; JRR to Frances B. Tucker, June 26, 1787, April 30, 1787, TC UVA.

84. JRR to Tudor Randolph, December 13, 1813, JRR UVA.

85. Ibid.

86. JRR to St. George Tucker, September 13, 1787, Bruce 1: 81; JRR to Frances B. Tucker, September 27, 1787, TC UVA.

87. St. George Tucker to Richard Randolph, Theodorick Randolph, and JRR, December 17, 1787, Bryan.

88. JRR memo TC UVA; JRR to Tudor Randolph, December 13, 1813, JRR UVA.

89. Garland 1: 25.

90. Stokes, "Virginia Portrait," 55.

91. "My dear and honored mother died about ten days after we reached home." JRR Memo, JRR UVA.

92. JRR to Tudor Randolph, December 13, 1813, JRR UVA. Randolph expresses the same sentiment in JRR to Henry St. George Tucker, Bruce 1: 34.

93. Bruce 1: 34.

94. Bruce 1: 94. A letter from Randolph to Tucker dated February 5, 1788, seemingly places Randolph at Columbia University less than a month following the death of his mother. In all likelihood the letter is misdated and was written February 5, 1789. Several other letters support this conclusion. Randolph wrote to Tucker in May 1788, asking "to let me know to where I am to go." Also Randolph notes in a letter to Tudor Randolph that he entered Columbia in May 1788. JRR to St. George Tucker, May 13, 1788, JRR LC; JRR to Littleton W. Tazewell, June 1788, Garland 1: 25; JRR to Tudor Randolph, December 13, 1813, JRR UVA.

95. JRR to St. George Tucker, May 13, 1788, JRR LC. Randolph later would allege that Dr. Witherspoon embezzled from funds provided by Tucker. As with the charges of cruelty against Maury, this allegation against Witherspoon has scant evidence to support it. The sole contemporary suggestion of financial irregularity at Princeton is found in a letter from Theodorick Randolph to St. George Tucker written two years after John Randolph had withdrawn. "I saw Dr. Witherspoon," Theodorick wrote, "and mentioned to him that you wished for a settlement between him and my father's estate. . . . He answered . . . that he was ready to settle, and that there was a balance in his hands." The tone of this letter suggests more bookkeeping error than intentional theft. Theodorick Randolph to St. George Tucker, January 18, 1790, JSB VHS; JRR to Tudor Randolph, December 13, 1813, JRR UVA.

96. Kierner, Scandal at Bizarre, 20.

97. JRR to St. George Tucker, May 13, 1788, JRR LC.

98. JRR to Tudor Randolph, December 13, 1813, JRR UVA.

99. Richard Randolph to Frances Tucker, October 28, 1787, TC WM, Doyle, "The Randolph Scandal." Richard Randolph squandered his Princeton tuition funds on clothes

and public balls, prompting a stern rebuke from Frances Tucker. Hamilton, *Tuckers of Virginia*, 54–55.

100. Frohnen, *The Anti-Federalists*, 686; Chernow, *Hamilton*, 266.

101. JRR to St. George Tucker, March 1, 1789, JRR LC; JRR to St. George Tucker, July 30, 1788, NYPL; JRR to Josiah Quincy, October 18, 1813, JRR LC. See JRR to Littleton Tazewell, June 1788, Garland 1: 25; JRR to St. George Tucker, June 15, 1788, February 19, 1789, JRR LC; JRR to Littleton Tazewell, April 30, 1789, Garland 1: 26.

102. JRR to St. George Tucker, July 30, 1788, NYPL.

103. JRR to Tudor Randolph, December 13, 1813, JRR UVA; JRR to St. George Tucker, September 17, 1788, February 5, 1789, JRR LC. Randolph's references are to the following works: *Ab Urbe Condita*, a history of Rome by Titus Livius; Xenophon's *Anabasis*, often read by students of Greek, or *Hellenica*, a primary source of events in Greece from 411 to 362 BC; *De Officiis* (*On Duties*) by Marcus Tullius Cicero; and a collection of orations by Demosthenes, the orator of ancient Athens.

104. JRR to St. George Tucker, June 15, 1788, JRR LC. The Latin phrase translates: "The man is wise who talks little."

105. Garland 1: 24; JRR to St. George Tucker, June 15, 1788, January 25, 1789, JRR UVA; JRR to St. George Tucker, December 25, 1788, HuL; JRR to Tudor Randolph, December 13, 1813, JRR UVA.

106. JRR to St. George Tucker, September 24, 1788, JRR LC.

107. Garland 1: 24; Kirk, *Randolph*, 31.

108. JRR to St. George Tucker, August 19, 30, 1789, JRR LC; but see JRR to St. George Tucker, September 17, 24, 1788, JRR LC; JRR to St. George Tucker, December 25, 1788, HuL.

109. Stokes, "Virginia Portrait," 14.

110. St. George Tucker to Theodorick Randolph and JRR, June 29, 1788, Bryan.

111. JRR to St. George Tucker, December 25, 1788, HuL; JRR to Tudor Randolph, December 13, 1813, JRR UVA; JRR to St. George Tucker, August 12, 19, 1788, JRR LC.

112. JRR to Henry Rutledge, April 26, 1790, PaH.

113. Stokes, "Virginia Portrait," 23. See also Doyle, "The Randolph Scandal," 306 (describing Theodorick as "tubercular, alcoholic, and another Randolph academic failure") and Dawidoff, *Education of Randolph*, 97 (Theodorick "had been a distracting and corrupting influence, dissipated and self-destructive").

114. JRR to Tudor Randolph, December 13, 1813, JRR UVA.

115. JRR to St. George Tucker, July 13, 1788, JRR LC.

116. Ibid.; St. George Tucker to JRR, August 13, 1788, Bryan.

117. JRR to St. George Tucker, August 25, 1788, JRR LC; December 25, 1788, HuL; January 25, 1789, September 11, 1789, August 30, 1789, JRR LC.

118. JRR to St. George Tucker, January 17, 1790, JRR LC.

119. JRR to St. George Tucker, January 25, 1789, JRR LC; JRR to "Jack," June 30, 1789, NYPL.

120. JRR to St. George Tucker, August 30, 1789, JRR LC. Theodorick likewise requested to leave New York for Philadelphia. Theodorick Randolph to St. George Tucker, November 12, 1789, JSB VHS.

121. Garland 1: 40; JRR to St. George Tucker, August 4, 1788, JRR LC.

122. *AC*, 17th Cong., 1st sess., 934; 19th Cong., 1st sess., 140, 399. Bruce 1: 74. Fisher Ames was a Federalist Congressman from Massachusetts and one of the era's leading orators.

123. Bruce 1: 74, 94–95; Garland 1: 26.

124. JRR to St. George Tucker, August 1, 1789, JRR LC.

125. JRR to St. George Tucker, September 11, 1789, JRR LC.

126. Garland 1: 28.

127. JRR to St. George Tucker, August 1, 1789, JRR LC.

128. JRR to St. George Tucker, September 11, 1789, JRR LC. "His frequent attendance at congressional debates . . . whetted an appetite for politics, shaped his views, and provided an insight and perspective available to few youths of his time and of great significance to his latter career." Jordan, "Art of Winning Elections," 392.

129. *Register of Debates in Congress*, 19th Cong., 1st sess., 399.

130. Kirk, *Randolph*, 19.

131. JRR to St. George Tucker, August 20, 30, 1789, JRR LC. See JRR to [James] Brown, March 19, 1790, NYPL; JRR to Henry Rutledge, May 15, 1790, PaH.

132. JRR to Henry Rutledge, April 26, 1790, PaH.

2. MACBETH HATH MURDERED SLEEP

1. Conway, *Life of Edmund Randolph*, 135.

2. JRR to St. George Tucker, January 27, [1791], JRR LC; JRR notation on Hume's *Treatise of Human Nature*, Bruce 1: 93. The books to which Randolph refers are: *An Essay on the Nature and Immutability of Truth in Opposition to Sophistry and Skepticism*, by James Beattie; *Elements of Criticism*, by Henry Kames; and *The History of Ancient Greece*, by John Gillies.

3. JRR to Joseph Bryan, May [30], 1804, Bruce 2: 577.

4. JRR to Tudor Randolph, December 13, 1813, JRR UVA; Bruce 2: 564.

5. JRR to St. George Tucker, October 19, 1790, JRR LC.

6. JRR to Theodore Dudley, October 6, 1807, Dudley, 36.

7. St. George Tucker to JRR, August [18], 1791, Bryan; JRR to St. George Tucker, November 5, 1791, TC UVA. Randolph still chafed under Tucker's financial management. "I wish, my dear Papa," he wrote, "would pay my board, etc., and allow me what he thinks a sufficiency for my clothes and pocket expenses, or make me my own Banker and let me manage for myself." JRR to St. George Tucker, October 19, 1790, JRR LC.

8. JRR to Theodore Dudley, October 6, 1811, Dudley, 107.

9. JRR to Henry M. Rutledge, February 24, 1791, PaH.

10. JRR to Henry M. Rutledge, March 25, 1791, PaH.

11. JRR to Henry M. Rutledge, July 16, 1791, WCB. Alan Crawford writes that Randolph at this time began to write letters to Nancy Randolph, younger sister of Richard Randolph's wife, Judith. "She had no interest in Jack," Crawford writes, "but he seemed insistent on courting her." *Unwise Passions*, 62–63. No letters from Randolph to Nancy from this period have come to light, and Nancy Randolph is the only source for the story.

12. JRR to Elizabeth T. Coalter, March 27, 1828, WCB; Bruce 2: 324–25.

13. Wilson and Fiske, *Appleton's Cyclopedia*, 5: 178. Both Bruce and Garland cite an undated letter in which William Thompson assures Randolph that Maria Ward (Randolph's fiancée) was "unaffected by this tale which has disturbed your peace." This might be evidence of that same story about Randolph's alleged romantic escapades. Bruce 2: 326–27; Garland 1: 182.

14. Stokes, "Early Life," 86–89.

15. JRR to Henry M. Rutledge, February 24, 1791, PaH.

16. St. George Tucker to JRR, August [18], 1791, Bryan.

17. JRR to St. George Tucker, November 17, 1790, JRR LC.

18. JRR to Henry M. Rutledge, February 24, 1791, PaH.

19. Ibid.; JRR to St. George Tucker, January 27, [1791], JRR LC.

20. JRR to Tudor Randolph, December 13, 1813, JRR UVA; JRR to Ann C. R. [Nancy] Morris, October 31, 1814, PrU.

21. Henry Lee to St. George Tucker, June 29, 1792, TC UVA.

22. Diary of John Randolph, JRR LVA. See JRR to Tudor Randolph, December 13, 1813, JRR UVA (The fever "brought me to the brink of the grave").

23. JRR to Henry M. Rutledge, March 25, 1791, PaH; but see JRR to Tudor Randolph, December 13, 1813, JRR UVA, in which Randolph calls the second Mrs. Tucker a "shrew and a vixen."

24. Dawidoff, *Education of Randolph*, 98–99; Doyle, "The Randolph Scandal," 313; Carson, "That Ground Called Quiddism," 72.

25. JRR to Tudor Randolph, December 13, 1813, JRR UVA.

26. The author is indebted to Munsey S. Wheby, M.D., M.A.C.P., professor emeritus, University of Virginia Medical School, for his assistance in analyzing Randolph's health. Dr. Wheby reviewed contemporary accounts of Randolph's condition in order to reach his diagnosis. "The description provided in your account . . . establish[es] the unequivocal diagnosis of Klinefelter syndrome. . . . He may have had Systemic Lupus Erythematosus. He may have had pulmonary tuberculosis. Either of these two could have been the cause of death. I favor Lupus because it can tie together the multisystem disorders and it can be associated with Klinefelter syndrome." Wheby to author, August 6, 2009. The same conclusion was reached by Andrew Burstein in *America's Jubilee.* "Most probably," Burstein writes, "John Randolph had the genetic condition known as Klinefelter's syndrome. In approximately one in every eight hundred live male births, the individual will have two X and one Y chromosome. These individuals are often tall, with narrow shoulders and disproportionately long limbs. . . . While symptoms vary, they also are known, like Randolph, to have light facial hair, and are predisposed to hyperactivity." *America's Jubilee*, 202–3.

27. Wattendorf and Muenke, "Klinefelter Syndrome," 2259; Visootsak and Graham, "Klinefelter Syndrome and Other Sex Chromosomal Aneuploidies," 42.

28. William Stokes offers the theory that Randolph "may have been afflicted with syphilis . . . which could explain both his dementia and his possible eunuchoidal tendency." Stokes, "Early Career," 297, 298. While Randolph's escapades in New York and Philadelphia certainly exposed him to sexual diseases, his predominant physical infirmities were apparent prior to those college years.

29. "Dr. Francis West's Reminiscences of the Last Moments of the Honorable John Randolph of Roanoke," JRR UVA.

30. Ibid.

31. JRR to Theodore Dudley, December 19, 1819, Dudley, 207.

32. Bruce 2: 318–22.

33. See Doyle, "The Randolph Scandal," 313, 315 ("Randolph's androgyny undoubtedly worked against him. . . . His persona fused masculine and feminine characteristics"); Burstein, *America's Jubilee*, 185 ("ambiguous sexuality"); and Carson, "That Ground Called Quiddism," 72 ("forever denied the ability to express himself sexually").

34. Malone, *Jefferson* 4: 444.

35. JRR to Theodore Dudley, February 5, 1822, Dudley, 252.

36. "Notes of Evidence," *Commonwealth v. Randolph*, Cullen and Johnson, *Papers of John Marshall* 2: 174–75.

37. Randolph's diary includes the entry: "To Bizarre in August . . . to Carter Page's and Randolph Harrison's [Glenlyvar] for the first time." His memorandum of 1796 states: "1792—Aug. reached Bizarre. Oct. 1 at Glenlyvar!!!" Randolph Harrison lists Randolph as part of the party that "arrived at his House on Monday the first of October before dinner." "Notes of Evidence," 170, 174; JRR Diary, JRR VHS; JRR to Tudor Randolph, December 13, 1813, JRR UVA.

38. Kierner, *Scandal at Bizarre*, 3; JRR Diary, JRR VHS.

39. "Notes of Evidence," 168–75.

40. Ibid. 171, 174.

41. JRR Diary, JRR VHS.

42. "I omitted to state that, in the winter of 1792–3, I spent some weeks at William & Mary College, and made a slight beginning in Mathematics and Natural Philosophy." JRR to Tudor Randolph, December 13, 1813, JRR UVA.

43. Richard Randolph to St. George Tucker, March 14, 1793, JSB VHS.

44. *Virginia Gazette and General Advertiser*, April 17, 1793.

45. Thomas Jefferson to Martha Jefferson Randolph, April 28, 1793, Boyd, *Jefferson Papers* 25: 621; Testimony of Mrs. Martha Randolph, "Notes of Evidence," 168–69.

46. Meade, *Patrick Henry*, 418–19. See Editorial Note in "Notes of Evidence," 165, n. 2. Richard Randolph's hearing was not a trial but an examination before judges sitting as a grand jury. The court would decide if sufficient evidence existed for a trial.

47. Kierner, *Scandal at Bizarre*, 55.

48. "Notes of Evidence," Deposition of Carter Page, 168.

49. "Notes of Evidence," Testimony of Martha Randolph, 168–69.

50. "Notes of Evidence," Testimony of Randolph Harrison, 170–71.

51. "Notes of Evidence," Testimony of Mrs. Randolph Harrison, 171–72.

52. "Notes of Evidence," Mrs. Judith Randolph, 175. Judith Randolph testified that "she was awake the whole night" and "that a child could not have been born or carried out of the room without her knowledge." Shortly before the beginning of the trial, she wrote: "I have endeavored to recall to my mind every circumstance which happened during our visit to Mrs. Harrison's last October, which, as they made no impression on me at the time, had entirely escaped my memory. I perfectly recollect Nancy's complaining one

night of being ill, and went into the room to see . . . whether it was necessary for her to take any medicine; but I did not think anything of her indisposition." Judith Randolph to St. George Tucker, April 21, 1793, JSB VHS. See also Judith Randolph to Eliza Pleasants, March 15, 1793, JSB VHS (denying any wrongdoing); Kierner, *Scandal at Bizarre*, 85–86.

53. "Notes of Evidence," Testimony of John Randolph, 174–75.

54. JRR diary, JRR VHS.

55. JRR to Littleton W. Tazewell, September 18, 1807, UNC; Bruce 1: 123–26; Stokes, "Early Life," 10–11, 26.

56. JRR to St. George Tucker, January 26, 1794, HuL.

57. By 1793, "both Jefferson and Madison, when seeking to determine political affiliation, made use of opinion about the French Revolution as a conclusive test." Ammon, "Jeffersonian Republicans in Virginia," 159.

58. JRR to St. George Tucker, May 25, 1793, JRR LC.

59. JRR to Tudor Randolph, December 13, 1813, JRR UVA. "I have made but small progress in Blackstone since I wrote last," Randolph wrote. "Mr. E[dmund] Randolph is out of town. He appointed Tuesday last for examining his students; I attended, but did not see him." JRR to St. George Tucker, August 25, 1793, JRR LC.

60. Johnson, *Randolph of Roanoke*, 63.

61. JRR to St. George Tucker, January 26, 1794, HuL.

62. JRR to St. George Tucker, March 1, 1794, HuL.

63. JRR to St. George Tucker, January 26, 30, 1794; March 1, 1794, HuL.

64. JRR to Tudor Randolph, December 13, 1813, JRR UVA; JRR to Henry M. Rutledge, December 28, 1795, PaH.

65. JRR to Tudor Randolph, December 13, 1813, JRR UVA; Garland 1: 63.

66. E. S. Thomas, *Reminiscences of the Last Sixty-five Years*, in Garland 1: 65.

67. JRR to St. George Tucker, February 22, 1796, JRR LC.

68. Sharp, *American Politics in the Early Republic*, 117; Magrath, *Yazoo*, 26.

69. Sharp, *American Politics in the Early Republic*, 117.

70. Thomas Jefferson to Edward Rutledge, November 30, 1795, Boyd, *Jefferson Papers* 28: 542.

71. Sharp, *American Politics in the Early Republic*, 151.

72. Adams, *Randolph*, 25; Bruce 1: 166.

73. JRR to Tudor Randolph December 13, 1813, JRR UVA.

74. JRR to John Brockenbrough, September 25, [1818], Shorey, 18. The complete quote reads as follows: "Very early in life I imbibed an absurd prejudice in favor of Mahomedanism and its votaries. The crescent had a talismanic effect on my imagination, and I rejoiced in all its triumphs over the cross (which I despised) as I mourned over its defeats; and Mahomet II himself did not more exult than I did, when the crescent was planted on the dome of St. Sophia, and the cathedral of the Constantines were converted into a Turkish mosque." In 2007 when Keith Ellison, a Muslim, was sworn in as a member of Congress, these words were used to support the proposition that Randolph, not Ellison, was the first Muslim to serve. See David Barton, "An Historical Perspective on a Muslim Being Sworn into Congress on the Koran," *Wallbuilders Newsletter*, January 2007. The facts do not support this conclusion. Randolph never converted to Islam or adopted any

of its practices. His "prejudice in favor" of Islam was part of his embrace of French revolutionary principles and rejection of Christianity.

75. JRR to "Citizen" Creed Taylor, [1797], HuL.

76. JRR to Henry M. Rutledge, April 29, 1797, PaH.

77. JRR to Judith Randolph, January 20, 1816, JRR LVA.

78. Randolph's contemporary account reads: "First intelligence of my brother's illness rec'd on the Amelia side of [Genito] bridge. . . . Next day at Bizarre, funeral over." JRR Memo, JRR UVA.

79. Carter, *Journals of Latrobe*, 143.

80. Ibid., 144; Nancy Randolph to St. George Tucker, June 1796, TC WM.

81. JRR to St. George Tucker, July 18, 1796, RMWC. Randolph wrote this letter "in such a state of stupor that I know not what I wrote." JRR to St. George Tucker, July 20, 1796, RMWC.

82. Bruce 1: 104.

83. "Since I saw you, I have been deprived by a sentence of the Federal Court of more than half my Fortune. 'Tis an iniquitous affair." JRR to Henry M. Rutledge, April 29, 1797, PaH. See JRR to N. B. Tucker, January 2, 1822, TC UVA ("Coming of age without a shilling; receiving an estate burthened with debt, even with petty claims"); JRR to John Brockenbrough, July 24, 1824, Shorey, 53 ("Here, then, am I, where I ought to have been thirty years ago—and where I would have been, had I not been plundered and oppressed during my nonage, and left to enter upon life overwhelmed with a load of DEBT, which the profits of a nineteen years' minority ought to have more than paid").

84. JRR to Tudor Randolph, December 13, 1813, JRR UVA; JRR to L. W. Tazewell, February 27, 1826, UNC; JRR to Theodore Dudley, December 13, 1811, Dudley, 109; Garland 1: 60; Jordan, "Art of Winning Elections," 393.

85. JRR to J. R. Bryan, December 29, 1830, *New York Times*, April 20, 1854.

86. JRR to Tudor Randolph, December 13, 1813, JRR UVA; JRR to L. W. Tazewell, February 27, 1826; JRR to St. George Tucker, June [24], 1797; JRR to James Brown, May 31, 1798, PrU; JRR to St. George Tucker, June 2, 1798, RMWC. At his death in 1833, Randolph owned 8,207 acres of productive land in Charlotte County and an estimated 383 slaves. *National Register of Historic Places Inventory*, "Roanoke Plantation," filed by the Virginia Historic Landmarks Commission Staff, August 1972, U.S. Department of Interior, National Park Service; Jordan, "Art of Winning Elections," 393, n. 14.

87. JRR to St. George Tucker, January 30, [1798], RMWC.

88. JRR to Theodore Dudley, November 15, 1807, Dudley, 40.

89. Randolph's diary shows four trips to the Hermitage between November 30 and December 17, 1795. JRR Diary, JRR VHS.

90. Martha Archer to Mrs. John L. Williams, June 4, 1878, Meade, "Some New Information," 256, 262.

91. Meade, "Some New Information," 259.

92. Ibid., 259–60.

93. Garland 1: 182, 184.

94. Bruce 1: 326–27.

95. JRR to Elizabeth T. Coalter, March 25, 1826, WCB. Robert Meade writes that

Maria Ward burned "a packet of love letters" written by Randolph. Meade, "Some New Information," 264.

96. "Perhaps it is a universal truth," James Madison wrote to Jefferson, "that the loss of liberty at home is to be charged to provisions [against] danger real or pretended from abroad." James Madison to Thomas Jefferson, May 13, 1798, Boyd, *Jefferson Papers* 30: 348.

97. Sharp, *American Politics in the Early Republic,* 176–78; Smith, *John Adams* 2: 975–78.

98. Dawidoff, *Education of Randolph,* 162.

99. The Virginia Resolution used less strident language than that employed in the Kentucky Resolution. The word "nullification" does not appear. See Burstein and Isenberg, *Madison and Jefferson,* 339–40.

100. JRR to Creed Taylor, September 16, [1798], JRR UVA.

101. George Washington to Patrick Henry, January 15, 1799, Twohig, *Papers of Washington* 3: 317–20.

102. Ibid., 318–19.

103. Meade, *Patrick Henry,* 447–48. At that time, Charlotte Courthouse was generally referred to as "Marysville," after Mary Hill Read, the wife of the town's founder, Clement Read. Ailsworth, *Charlotte County.*

104. W. W. Henry, *Henry* 2: 448.

105. Meade, *Patrick Henry,* 448–50.

106. W. W. Henry, *Henry* 2: 607–10.

107. Garland includes in his biography what he calls a "tolerable approximation" of Randolph's remarks based on "faint tradition." Garland 1: 133–41. A brief account of the debate is included in James W. Alexander, *The Life of Archibald Alexander* (Philadelphia: Presbyterian Board of Publication, 1870), 188–89. There is no evidence to support either version. See Tucker, "Garland's Life of Randolph," 41, 56 (Tucker vigorously contests Garland's account of Randolph's speech). Several accounts report that Randolph stepped into the tavern after his speech to pay his respects to Henry. "Young man," Henry allegedly said, "you call me father; then, my son, I have something to say unto thee: keep justice, keep truth, and you will live to think differently." As Randolph left him, Henry turned to those in his company and pronounced a verdict: "He is a young man of great promise. Cherish him." Randolph never recited such a story. Meade, *Patrick Henry,* 450–51. In another fanciful anecdote, a local farmer assesses Randolph's performance with the quip: "I tell you what, the young man is no bug-eater neither." W. W. Henry, *Henry,* 611.

108. JRR to Francis Scott Key, February 17, 1814, Garland 2: 30.

3. ASK MY CONSTITUENTS

1. "John Randolph—A Personal Sketch," 139.

2. *AC,* 6th Cong., 1st sess., 228.

3. Ibid., 252–54.

4. Ibid., 257, 260.

5. Ibid., 296–300.

6. Ibid., 297, 298, 300.

7. Ibid., 367.

8. Thomas Jefferson to Thomas Mann Randolph, January 13, 1800, Boyd, *Jefferson Papers* 31: 305.

9. The account which follows of the events at the Chestnut Theatre is taken from *AC*, 6th Cong., 1st sess., 377–88, 426–507.

10. Thomas Jefferson to Martha Jefferson Randolph, January 21, 1800, Boyd, *Jefferson Papers* 31: 331.

11. JRR to John Adams, January 11, 1800, *AC*, 6th Cong., 1st sess., 372–73.

12. Abigail Adams to John Quincy Adams, February 8, 1800, Smith, *Adams* 2: 1023.

13. John Adams to "Gentlemen of the House of Representatives," January 14, 1800, *AC*, 6th Cong., 1st sess., 372.

14. *AC*, 6th Cong., 1st sess., 384.

15. Ibid., 432.

16. Ibid., 457.

17. Ibid., 500.

18. Ibid., 502.

19. JRR to Joseph H. Nicholson, February 4, 1800, JRR LC. A touch of melancholy crept into Randolph's comments in the wake of the Playhouse Incident. "I, too, am wretched; misery is not your exclusive charter," he wrote to Joseph Bryan. "I have for some months meditated a temporary relinquishment of my country." Randolph attributed this feeling to unidentified "events which happened before I took my seat in Congress." JRR to Joseph Bryan, February 20, 1800, Garland 1: 180.

20. JRR to Joseph H. Nicholson, February 7, 1800, JRR LVA.

21. Thomas Jefferson to Mary Jefferson Eppes, January 17, 1800, Boyd, *Jefferson Papers* 31: 314.

22. JRR to Judith Randolph, April 19, [1800], Bryan.

23. JRR to Francis Scott Key, February 17, 1814, Garland 2: 30–32.

24. *AC*, 6th Cong., 1st sess., 547–48, 661–62.

25. JRR to J. H. Nicholson, May 14, 1800, JRR LC.

26. JRR to J. H. Nicholson, June 21, 1800, JRR LC.

27. JRR to J. H. Nicholson, July 1, 1800, JRR LC.

28. JRR to J. H. Nicholson, July 4, 1800, JRR LC; see JRR to J. H. Nicholson, July 1, August 12, September 26, December 17, 1800; JRR LC.

29. JRR to J. H. Nicholson, July 4, 1800, JRR LC.

30. JRR to J. H. Nicholson, August 12, 1800, JRR LC.

31. JRR to J. H. Nicholson, July 1, 1800, JRR LC.

32. JRR to J. H. Nicholson, September 26, 1800, JRR LC.

33. JRR to Joseph Bryan, May 28, 1804, Bryan.

34. JRR to J. H. Nicholson, December 16, 1800, JRR LC.

35. JRR to J. H. Nicholson, December 17, 1800, JRR LC.

36. Malone, *Jefferson* 3: 492.

37. John Adams to Elbridge Gerry, December 30, 1800, Malone, *Jefferson* 3: 500.

38. JRR to J. H. Nicholson, December 17, 1800, JRR LC.

39. JRR to J. H. Nicholson, January 1, 1801, JRR LC.

40. JRR to J. H. Nicholson, December 17, 1800, JRR LC.

41. JRR to J. H. Nicholson, January 1, 1801, JRR LC.

42. JRR to St. George Tucker, February 11, 1801, Bruce 1: 168; JRR to James Monroe, February 11, 12, 1801, JRR LC.

43. JRR to St. George Tucker, February 14, 1801, Bruce 1: 168–69.

44. Malone, *Jefferson* 3: 504–5; Isenberg, *Fallen Founder*, 218–20. One study attributes Bayard's vote to frayed nerves. Elkins and McKitrick, *Age of Federalism*, 749. See also Burstein and Isenberg, *Madison and Jefferson*, 360 ("No evidence exists to prove that either Burr or Jefferson made any meaningful promises to any Federalist electors").

45. JRR to James Monroe, February 17, 1801, JRR LC.

46. JRR to James Monroe, February 20, 1801, JRR LC.

47. JRR to William Thompson, February 1800, Bruce 2: 552–53.

48. JRR to J. H. Nicholson, July 18, 1801, JRR LC.

49. JRR to J. H. Nicholson, July 18, 1801, JRR LC. The phrase *"te deum"* is an abbreviated form of the phrase *"te deum laudumus"*—"We praise thee, O God."

50. JRR to St. George Tucker, October 10, 1801, RMWC; JRR to J. H. Nicholson, October 1, 1801, JRR LC.

51. JRR to J. H. Nicholson, November 1, 1801, JRR UVA.

4. MASTER OF THE HOUSE

1. *AC*, 7th Cong., 1st sess., 725.

2. Ibid., 606.

3. James A. Bayard to Alexander Hamilton, March 8, 1801, Boyd, *Jefferson Papers* 33: 137, "Editorial Note."

4. JRR to St. George Tucker, January 15, 1802, RMWC.

5. Foner, *Writings of Jefferson*, 335–42.

6. *AC*, 11th Cong., 1st sess., 68–69.

7. Clyde N. Wilson, "Nathaniel Macon," Wilson, *From Union to Empire*, 61–65. Macon's biographer wrote that Macon "had developed in Congress more of the character of a judge than of a party leader. . . . [H]e knew the history of the House, its precedents in all important measures . . . [and] he had the confidence of the President." Dodd, *Life of Macon*, 172. Noble Cunningham wrote that Macon was not an "aggressive leader," but "had a consistently Jeffersonian record, no important enemies, and a certain unassuming honesty and integrity which made him a popular choice for the speakership." *Jeffersonian Republicans in Power*, 73.

8. Adams, *History* 1: 267; Adams, *Randolph*, 54.

9. Some Federalists detected antagonism between Randolph and Giles. "Randolph is ambitious of being at the head of the Virginians," James Bayard wrote. "It is impossible that Giles will be content to act under him." Roger Griswold agreed, writing that "Giles thinks the first representative of the Ancient Dominion ought certainly on all important occasions to take the lead, and Johnny Randolph is perfectly astonished that his

great abilities should be overlooked." James A. Bayard to John Rutledge, December 20, 1801, Roger Griswold to John Rutledge, December 14, 1801, Rutledge Papers, University of North Carolina, in Cunningham, *Jeffersonian Republicans in Power*, 73–74.

10. JRR to [St. George Tucker], December 26, [1801], MiH.

11. Ibid.

12. *AC*, 7th Cong., 1st sess., 350.

13. Ibid.

14. Ibid., 356.

15. JRR to St. George Tucker, January 15, 1802, RMWC.

16. Adams, *History* 1: 55. William Pitt the Younger, prime minister of Great Britain (1783–1801, 1804–6), displayed great skill at consolidating the power of his office.

17. Wilson, "Macon," 63. Macon "lived with Randolph and Joseph Nicholson in a small house near the present Treasury department." Dodd, *Life of Macon*, 173.

18. William Dodd writes that the "two were often seen together, Macon, now forty-three years old, a tall well-proportioned, healthy physique; Randolph, only twenty-eight, slender, delicate-looking, sallow-complexioned, with the promise of scarce another decade of life." *Life of Macon*, 174.

19. Manasseh Cutler to Major Burnham, March 4, 1802, Cutler, *Life of Cutler*, 91–92.

20. Thomas Jefferson to Barnabas Bidwell, July 5, 1806; Thomas Jefferson to William A. Burwell, September 17, 1806, TJ LC.

21. Thomas Jefferson to JRR, November 19, 1804, TJ LC; Thomas Jefferson to JRR, Bruce 1: 268–69; Malone, *Jefferson* 4: 409–10.

22. A precise characterization of the relationship between Randolph and Jefferson has eluded historians. Hugh Garland writes that the two "were intimate friends . . . on terms of unreserved intercourse." Lemuel Sawyer states that Randolph was in Jefferson's confidence from the beginning of the administration. Joseph Baldwin, relying on Garland, describes the relationship as "cordial, politically and socially." A modern take was offered by Alan Crawford, who writes, with little substantiation, that Jefferson "[expressed] to Jack, and sometimes to Jack alone, his administration's legislative goals." A less effusive view was offered by Henry Adams. "No member of the House," Adams wrote, "wielded serious influence over the President, or represented with authority the intentions of the party." Dumas Malone writes that Jefferson's primary congressional liaison during this session was William Giles and describes the president's relationship with Randolph as "friendly without being intimate." Noble Cunningham writes that Jefferson "accepted Randolph's position of party leadership, took him into his confidence . . . [but] there is no evidence that he was ever popular with the President." Forrest McDonald writes that Randolph's leadership "caused the president some discomfort." Garland 1: 191; Adams, *History* 1: 269; Malone, *Jefferson* 4: 443; Cunningham, *Jeffersonian Republicans in Power*, 76; Sawyer, *Randolph*, 24–25; Baldwin, *Party Leaders*, 174; Crawford, *Unwise Passions*, 154; McDonald, *Presidency of Jefferson*, 40.

23. *AC*, 7th Cong., 1st sess., 631.

24. Ibid., 519.

25. Adams, *History* 1: 267.

26. Thomas Jefferson to James Monroe, May 4, 1806, TJ LC.

27. William Plumer to William Plumer Jr., February 22, 1803, Plumer, *Life of William Plumer,* 256.

28. *AC,* 7th Cong., 1st sess., 354; *Public Statutes at Large* 2: 148.

29. *AC,* 7th Cong., 1st sess., 439–40.

30. Ibid., 1028.

31. Ibid., 1033, 1035.

32. Ibid., 1166–67.

33. Ibid., 1177.

34. Ibid.

35. Ibid., 677.

36. Ibid., 530.

37. Ibid., 579, 761.

38. Ibid., 734.

39. Ibid., 567.

40. Ibid., 782.

41. Ibid., 602.

42. Ibid., 612.

43. Ibid., 646, 650.

44. Ibid., 651, 653.

45. Ibid., 658, 659.

46. Ibid., 660.

47. Ibid., 661.

48. Ibid.

49. "With *McCulloch,*" Kent Newmyer writes, "the Constitution became, as Charles Evans Hughes later put it, 'what the judge says it is.'" Newmyer, "John Marshall and the Southern Constitutional Tradition," in Hall and Ely, *An Uncertain Tradition,* 109. See also Tate, *Conservatism and Southern Intellectuals,* 10 ("By 1819 the primary enemy of the Old Republicans shifted to the Marshall Court").

50. *AC,* 7th Cong., 1st sess., 664.

51. Thomas Jefferson to Joel Barlow, May 3, 1802, Ford, *Writings of Jefferson* 8: 149.

52. *AC,* 12th Cong., 2nd sess., 783–84.

53. *AC,* 7th Cong., 1st sess., 1283; Adams, *Randolph,* 73.

54. JRR to J. H. Nicholson, May 9, 1802, JRR LC.

55. Ibid.

56. See JRR to Richard E. Meade, September 26, 1802, JRR UVA (Judith's irregular health; Nancy's "indisposition").

57. JRR to J. H. Nicholson, October 31, 1802, JRR LC.

58. Both Samuel Smith and Joseph Nicholson had some support for House leader, but neither mounted a challenge to Randolph. Cunningham, *Jeffersonian Republicans in Power,* 75.

59. William Plumer to Nicholas Emery, January 1803, Plumer, *Life of William Plumer,* 248.

60. JRR to James Monroe, January 3, 1803, JRR LC.

61. *AC,* 7th Cong., 2nd sess., 335–36.

62. Adams, *Randolph*, 80. Dumas Malone wrote that "Macon, Randolph, and Nicholson constituted a congressional triumvirate comparable to the executive triumvirate of Jefferson, Madison, and Gallatin." *Jefferson* 4: 446.

63. JRR to J. H. Nicholson, June 14, [1803], JRR LC; JRR to Betty T. Coalter, June 17, 1803, JRR CaP.

64. JRR to Albert Gallatin, June 4, 1803, Adams, *Randolph*, 83–84.

65. JRR to J. H. Nicholson, June 14, [1803], JRR LC.

66. JRR to James Monroe, June 15, 1803, JRR LC.

67. Jefferson "had to assume logically that since the Constitution did not specifically grant the government authority to obtain new land, it prohibited the acquisition of territory regardless of size." DeConde, *This Affair of Louisiana*, 182. For further discussion on the constitutionality of the Louisiana Purchase, see Brown, *Constitutional History*, 14–22; Kukla, *A Wilderness So Immense*, 301–6; and Kastor, *The Nation's Crucible*, 46.

68. *AC*, 8th Cong., 1st sess., 382.

69. Ibid., 389.

70. Ibid., 406, 409.

71. Ibid., 415.

72. JRR to Creed Taylor, January 31, 1802, JRR UVA.

73. JRR to Thomas Jefferson, October 25, 1803, JRR LVA.

74. "The Louisiana Purchase was an act 'beyond the Constitution,' Jefferson believed." Kukla, *A Wilderness So Immense*, 301. See also DeConde, *This Affair of Louisiana*, 181, 183–84; Brown, *Constitutional History*, 14–22. Jefferson ultimately accepted the position advocated by Albert Gallatin. "The existence of the United States as a nation," Gallatin wrote, "presupposes the power enjoyed by every nation of extending their territory by treaties." Gallatin to Jefferson, January 13, 1803, Adams, *Writings of Gallatin* 1: 113.

75. *AC*, 8th Cong., 1st sess., 436.

76. Ibid., 438. Randolph's view was later confirmed by John Marshall. "The Constitution confers absolutely on the Government of the Union," Marshall wrote in *American Insurance Co. v. Canter*, "the power of making war, and of making treaties; consequently, that Government possesses the power of acquiring territory, either by conquest or by treaty."

77. *AC*, 8th Cong., 1st sess., 440.

78. JRR to James Monroe, November 7, 1803, JRR LC.

79. Brown, *Plumer's Memorandum*, 24–25.

80. *AC*, 8th Cong., 1st sess., 627.

81. JRR to Thomas Jefferson, November 30, 1803, JRR LVA.

82. Thomas Jefferson to JRR, December 1, 1803, Ford, *Writings of Jefferson* 8: 281–82.

5. AN EVIL DAILY MAGNIFYING

1. Cleaves, *Old Tippecanoe*, 45.

2. *American State Papers* 1, *Public Lands*, No. 76, Indiana Territory, 146.

3. William Bruce calls the report "one of the most notable productions of [Randolph's] pen." Bruce 2: 244.

4. "On slavery [Randolph] adopted an approach that was as ambiguous and

unpredictable—and as sassy—as his pronouncements were on every other matter he addressed." Burstein, *America's Jubilee*, 191.

5. Ford, *Deliver Us from Evil*, 17.

6. Quincy, *Figures of the Past*, 212–13.

7. Ibid. 212.

8. JRR to Josiah Quincy, March 22, 1814, JRR LC.

9. JRR to Littleton Waller Tazewell, January 8, 1804, UNC; JRR to [N. B. Tucker, April 15, 1816], TC UVA; JRR to George Logan, February 13, 1813, PaH; Kirk, *Randolph*, 156–61. Randolph "was never more sincere than in his frequent profession of hatred for the institution [of slavery]." Forbes, *The Missouri Compromise*, 98.

10. Sheads, "Nicholson," 135. See JRR to James Garnett, February 17, 1811, JMG (Randolph states that "the fate to which my poor, miserable Slaves would . . . be exposed" is what prevents his emancipating them). Garland incorrectly states that Randolph was prevented from emancipating his slaves because they were included in the mortgage upon the Randolph estate. Garland 2: 150. The reader will recall that Randolph paid off his father's debt. Bruce implies, without evidence, that Randolph sold slaves in paying off that debt. Bruce 2: 358.

11. See JRR to James Garnett, December 22, 1818, JMG; JRR to James Garnett, July 13, 1818, JMG ("My negroes are attended to in sickness and health, their comfort provided as far as practicable and their labour abridged by being judiciously directed as well by mechanical contrivances").

12. Mathias, "John Randolph's Freedmen: The Thwarting of a Will," 264.

13. JRR to Harmanus Bleecker, November 16, 1818, HB.

14. JRR to Harmanus Bleecker, October 10, 1818, HB.

15. *Register of Debates*, 19th Cong., 1st sess., 118.

16. Clarkson, *Essay*, 259.

17. *Ibid.*, 95. Both Jefferson and Randolph, Douglas Egerton writes, "harbored serious doubts about the peculiar institution, they were unnerved by the thought of dozens of men dying for the crime of yearning to be free." Egerton, *Gabriel's Rebellion*, 93.

18. JRR to Harmanus Bleecker, October 10, 1818, HB.

19. *Register of Debates*, 19th Cong., 1st sess., 118.

20. Egerton, *Gabriel's Rebellion*, 21–22, 50–53, 55–57, 67–73; Ford, *Deliver Us from Evil*, 49–54.

21. JRR to J. H. Nicholson, September 26, 1800, JRR LC.

22. Ibid.

23. Matthew Mason writes in his study of slavery that Randolph was "alarmed to hear [Gabriel and other slaves] speaking in terms of their rights and of vengeance." He states that Randolph "fretted" about the spirit displayed by the condemned men. Mason, *Slavery and Politics*, 17. In fact, Randolph's comments do not show surprise or alarm but recognition of the inherent dangers of slavery and the natural desire for liberty. "Perhaps," Douglas Egerton writes in his history of the rebellion, "the slumbering consciences of these old revolutionaries were awakened by the political nature of much of the testimony." *Gabriel's Rebellion*, 102. Lacy Ford calls Randolph's comment "the most troubling assessment of Gabriel's Rebellion." *Deliver Us from Evil*, 54.

24. Ford, *Deliver Us from Evil*, 17. "In the post-Revolutionary upper South," Ford

writes, "practical doubts about the fundamental vulnerability to unrest of a society with a large population of slaves merged with triumphant republican ideals and an emerging Christian morality to raise serious reservations about the future of slavery in the United States, or at least in the upper South." *Deliver Us from Evil*, 23.

25. JRR to Littleton W. Tazewell, January 8, 1804, UNC.

26. JRR to [N. B. Tucker, April 15, 1816], TC UVA. This view of emancipation may have been one of the reasons Randolph attended with Henry Clay a meeting of the African Colonization Society. Bruce 2: 247–48, citing the *National Intelligencer,* December 24, 1816. But ten years later, Randolph expressed the belief that the society was motivated by "morbid sensibility, religious fanaticism, vanity, and the love of display." JRR to John Brockenbrough, February 20, 1826, Shorey, 67.

27. Ford, *Deliver Us from Evil*, 147.

28. JRR to Harmanus Bleecker, July 26, 1814, HB. See also JRR to J. R. Clay, February 12, 1829, JRR LC ("People may say what they please, but I have found no better friends than among my own servants"); JRR to J. R. Clay, June 12, 1829, JRR LC ("My faithful servants, who are my best friends, always inquire kindly after you").

29. JRR to John Brockenbrough, August 1, 1814, Shorey, 10–11.

30. JRR to Harmanus Bleecker, July 26, 1814, HB.

31. JRR to Nathan Loughborough, April 30, 1828, JRR LVA.

32. Ford, *Deliver Us from Evil*, 147.

33. JRR to James Garnett, July 13, 1818, JMG.

34. JRR to Harmanus Bleecker, November 16, 1818, HB.

35. JRR to Walter Coles, June 11, 1821, JRR UVA.

36. Ford, *Deliver Us from Evil*, 147.

37. JRR to N. B. Tucker, January 2, 1822, TC UVA.

38. JRR to John Brockenbrough, August 1, 1814, Shorey, 10–11.

39. JRR to James Garnett, January 12, 1812, JMG.

40. JRR to James Garnett, November 24, 25, 1832, JMG.

41. Ford, *Deliver Us from Evil*, 147.

42. JRR to Littleton Waller Tazewell, January 8, 1804, UNC.

43. JRR to James Garnett, February 17, 1811, JMG.

44. JRR to George Logan, February 13, 1813, PaH.

45. Ford, *Deliver Us from Evil*, 147.

46. Tate, *Conservatism and Southern Intellectuals*, 34.

47. "As divided as the Southern mind may have been on these issues, it was united behind the idea that slavery was and must remain an issue for Southerners alone to deal with. . . . Southern slaveholders felt besieged both from without and within." Mason, *Slavery and Politics*, 30.

48. Quincy, *Figures of the Past*, 212–13.

49. JRR to John Brockenbrough, February 24, 1820, Shorey, 27.

50. *Register of Debates*, 19th Cong., 1st sess., 117.

51. Ibid., 117–18.

52. Ibid., 119.

53. Ibid., 118.

54. Ibid., 130.

55. Ibid.

56. Ibid., 127–28.

57. Ibid. 118.

6. YAZOO MEN

1. Thomas Jefferson to John Dickinson, December 19, 1801, TJ LC.

2. Marshall "made two fundamental points. . . . First, in a conflict between the Constitution and an act of Congress, the Constitution must prevail. . . . Second, and just as important, the judiciary would be the final arbiter of that conflict between a law and the Constitution." Sloan and McKean, *The Great Decision,* 163–64. The abiding significance of *Marbury,* these authors conclude, "is that it stands for a system in which independent courts have the last word on the Constitution, and on the requirements of law." *The Great Decision,* 178. Historian James MacGregor Burns writes that Marshall's words "laid the basis for a power of judicial review . . . so absolute and sweeping that it would eventually create a *supremacy* of the Supreme Court." *Packing the Court,* 31.

3. Marshall "saw judicial review as a mechanism for asserting the rightful authority of the new government, especially when confronted with the claims of the states' rights school that the Constitution strictly limited federal powers." Magrath, *Yazoo,* 61.

4. Thomas Jefferson to Abigail Adams, September 11, 1804, Cappon, *Adams-Jefferson Letters,* 279.

5. Thomas Jefferson to Elias Shipman, July 12, 1801, TJ LC.

6. Lillich, "The Chase Impeachment," 49, 51, note 6. "Even the Federalist district judges who sat with him found him short-tempered, harsh, and mercurial—traits Chase exhibited throughout his career." Hoffer and Hull, *Impeachment in America,* 229. "Irascible, overbearing, and partisan, Chase had made himself a convenient target by his intemperate conduct." Hobson, "The Marshall Court," 53. Chief Justice John Marshall "had little sympathy for Chase's free-wheeling partisanship on the bench." Smith, *John Marshall,* 337. See also Newmyer, *Marshall and the Heroic Age of the Supreme Court,* 179 (describing Chase as "arrogant, imperious, and intemperate").

7. President John Adams questioned the fairness and legality of the trial and pardoned Fries.

8. Hoffer and Hull, *Impeachment in America,* 230. "Chase made it clear from the first that he intended to impose his own will upon the conduct of the trial." Elsmere, *Chase,* 119–20. "Affidavits circulated stating that Justice Chase intended to 'teach the lawyers in Virginia the difference between the liberty and the licentiousness of the press' and that he had ordered the marshal to exclude all Republicans from the jury." Stone, *Perilous Times,* 62.

9. Hoffer and Hull, *Impeachment in America,* 230.

10. Lillich, "The Chase Impeachment," 50. For reaction to Chase's charge, see Elsmere, *Chase,* 162–67.

11. Thomas Jefferson to J. H. Nicholson, May 13, 1803, TJ LC.

12. Randolph had handled the impeachment of Judge John Pickering of New

Hampshire, the first federal judge to be impeached and convicted. Pickering, however, had been insane, and his removal was supported by both parties. It provided little useful precedent. Ellis, *The Jeffersonian Crisis,* 69–75.

13. *AC,* 8th Cong., 1st sess., 819.

14. Ibid., 1238–39.

15. Magrath, *Yazoo,* 3, 6–7.

16. White, *Statistics of the State of Georgia,* 50.

17. Haskins, *The Yazoo Land Companies,* 26–27.

18. Magrath, *Yazoo,* 13–14; Knight, *A Standard History of Georgia,* 392–93.

19. Magrath, *Yazoo,* 35–36.

20. Peter Magrath writes of Randolph's opposition: "As an agrarian of the Virginia plantation aristocracy, Randolph saw the land speculators as a species of the financial capitalists whom he despised. Federal recognition of the claims would mean a repudiation of the validity of the Georgia repeal act, and this ran counter to his conviction that federal powers under the Constitution should be strictly construed so as not to trespass on the more important rights of the State." Magrath also attributes Randolph's motivation to hatred of Madison and his being "a natural oppositionist." *Yazoo,* 41.

21. *AC,* 8th Cong., 1st sess., 1039.

22. Ibid., 983–84.

23. William Plumer to J. Mason, February 14, 28, 1804, in Brant, *Madison* 4: 233–34; William Plumer to John Park, February 15, 1804, in Cunningham, *Jeffersonian Republicans in Power,* 77.

24. Manasseh Cutler to Captain F. Poole, February 13, 1804, Cutler, *Life of Cutler,* 161–63.

25. Sawyer, *Randolph,* 42; Cutler, *Life of Cutler,* 161–63.

26. Sawyer, *Randolph,* 42; Brant, *Madison* 4: 233; Cunningham, *Jeffersonian Republicans in Power,* 77.

27. Sawyer *Randolph,* 42.

28. Brant, *Madison* 4: 233; Cunningham, *Jeffersonian Republicans in Power,* 77; Cutler, *Life of Cutler,* 161–63.

29. *AC,* 8th Cong., 1st sess., 1039–40.

30. Ibid., 1109–10.

31. Ibid., 1109.

32. Ibid., 1115.

33. Ibid., 1104. Randolph's "ten-year assault on Madison as a 'Yazoo man,'" Irving Brant wrote, "was a calculated prostitution of the truth to political demagogy and neurotic jealousy." *Madison* 4: 240.

34. Brown, *Plumer's Memorandum,* 122–23.

35. Ibid., 122. Representative Simeon Baldwin of Connecticut wrote: "This Randolph . . . despising the feebleness of his partisans . . . attempts to manage them with so much aristocratic hauteur, that they sometimes grow unmanageable and rebel, but they have nobody else who really possess the talents responsible for a leader." Simeon Baldwin to Mrs. Baldwin, February 15, 1804, Baldwin Family Papers, Yale University, in Cunningham, *Jeffersonian Republicans in Power,* 77.

36. JRR to Albert Gallatin, October 14, 1804, Adams, *Randolph*, 117.

37. JRR to Richard E. Meade, July 27, 1804, Meade, "Some New Information," 256.

38. JRR to James Monroe, July 20, 1804, JRR LC. Upon reflection, Randolph revised his somewhat flippant summation. "I feel for Hamilton's *immediate connexions*," he wrote to Nicholson, "real concern, for Himself, *nothing* for his party, and those 'soi-disant' republicans who have been shedding *'crocodile tears'* over him, *contempt. . . .* Burr's is, indeed, an incomparable defeat; he is cut off from hope of a retreat among the Federalists; not so much because he has overthrown their idol, as because he cannot answer their purpose. . . . In his correspondence with Hamilton, how visible is his ascendency over him, and how sensible does the letter appear of it. . . . On one side [Hamilton] there is labored obscurity, much equivocation, and many attempts at evasion, not unmixed with a little blustering; on the other [Burr] an unshaken adherence to his object, and an undeviating pursuit of it, not to be eluded or baffled." JRR to J. H. Nicholson, August 27, 1804, JRR LC.

39. JRR to George Hay [October 1804], JRR UVA.

40. Henry St. George Tucker to St. George Tucker, March 3, 1805, TC UVA.

41. The eight Articles of Impeachment addressed the following acts: (1) misconduct at the Fries trial, (2) allowing a biased juror at the Callender trial, (3) refusing to permit John Taylor to testify at the Callender trial, (4) intemperate conduct and "vexatious interruption" at the Callender trial, (5) issuing a bench warrant instead of a summons at the Callender trial, (6) refusing a continuance at the Callender trial, (7) the charge to the grand jury in Newcastle, Delaware, and (8) the charge to the grand jury in Baltimore. Smith and Lloyd, *Trial of Samuel Chase*, 5–8.

42. Fisher Ames to Thomas Dwight, January 20, 1805, Ames, *Works of Ames* 1: 338.

43. Adams, *Memoirs of John Quincy Adams* 1: 323.

44. JRR to James Monroe, February 28, 1804, JRR LC.

45. Adams, *Memoirs of John Quincy Adams* 1: 322.

46. Ibid., 323.

47. JRR to Richard E. Meade, December 1, 1804, JRR UVA.

48. JRR to J. H. Nicholson, January 15, 1805, JRR LC; JRR to Richard E. Meade, January 14, 1805, JRR UVA.

49. JRR to St. George Tucker, January 30, 1805, RMWC.

50. *AC*, 8th Cong., 2nd sess., 1022.

51. Adams, *Randolph*, 126. Dumas Malone called the speech "verbal terrorism." Malone, *Jefferson* 4: 451.

52. *AC*, 8th Cong., 2nd sess., 1026.

53. Ibid.

54. Ibid., 1031.

55. Ibid., 1028.

56. Ibid., 1029–30.

57. Ibid., 1031–32. Forrest McDonald writes "it seems entirely probable that [Randolph's charges] were well founded." *Presidency of Jefferson*, 88.

58. *AC*, 8th Cong., 2nd sess., 1032.

59. Ibid., 1033.

60. Ibid., 1099.

61. Brown, *Plumer's Memorandum*, 269. Manasseh Cutler called it a *"fire and brimstone* speech." Cutler diary, January 29, 1805, Cutler, *Life of Cutler*, 182.

62. "What Randolph thus said was to a great extent true." Adams, *Randolph*, 129. "[A] denial of the validity of the rescinding act meant a denial of his most cherished theories of government." Haskins, *Yazoo Land Companies*, 33.

63. *AC*, 8th Cong., 2nd sess., 1032.

64. Ibid., 1103–4.

65. Ibid., 1104.

66. Manasseh Cutler to Dr. Torrey, February 2, 1805, Cutler, *Life of Cutler*, 186–88. Randolph viewed the published account of the Yazoo speech as "a tame and vapid copy of a spirited original." JRR to St. George Tucker, February 22, 1805, RMWC.

67. *AC*, 8th Cong., 2nd sess., 1174.

68. Richmond *Enquirer*, November 5, 1805.

69. Brown, *Plumer's Memorandum*, 370. Jefferson's secretary, William Burwell, was convinced that Randolph was "determined to oppose [the administration] unless he was made the sole leader in the Government." Cunningham, *Jeffersonian Republicans in Power*, 84.

70. Brant, *Madison* 4: 249–50.

71. Adams, *History* 2: 219; Luconi, "Madison and Impeachment," 203.

7. THE *TERTIUM QUID*

1. Henry St. George Tucker to St. George Tucker, March 3, 1805, TC UVA.

2. Lillich, "The Chase Impeachment," 63. Martin, "after the death of Patrick Henry, was generally regarded as the greatest trial lawyer in the country." Smith, *John Marshall*, 343.

3. *AC*, 8th Cong., 2nd sess., 106.

4. Ibid., 142.

5. Ibid., 148.

6. Ibid., 150.

7. Ibid., 153.

8. The numerous articles "diluted the effect of the one charge where the Republicans were certain to muster impeachment votes [the charge to the Baltimore grand jury]." Lillich, "The Chase Impeachment," 58–59.

9. "Because Randolph did not yet name the demon, Chase's counsel did not attempt to slay it." Hoffer and Hull, *Impeachment in America*, 241.

10. *AC*, 8th Cong., 2nd Sess., 165.

11. Brown, *Plumer's Memorandum*, 280. Albert Beveridge offered a different view of Randolph's opening argument, calling it "a speech of some skill." Beveridge, *Life of Marshall* 3: 187.

12. Richmond *Enquirer*, March 12, 1805.

13. John Quincy Adams to John Adams, March 8, 1805, Ford, *Writings of Adams* 3: 106.

14. "Plainly Marshall was still fearful of the outcome of the Republican impeachment

plans, not only as to Chase, but as to the entire Federalist membership of the Supreme Court." Beveridge, *Marshall* 3: 196.

15. Smith and Lloyd, *Trial of Chase*, 255–56, 259; *AC*, 8th Cong., 2nd sess., 263–64, 266.

16. Brown, *Plumer's Memorandum*, 291.

17. "The virulence of the party prosecuting," Timothy Pickering wrote, "and the aggravated evidence of angry irritated opponents, had thrown some light clouds over the Judge's character; but in the course of the trial, I am inclined to think that these will be dissipated." Timothy Pickering to Rufus King, February 15, 1805, King, *Life of King* 4: 439. "The general sentiment here even among political adversaries of the Judge is that he will be honorably acquitted." *Baltimore Federal Gazette*, February 18, 1805.

18. Adams, *Memoirs of John Quincy Adams*, 353. Giles's biographer writes that the senator "did have extraordinary relations with John Randolph, manager, but he did not allow these things to prevent his judging the case with fairness." Anderson, *Giles*, 97.

19. JRR to J. H. Nicholson, February 1805, JRR LC.

20. Ibid.

21. Hoffer and Hull, *Impeachment in America*, 242–44.

22. *AC*, 8th Cong., 2nd sess., 354.

23. Ibid., 356–60.

24. Ibid., 360.

25. Ibid.

26. Ibid., 363.

27. "[T]he Senate Chamber could not contain even a small part of the throng that sought the Capitol to hear the celebrated lawyer." Beveridge, *Marshall* 3: 201.

28. *AC*, 8th Cong., 2nd sess., 433.

29. Ibid., 434.

30. Ibid., 489.

31. Ibid., 452–53.

32. "Friendship, ideology, and long practice as an advocate combined to make [Martin's] the most striking performance at the bar of the Senate." Hoffer and Hull, *Impeachment in America*, 248.

33. *AC*, 8th Cong., 2nd sess., 560.

34. Ibid., 583.

35. Henry St. George Tucker to St. George Tucker, March 3, 1805, JRR LC.

36. Cutler diary, February 27, 1805, Cutler, *Life of Cutler*, 184.

37. Bruce 1: 214; Adams, *Randolph*, 147.

38. Adams, *Memoirs of John Quincy Adams*, 359

39. Henry St. George Tucker to St. George Tucker, March 3, 1805, TC UVA ("He was extremely unwell, scarcely able to support himself during his argument"); Adams, *Memoirs of John Quincy Adams* 1: 354 ("Mr. Randolph, the chairman, appeared to be much indisposed").

40. "Although he was a gifted orator, Randolph lacked an understanding of the rules of evidence and had no experience in building a case before a jury." Smith, *John Marshall*, 344.

41. *AC*, 8th Cong., 2nd sess., 642, 644.

42. Ibid., 642, 645–46, 651.

43. Ibid., 643.

44. Ibid., 648–50.

45. Ibid., 658.

46. Ibid., 642, 645, 650, 658.

47. Ibid., 649, 659.

48. Ibid., 655–56.

49. "In the midst of his harangue, the fellow cried like a baby, with clear, sheer madness." Manasseh Cutler to Dr. Torrey, March 1, 1805, Cutler, *Life of Cutler*, 193. "Here the overwrought and exhausted man broke into tears" but "closed in a passage of genuine power." Beveridge, *Marshall* 3: 216.

50. *AC*, 8th Cong., 2nd sess., 662.

51. Brown, *Plumer's Memorandum*, 302. "The danger of Chase's acts was no longer framed within the scaffolding of a coherent legal doctrine, but dumped upon a jerry-built analogy between the Federalist party and the Tories." Hoffer and Hull, *Impeachment in America*, 252.

52. "While Nicholson and Campbell were to acquit themselves well, the rest were pedestrian lawyers. . . . [B]y every objective standard they were poorly prepared in their own right." Lillich, "The Chase Impeachment," 63, 71. It is also possible that several acquittal votes were cast to diminish Randolph's influence. Ellis, *Jeffersonian Crisis*, 103.

53. Adams, *History* 2: 240. "In private . . . [Madison] could not refrain from rejoicing over the political blow to Randolph and his radical allies." Luconi, "Madison and Impeachment," 203. John Quincy Adams noted that Madison "appeared much diverted at the petulance of the managers on their disappointment." Adams, *Memoirs of John Quincy Adams* 1: 365. Noble Cunningham writes that Jefferson was "disappointed" with the outcome. *Jeffersonian Republicans in Power*, 81.

54. An interesting view of Chase's guilt is offered by Raoul Berger. He concludes that "Chase's conduct was not merely an oppressive misuse of power, but in two respects it was illegal as well. . . . [I]t furnished grounds for impeachment under English law, to which the Founders looked for guidance. . . . By his conduct Chase destroyed confidence in the impartial administration of justice. . . . That is the lesson that needs to be drawn from the richly justified attempt to bring him to justice, not that his acquittal represents a triumph over gross partisanship." *Impeachment: The Constitutional Problems*, 249–51.

55. John Quincy Adams to John Adams, March 14, 1805; Ford, *Writings of Adams* 3: 114.

56. JRR to J. H. Nicholson, March 4, 1805, JRR LC.

57. JRR to J. H. Nicholson, April 12, 1805, JRR LC; JRR to David Parish, April 12, 1805, Bruce 2: 671.

58. JRR to J. H. Nicholson, March 17, 1805, JRR LC.

59. Beverley Tucker to St. George Tucker, August 4, 1805, TC UVA.

60. JRR to Harmanus Bleecker, November 16, 1818, HB.

61. Richmond *Enquirer*, July 12, 1805.

62. JRR to J. H. Nicholson, April 18, 1805, JRR LC.

63. Ibid.

64. JRR to J. H. Nicholson, August 25, 1805, JRR LVA; JRR to J. H. Nicholson, October 12, 1805, JRR LC.

65. "Randolph had come to see the partnership of the president and his secretary of state as phony republicanism." Burstein and Isenberg, *Madison and Jefferson*, 435.

66. JRR to J. H. Nicholson, March 29, 1805, JRR LC.

67. JRR to J. H. Nicholson, April 30, 1805, JRR LC.

68. Ibid.

69. JRR to J. H. Nicholson, August 25, 1805, JRR LVA.

70. JRR to Albert Gallatin, October 25, 1805, Adams, *Writings of Gallatin*, 331–33.

71. JRR to Ann C. R. Morris, October 31, 1814, JRR UVA; Ann C. R. Morris to JRR, January 16, 1815, PrU.

72. Bruce 2: 276, 288.

73. Richmond *Enquirer*, October 10, 1806.

74. Ibid., September 19, 1806.

75. Norman Risjord writes that Randolph "fully expected to receive this appointment" and was "disappointed" that he did not. *The Old Republicans*, 33–34. Irving Brant concludes that Randolph "pointed to his availability for the expected vacancy at London." *Madison* 4: 311. Jefferson biographer George Tucker wrote that the president and Madison "had seen enough of Mr. Randolph to know that his defects of temper rendered him unfit for such a situation—that he could neither be expected to yield implicit obedience to the views of those who employed him, nor be capable of the address or patient research or temperate logic for effecting them." Bruce 1: 265. Finally, Nancy Randolph Morris wrote that Randolph was "elated with the prospect of a foreign mission" and "as usual, you rode your new Hobby to the annoyance of all who like me were obliged to listen. Your expected voyage enchanted you so much that you could not help talking of it even to your deaf nephew: 'Soon, my boy, we shall be sailing over the Atlantic.' But . . . [it] appeared soon after that Mr. Jefferson and Mr. Madison, knowing your character, had prudently declined a compliance with your wishes." Anne Morris to JRR, January 16, 1825, JRR UVA. Randolph did discuss traveling to London in two letters written during this period. Neither letter references an anticipated or desired diplomatic purpose for the trip. In his letter to Joseph Nicholson, Randolph seems to want to get away in wake of the Chase trial. "'Tis not in my power to express one half of what I have felt within a few weeks," he wrote. "Suffice to say that no circumstance has occurred, or *can now happen*, to induce me to abandon my proposed trip to Europe." JRR to J. H. Nicholson, April 29, 1805, JRR LC. He expressed similar sentiments to Albert Gallatin. JRR to Albert Gallatin, October 25, 1805, Adams, *Gallatin*, 331–33. The purpose of the proposed trip to London was to secure a proper education for his deaf nephew, St. George Randolph, which might explain Nancy's recollection of Randolph's discussing it with the boy. See JRR to St. George Tucker, December 17, 1805, RMWC. There exists no evidence that Randolph sought or expected this appointment.

76. Richmond *Enquirer*, October 10, 1806.

77. Malone, *Jefferson* 5: 67–68. See also Quincy, *Life of Quincy*, 94 ("Jefferson's friends . . . had selected Barnabas Bidwell of Massachusetts").

78. Quincy, *Life of Quincy*, 94.

79. Brown, *Plumer's Memorandum*, 338.

80. Quincy, *Life of Quincy*, 95.

81. Foner, *Writings of Jefferson*, 363, 364, 365.

82. Ibid., 365.

83. Bruce 1: 225. "Reactions in the House [to Jefferson's message] ranged from anger to dismay." Carson, "That Ground Called Quiddism," 81.

84. *AC*, 9th Cong., 1st sess., 946.

85. Thomas Jefferson to Albert Gallatin, December 7, 1805, Adams, *Gallatin* 1: 282.

86. *Decius*, Richmond *Enquirer*, August 15, 1806; Risjord, *Old Republicans*, 46–47; Malone, *Jefferson* 5: 72.

87. Cunningham, *Jeffersonian Republicans in Power*, 82.

88. Adams, *History* 2: 240. Madison, his biographer wrote, "having no public or social motive for frequent contact [with Randolph,] sought none. That was enough to make Randolph his enemy." Brant, *Madison* 4: 232. Randolph once said that he "had not been in the habit of paying great deference to the political opinions of the late General [Alexander] Hamilton, or to those of the negotiator of the Treaty of London [John Jay], nor did he think the third member of the gentleman's political trinity [James Madison] entitled to more consideration than his worthy co-adjustors." *AC*, 10th Cong., 1st sess., 944.

89. *AC*, 9th Cong., 1st sess., 947.

90. Ibid.

91. Ibid., 946; JRR to St. George Tucker, December 17, 1805, RMWC.

92. Adams, *Randolph*, 168.

93. Ibid., 169; Malone, *Jefferson* 5: 73; *Decius*, Richmond *Enquirer*, August 15, 1806.

94. Adams, *Randolph*, 166.

95. JRR to J. H. Nicholson, December 1805, Adams, *Randolph*, 170.

96. *AC*, 9th Cong., 1st sess., 1117.

97. Ibid., 1117–18.

98. JRR to George Hay, January 3, 1806, JRR UVA.

99. Bruce 1: 231.

100. Thomas W. Thompson to Daniel Webster, January 10, 1806, Wiltse, *Papers of Webster* 1: 74–75.

101. Adams, *Randolph*, 172.

102. McDonald, *Presidency of Jefferson*, 104.

103. Thomas Jefferson to William Duane, April 30, 1811, TJ LC.

104. JRR to Caesar Rodney, February [12], 1806, JRR LVA.

105. JRR to Caesar Rodney, February 28, 1806, JRR LVA. Randolph was not alone in this view. John Taylor of Caroline "was convinced that it was Madison's influence which had led to this betrayal of Republicanism, and . . . that Madison had always been a Federalist." Ammon, "Jeffersonian Republicans," 157.

106. JRR to Theodore Dudley, January 31, 1806, Dudley, 9.

107. JRR to Theodore Dudley, February 15, 1806, Dudley, 15.

108. Brant, *Madison* 4: 313.

8. MYSTERY OF AFFECTION AND FAITH

1. Thomas Jefferson to William Duane, March 22, 1806, TJ LC.

2. Thomas Jefferson to James Monroe, May 4, 1806, TJ LC.

3. Ibid.

4. Howe, *Historical Collections of Virginia*, 223. H. J. Eckenrode in his study of the Randolph family identifies the portrait as "John Randolph of Roanoke as a boy." *The Randolphs*, 225.

5. Adams, *Randolph*, 160. Stuart's painting is "justly regarded as one of the most beautiful productions of the painter's brush." *Works of Stuart*, 38.

6. JRR to James M. Garnett, April 27, [1806], JMG.

7. JRR to James M. Garnett, June 19, 1806, JMG.

8. *AC*, 9th Cong., 1st sess., 72–73; Adams, *History* 3: 709–10.

9. JRR to J. H. Nicholson, February 20, 1806, JRR LC.

10. Adams, *Randolph*, 173. Richard Weaver wrote that Randolph's "opposition was to a consistent trend which he saw as carrying the nation away from republican principles, which in his mind constituted the anchor of liberty." "Two Types of American Individualism," Curtis and Thompson, *Southern Essays of Weaver*, 80.

11. *AC*, 9th Cong., 1st sess., 557.

12. Ibid., 560.

13. Ibid.

14. Ibid., 559.

15. Ibid., 562.

16. Ibid., 556.

17. "At first Randolph had most of the southern members with him," Forrest McDonald writes, "for all that was at stake was American commercial prosperity, which they were not at all loathe to sacrifice. But then he went too far." *Presidency of Jefferson*, 108.

18. Benjamin Tallmadge to Manasseh Cutler, February 19, 1806, Cutler, *Life of Cutler*, 326–27.

19. *AC*, 9th Cong., 1st sess., 561, 566, 567.

20. Carson, "That Ground Called Quiddism," 88; Haynes, "Letters of Taggart," 198.

21. *AC*, 9th Cong., 1st sess., 565.

22. Ibid., 565, 566. Randolph called Madison "as mean a man for a Virginian as John Quincy Adams was for a Yankee." Bruce 1: 253. Madison's pamphlet, *An Examination of the British Doctrine, Which Subjects to Capture Neutral Trade, Not Open in Time of Peace*, was, Bradford Perkins writes, "too verbose and too complicated for ordinary readers" and "merited John Randolph's scornful comment." Perkins, *Prologue to War*, 43.

23. Col. [Benjamin] Tallmadge to Manasseh Cutler, April 2, 1806, Cutler, *Life of Cutler*, 327.

24. *AC*, 9th Cong., 1st sess., 563, 564, 569.

25. Ibid., 573.

26. Brown, *Plumer's Memorandum*, 444.

27. Thomas W. Thompson to Daniel Webster, March 10, 1806, Wiltse, *Papers of Webster* 1: 81.

28. Joseph Bryan to JRR, April 23, 1806, JSB VHS.

29. Richmond *Enquirer*, March 21, 1806. Randolph's speech has been praised for "the range and brilliance of is observations," and dubbed "unquestionably one of the most brilliant speeches ever uttered in Congress." Dawidoff, *Education of Randolph*, 190; Bruce 1: 245. Norman Risjord wrote that the speech "erected a stable platform for conservative discontent." *The Old Republicans*, 57. Russell Kirk concluded that the speech means "more in these times of American incertitude than ever it did before." *Randolph*, 25. The speech routinely appeared in nineteenth-century studies of American oratory. *See: American Eloquence: A Collection of Speeches and Addresses by the Most Eminent Orators of America* (New York: D. Appleton and Co., 1857); *American Oratory from the Speeches of Eminent Americans* (Philadelphia: Desilver, Thomas & Co., 1836); *Library of Oratory* (Philadelphia: E. C. & J. Biddle, 1845); and *Orations of American Orators* (New York: Colonial Press, 1900).

30. *AC,* 9th Cong., 1st sess., 592.

31. "Both the nature of the carrying trade and the consequences of forceful policy in its defense doomed the Gregg Resolution in the Ninth Congress." Spivak, *Jefferson's English Crisis,* 45.

32. Thomas Jefferson to James Monroe, March 18, 1806, TJ LC. Outwardly, Jefferson continued to affect bewilderment at Randolph's behavior. Senator Plumer quotes Jefferson as saying: "Mr. Randolph's late conduct is very astonishing and has given me much uneasiness. I do not know what he means." Brown, *Plumer's Memorandum,* 471.

33. Ammon, *Monroe,* 242–47. "The Randolph-Monroe movement . . . seemed serious both because of its ideological earnestness and its possession, in Monroe, of a nationally respected candidate." Ketcham, *Madison,* 467.

34. JRR to James Monroe, March 20, 1806, JRR LC.

35. JRR to James Monroe, April 22, 1806, JRR LC.

36. JRR to James Monroe, September 16, 1806, JRR LC.

37. Thomas Jefferson to James Monroe, May 4, 1806, TJ LC.

38. Ibid.

39. James Monroe to JRR, November 12, 1806, Ammon, *Monroe,* 257.

40. Plumer attributes this phrase to Randolph. Brown, *Plumer's Memorandum,* 465.

41. Adams, *History* 3: 173.

42. Benjamin Tallmadge to Manasseh Cutler, February 19, 1806, Cutler, *Life of Cutler,* 326–27.

43. *AC,* 9th Cong., 1st sess., 775. Principal members of the Quid faction included James Garnett of Virginia, Joseph Bryan of Georgia, Joseph Nicholson of Maryland, Richard Stanford of North Carolina, Christopher Clark of Virginia, Phillip Thompson of Virginia, and Edwin Gray of Virginia. Nathaniel Macon was a fellow-traveler of the Quids.

44. *AC,* 9th Cong., 1st sess., 909.

45. Adams, *History* 3: 173; *AC,* 9th Cong., 1st sess., 983.

46. Richmond *Enquirer,* April 4, 1806.

47. *AC*, 9th Cong., 1st sess., 928.

48. Ibid., 1110.

49. Ibid., 984.

50. Ibid., 1023.

51. Ibid., 14, 319, 105.

52. Ibid., 985.

53. Ibid., 988.

54. Ibid.

55. Malone, *Jefferson* 5: 128. "No doubt," Malone wrote, "this high-spirited, thin-skinned young man was painfully aware that he had achieved less than had been expected of him."

56. *AC*, 9th Cong., 1st sess., 1102.

57. Ibid., 1103.

58. Thomas Randolph's biographer writes that John Randolph "was almost certainly referring to Findley." Gaines, *Thomas Mann Randolph*, 61. Dumas Malone agreed, writing "there could be little doubt that the orator had [Findley] in mind." *Jefferson* 5: 128. Joseph Bryan provides contemporary confirmation in a letter to Randolph. "I have seen some account of Findley's conduct on the last day of the session, as well as his speech. I have also seen the speech of that scoundrel Jackson. Your conduct to him was proper—or rather I would say to both." Joseph Bryan to JRR, June 3, 1806, JSB VHS.

59. *AC*, 9th Cong., 1st sess., 1104–5.

60. Richmond *Enquirer*, June 17, 1806.

61. Ibid.

62. *AC*, 9th Cong., 1st sess., 1106.

63. Richmond *Enquirer*, June 17, 1806.

64. JRR to J. H. Nicholson, April 27, 1806, JRR LC.

65. JRR to James M. Garnett, April 27, [1806], JMG; JRR to Joseph Scott [November 9], 1806, HuL.

66. JRR to Joseph Scott, [November 9], 1806, HuL; JRR to Joseph H. Nicholson, October 24, 1806, JRR LC.

67. JRR to James M. Garnett, April 27, [1806], JMG; JRR to Caesar Rodney, November 20, 1806, JRR UVA.

68. JRR to Joseph Scott, [November 9], 1806, HuL.

69. JRR to James Garnett, May 11, 1806, JMG.

70. See JRR to James Garnett, April 27, May 11, June 4, 1806 JMG; JRR to J. H. Nicholson, June 3, 1806, Adams, *Randolph*, 196–97.

71. JRR to James Garnett, May 1806, JMG.

72. "A nobler spirit," Ritchie would write later that year in an editorial about Randolph, "lives not among the sons of men." Richmond *Enquirer*, September 2, 1806.

73. Ambler, *Thomas Ritchie*, 35.

74. JRR to James Garnett, July 5, 1806, JMG; JRR to J. H. Nicholson, June 3, 1806, Adams, *Randolph*, 196–97.

75. Richmond *Enquirer*, July 1, 1806.

76. Thomas Jefferson to Thomas Mann Randolph, July 13, 1806, TJ LC.

77. JRR to James Garnett, June 19, June 4, 1806, JMG.

78. JRR to J. H. Nicholson, July 7, 1806, JRR LC.

79. *Decius,* Richmond *Enquirer,* August 15, 1806.

80. Ibid.

81. Joseph Bryan to JRR, September 12, 1806, JSB VHS. Somewhat surprisingly, the *Enquirer* agreed to publish the Decius letter. "[The] Press is free for the publication of all opinions and statements," Ritchie wrote, and "however he may lament . . . the temporary warmth, and the petty schism . . . he cannot but rejoice at the discussion." Richmond *Enquirer,* August 15, 1806.

82. Malone, *Jefferson* 5: 161–62; Thomas Jefferson to William A. Burwell, September 17, 1806, TJ LC.

83. Thomas Jefferson to William A. Burwell, September 17, 1806, TJ LC.

84. Richmond *Enquirer,* September 2, October 24, 1806.

85. Thomas Jefferson to Barnabas Bidwell, July 5, 1806, TJ LC.

86. JRR to J. H. Nicholson, October 24, 1806, JRR LC.

87. On the alleged Jefferson-Walker affair, see Malone, *Jefferson* 1: 153–55, 447–51; 5: 216–23.

88. JRR to J. H. Nicholson, June 24, 1806, JRR LC.

89. JRR to James Monroe, July 3, September 16, 1806, JRR LC.

90. JRR to J. H. Nicholson, October 24, 1806, JRR LC.

91. JRR to James Garnett, September 4, 1806, JMG.

92. JRR to James M. Garnett, October 28, 1806, JMG.

93. Joseph Bryan to JRR, November 28, 1806, JSB VHS.

9. HOUSE CYNOSURE

1. Randolph recorded in his diary that, when Albert Gallatin told Jefferson that Randolph would remain chairman of Ways & Means, the president responded "That will never do." JRR Diary, JRR VHS.

2. *AC,* 9th Cong., 2nd sess., 111.

3. Ibid.

4. Nathanial Macon to Joseph H. Nicholson, December 2, 1806, Nicholson Papers, in Dodd, *Life of Macon,* 209.

5. *AC,* 9th Cong., 2nd sess., 115, 130.

6. Brown, *Plumer's Memorandum,* 608. On the other hand, Randolph did attempt to maintain a degree of cordiality. "Have you any recollection of my *refusing* to drink the President" he wrote about one rumor, "when given as a toast by the master of the feast?" Randolph had no memory of "such an act of rudeness." JRR to Richard Meade, January 3, 1807, JRR UVA.

7. Foner, *Writings of Jefferson,* 373. Randolph's words may have seemed "too contemptuous . . . but events had borne out his prediction that [the non-importation act] would not greatly alarm the British government." Malone, *Jefferson* 5: 476.

8. JRR to Joseph H. Nicholson, December 10, 1806, JRR LC.

9. JRR to James Monroe, December 5, 1806, JRR LC.

10. JRR to Joseph H. Nicholson, December 10, 1806, JRR LC.

11. JRR to Joseph Scott, January 12, 1807, JRR UVA.

12. JRR to James Monroe, December 5, 1806, JRR LC.

13. *AC*, 9th Cong., 2nd sess., 294–95.

14. Ibid., 350.

15. Ibid., 418.

16. Ibid., 421. "Yesterday we had a most extraordinary bill from the Senate," Randolph wrote, "for suspending the privilege of the Writ of Habeas Corpus. The details of the bill were, if possible, more objectionable than its principle and . . . was stuffed with arbitrary and detestable provisions." JRR to J. H. Nicholson, January 27, 1807, JRR LC.

17. *AC*, 9th Cong., 2nd sess., 483.

18. Ibid., 626.

19. Ibid., 686–87.

20. Hoffer, *Treason Trials*, 37, 42–45; Wheelan, *Jefferson's Vendetta*, 126–28.

21. Hoffer, *Treason Trials*, 38–41; Wheelan, *Jefferson's Vendetta*, 110.

22. For conflicting interpretations of Burr's plans and guilt, see Isenberg, *Fallen Founder*, 271–72, 282–316; Abernethy, *The Burr Conspiracy*, 10–40, 61–118, 138–226; Wheelan, *Jefferson's Vendetta*, 131–52; Melton, *Aaron Burr*, 51–145; Malone, *Jefferson* 5: 215–66; and Burstein and Isenberg, *Madison and Jefferson*, 441–46.

23. Foner, *Writings of Jefferson*, 370.

24. JRR to James Monroe, December 5, 1806, JRR LC.

25. JRR to Joseph H. Nicholson, December 21, 1806, JRR LC; *AC*, 9th Cong., 2nd sess., 336. George Hoadley, Washington correspondent for Philadelphia's *Gazette of the United States,* reported that Randolph's speeches on the Burr resolution were "by far the most interesting speeches I ever heard." Like so many others, Hoadley felt the need to describe Randolph. "He is tall and very slim and resembles a tall boy more than a man," Hoadley wrote to his father. "His features are small and his countenance pale and one would be at a loss to conjecture from his face whether he's young or old. His voice is singular and resembles a girl's or a small boy's but it's very clear and distinct." George Hoadley to Timothy Hoadley, January 23, 1807, Hoadley Papers, Virginia Historical Society.

26. Foner, *Writings of Jefferson*, 376.

27. JRR to Joseph H. Nicholson, March 25, 1807, JRR LC. The Latin phrase translates: "How changed from what he once was."

28. Hoffer, *Treason Trials*, 131–35.

29. Thomas Jefferson to William Branch Giles, April 6, 1807, TJ LC. See also Hoffer, *Treason Trials*, 136 ("In the preceding months, Jefferson had acted in the role of judge, prosecutor, and jury"); Wheelan, *Jefferson's Vendetta*, 100 ("President Jefferson had appropriated $11,000 from the government's 'continuing fund' for U.S. Attorney George Hay to hire prosecutors").

30. Scott, *Memoirs* 1: 16.

31. Carpenter, *Trial of Col. Burr* 1: 7–10.

32. Ibid., 12.

33. Beveridge, *Marshall* 3: 413; Melton, *Aaron Burr*, 176.

34. JRR to Joseph H. Nicholson, May 27, 1807, JRR LC.

35. JRR to James Monroe, May 30, 1807, JRR LC. The "Greek Kalends" referred to a point in time that does not or will not exist.

36. JRR to James Monroe, May 30, 1807, JRR LC.

37. Abernethy, *Burr Conspiracy*, 239.

38. Ibid.

39. JRR to Joseph H. Nicholson, June 28, 1807, JRR LC. "Burr declares that W[ilkinson] has for ten years received 3,000 dollars annually, as a Spanish officer," Randolph wrote, "that he (W) drew ten thousand dollars out of the Treasury of Spain when he took possession of N. Orleans for the U.S. and . . . sufficient evidence will be found in his (Burr's) portfolio in possession of his daughter . . . sufficient to damn W forever." JRR to Edward Dillon, February 21, [1808], DP.

40. Lemuel Sawyer writes, with no evidence, that Randolph proposed the indictment of Wilkinson. Sawyer, *Randolph*, 28.

41. JRR to Joseph H. Nicholson, June 25, 1807, JRR LC. In January 1808, Randolph commented further on the failure to indict Wilkinson. "This motion," he said in a speech to the House, "was overruled upon this ground: that the treasonable (overt) act having been alleged to be committed in the State of Ohio, and General Wilkinson's letter to the President of the United States having been dated, although but a short time, prior to that act, this person had the benefit of what lawyers would call a legal exception, or a fraud." *AC*, 10th Cong., 1st sess., 1397.

42. JRR to Joseph H. Nicholson, June 25, 1807, JRR LC.

43. *AC*, 10th Cong., 1st sess., 1397–98.

44. Carpenter, *Trial of Col. Burr* 1: 123–24; George Hay to Thomas Jefferson, in Beveridge, *Marshall* 3: 467.

45. JRR to Joseph H. Nicholson, June 25, 1807, JRR LC.

46. *AC*, 11th Cong., 1st sess., 62.

47. JRR to James Wilkinson, December 25, 1807, Bouldin, *Home Reminiscences*, 138. Wilkinson tried to bait Randolph into changing his decision by posting handbills throughout Washington that read: "Hector unmasked . . . I denounce John Randolph, M.C., to the world as a prevaricating, base, calumniating scoundrel, poltroon and coward." Randolph continued to ignore him. Sawyer, *Randolph*, 36.

48. See generally Cray, "Remembering the USS Chesapeake," 445 *et seq.*

49. JRR to Joseph H. Nicholson, June 28, 1807, JRR LC.

50. JRR to Joseph H. Nicholson, July 21, 1807, Adams, *Randolph*, 224–25. Randolph also wrote: "There is but one sentiment as far as I can learn and what *that sentiment* is you might easily conjecture." JRR to [Thomas Nelson] August 23, 1807, PaH. See also JRR to Theodore Dudley, August 23, 1807, Dudley, 32–33.

51. See *AC*, 10th Cong., 1st sess., 838, 1168.

52. JRR to James Garnett, August 31, 1807, JMG.

53. *AC*, 10th Cong., 1st sess., 793–94.

54. John Taylor of Caroline to Wilson Nicholas, November 30, 1807, in Risjord, *Old Republicans*, 82.

55. Albert Gallatin to Hannah Gallatin, October 30, 1807, New York Historical Society.

56. Malone, *Jefferson* 5: 476.

57. John Taylor of Caroline to Wilson Nicholas, November 30, 1807, Risjord, *Old Republicans*, 82.

58. *AC,* 10th Cong., 1st sess., 849.

59. Ibid., 1003.

60. John Taylor of Caroline to James Garnett, December 17, 1807, Kirk, *Randolph,* 139–40.

61. "I voted against it upon this ground: that the course which the Government has thought fit to pursue, whether precisely proper or not, having been acquiesced in by Congress and by the nation, ought not now to be abandoned, without an imperious necessity for such a step: that to depart from it under the pressure of the French decree would . . . be neither more nor less than to enter it up as final and conclusive. What indeed could Bonaparte require more from us than a non-importation and non-exportation law?" JRR to L. W. Tazewell, December 24, 1807, UNC.

62. JRR to Joseph H. Nicholson, December 24, 1807, JRR LC.

63. Albert Gallatin to Thomas Jefferson, December 18, 1807, Adams, *Gallatin* 1: 368.

64. JRR to Joseph Scott, January 25, 1808, HuL.

65. Ibid., February 15, 1808, HuL.

66. Ibid., February 18, 1808, HuL.

67. Ammon, *Monroe,* 271–75.

68. Thomas Jefferson to James Monroe, February 18, 1808, TJ LC.

69. Washington *National Intelligencer,* March 7, 1808. See also Brant, *Madison* 4: 432–34; Cunningham, *Jeffersonian Republicans in Power,* 114–17.

70. Nathaniel Macon to Joseph H. Nicholson, June 1, 1806, Dodd, *Life of Macon,* 204.

71. JRR to James Garnett, May 27, 1808, JMG.

72. Richmond *Enquirer,* November 18, 1808.

73. Garland 1: 278.

74. JRR to James Garnett, July 24, 1808, JMG.

75. JRR to James Garnett, August 31, 1808, JMG.

76. Josiah Jackson to James Madison, June 1, 1809, Rutland, *Papers of Madison, Presidential Series* 1: 218.

77. JRR to Joseph Scott, August 8, 1808, HuL.

78. JRR to Joseph H. Nicholson, August 25, 1808, JRR LC.

79. JRR to Joseph H. Nicholson, March 16, 1808, JRR LC.

80. Thomas Jefferson to James Madison, March 30, 1809, Rutland, *Papers of Madison* 1: 91. Jefferson's observation was prescient. As Monroe began to repair his relationship with Madison, Randolph reacted predictably. He wrote to Monroe about reports that "you have . . . volunteered explanations . . . of the differences heretofore subsisting between yourself and [the] administration, which amount to a dereliction of the ground which you took after your return from England, and even of your warmest personal friends. . . . it would be disingenuous to conceal that it has created unpleasant sensations not in me only but in others." JRR to James Monroe, January 14, 1811, JRR LC. See Bruce 1: 344–45; Adams, *Randolph,* 243–44.

81. JRR to Edward Dillon, [January 7, 1809], DP.

82. See JRR to James M. Garnett, August 14, 1810; July 7, August 7, 1811, JMG.

83. JRR to James M. Garnett, March 20, 1810, JMG.

84. Francis W. Gilmer, *Sketches of American Orators* (1816), in Bruce 2: 77–78.

85. Bruce 1: 324–25.

86. Randolph's health during this time ranged from "as good as I have enjoyed for many years" to "indifferent" to "unusually bad." JRR to Theodore Dudley, June 24, 1809, Dudley, 68; JRR to James M. Garnett, September 14, 1809, JMG; JRR to F. B. T. Coalter, January 10, 1809, JRR UVA. Generally, Randolph rarely passed a day "without pain or disquietude." JRR to F. B. T. Coalter, August 19, 1811, JRR UVA. See JRR to St. George Tucker, March 13, 1810, Bruce 2: 304 ("Indeed, exemption from pain has become with me a highly pleasurable sensation").

87. Adams, *History* 4: 379. "How orotund and superficial the addresses of Webster and Clay now seem," Russell Kirk wrote of Randolph's speeches, "by the side of this darting passion!" *The Conservative Mind*, 157–58.

88. *AC*, 11th Cong., 1st sess., 68–69.

89. Quincy, *Life of Quincy*, 234.

90. *AC*, 10th Cong., 1st sess., 834, 2136; 10th Cong., 2nd sess., 599.

91. Ibid., 2nd sess., 1338.

92. Ibid., 1464.

93. Koenig, "Consensus Politics," 75.

94. *AC*, 10th Cong., 2nd sess., 1335, 596.

95. Bruce 2: 202.

96. Sparks, *Memoirs of Fifty Years*, 226.

97. *AC*, 10th Cong., 1st sess., 1890.

98. Ibid., 2037.

99. Ibid., 2048–49.

100. Bruce 2: 321.

101. JRR to Theodore Dudley, January 9, 1812, Dudley, 116 ("Speaking, as I always do, from the impulse of the moment, the *verba ardentia* cannot be recalled. The glowing picture fades, the happy epithet, the concise and forcible expression is lost, never again to be retrieved"); JRR to Francis W. Gilmer, March 15, 1817, JRR UVA ("I never prepared myself to speak but on two questions—the Connecticut Reserve and the first discussion of the Yazoo claims"); JRR to James Garnett, August 12, 1811, JMG ("I made a very vehement speech in imagination to Mr. Speaker—a better one I dare swear, than I shall be able to produce when the occasion arrives").

102. JRR to F. S. Key, February 17, 1814, Garland 2: 30–32. John Quincy Adams had another view. He called Randolph's speeches "a farrago of commonplace political declamation, mingled up with a jumble of historical allusions, scraps of Latin from the Dictionary of Quotations, and a continual stream of personal malignity to others, and of inflated egotism." *Memoirs of John Quincy Adams* 7: 472.

103. Quincy, *Figures of the Past*, 212.

104. Ibid., 213.

105. Adams, *History* 4: 379.

106. JRR to James Garnett, March 20, 1810, JMG.

107. JRR to Joseph H. Nicholson, February 18, 1810, JRR LC.

108. JRR to F. B. T. Coalter, April 6, 1810, JRR UVA; JRR to Joseph Scott, May 3, 1810, HuL.

109. JRR to Joseph H. Nicholson, December 4, 1809, JRR LC.

110. Ibid.

111. JRR to James M. Garnett, September 14, 1809, JMG.

112. *AC*, 10th Cong., 1st sess., 883.

113. Bruce 2: 203–4.

114. *AC*, 10th Cong., 1st sess., 2087, 2257; 10th Cong., 2nd sess., 688.

115. Nathaniel Macon to Joseph H. Nicholson, April 14, 1808, Adams, *Randolph*, 234–35.

116. Albert Gallatin to William Henry Harrison, September 27, 1809, Adams, *Gallatin* 1: 463.

117. *AC*, 10th Cong., 1st sess., 1781.

118. Ibid., 1021.

119. Ibid., 683.

120. John Greenleaf Whittier, "Randolph of Roanoke," Lounsbury, *Yale Book of American Verse*, 134–38.

10. OF ROANOKE

1. Langguth, *Union 1812*, 134–35; Buel, *America on the Brink*, 40, 44. "At one stroke, it had doomed ships to decay, sailors to starvation, and crops to destruction." Brown, "Embargo Politics," 199.

2. *AC*, 10th Cong., 2nd sess., 1466.

3. Ibid., 1340.

4. Ibid., 1501.

5. Ibid., 1342. Randolph repeated this view to Nicholson: "As to what we are to do, my first step would be to repeal all the laws restricting trade, and as we will not, or cannot, protect it, let it shift for itself. As to our navy, it may sail out of port and sail back again—and the officers of our army may continue to edit Journals, and (by way of keeping their courage alive) cane members of congress in the Capitol." JRR to J. H. Nicholson, December 4, 1809, JRR LC.

6. JRR to Joseph Scott, March 2, 1809, HuL.

7. JRR to St. George Tucker, November 14, 1809, Bruce 2: 304–5.

8. JRR to James Garnett, December 25, 1809, JMG; JRR to J. H. Nicholson, December 4, 1809, JRR LC.

9. JRR to Theodore Dudley, February 4, 1811, Dudley, 83–84.

10. JRR to James Garnett, September 14, 1809, JMG. Randolph treated himself with various does of "calomel" and "rhubarb." He commented that the "physick operates badly." See JRR Diary, July 14, October 2, October 3, 1811, JRR VHS; JRR to Theodore Dudley, July 15, 1811, Dudley, 90.

11. JRR to James Garnett, November 6, 1810, JMG. The gunpowder, "Pigon and Andrews," was an English-manufactured brand. Randolph was apparently unwilling to rely on locally manufactured gunpowder, which tended to vary in composition and quality. "As you are a brother sportsman, I must caution you against pouring the powder from the charger on top of the flask, into your gun. I did so, the other day, a part of the wadding of the preceding charge remained in the barrel, *on fire*. The train communicated

and the contents of the flask (*about half a pound of the strongest gunpowder*) exploded in my hand which was burnt, and contused most dreadfully." JRR to [John Taylor], November 13, 1810, JRR MiH.

12. See JRR to James Garnett, September 14, 1809, JMG ("My health is very indifferent, and my spirits worse"); JRR to James Garnett, December 25, 1809, JMG (My "body [and I fear my mind also]" are "peculiarly sensible to the impression of pain").

13. JRR to James Garnett, August 7, 1811, JMG.

14. JRR to James Garnett, June 24, 1811, JMG.

15. JRR to Theodore Dudley, August 11, 1811, Dudley, 95.

16. Ibid., October 13, 1811, Dudley, 109.

17. JRR to James Garnett, June 29, 1810, August [5], 1811, JMG; to Theodore Dudley, August 4, 11, 12, 1811, Dudley, 96, 98.

18. JRR to Ryland Randolph, September 13, 1811, TC UVA.

19. JRR to James Garnett, July 31, 1810, JMG. Randolph was not always as nonchalant about his farming woes, once writing: "I shall perish and come to jail—unless I abandon a fruitless pursuit of public business and attend to my own concerns." JRR to James Garnett, June 29, 1810, JMG.

20. JRR to James Garnett, June 29, 1810, JMG.

21. Ibid., October 7, 1811, JMG. One overseer, William Curd, did not receive such blanket condemnation. Randolph wrote that Curd "was of great skill and judgment in his calling, indefatigable, laborious, well behaved and *honest!!!*" When Curd was struck by a fever, Randolph nursed him for more than ten days and was devastated when he died. "I shall never look upon his like again," he wrote. JRR to John Taylor, September 22, 1811, MiH; JRR to Ryland Randolph, September 13, 1811, TC UVA; JRR to James Garnett, September 15, 1811, to James Garnett, JMG; JRR to Theodore Dudley, September 15, 22, October 13, 1811, Dudley, 103, 104, 109.

22. JRR to James M. Garnett, May 27, 1811, JMG.

23. JRR to Richard K. Randolph, August 12, 1811, JRR LC.

24. JRR to James M. Garnett, May 27, 1811, JMG.

25. JRR to Richard K. Randolph, August 12, 1811, JRR LC.

26. Bouldin, *Home Reminiscences*, 78.

27. JRR to Elizabeth T. Coalter, April 10, 1824, Bruce 2: 737–38. Bruce writes that Randolph sought to distinguish himself from "Possum Jack," the man who attacked him over the payment of a debt. Randolph's letter to Elizabeth Coalter does not identify the other Randolphs, referring to them as only "J.R. junr. and J.R." See JRR to Elizabeth T. Coalter, February 27, 1824, CaP ("Always write 'of Roanoke' on your superscription. There is another J.R. and I am sorry for it"); JRR to Elizabeth Coalter, March 6, 1824, Bryan ("Leave out your 'hon[orable],' I am 'of Roanoke'").

28. JRR to Joseph H. Nicholson, August 15, 1809, JRR LC.

29. JRR to James Monroe, January 1, 1809, JRR LC. Randolph was right about Smith, who proved to be a less-than-competent secretary of state, openly criticizing the administration and bickering with his colleagues. Madison demanded his resignation in 1811. "Memorandum as to Robert Smith," April 1811, Rutland, *Papers of James Madison, Presidential Series* 3: 255–63.

30. JRR to Joseph H. Nicholson, December 4, 1809, JRR LC.

31. JRR to James Garnett, December 25, 1809, JMG. See also JRR to J. H. Nicholson, December 4, 1809, JRR LC ("I am very seriously ill with a most distressing and obstinate complaint—chronic diarrhea").

32. "War!" Randolph huffed on hearing of the resolution. "*War* carried on by Giles and Smilie and Willis Alston!" JRR to Joseph H. Nicholson, February 18, 1810, JRR LC.

33. JRR to James Garnett, December 25, 1809, JMG. The first "Mucius" letter was published in the *Spirit of 'Seventy-Six* on January 12, 1810. It appeared written under the name "Philo-Laos," a name supplied by the editor and corrected in the subsequent letter. The second letter was published on January 26 and the third on April 17, 1810. Another letter under the name "Leontius" appeared on February 9, 1810, but is unclear if Randolph was the author. Rutland, *Papers of Madison, Presidential Series* 1: 175–77, 208–9, 226–27, 303–4. Joseph Bryan confirmed that Randolph was the author of the first two "Mucius" letters. Joseph Bryan to JRR, May 27, 1810, JSB VHS.

34. The second "Mucius" letter passed comments on the many actors in the long-running controversy with Great Britain. Randolph praised George Washington, dismissed John Adams as "a rank Englishman," dubbed Thomas Jefferson "a finished Frenchman," called Secretary of State Smith "notoriously incompetent," and judged his old enemy, General James Wilkinson, to be in the "last stage of putrefaction."

35. *AC*, 11th Cong., 2nd sess., 1609–11.

36. Ibid., 1612, 1702–3.

37. Ibid., 1612.

38. "The outcome was technically a draw. . . . In effect, that was a victory for Randolph." Brant, "Eppes, Randolph, & Adams," 252.

39. Adams, *History* 5: 209. An alternative view is offered by Norman Risjord, who wrote that Randolph "led the House from one pointless debate to another in his crusade to re-establish the old 'principles of 1798.'" *Old Republicans*, 101.

40. Joseph Nicholson to Albert Gallatin, December 25, 1809, Brant, *Madison* 5: 130.

41. *AC*, 11th Cong., 3rd sess., 786.

42. Sawyer, *Randolph*, 42.

43. JRR to Joseph H. Nicholson, January 28, 1811, JRR LC.

44. Ibid.

45. Sawyer, *Randolph*, 42. Sawyer writes that Randolph was fined twenty dollars as a result of the altercation. There are no comments from Randolph to confirm that part of the incident.

46. JRR Diary, January 23, 1811, JRR VHS.

47. JRR Diary, January 27, 1811; Bruce 1: 365.

48. JRR to James Garnett, April 7, 1811, JMG.

49. Ibid.; Bruce 1: 365; Sawyer, *Randolph*, 40.

50. Sawyer, *Randolph*, 40.

51. JRR to James Garnett, April 7, 1811, JMG.

52. Ibid., May 5, 1811, JMG; JRR to Joseph H. Nicholson, March 3, [1811], JRR LC.

53. JRR to J. H. Nicholson, June 24, 1811, JRR LC.

54. JRR to James Garnett, March 19, 1811, JMG.

55. JRR to Joseph H. Nicholson, March 19, 1811, JRR LC; JRR to James Garnett, March 19, 25, 1811, JMG.

56. JRR Diary, April 1, 1811, JRR VHS.

57. JRR Diary, April 1, 8, 15, 22, 1811, JRR VHS; JRR to James Garnett, April 11, 16, 1811, JMG; JRR to Theodore Dudley, April 11, 1811, Dudley, 86–87.

58. JRR to Richard K. Randolph, April 29, 1811, JRR LC; JRR to James Garnett, April 16, 20, 1811, JMG.

59. JRR to James Garnett, April 16, 1811, JMG. Randolph expressed "a loss to divine the cause of that 'diabolical spirit' . . . exerted against me. . . . If the persons to whom I am thus obnoxious could look into my bosom they would, I presume, dismiss their resentments." JRR to James M. Garnett, March 25, 1811, JMG.

60. JRR to James M. Garnett, April 24, 1811, JMG.

61. Buel, *America on the Brink*, 127.

62. "More properly categorized as a loose grouping rather than a cohesive faction, [the War Hawks] differed widely in how to implement their views, but were united in their desire for an end to the temporizing of the last four years." Heller, *Democracy's Lawyer*, 95.

63. Bruce 1: 370; Garland 1: 303–11.

64. Burstein and Isenberg write that Madison, who did not expect London to repeal the Orders in Council and was equally distrustful of France, "fell for Napoleon's gambit nonetheless and played into French hands." *Madison and Jefferson*, 485. Robert Remini asserts that Madison was "duped." *Henry Clay*, 75.

65. Sargent, *Public Men and Events* 1: 130.

66. "[Macon] will not be speaker," Randolph wrote. "The friends of Mr. Madison hate him and will elect Mr. Henry Clay of Kentucky who is a young man never before in this House." JRR to John St. George Randolph, November 4, 1811, Duke.

67. Sargent, *Public Men and Events* 1: 130.

68. "You may recollect," Congressman J. A. Harper wrote, "that at the last session his dog created much disturbance and even quarreling . . . [Clay] immediately ordered the doorkeeper to take *her* out (for she is a female)." J. A. Harper to William Plumer, December 2, 1811, Papers of William Plumer, in Brant, *Madison* 5: 381. See also Heidler, *Henry Clay*, 87–88.

69. *AC*, 12th Cong., 1st sess., 376.

70. Ibid., 377.

71. Ibid., 422.

72. Ibid., 424–26.

73. Ibid., 426.

74. Grundy's reply was not "a reasoned justification of war so much as an appeal to the militant sentiment of the frontier." Wiltse, *Calhoun* 1: 58. "Grundy held impressive credentials as a lawyer and judge . . . but he was no match for Randolph on this day." Vipperman, *William Lowndes*, 81. An early biographer of Grundy writes that his subject "was a western man . . . much more vexed at the supposed intrigues which the British were carrying on with the Indians than with the destruction of ocean commerce." He notes that Grundy's speech contained "a rather unusual distinction" and "a political mistake," and

that it was necessary for Calhoun to come "to the rescue of Grundy." Parks, *Felix Grundy,* 40–43. Grundy's most recent biographer comments that Grundy's speech "straightforwardly assessed the causes for war." Heller, *Democracy's Lawyer,* 98.

75. JRR to Joseph H. Nicholson, December 20, 1811, JRR LC.

76. JRR to John Taylor, December 13, 1811, MiH.

77. JRR to James Garnett, December 13, 1811, JMG.

78. JRR to Joseph H. Nicholson, December 20, 1811, JRR LC.

79. JRR to Joseph H. Nicholson, December 3, [1811], JRR LC; Bruce 2: 589.

80. JRR to Theodore Dudley, December 12, 1811, Dudley, 114–15; JRR to James Garnett, January 12, 1812, JMG.

81. *AC,* 12th Cong., 1st sess., 441.

82. Ibid., 441–42.

83. Ibid., 441–42.

84. Ibid., 449.

85. Ibid., 449.

86. Ibid., 445–46.

87. Ibid., 446.

88. Ibid., 448.

89. Ibid., 447.

90. Coit, *Calhoun,* 75.

91. Wharton, *Social Life in the Early Republic,* 152.

92. *AC,* 12th Cong., 1st sess., 450.

93. Ibid., 450–51.

94. Tate, *Conservatism and Southern Intellectuals,* 68–69.

95. *AC,* 12th Cong., 1st sess., 452, 454.

96. Ibid., 454.

97. Ibid., 454–55.

98. Randolph's "relentless warnings were effective enough to take something of the shine off the War Hawk agenda." Heidler, *Henry Clay,* 87.

99. *AC,* 12th Cong., 1st sess., 476.

100. Ibid., 476–77.

101. Ibid., 477.

102. Ibid., 479.

103. Ibid., 480.

104. Ibid.

105. Richmond *Enquirer,* December 24, 1811.

106. Coit, *Calhoun,* 77.

107. Wiltse, *Calhoun* 1: 59.

108. *AC,* 12th Cong., 1st sess., 490.

109. Ibid., 525.

110. JRR to James Garnett, January 20, 1812, JMG.

111. See *AC,* 12th Cong., 1st sess., 341 ("moved for the reading of the documents; which being objected to, he called for the yeas and nays"), 356–57 ("This motion was opposed by Mr. Randolph . . . in a speech of considerable length"), 394 ("A motion was made by

Mr. Randolph to recommit the report"), 402 ("Mr. Randolph moved that the bill and amendments be postponed until Friday next"), 419 ("Mr. Randolph, wishing time, moved that the report lie on the table"), and 558 ("A motion was made by Mr. Randolph to refer the bill and report").

112. *AC,* 12th Cong., 1st sess., 720.

113. Ibid., 709.

114. JRR to Richard K. Randolph, February 7, 1812, JRR LC.

115. JRR to James Garnett, February 1, 1812, JMG.

116. Ibid., February 5, 1812, JMG.

117. On the Madison-Monroe rapprochement, see Burstein and Isenberg, *Madison and Jefferson,* 473–74.

118. JRR to James Garnett, April 2, 1812, JMG.

119. *AC,* 12th Cong., 1st sess., 1590.

120. Ibid., 1593.

121. JRR to James Garnett, April 21, 1812, JMG.

122. Coit, *Calhoun,* 75.

123. Buel, *America on the Brink,* 135–39, 142–54.

124. JRR to James Garnett, April 21, 1812, JMG. See Hickey, *The War of 1812,* 41 ("Republicans in Congress were also sending mixed signals").

125. *AC,* 12th Cong., 1st sess., 1451.

126. Ibid., 1451, 1454, 1461.

127. Ibid., 1461–62.

128. Ibid., 1462.

129. Ibid., 1468.

130. Clay and Randolph took the debate to the pages of the *National Intelligencer.* Clay repeated his interpretation of the House Rules and stated that Randolph had "patiently and repeatedly" developed his views on the floor. The time finally came, he wrote, when the House had to proceed. Randolph responded with a lengthy letter accusing the House of "outstripping a British House of Commons . . . in prostrating, from motives of caprice, temporary convenience, or party spirit, any one of the great fundamental principles, without a religious observance of which, no free Government can endure." Henry Clay to the *National Intelligencer,* July 2, 1812; JRR to the *National Intelligencer,* June 17, 1812; *AC,* 12th Cong., 1st sess., 1469–79. See Heidler, *Henry Clay,* 96–98, 97 ("Beneath all the bombast was a kernel of truth, for Clay had indeed used parliamentary procedure to silence opponents, a practice that would eventually give him a reputation as a dictator. But Randolph's anger was not just bluster").

131. JRR to John Taylor, June 16, 1812, MiH.

11. AN IRRECLAIMABLE HERETIC

1. JRR to Freeholders of Charlotte, Prince Edward, Buckingham, and Cumberland, Garland 1: 302.

2. JRR to Josiah Quincy, July 24, August 16, 1812, Quincy, *Life of Quincy,* 268–71.

3. Jordan, *Political Leadership in Jefferson's Virginia*, 177.

4. Richmond *Enquirer*, April 5, 1811. In addition to these actions, the Georgia town of Randolph changed its name to "Jasper." Kirk, *Randolph*, 142.

5. JRR to James Garnett, August 2, 1812, JMG; JRR to Josiah Quincy, August 16, 1812, Quincy, *Life of Quincy*, 270–71.

6. See JRR to James M. Garnett, September 14, 1812, JMG ("Eppes was extremely feeble and the countenance of his friends betrayed evident mortification. His display was hooted. . . . [S]ome said that any school boy of sixteen could have done better"); JRR to Richard K. Randolph, September 17, 1812, JRR LC (Eppes "was more feeble than I ever heard him and disappointed all expectations"); JRR to James M. Garnett, October 1, 1812, JMG (Randolph has met Eppes "at three successive courts and shall confront him again").

7. Bouldin, *Home Reminiscences*, 55.

8. JRR to Richard K. Randolph, October 11, 1812, JRR UVA.

9. JRR to James Garnett, August 9, 1812, JMG; JRR to Harmanus Bleecker, August 16, 1812, HB.

10. JRR to Freeholders of Charlotte, Prince Edward, Buckingham, and Cumberland, Garland 2: 301–2; JRR to James Garnett, September 14, 1812, JMG. Randolph did not identify the "single individual," but it is likely a reference to James Madison. He would later express the same sentiment in writing about the reaction of his sister-in-law upon learning that her husband's unit had been ordered to march. "I never witnessed such agony," Randolph wrote. "Would to God that James Madison could have heard this tribute of his subjects to the wisdom and mercy of his reign." JRR to James Garnett, June 25, 1813, JMG.

11. JRR to Richard K. Randolph, September 17, 1812, JRR UVA; JRR to James Garnett, September 14, 1812, JMG.

12. JRR to Richard K. Randolph, September 17, 1812, JRR UVA.

13. JRR Diary, October 5, 1812, JRR VHS; Jordan, *Political Leadership in Jefferson's Virginia*, 162, n. 21.

14. JRR to Richard K. Randolph, October 11, 1812, JRR UVA. It was reported that one Randolph speech at Charlotte "almost brought on a free fight." Eckenrode, *The Randolphs*, 206.

15. JRR to Josiah Quincy, August 2, 1812, Quincy, *Life of Quincy*, 269–70.

16. JRR to James Garnett, December 15, 1812, JMG; JRR to John Taylor, December 15, 1812, MiH.

17. JRR to John Taylor, December 15, 1812, MiH.

18. JRR to James Garnett, January 26, 1813, JMG. See JRR to James Garnett, January 22, February 4, 1813, JMG.

19. JRR to Theodore Dudley, November [19], 1812, Dudley, 126.

20. *AC*, 12th Cong., 2nd sess., 184–85.

21. JRR to James Garnett, January 26, 1813, JMG.

22. *AC*, 12th Cong., 2nd sess., 781.

23. Ibid.

24. Ibid., 782.

25. Ibid., 783.

26. Ibid., 784.

27. Ibid., 786.

28. Ibid., 789.

29. Ibid., 789.

30. JRR to Theodore Dudley, February 11, 18, 1813, Dudley, 136, 137.

31. JRR to Theodore Dudley, March 5, 1813, Dudley, 139.

32. JRR Diary, JRR VHS.

33. JRR to Harmanus Bleecker, March 28, 1813, HB.

34. Ibid.; Judith Randolph to St. George Tucker, April 4, 1813, TC.

35. JRR to Josiah Quincy, April 19, 1813, Quincy, *Life of Quincy*, 329–30.

36. Bradshaw, *History of Prince Edward County*, 179.

37. JRR to Charles Goldsborough, August 7, 1813, JRR UVA; JRR to Theodore Dudley, April 16, 1813, Dudley, 141; JRR to Josiah Quincy, April 19, 1813, Quincy, *Life of Quincy*, 329–30.

38. JRR to Francis Scott Key, May 22, 1813, Garland 2: 13.

39. JRR to Richard K. Randolph, May 17, 1813, JRR LC; JRR to James Garnett, May 15, 1813, JMG. Irving Brant writes that Randolph's defeat "gave Madison particular satisfaction." Brant, *Madison* 6: 179. A recent study calls it a "bright spot for Madison and Jefferson." Burstein and Isenberg, *Madison and Jefferson*, 526.

40. JRR to James Garnett, May 15, 1813, JMG.

41. JRR to Harmanus Bleecker, April 22, 1813, HB.

42. JRR to Richard K. Randolph, May 17, 1813, JRR LC.

43. JRR to Francis Scott Key, May 10, 1813, Garland 2: 13.

44. Ibid., May 22, 1813, Garland 2: 13; JRR to Josiah Quincy, June 20, 1813, Quincy, *Life of Quincy*, 332.

45. JRR to James Garnett, May 15, 1813, JMG. See also JRR to Francis Scott Key, May 10, 1813, Garland 2: 13.

46. JRR to John Brockenbrough, June 2, 1813, Shorey, 6.

47. JRR to Richard K. Randolph, June 7, 1813, JRR UVA.

48. JRR to F. S. Key, July 17, 1813, Garland 2: 16.

49. JRR to Thomas Robinson, July 9, 1813, Duke. JRR to F. S. Key, September 12, 1813, Garland 2: 19–22; May 7, 1814, Garland 2: 35–36.

50. JRR to John Brockenbrough, June 2, 1813, Shorey, 5; JRR to Thomas Robinson, June 2, 1813, Duke; JRR to F. S. Key, June 3, 1814, Garland 2: 39; JRR to F. S. Key, July 14, 1814, Garland 2: 39–40.

51. JRR to John Brockenbrough, July 15, 1814, Shorey, 9.

52. JRR to John Brockenbrough, June 2, 1813, Shorey, 5; JRR to Harmanus Bleecker, June 13, 1813, HB.

53. JRR to John Brockenbrough, June 2, 1813, Shorey, 5.

54. JRR to Francis Scott Key, September 12, 1813, Garland 2: 21.

55. JRR Diary, JRR VHS.

56. JRR to Elizabeth Coalter, January 30, 1822, WCB; JRR to John Brockenbrough, [March 3, 1824], Shorey, 50–51.

57. John Marshall to JRR, March 6, 1828, JRR UVA.

58. Russell Kirk wrote that Marshall was "one of the few leaders of the age whom Randolph respected and loved." *The Conservative Mind,* 156.

59. JRR to Josiah Quincy, March 22, 1814, Quincy, *Life of Quincy,* 350, 352. See also JRR to F. S. Key, March 20, 1814, Bruce 1: 9; JRR to Thomas Marsh Forman, April 7, 1814, JRR VHS.

60. JRR to Harmanus Bleecker, January 28, 1814, HB.

61. Ibid., April 4, 1814, HB. See also JRR to Richard K. Randolph, February 15, 1814, JRR LC (Randolph "most entertained" by reading Burke); JRR to F. S. Key, February 17, 1814, Garland 2: 30–32 (Randolph calls Burke "the father of political wisdom"); JRR to Harmanus Bleecker, July 26, 1814, HB (Randolph reading Burke and Byron); JRR to John Brockenbrough, August 1, 1814, Shorey, 10–11 (Randolph reading Burke's *Remarks on the Policy of the Allies with Respect to France*); and JRR to Henry Rutledge, July 11, 1818, JRR LVA (Randolph describes Burke as "the great master of political philosophy").

62. Tate, *Conservatism and Southern Intellectuals,* 65.

63. JRR to Theodore Dudley, January 31, 1806, Dudley, 9 ("I send you . . . letters written by the great Mr. Pitt, afterwards Earl of Chatham. . . . You know my opinion of Lord Chatham: that he was at once the greatest *practical* statesman that ever lived, and the most transcendent orator. With all this, he was a truly *good* man"); JRR to Theodore Dudley, February 2, 1806, Dudley, 11–12 (JRR endeavors "to avail myself of the wisdom and experience" of Pitt); and JRR to Theodore Dudley, January 8, 1807, Dudley, 25–27 ("Let me recommend to you another perusal of Lord Chatham's letters to his nephew").

64. JRR to James Garnett, March 25, 1811, JMG. ("I must, therefore, refer you to Burke's second letter on the French Revolution, in which he palliates (to say the least of it) the conduct of those whose strong disgust turned them away from the spectacle of a degraded country").

65. Garland 1: 58.

66. Nathaniel Beverley Tucker, "Garland's Life of Randolph," 46.

67. Tate, *Conservatism and Southern Intellectuals,* 26. See Kirk, *Randolph,* 34–35, 43–45.

68. Huebner, *The Southern Judicial Tradition,* 31; Horsnell, "Spencer Roane," 120.

69. Huebner, *The Southern Judicial Tradition,* 18, 31; Horsnell, "Spencer Roane," 62–119; Moncure, "The Court Decision that Nearly Destroyed the Episcopal Church" 4, 12.

70. Richmond *Enquirer,* June 11, 1819.

71. Miller, *Juries and Judges Versus the Law,* 118.

72. JRR to John Brockenbrough, [1821], Shorey, 32.

73. JRR to John Brockenbrough, [February 23, 1820], Shorey, 26.

74. JRR to James Garnett, March 22, 1820, JMG. When Roane died, Randolph praised him as "a rallying point for the friends of states' rights." He then noted the trait that drew them together. Roane "had the judgment to perceive, and the candor to acknowledge, the consistency of my public conduct with my avowed principles." JRR to John Brockenbrough, [March 22, 1824], Shorey, 52.

75. Huebner, *The Southern Judicial Tradition*, 10.

76. JRR to F. S. Key, September 12, 1813, Garland 2: 20.

77. JRR to John Brockenbrough, June 2, 1813, Shorey, 6; JRR to F. S. Key, February 17, 1814, Garland 2: 31.

78. JRR to Josiah Quincy, March 22, 1814, Quincy, *Life of Quincy*, 350, 352.

79. JRR to Josiah Quincy, January 29, 1814, Quincy, *Life of Quincy*, 349.

80. JRR to Harmanus Bleecker, July 25, 1813, HB; JRR to Josiah Quincy, January 29, 1814, Quincy, *Life of Quincy*, 349. Randolph often included references to Madison while discussing topics unrelated to politics. "My good friend, I am no patriot. I am thinking much more of my crop (ruined by a deluge of rain), of my debts and taxes, and the scanty means of paying either, than of the President's health or the new furbishing of Mrs. M's with-drawing-Rooms." JRR to James Garnett, August 7, 1813, JMG.

81. JRR to Richard K. Randolph , February 15, 1814, JRR LC.

82. JRR to John Brockenbrough, August 1, 1814, Shorey, 10.

83. JRR to Josiah Quincy, June 20, 1813, Quincy, *Life of Quincy*, 332; JRR to Harmanus Bleecker, July 25, August 22, 1813, HB.

84. JRR to Francis Scott Key, October 17, 1813, Garland 2: 26.

85. JRR to Josiah Quincy, October 18, 1813, Quincy, *Life of Quincy*, 337–39.

86. JRR to St. George Tucker, April 11, 1814, TC UVA.

87. Ibid., April 14, 1814, TC UVA.

88. [St. George Tucker] to [JRR, April 15, 1814], TC UVA.

89. Bruce 2: 271. "Of all the misfortunes of my life, one only excepted," Tucker wrote, "I have felt the bitterness of that by which the affections of one whom I had educated and regarded from early childhood in the same light as if he had been my own son, [now] been alienated from me, as the greatest and most afflicting." St. George Tucker to Henry St. George Tucker, March 10, 1816, TC UVA. In 1817, Randolph wrote Tucker one last letter. "I deem it my duty," he wrote, "to bring back to your perhaps bewildered memory, some of those things of which it is my earnest and sincere prayer that you may truly repent. . . . The germ of piety was sown in my opening heart by a mother's hand—the sneer of skepticism, the open . . . habitual profanity of yourself and your companions . . . men of splendid genius would not kill the tender bud. It is survived the evil example and the infidel books which I heard praised and read, some of which were put into my hands by those to whom my opening manhood was carelessly confided." Randolph recited the familiar complaints of abuse, neglect, and financial mismanagement that had come to characterize his view of life with Tucker. "Repent," he concluded. "Make atonement as far as possible . . . and may God have mercy upon you, and may his mercy be for me as I sincerely and from my heart forgive you." JRR to [St. George Tucker], February 28, 1817, JRR UVA. There might have been some truth in Randolph's recollection regarding Tucker's religious beliefs. Tucker was something of a religious skeptic. His biographer writes that, "although Tucker believed in a rational Creator before and after his marriage, many of his friends noticed a change in his religious attitudes during his years with [Frances Bland Tucker]. Robert Andrews, a college chum and an ordained Episcopal minister, wrote 'I was pleased to observe that amongst the benefits you have derived from matrimony, some knowledge of what the Scriptures contain is one.'" Hamilton, *Tuckers of Virginia*, 52.

90. JRR to F. S. Key, September 26, 1814, Garland 2: 22.

91. JRR to James Garnett, June 25, 1813, JMG.

92. JRR Diary, August 1814, JRR VHS ("I set out for Richmond and made a tender of my services to the Govr").

93. JRR to F. S. Key, September 8, 1814, Garland 2: 45; JRR to Theodore Dudley, September 2, 1814, Dudley, 159.

94. JRR to [unknown], September 14, 1814, JRR UVA.

95. JRR to Harmanus Bleecker, September 23, 1814, HB.

96. Randolph wrote that he was approached by two "good men and true," but who nevertheless asked too many personal questions. "Gentlemen," Randolph said, "I am a free man, not responsible to anyone for my movements." "But," one of the men protested, "you are responsible to us, for you are free against our consent." JRR to James Garnett, December 31, 1813, JMG.

97. JRR to Richard Stanford, April 9, 1814, JMG.

98. JRR to Harmanus Bleecker, June 2, 1814, JRR HB; JRR Diary, July 18, 1814, JRR VHS.

99. Daniel Webster to William Sullivan, October 17, 1814, Wiltse, *Papers of Webster* 1: 171.

100. Tudor Randolph, Judith's son and Nancy's nephew, arrived at Morrisania on August 4, 1814. Gouverneur Morris wrote to Randolph inviting him and Judith to come to Tudor's side if they so desired. In the meantime, he would provide all necessary care for the boy. The situation seemed stable enough for Judith to remain in Virginia, but by late September, Tudor's condition worsened. Judith left immediately for New York, with Randolph to follow.

101. See Crawford, *Unwise Passions*, 173–77, 184–86, 191–204; Adams, *Morris*, 283–88.

102. JRR to Theodore Dudley, October 13, 1814, Dudley, 161.

103. Ibid., October 23, 1814, Dudley, 163.

104. Ibid., October 13, 1814, Dudley, 162.

105. JRR to Richard Stanford, October 13, 1814, JMG.

106. JRR to Theodore Dudley, October 23, 1814, Dudley, 163.

107. JRR to Ann C. R. "Nancy" Morris, October 31, 1814, JRR UVA.

108. JRR to Richard Randolph, October 24, 1814, JRR LC. "I am very seriously injured." Randolph wrote to Theodore Dudley about the accident. "The patella is, in itself, unhurt; but the ligaments are very much wrenched, so that a tight bandage alone enables me to hobble from one room to another with the help of a stick." JRR to Theodore Dudley, November 17, 1814, Dudley, 164. See also JRR to Edward Cunningham, November 18, 1814, JRR VHS ("I am a worse cripple than ever & I fear for life").

109. "Statement of affairs with D. B. Ogden," November 23, 1814, TC UVA. The account herein of Randolph's meeting with Ogden is taken from this memorandum.

110. Marshall did not disclose any confidences to Morris but did state that "suspicion has never reached my ears" regarding Nancy Randolph. Smith, *John Marshall*, 387.

111. "Statement of affairs with D. B. Ogden."

112. Ogden owed "large sums of money" to Morris and to other creditors. He "deeply resented his uncle's marriage," and the birth of Gouverneur Jr. "cut him off from his inheritance." Adams, *Morris*, 293, 294.

113. "To no persons but Mr. Bleecker, Commodore Decatur . . . and one other did I communicate a half design which subsequent circumstances have compelled me to lay aside all thoughts of neither of them." JRR to Richard Stanford, November 15, 1814, JRR UVA. Apparently, Randolph shared the letter with Congressman Stanford. See JRR to Richard Stanford, December 2, 1814, JRR UVA ("What do you think of my letter to Mrs. Morris sent to you to be addressed?").

114. Christopher Doyle writes that Randolph "boldly reactivated public discussion of the scandal." He asserts that Randolph's "timing mattered . . . [his] focus mattered" and that the "androgynous congressman" took this step for political reasons. "The Randolph Scandal," 301, 304. The author does not concur with this conclusion for several reasons. First, Randolph's re-election to the House was all but assured before he departed for Morrisania. Second, he did not release his letter to the public. Third, the matter would have remained private had Nancy Morris not sent copies of her response to Randolph's political enemies. Fourth, Randolph had never resorted to such tactics in any election, nor would he in subsequent elections. Finally, the events at Glenlyvar and Richard's sudden death were never far from Randolph's thoughts. His unexpected reunion with Nancy Morris and the allegations of David Ogden were provocation enough to write this letter. Politics was no consideration whatsoever.

115. JRR to Ann C. R. Morris, October 31, 1814, JRR UVA.

116. Ibid.

117. Ibid.

12. DYING, SIR, DYING

1. JRR to [unknown], January 7, 1815, Richmond *Enquirer,* April 1, 1815.

2. Ibid.

3. JRR to Harmanus Bleecker, February 4, 1815, HB.

4. Morris's biographers agree that Randolph's letter had no impact on the marriage. See Adams, *Morris,* 295 ("it did not faze his devotion to his wife"); and Kirschke, *Gouverneur Morris,* 263 ("Morris was not put off by this history, of which he was sufficiently aware").

5. Ann C. R. Morris to JRR, January 16, 1815, PrU.

6. Ibid.

7. Ibid.

8. JRR to William Branch Giles, March 12, 1815, NYPL. Giles had received the letter from Nancy Morris. "By this day's mail," she wrote, "I send (in three packages) a copy of my answer to Mr. Randolph's letter. I am anxious that it should be seen in Richmond with the certified copy of his." Ann C. Morris to William B. Giles, February 7, 1815, JRR LVA. See also Ann C. Morris to William B. Giles, February 17, 1815, JRR LVA (Nancy "anxious to know whether all the packages [arrived] . . . determined it shall be seen in Virginia"). Mrs. Morris sent a similar letter to John W. Eppes. Randolph wrote that "Mr. G. M. [Gouverneur Morris] and his *amicable* consort [have] distributed throughout this district for the purpose of influencing the election a number of libels on my character." JRR to Harmanus Bleecker, April 18, 1815, HB. See also Ann C. Morris to [unknown],

May 30, 1828, JRR LVA ("I will come forward to shew how corrupt that branch of the Randolph family has always been—fortunate indeed is it for mankind that the wisdom and mercy of God determined it should be extinct—when providence rescued me from their merciless fangs, I determined to return good for evil").

9. JRR to Harry Heth, March 29, 1815, JRR UVA.

10. JRR to Harmanus Bleecker, April 18, 1815, HB.

11. Ibid.

12. JRR to Judith Randolph, January 20, 1816, JRR LVA. See also JRR to Theodore Dudley, December 27, 1814, Dudley, 169–70 ("I hope you did not communicate to your mother any part of my letter except that which contained the request that she would relate the circumstances of my brother's death").

13. Dawidoff, *Education of Randolph*, 101.

14. JRR to Rev. William Meade, May 19, 1815, JRR LC.

15. JRR to John Brockenbrough, [May 29, 1815], Shorey, 12; JRR to James Garnett, May 20, 1815, JMG.

16. This portion of Key's letter was quoted by Randolph in a letter to John Brockenbrough. "I have received a letter from Frank Key," Randolph wrote, "that I would not exchange for the largest bundle of bank notes that you ever signed. Hear him." He then inserts a lengthy excerpt, from which comes this selection. JRR to John Brockenbrough, [May 29, 1815], Shorey, 12.

17. JRR to Francis Scott Key, [May 31], 1815, Garland 2: 65.

18. Ibid., 66.

19. JRR to Francis Scott Key, [May] 1815, Garland 2: 67–68.

20. His double-mindedness on the subject was shown when, within a single week, he wrote to James Garnett that he had "at last found peace—that peace which passeth all understanding, verily the peace of God," and also wrote to Reverend Meade that "no coincidence of circumstances . . . could contribute to make me tolerably happy, without better assurance than I have of reconciliation to God." JRR to James Garnett, September 7, 1815, JMG; JRR to Rev. William Meade, September 1, 1815, JRR LC.

21. James Madison, Address to Congress, *AC*, 13th Cong., 3rd sess., 14.

22. Richmond *Enquirer*, December 31, 1814. In the same issue, the *Enquirer* approvingly quoted a column from the Boston *Centinel* comparing Randolph to "a wild and ungovernable horse, [who] gallops through the public highways, treading down everyone in his course, whether friend or foe."

23. Richmond *Enquirer*, April 1, 1815. See also Richmond *Enquirer*, March 25, 29; April 1, 5, 8, 15, 16, 1815 for editorials and letters regarding Randolph's election bid.

24. JRR to Harmanus Bleecker, April 18, 1815, HB.

25. JRR to Francis Scott Key, April 25, 1815, Garland 2: 48.

26. Richmond *Enquirer*, April 26, 1815.

27. JRR to Francis Scott Key, October 23, 1815, Bruce 1: 559.

28. JRR to Harmanus Bleecker, February 4, 1816, HB; *AC*, 14th Cong., 1st sess., 1158.

29. JRR to Harmanus Bleecker, February 4, 1816, HB.

30. JRR to James Garnett, February 4, 1816, JMG.

31. JRR to Harmanus Bleecker, February 4, October 7, 1816, HB.

32. *AC*, 14th Cong., 1st sess., 728.

33. Ibid., 533, 536.

34. JRR to Richard K. Randolph, March 22, 1816, JRR LC; JRR to Harmanus Bleecker, April 16, 1816, HB.

35. JRR to Harmanus Bleecker, March 21, 1816, HB. See also JRR to Richard K. Randolph, March 22, 1816, JRR LC ("The conduct of the minority [as it is called] during the present session has satisfied me that they possess neither the courage, the talent, nor the integrity to conduct an opposition").

36. JRR to Editor, *National Intelligencer,* January 6, 1816, JRR LC.

37. JRR to Edward Booker, February 9, 1816, JRR LC.

38. Ibid.

39. JRR to George Logan, April 27, 1816, PaH.

40. JRR to James Garnett, April 16, 1816, April 23, 1816, JMG; JRR to Harmanus Bleecker, April 16, 1816, HB. See also JRR to David Parish, April 12, 1816, JRR LC; JRR to George Logan, April 27, 1816, PaH.

41. JRR to John H. Rice, March 16, 1816, Bruce 2: 509.

42. Ibid.

43. JRR to Harmanus Bleecker, January 30, 1816, HB; JRR to James Garnett, January 31, 1816, JMG.

44. Elijah H. Mills to [unknown], January 19, 1816, Bruce 2: 408–9.

45. Lewis H. Machen to Caroline Webster, [date unknown], 1816, *Letters of A. W. Machen,* in Bruce 2: 81.

46. See *AC,* 14th Cong., 1st sess., 677 ("Mr. Randolph . . . commenced a speech in a rather desultory but pointed manner"); 678 ("Mr. Randolph resumed his discourse, which he concluded just before sunset"); 739 ("Mr. Randolph . . . went much at length into this abuse"); 764 ("Mr. Randolph . . . spoke on the subject nearly four hours"); and 856 ("Mr. Randolph . . . delivered a speech of three hours on the opposite side of . . . Mr. Calhoun").

47. *AC,* 14th Cong., 1st sess., 873–74.

48. Ibid., 723.

49. Ibid., 721.

50. Ibid., 687.

51. Ibid., 685.

52. Ibid., 840–41, 844–45. See Tate, *Conservatism and Southern Intellectuals,* 8–10.

53. "Randolph's answer was one which Calhoun passed over at the time, but to which he paid tribute many years later." Wiltse, *Calhoun* 1: 108.

54. Remini, *Clay,* 139.

55. Wiltse, *Calhoun* 1: 108–9.

56. Adam Tate writes that "[an] economic system promoting liberty would have only hard money, regulated by supply and demand through the just exchange of goods among a consenting people. A tyrannical economic system ran on paper money, regulated by capitalist interests and the banks, which made money without industry." *Conservatism and Southern Intellectuals,* 57.

57. Brant, *Madison* 3: 328–29.

58. "Dependence was antithetical to republicans, and because Hamilton's system encouraged dependence, it endangered republicanism." Tate, *Conservatism and Southern Intellectuals*, 57.

59. JRR to James Garnett, February 2, 1816, JMG.

60. *AC*, 14th Cong., 1st sess., 1113.

61. Ibid., 1111–12.

62. JRR to [unknown], March 4, 1816, PaH.

63. *AC*, 14th Cong., 1st sess., 1338.

64. Ibid., 1338–39.

65. Ibid., 1339.

66. JRR to David Parish, February 3, 1816, JRR UVA.

67. JRR to Harmanus Bleecker, March 12, 1816, HB. See JRR to James Garnett, January 15, 1816, JMG ("I am very sick, hardly able to write"); JRR to Theodore Dudley, April 11, 1816, Dudley, 176 ("My own health is not much better"). Randolph's health was further damaged by yet another fall down "a steep staircase." He "sprained both . . . thumbs, and several fingers of each hand." JRR to Theodore Dudley, February 18, 1816, Dudley, 174.

68. JRR to Theodore Dudley, December 28, 1816, Dudley, 180.

69. JRR to Richard K. Randolph, June 9, 1816, JRR LC. Randolph again reached out to Francis Key. "My mind is filled with misgivings and doubts and perplexities that leave me no repose," he wrote. "Of the necessity for forgiveness I have the strongest conviction; but I cannot receive any assurance that it has been accorded to me. In short, I am in the worst conceivable situation as its respects my internal peace and future welfare." JRR to F. S. Key, May 7, 1816, Garland 2: 86–87. "To me the world is a vast desert," he wrote again to Key, "and there is no merit in renouncing it, since there is no difficulty. There never was a time when it was so utterly destitute of allurement for me. . . . I look out towards the world, and find a wilderness, peopled indeed, but not with flesh and blood—with monsters tearing one another to pieces for money or power, or some other vile lust. JRR to F. S. Key, June 16, 1816, Garland 2: 88.

70. JRR to David Parish, February 3, 1816, JRR UVA. See also JRR to Edward Booker, February 9, 1816, JRR LC ("I am utterly ignorant of the intrigues and corruptions going on here for the Presidency").

71. JRR to Harmanus Bleecker, October 27, 1816, HB.

72. JRR to F. S. Key, October 25, 1816, Garland 2: 89.

73. Garland 2: 92; Moore, *American Eloquence* 2: 158. See Bouldin, *Home Reminiscences*, 62 ("John, I am dying; I shall not live through the night").

13. THE MORAL AUTHORITY OF MY HEART

1. JRR to Mrs. Joseph Clay, March 14, 1820, Bruce 2: 461–62.

2. JRR to Theodore Dudley, August 3, 1807, Dudley, 29.

3. See JRR to Theodore Dudley, July 12, 1807, Dudley, 28 ("some knowledge of the Greek is almost indispensable to the profession for which you are designed."); JRR to Theodore Dudley, August 7, 1807, Dudley, 30 (requesting "a description of your studies

for a week, under the several heads of Greek, Latin, French, mathematics"); JRR to Theodore Dudley, November 15, [1809], Dudley, 76–77 ("I am very anxious that you should speak French, and read Italian, Spanish and German").

4. JRR to Elizabeth Coalter, March 21, 1824, Bryan.

5. JRR to Theodore Dudley, February 12, 1809, Dudley, 64.

6. Ibid., January 31, 1806, Dudley, 11; February 2, 1806, Dudley, 11; February 2, 1811, Dudley, 12. See also JRR to Theodore Dudley, January 31, 1806, Dudley, 9 ("I send you by the New Orleans mail, 'letters written by the great Mr. Pitt, afterwards Earl of Chatham, to his nephew, when at college'"); January 8, 1807, Dudley, 25 ("Let me recommend to you another perusal of Lord Chatham's letters to his nephew"); JRR to Theodore Dudley and Tudor Randolph, November 2, 1808, Dudley, 54 ("Read Lord Chatham's Letters again. Think that I speak to you in his words").

7. JRR to Theodore Dudley, December 19, 1807, Dudley, 43; February 12, 1808, Dudley, 45–46.

8. JRR to Theodore Dudley, February 12, 1808, Dudley, 45–46.

9. JRR to Elizabeth T. Coalter, February 1, 1828, Bruce 2: 535–36.

10. JRR to Theodore Dudley, February 2, 1811, Dudley, 12.

11. See JRR to Theodore Dudley, January 31, 1806, Dudley, 10; March 1, 1806, Dudley, 17; July 24, 1806, Dudley, 22; September 11, 1806, Dudley, 23; March 13, 1808, Dudley, 49–50; March 18, 1808, Dudley, 51; January 17, 1809, Dudley, 61; JRR to T. M. F. Bryan, October 11, 1823, JRR UVA.

12. JRR to Elizabeth T. Coalter, February 19, 1823, Bryan.

13. JRR to John St. George Randolph, December 13, [1812], LC.

14. JRR to Theodore Dudley, March 7, 1814, Dudley, 154.

15. JRR to St. George Randolph, September 6, 1806, JRR Duke.

16. Ibid.

17. JRR to Mrs. Joseph Clay, March 14, 1820, Bruce 2: 461.

18. JRR to Theodore Dudley, February 15, 1806, Dudley, 15.

19. Ibid., January 8, 1807, Dudley, 25; January 8, 1807, Dudley, 27.

20. JRR to Theodore Dudley, October 29, 1810, Dudley, 71.

21. JRR to Theodore Dudley and Tudor Randolph, October 6, 1807, Dudley, 36.

22. Ibid.

23. JRR to Theodore Dudley, December 30, 1821, Dudley, 232.

24. JRR to William Thompson, May 13, 1804, Bruce 2: 562–63.

25. See JRR to Theodore Dudley, March 1, 1806, Dudley, 18 ("Your fate, my dear Theodorick, is in your own hands. Like Hercules, every young man has his choice between *pleasure*, falsely so called, and *infamy*, or laborious virtue and a fair fame"); August 30, 1807, Dudley, 34 ("Whether you prove a useful or creditable member of society or not, depends altogether upon yourself"); August 30, 1807, Dudley, 34 ("Yes, my dear Theodore, your destiny is in your own hands"); and JRR to Theodore Dudley and Tudor Randolph, July 20, 1806, Dudley, 20 ("Whether such is to be your future character, respected and esteemed by all good men, or whether you shall become mere vulgar beings, whose only business is *fruges consumere*, will altogether depend upon your present exertions").

26. JRR to Theodore Dudley, January 8, 1807, Dudley, 25–26.

27. Ibid. See also JRR to Theodore Dudley, February 22, 1822, Dudley, 245 ("What,

then, are we to expect from a generation that has been taught to cherish this not 'fair defect' of our perverted nature; to nourish and cultivate, as 'amiable and attractive,' what, at the bottom, is neither more nor less than the grossest selfishness, a little disguised under the romantic epithet of 'sensibility!'").

28. JRR to F. B. T. Coalter, December 10, 1812, LVA.

29. JRR to Theodore Dudley, January 21, 1822, Dudley, 236; February 4, 1822, Dudley, 248–49.

30. JRR to Theodore Dudley, November 16, 1810, Dudley, 75.

31. JRR to Elizabeth T. Coalter, January 19, 1822 Bryan.

32. JRR to Elizabeth Coalter, January [31], 1824, Bryan.

33. Ibid., March 12, 1824, Bryan; March 6, 1824, Bryan.

34. JRR to Elizabeth T. Coalter, February 12, 1826, Bryan.

35. Ibid., [February 6, 1823], Bryan.

36. T. M. F. Bryan to John Randolph Bryan, October 16, 1827, Bruce 2: 465.

37. John Randolph Bryan to [Robertson], March 27, 1878, Bruce 2: 466.

38. Elizabeth Coalter Bryan to Mrs. St. George Tucker, August 15, 1833, Bruce 2: 541.

39. JRR to Theodore Dudley, December 19, 1819, Dudley, 206.

14. TWO SOULS

1. JRR to Edward Cunningham, March 18, 1817, JRR VHS. See also JRR to Edward Booker, April 2, 1817, JRR UVA ("I have been at the point of death for ten days. . . . [N]othing is farther from my thoughts than to become a candidate at the next Congress"); JRR to Henry M. Rutledge, August 2, 1817, JRR UVA ("I have been urged to return to public life, but I have done with it forever. I feel myself utterly unfit for intercourse with mankind").

2. JRR to Charles Mercer, December 15, 1817, PrU.

3. Stokes and Berkeley, *Papers of Randolph*, 105–6.

4. JRR to Harmanus Bleecker, July 20, 1817, HB.

5. Dudley, 203–4. At some point, Dudley had enough of Randolph's abuse and left Roanoke. "I consider myself under obligations to you that I can never repay," Randolph wrote. "I have considered you as a blessing sent to me by Providence, in my old age, to repay the desertion of my other friends and nearer connexions." JRR to Theodore Dudley, August 1818, Dudley, 203. Dudley returned and remained for two more years.

6. Dudley's complete description deserves repeating. "In his dark days, when the evil genius predominated, the austere vindictiveness of his feelings towards those that a distempered fancy depicted as enemies, or as delinquent in truth or honour, was horribly severe and remorseless. Under such circumstances of mental alienation, I sincerely believe . . . that had our blessed Saviour, accompanied by his Holy Mother, condescended to become again incarnate, revisited the earth, and been domiciliated with him one week, he would have imagined the former a rogue, and the latter no better than she should be. On the contrary, when the benevolent genius had the ascendant, no one ever knew better how to feel and express the tenderest kindness, or to evince, in countenance and manner, gentler benevolence of heart." Dudley, 203–4.

7. JRR to John Brockenbrough, [August 1819], Shorey, 23. Randolph's equilibrium

was also affected by the financial Panic of 1819. He lost more than $16,000 by "the sudden failure of a commercial house in Richmond." JRR to Harmanus Bleecker, May 22, 1819, HB. See also JRR to Henry M. Rutledge, May 3, 1819, JRR LC ("the distress here in the commercial world is greater than it has been since 1784–5, when the same causes, peace and paper money, plunged the town in ruin").

8. JRR to Harmanus Bleecker, March 15, 1818, HB.

9. JRR to F. W. Gilmer, July 10, 1818, JRR LVA.

10. JRR to F. S. Key, September 25, 1818, Garland 2: 103.

11. "It is true," Randolph wrote, "that I am about to be placed in the political cockpit . . . the manner of application was unusual and I believe unprecedented in this country. . . . [A] letter was addressed to me by respectable Freeholders from each of the counties that compose the district . . . claiming my services on the ground of Union . . . and of a previous pledge on my part not to withhold my services." JRR to Harmanus Bleecker, March 25, 1819, HB. See also JRR to F. S. Key, May 3, 1819, Garland 2: 105 ("Very contrary to my judgment, and yet more against my feelings, I am again a public man").

12. JRR to Rev. William Meade, December 21, 1818, JRR LC.

13. JRR to James M. Garnett, January 11, 1820, JMG. See also JRR to Harmanus Bleecker, January 23, 1820, HB ("I am well enough received here . . . by all but some ultra-federalists turned courtiers and place hunters").

14. JRR to Harmanus Bleecker, January 23, 1820, HB.

15. AC, 16th Cong., 1st sess., 819.

16. JRR to H. M. Rutledge, March 20, 1820, Duke.

17. JRR to James M. Garnett, January 29, 1820, JMG.

18. A recent study points out that the compromise was not Clay's creation. "Actually, Clay never publicly spoke for or against the Missouri Compromise, and he was in fact doubtful that it would calm rancor or long quell disunion." Heidler, Henry Clay, 147.

19. See generally Forbes, The Missouri Compromise, 95–98, 112–16.

20. AC, 16th Cong., 1st sess., 1464; JRR to James M. Garnett, February 9, 1820, JMG.

21. Randolph "clearly feared that compromise would have negative social effects including a hardening of southern attitudes toward slavery, in addition to the growth of fanaticism regarding the social issue of slavery." Tate, Conservatism and Southern Intellectuals, 71.

22. Thomas Jefferson to John Holmes, April 22, 1820, Foner, Writings of Jefferson, 767.

23. JRR to Joseph Clay, February 20, 1820, JRR UVA.

24. Moore, The Missouri Controversy, 96.

25. Kirk, Randolph, 69.

26. AC, 16th Cong., 1st sess., 925–26. In this same speech, Randolph said he would carry "the war [against the slave trade] into the enemy's country, even into Africa, and endeavor to put it down there."

27. Boston Daily Advertiser, February 5, 1820, Moore, The Missouri Controversy, 93.

28. AC, 16th Cong., 1st sess., 1453–54; JRR to John Brockenbrough, [February 23, 1820], Shorey, 24.

29. JRR to John Brockenbrough, [February 23, 1820], Shorey, 24; Bruce 1: 449.

30. The Annals record that Randolph spoke "for more than two hours" on February 22, 1820; on February 25; for "more than four hours" on February 26; and "more than

three hours" on March 1. *AC,* 16th Cong., 1st sess., 1454, 1539, 1541, 1572. Bruce writes that "bad blood" between Randolph and the publishers of the *Annals,* Gales & Seaton, accounts for the lack of reporting. He also proffers that Randolph might have failed to revise and submit his remarks. Bruce 1: 448.

31. Moore, *The Missouri Controversy,* 93.

32. Sparks, *Memoirs of Fifty Years,* 226.

33. Adams, *Memoirs of John Quincy Adams* 4: 532.

34. JRR to John Brockenbrough, February 23, 1820, Shorey, 25.

35. Garland 2: 127; Bruce 1: 449.

36. Bruce 1: 449.

37. *AC,* 16th Cong., 1st sess., 1539, 1541.

38. JRR to H. M. Rutledge, March 20, 1820, Duke.

39. Bruce 1: 449.

40. JRR to James M. Garnett, February 9, 1820, JMG; JRR to Harmanus Bleecker, March 11, 1820, HB; JRR to John Brockenbrough, February 23, 24, 1820, Shorey, 26, 27.

41. JRR to John Brockenbrough, February 24, 1820, Shorey, 27.

42. *AC,* 16th Cong., 1st sess., 1572.

43. Moore, *The Missouri Controversy,* 104, citing the Pittsburgh *Statesman,* April 26, 1820. The term "doughfaces" was probably drawn from a game in which children placed wet dough on their faces and attempted to frighten one another.

44. JRR to Elizabeth J. C. Clay, March 20, 1820, Kirk, *Randolph,* 171.

45. *AC,* 16th Cong., 1st sess., 1589.

46. Ibid., 1590. Robert Forbes calls Clay's action a "somewhat underhanded parliamentary maneuver." Forbes, *The Missouri Compromise,* 98.

47. Garland 2: 130.

48. "The Missouri debate allowed the political ideas of the Old Republicans to influence the rest of the South, and during the 1820s many southerners rediscovered states' rights political ideology." Tate, *Conservatism and Southern Intellectuals,* 75.

49. "The Missouri Compromise boosted the reputations of Randolph and [John] Taylor [of Caroline] in the south and gave new life to sectionalism in national political dialogue." Tate, *Conservatism and Southern Intellectuals,* 75.

50. Little evidence survives documenting the friendship between Randolph and Decatur. Garland writes that Randolph and Decatur were "friends and . . . kindred spirits." Bruce describes the relationship as a "tie of genuine friendship." Garland 2: 136; Bruce 2: 624. An early biographer of Decatur relates an anecdote about the two men engaging in a discussion about religion. Mackenzie, *Decatur,* 344–45. That story is repeated by Decatur's most recent biographer, but no other comments are made about their relationship. Allison, *Stephen Decatur,* 209. Another biographer states only that Randolph was "one of the commodore's most fervent supporters." de Kay, *Rage for Glory,* 4. No letters between the two men or anecdotes have survived. Randolph apparently turned to Decatur for advice during the exchange of letters with Nancy Morris. Perhaps he provided some details of their friendship in his two speeches on the House floor delivered in the wake of Decatur's death, but the speeches are not published. See *AC,* 16th Cong., 1st sess., 1670, 1675. See Lewis, "Decatur in Portraiture," 365 ("Randolph had been . . . one of Decatur's most intimate friends").

51. Statement of Judge William Leigh, Bruce 2: 335.

52. Lewis, *The Romantic Decatur*, 233.

53. Shorey, 29–30; Bruce 2: 334.

54. *AC*, 16th Cong., 1st sess., 1670, 1675.

55. Bruce 2: 335.

56. Adams, *Memoirs of John Quincy Adams* 5: 36.

57. Bruce 2: 334.

58. Garland 2: 137.

59. JRR to Francis W. Gilmer, July 1, 1820, Bryan; JRR to Elizabeth T. Coalter, December 29, 1822, Bryan.

60. JRR to Francis W. Gilmer, July 1, 1820, Bryan; JRR to Richard K. Randolph, August 14, 1820, JRR LC. Randolph's references are to Geoffrey Chaucer and John Dryden.

61. JRR to Theodore Dudley, June 10, 1821, Dudley, 219.

62. Ibid., June 24, 1821, Dudley, 222.

63. JRR to Elizabeth T. Coalter, June 12, 1821, Bryan.

64. JRR to Theodore Dudley, June 10, 1821, Dudley, 220.

65. Bruce 2: 409. Randolph found he was "in much better spirits than when I wrote last. Indeed I am at length entirely satisfied that the greater part of my mental sufferings are attributable to bodily disease." JRR to James M. Garnett, August 21, 1821, JMG

66. JRR to Harmanus Bleecker, January 30, 1821, HB.

67. Bruce 2: 314.

68. JRR to [unknown], January 1821, JRR LVA; JRR to John Brockenbrough, November 26, 1820, Shorey, 31; JRR to Harmanus Bleecker, December 29, 1821, HB; JRR to James M. Garnett, January 9, 1822, JMG.

69. JRR to F. W. Gilmer, December 24, 1820, JRR LVA.

70. JRR to Francis W. Gilmer, July 22, 1821, Bryan.

71. JRR to John Brockenbrough, January 19, [1822], Shorey, 44.

72. Ibid., January 18, 1822, Shorey, 44.

73. JRR to Theodore Dudley, January 27, 1822, Dudley, 240–41.

74. *AC*, 17th Cong., 1st sess., 818.

75. Ibid., 819–20.

76. Ibid., 818, 847.

77. Ibid., 863.

78. Ibid., 942, 945.

79. JRR to John Brockenbrough, February 7, 1822, Shorey, 47.

80. *AC*, 17th Cong., 1st sess., 823, 821, 932.

81. JRR to [unknown], February 7, 1822, Garland 2: 161–62, 168.

82. *AC*, 17th Cong., 1st sess., 944.

83. JRR to John Brockenbrough, February 7, 1822, Shorey, 47. A reference to 1 Samuel 4:21: "Then she named the child Ichabod, saying 'The glory has departed from Israel!' because the ark of God had been captured."

84. Garland 2: 175.

85. Bruce 2: 442.

86. Bruce 1: 471–72.

87. Bruce 2: 336.

88. JRR to Richard K. Randolph, May 23, 1823, JRR LC.

89. Ibid.; JRR to Elizabeth Coalter, August 25, 1823, Duke; JRR to James Garnett, September 26, 1823, JMG; JRR to T. M. F. Bryan, October 11, 1823, JRR UVA; JRR to William Barksdale, October 24, 1823, JRR LC.

90. JRR to James M. Garnett, November 1823, JMG.

15. A FIG FOR THE CONSTITUTION

1. JRR to his constituents, March 16, 1822, Adams, *Randolph*, 269–70.

2. *Messages and Papers of the Presidents* 2: 785–86.

3. Remini, *Clay*, 219.

4. Bruce 2: 203.

5. JRR to James M. Garnett, [January 1, 1824], JMG.

6. JRR to William Barksdale, October 24, 1823, JRR LC.

7. Ammon, Monroe, 549.

8. *AC,* 18th Cong., 1st sess., 805–6. Clay introduced a companion resolution warning Spain not to attempt to regain her former holdings in the Americas. *AC,* 18th Cong., 1st sess., 1104.

9. Ibid., 1112–13.

10. Ibid., 1113.

11. Ibid., 1114.

12. Ibid., 1116.

13. Ibid., 1086.

14. Ibid., 1099.

15. Ibid., 1093. Merrill Peterson calls Webster's speech on Greek independence "one of the most splendid ever heard in Congress." He notes that in wake of the speech, Clay embraced Webster "as a better Republican than boastful sentinels of party principle like John Randolph." *Great Triumvirate,* 77.

16. JRR to John Randolph Bryan, August 1, 1830, Bryan.

17. *AC,* 18th Cong., 1st sess., 1181.

18. Ibid., 1182.

19. Ibid.

20. Ibid.

21. Ibid.

22. Ibid., 1183.

23. Ibid.

24. Ibid., 1184.

25. Ibid.

26. Ibid., 1188.

27. Ibid.

28. Ibid., 1034–36.

29. Ibid., 1033.

30. JRR to James M. Garnett, January 15, 1824, JMG.

31. Ibid., January 14, 1824, JMG.

32. *AC,* 18th Cong., 1st sess., 1296–97.

33. Ibid., 1297. The literary reference is to *Le Bourgeois Gentilhomme* ("The Citizen Turned Gentleman") by the French playwright and actor Molière (Jean Baptiste Poquelin).

34. *AC,* 18th Cong., 1st sess., 1297–98.

35. Ibid., 1299.

36. Ibid.

37. Ibid., 1300. See W. W. Henry, *Patrick Henry* 2: 609.

38. *AC,* 18th Cong., 1st sess., 1301–2.

39. Ibid., 1303.

40. Ibid., 1307, 1308, 1309.

41. Ibid., 1306–7.

42. Ibid., 1308.

43. Ibid., 1299–300. Henry Adams wrote that Randolph's speech was a "masterpiece" that "warrants placing him in very high rank as a political leader." *Randolph,* 274, 278. Russell Kirk judged there had been "no better exposition of the argument for strict constitutional construction." *Randolph,* 105.

44. *AC,* 18th Cong., 1st sess., 1315.

45. Ibid., 1313.

46. Bruce 1: 451, note a.

47. Henry Clay to Francis T. Brooks, March 16, 1824, Hopkins, *Papers of Clay* 3: 674.

48. *AC,* 18th Cong., 1st sess., 1978–79, 1994–95, 2001.

49. JRR to F. W. Gilmer, March 9, 1824, Bryan. See also JRR to William J. Barksdale, March 9, 1824, JRR UVA (making identical comments about Clay).

50. *AC,* 18th Cong., 1st sess., 1469.

51. Ibid., 1480.

52. Ibid., 2289, 2290, 2314.

53. Ibid., 2315

54. Ibid., 2315–16.

55. Ibid., 2357.

56. Ibid., 2359–60.

57. Russell Kirk dubbed Randolph's opponents in this debate "latitudinarians of constitutional interpretation." *Randolph,* 107–9.

58. *AC,* 18th Cong., 1st sess., 2360.

59. Ibid., 2361.

60. Ibid.

61. Ibid., 2365.

62. Ibid., 2367.

63. Ibid., 2368. In Roman mythology, Mezentius was an Etruscan king noted for his cruelty. He was reported to have tied men face to face with corpses and let them die—a "Mezentian marriage."

64. Ibid., 2379.

65. JRR to William J. Barksdale, April 16, 1824, JRR LC.

66. Richmond *Enquirer*, July 9, 1824.

67. Ibid., July 15, 1824.

68. Wiltse, *Calhoun* 1: 289.

69. Coit, *Calhoun*, 166–67.

70. Adams, *Randolph*, 279.

71. Thomas Jefferson to Edward Livingston, April 4, 1824, Ford, *Writings of Jefferson* 10: 300.

72. Richmond *Enquirer*, May 25, 1824.

73. JRR to John Brockenbrough, July 24, 1824, Shorey, 53–54.

74. Ibid.

75. JRR to Elizabeth Coalter, December 2, 1824, CaP.

76. JRR to F. W. Gilmer, November 8, 1824, WCB; JRR to James Garnett, December 5, 1824, JMG.

77. Andrew Jackson to William B. Lewis, January 29, 1825, in Remini, *Andrew Jackson* 2: 87.

78. JRR to General Bailey, January 28, 1825, *New York Times*, May 5, 1877.

79. *Register of Debates*, 18th Cong., 2nd sess., 527.

80. Smith, *Forty Years*, 185–86.

81. Bouldin, *Home Reminiscences*, 168.

82. JRR to Daniel Webster, [February 20, 1825], Wiltse, *Papers of Webster* 2: 54.

83. Remini, *Webster*, 242–43.

84. Richmond *Enquirer*, May 25, 1824.

85. *Register of Debates*, 18th Cong., 2nd sess., 58; Remini, *Webster*, 242; Bruce 1: 496–97.

86. Memorandum of Thomas Hart Benton, February 25, 1825, Wiltse, *Papers of Webster* 2: 54–55.

87. JRR to Richard K. Randolph, February 25, 1825, JRR LC. See also JRR to F. W. Gilmer, February 25, 1825, Bryan; JRR to F. W. Gilmer, March 1, 1825, WCB.

88. Daniel Webster to Thomas H. Benton, February 25, 1825; JRR to Thomas H. Benton, August 25, 1825, Hart, "An Affair of Honor," 55, 56. This 1825 episode was the only near-duel between Randolph and Webster. An exchange of letters in 1816 between Randolph and Thomas Robertson of Louisiana has been frequently mischaracterized as a challenge between Randolph and Webster. On April 25, 1816, Randolph spoke in opposition to increasing the duty on imported sugar. *AC*, 14th Cong., 1st sess., 1438. Robertson "made a few remarks in reply," which were followed by "some further conversation between Mr. Randolph and Mr. Robertson." The unreported conversation was followed by a note from Robertson to Randolph. "Your observation, on taking your seat in the House of Representatives today," he wrote, "and your refusal when called upon, to explain, leaves me no other alternative than to demand that satisfaction which my insulted feelings require." Thomas B. Robertson to JRR, April 25, 1816, JRR LC. Randolph refused the challenge. JRR to Thomas B. Robertson, April [26], 1816, JRR LC. In 1870, George Curtis wrote that Randolph challenged Webster, calling Randolph's letter of April 26, 1816, to Robertson as, in fact, Webster's reply to Randolph refusing the duel. Curtis, *Life of Webster* 1: 154–55. Biographer Claude Fuess, relying on the same letter, repeats the

story. *Daniel Webster* 1: 189. An editorial note in Webster's Papers states that "a misunderstanding developed between Webster and [Randolph], when the former objected to the incorporation of a sugar tax in the tariff bill, the inclusion having been urged by Randolph. The disagreement led the Virginian to challenge Webster to a duel, but Webster declined." Wiltse, *Papers of Webster* 1: 197. Most recently, Robert Remini wrote that Randolph "sparred with Webster over the sugar duty and got so provoked that he challenged the New Hampshire representative to a duel! . . . The challenge was as ridiculous as Randolph himself, and Webster simply brushed it aside." Remini, *Webster,* 139–40. The confusion about this incident seems based upon a letter of April 30, 1816, in which Randolph forwards to Webster a copy of his response to Robertson. Webster's name was affixed at the bottom of the letter and, accordingly, readers have drawn the conclusion that Webster had failed to keep a copy of his response refusing the duel, and requested one from Randolph. In addition, the Randolph-to-Robertson letter in Randolph's papers is a copy not in his hand and carries the notation: "I presume a copy of Mr. Randolph's letter." This confusing record aside, the 1816 duel challenge was from Robertson to Randolph, not from Randolph to Webster. First, Webster took no part in the debate on the sugar tax on April 25, 1816—the debate during which the actionable words were spoken. Second, after the Robertson-Randolph debate on April 25, both Randolph and Webster voted against the amendment to incorporate the sugar tax. Third, all accounts in Webster biographies inaccurately report that Randolph *favored* the sugar tax. The record shows that Randolph spoke twice against the tax, on April 8 and again on April 25. Thus, the basis for the challenge—a disagreement over the sugar tax—does not exist. Fourth, none of the accounts in Webster biographies address the letter of April 25, 1816, from Robertson to Randolph issuing the challenge. Fifth, Webster spoke "at length" on the tariff on April 26, 1816. *AC,* 14th Cong., 1st sess., 1440–49. Webster's remarks were followed by a "debate of much length and no little warmth." At least thirteen congressmen participated in the debate; Randolph did not. These facts establish that the duel challenge was from Robertson to Randolph. Why then did Randolph send Webster a copy of his response to Robertson? Randolph's cover letter reads: "I now regret very much that I did not leave Georgetown with you this morning. I have just dined where you breakfasted this morning. . . . That reflection seems to add to the uncomfortable feeling of solitariness that now assails me. Below you have the 'copy' of the paper which you desired me to forward to you." JRR to Daniel Webster, April 30, 1816, Wiltse, *Papers of Webster* 1: 198. One might speculate that, as Randolph and Webster were on the same side in the debate over the sugar tax, they might have discussed the challenge, and Webster might have requested a copy for his information. While this answer is unsatisfactory, the letter from Randolph to Webster does generally support the proposition that the disagreement was not between these two men. Randolph would have hardly spoken so warmly to a challenger within a week of the challenge.

89. JRR to John Brockenbrough, [April 5, 1825], [June 1825], Shorey, 56. See also JRR to N. B. Tucker, May 27, 1825, TC UVA (Randolph wants to see Tucker "once more before I die and something tells me that that time is not far off").

90. JRR to William J. Barksdale, June 29, 1825, JRR LC; JRR to John Brockenbrough, [July 8, 1825], Shorey, 57.

91. A third ballot was taken. The result was Randolph 104, Tucker 80, abstentions 42. Thus a majority did not support Randolph's election.

92. Wiltse, *Calhoun* 1: 329.

16. THE PURITAN AND THE BLACKLEG

1. "In the aftermath of the election . . . Van Buren had a great deal of rethinking and reorganizing to do." Silbey, *Van Buren*, 45.

2. Van Buren, *Autobiography*, 205.

3. Ibid., 427. Along with his praise, Van Buren did note that Randolph "lacked a balance-wheel to regulate his passions and to guide his judgment."

4. Van Buren, *Autobiography*, 429. "Van Buren rather looked up to the aristocrat he believed this Virginian to be, much in the same way he deferred to [Jackson]. Apart from Randolph's pretensions, Van Buren found him vastly entertaining, drunk or sober, with his gift for invective, his colorful language, his amusing remembrances of times past; though he could be exasperated, even bored at times, with Randolph's lengthy wandering speeches . . . no one doubted his devotion to Jeffersonian principles." Niven, *Martin Van Buren*, 180–81. Van Buren attempted to "obtain a glimpse of the inner chambers of the man's real constitution," but Randolph pushed back at such familiarity. "You think you understand me already, but you are mistaken," he snapped. "You know nothing at all about me!" Van Buren, *Autobiography*, 426.

5. Bruce 2: 203. Randolph would later describe Van Buren as "too great an intriguer and besides wants personal dignity and weight of character. He is an adroit, dapper, little managing man, but he can't inspire respect, much less veneration." JRR to Andrew Jackson, March 18, 1832, Bruce 2: 13.

6. JRR to Thomas Marsh Forman, March 4, 1826, JRR VHS.

7. *Register of Debates*, 19th Cong., 1st sess., 400.

8. JRR to F. W. Gilmer, January 8, 1826, Bryan UVA.

9. JRR to John Brockenbrough, January 6, 1826, Shorey, 61.

10. *Register of Debates*, 19th Cong., 1st sess., 142, 407, 571, 590, 642, 674. Similar entries are found at *Register of Debates*, 19th Cong., 1st sess., 423 ("a speech of more than two hours"), 589 ("a speech of about two hours and a half"), 666 ("a speech of two hours), and 682 ("rejoined in a speech of two hours"). On February 13, 1826, Randolph wrote that he "just concluded a speech of nearly two hours." JRR to Thomas Marsh Forman, February 13, 1826, JR VHS.

11. Poore, *Reminiscences* 1: 68–69; Adams, *Randolph*, 297–98. It is not clear what Randolph was consuming while on the Senate floor. "I had rather die than drink, habitually, brandy and water," he wrote. "Genuine Madeira is the only thing, except good water, that I can drink with pleasure, or impunity." JRR to Theodore Dudley, February 5, 1822, Dudley, 250–53. John Quincy Adams asserted that Randolph drank "bottled porter," but also a mixture of "about one-third brandy and two-thirds water" which he called "toast-water." Adams, *Memoirs of John Quincy Adams* 7: 433, 472. Adams could have mistaken this mixture for another drink concoction of the same name. "My drink is toast and water," Randolph wrote, "made by boiling the latter, and pouring it on highly toasted

bread—so that it acquires the colour of Cognac brandy." JRR to Theodore Dudley, January 27, 1822, Dudley, 240.

12. Daniel Webster to [John Evelyn Denison], May 3, 1826, Wiltse, *Papers of Webster* 2: 107. Randolph appears to have known exactly what he was doing during these rambling speeches. Describing one speech, he wrote that he "closed with a tirade that, as Monroe would say, produced, for the time, great effect. . . . I began to give credit to what I saw in the newspapers—this was the conduct of a Tiberius." JRR to Littleton Tazewell, February 21, 1826, UNC.

13. Richmond *Enquirer,* January 16, 1827. This is probably a reference to one occasion on which Randolph wore six or seven overcoats. While speaking, he took them off, one by one, and piled them beside him. See Coit, *Calhoun,* 162–63.

14. Bruce 2: 409–10; Adams, *Randolph,* 263. John Quincy Adams described the "speeches of ten hours long" as "raving balderdash" that reviled "the absent and the present, the living and the dead." Adams, *Memoirs of John Quincy Adams* 7: 433.

15. "[On] one occasion . . . there were hardly a dozen senators in their seats, at least one of whom *appeared* to be pretty soundly asleep." *Niles' Register* 6 (May 13, 1826): 186.

16. Van Buren, *Autobiography,* 206.

17. Ibid.

18. Ibid., 428.

19. Wilson, *Papers of Calhoun* 6: 347.

20. *Register of Debates,* 19th Cong., 1st sess., 102.

21. Ibid., 125–26.

22. Kirk, *The Conservative Mind,* 161.

23. JRR to John Brockenbrough, February 10, 1826, Shorey, 65.

24. JRR to F. W. Gilmer, January 8, 1826, Bryan; JRR to John Brockenbrough, February 20, 1826, Shorey, 67.

25. JRR to John Brockenbrough, February 1, 1826, Shorey, 63.

26. Ibid., February 27, 1826, Shorey, 68.

27. *Register of Debates,* 19th Cong., 1st sess., 402. Dumas Malone writes that Randolph's words were "a balm to Jefferson's spirit." *Jefferson* 6: 481–82. Randolph's good will went only so far. "I have always believed," he wrote as news of Jefferson's troubled financial condition spread, "that St. Thomas of Cantingbury's jewels were Bristol stones—in other words, that he was insolvent. What else could be expected from his gimcracks and crack-brained notions and improvements?" JRR to John Brockenbrough, January 30, 1826, Shorey, 62.

28. Bruce 2: 409–10.

29. Van Buren, *Autobiography,* 209–10.

30. Andrew Burstein writes that Clay's support for the conference was to "counter British influence in Latin America, consistent with the Monroe Doctrine, and to strengthen ties with the newly independent republics of the Southern Hemisphere." Burstein, *America's Jubilee,* 193.

31. Silbey, *Van Buren,* 47.

32. *Register of Debates,* 19th Cong., 1st sess., 391.

33. Ibid., 394.

34. Ibid., 403.

35. Ibid., 392.

36. Ibid., 395.

37. Ibid., 401.

38. Merrill Peterson quotes an eyewitness, John K. Kane of Philadelphia, as saying that "the published account of Randolph's outburst was but a poor caricature of the original." Kane reports that Randolph said: "But we were the first to see on the stage of real life the blue-bonneted puritan of New England sharing the profits of the shuffle with the political Black Legs of the West!" *Great Triumvirate*, 140.

39. Henry Clay to JRR, March 31, 1826, JRR LC.

40. Henry Clay to Charles Hammond, April 19, 1826, Hopkins, *Papers of Clay* 5: 253–54.

41. Bruce 1: 517.

42. Peterson, *Great Triumvirate*, 141.

43. "Memorandum of Terms of Duel," JRR LC.

44. Heidler, *Henry Clay*, 198; Burstein, *America's Jubilee*, 197–98.

45. JRR to Thomas Forman Bryan, April 8, 1826, JRR VHS.

46. Account of James Hamilton, "Famous Duels," *New York Times*, August 4, 1856.

47. Thomas Hart Benton to Henry St. George Tucker, July 16, 1826, JRR LC.

48. Benton, *Thirty Years' View* 1: 70–74. See also Heidler, *Henry Clay*, 198–99; Burstein, *America's Jubilee*, 197–200.

49. Thomas Hart Benton to Henry St. George Tucker, July 16, 1826, JRR LC.

50. Heidler, *Henry Clay*, 199.

51. Jeanne and David Heidler write that Clay's first shot "tore through Randolph's trouser leg, missing flesh." *Henry Clay*, 199. Most accounts report that only Clay's second shot pierced Randolph's clothing.

52. Benton, *Thirty Years' View* 1: 75–77.

53. Henry St. George Tucker to Beverley Tucker, April 11, 1826, TC UVA.

54. JRR to John Brockenbrough, April 14, 1826, Shorey, 71.

55. Richmond *Enquirer*, April 18, 1826.

56. Ibid., January 16, 1827.

57. JRR to John Brockenbrough, August 8, 1826, Shorey, 75.

58. Ibid.

59. Ibid., 76.

60. JRR to John Brockenbrough, January 7, 1827, Shorey, 80.

61. Ibid., [January 1, 1827], Shorey, 79.

62. Ibid., January 12, 1827, January 13, 1827, Shorey, 82.

63. Ibid., January 14, 1827, Shorey, 83.

64. Richmond *Enquirer*, January 16, 1827.

65. Ibid.

66. JRR to John Brockenbrough, January 20, 1827, Shorey, 84.

67. Chitwood, *John Tyler*, 82.

68. JRR to J. R. Bryan, January 29, 1827, JRR Princeton.

69. JRR to John Brockenbrough, February 15, February 24, 1827, Shorey, 86, 89–90.

70. Ibid., December 21, 1827, Shorey, 99. "Old Prince Edward has come out manfully indeed," Randolph wrote of the election results, "and if anything could exhilarate me, it would be such a manifestation of the confidence of those who know me best." JRR to John Brockenbrough, February 26, 1827, Shorey, 91.

71. JRR to John Brockenbrough, April 10, 1828, Shorey, 103.

72. JRR to Maria Coleman, December 31, 1827, JRR LC.

73. Nathaniel Macon to [unknown], March 6, 1828, Macon Papers, North Carolina Historical Society, Bruce 2: 312.

74. JRR to John Brockenbrough, May 27, 1828, Shorey, 104. See also JRR to John Brockenbrough, September 4, 1827, Shorey, 96 ("sharp attack of bile . . . anxiety, distress"); JRR to John Brockenbrough, November 6, 1827, Shorey, 97 ("My good friend, I can't convey to you—language can't express—the thousandth part of the misery I feel"); JRR to J. R. Bryan, December 5, 1827, JRR UVA ("I write with difficulty & pain"); JRR to John Brockenbrough, December 15, 1827, Shorey, 98 ("I am dying as decently as I can"); JRR to Dennis A. Smith, [December 25, 1827], JRR UVA ("My lungs I once thought to be invulnerable, but Death takes the Bull by the horns"); JRR to James Garnett, February 10, 1828, JMG ("I am very ill—past all hope or desire of recovery"); JRR to Joseph Clay, April 18, 1828, JRR LC ("very ill, very ill indeed"); JRR to Timothy Pickering, April 24, 1828, MiH (Blood "pouring from my lungs"); JRR to Martin Van Buren, October 13, 1828, JRR LC ("I am suffering very severely from ill health and worse spirits"); JRR to Elizabeth T. Coalter, November 28, 1828, Bruce 2: 365–66 ("My cough is almost incessant, and I am sure that I must be an object of disgust to all except to those whose previous attachment overcomes or suppresses the feeling"); JRR to John Brockenbrough, November 29, 1828, Shorey, 111 ("My cough is very much worse, and the pain in my breast and side increased a good deal").

75. JRR to John Brockenbrough, May 30, 1828, Shorey, 105.

76. Ibid., June 3, 1828, Shorey, 106; JRR to William J. Barksdale, July 28, 1828, JRR LC; JRR to John Brockenbrough, 1828, MiH.

77. *Register of Debates,* 20th Cong., 1st sess., 1163–64.

78. Morse, *John Quincy Adams,* 212.

79. JRR to John Brockenbrough, December 7, 1828, Shorey, 111.

80. *Register of Debates,* 20th Cong., 1st sess., 1333.

81. JRR to Elizabeth T. Coalter, August 18, 1828, WCB.

82. JRR to Captain West, Bruce 2: 166–67, 358.

83. JRR to J. S. Skinner, March 2, 7, 8, May 21, 1828, *American Turf and Sporting Magazine* 4, no. 11 (July 1833): 574–78.

84. JRR to John Brockenbrough, May 30, 1828, Shorey, 105–6.

85. Ibid., March 7, 1829, Shorey, 127.

17. REMORSE

1. JRR to James Garnett, April 1, 1829, JMG; JRR to John Brockenbrough, April 28, 1829, Shorey, 131. See also JRR to John Brockenbrough, February 12, April 21, 1829, Shorey, 121–22, 129–30.

2. JRR to John Brockenbrough, February 12, 1829, Shorey, 122.

3. Nowhere, Russell Kirk wrote, "except at the federal constitutional convention, perhaps, were the fundamentals of government more thoroughly discussed—the problems of right and power, of suffrage and office, of property and poverty, of permanence and change. The East stood against the West. . . . [T]he old order defied the new; egalitarianism fought conservatism." *Randolph*, 71–72.

4. Bruce, *The Rhetoric of Conservatism*, 2.

5. Beveridge, *Marshall* 4: 479.

6. Pleasants, "Sketches of the Virginia Convention," 303.

7. Ibid., 304.

8. Bouldin, *Home Reminiscences*, 168–69.

9. Pleasants, "Sketches of the Virginia Convention," 148.

10. Grigsby, "The Virginia Convention," 80–81.

11. Richmond *Enquirer*, November 12, 1829.

12. Pleasants, "Sketches of the Virginia Convention," 148.

13. Grigsby, "The Virginia Convention," 41.

14. *Proceedings and Debates of the Virginia State Convention*, 313.

15. Ibid.

16. Ibid., 314.

17. Ibid., 316.

18. Grigsby, "The Virginia Convention," 44.

19. *Proceedings and Debates of the Virginia State Convention*, 316.

20. Ibid., 319.

21. Ibid., 319–20.

22. Pleasants, "Sketches of the Virginia Convention," 148.

23. *Proceedings and Debates of the Virginia State Convention*, 320–21.

24. Richmond *Enquirer*, November 17, 1829.

25. *Proceedings and Debates of the Virginia State Convention*, 716.

26. Grigsby, "The Virginia Convention," 42.

27. *Proceedings and Debates of the Virginia State Convention*, 480. See also *Proceedings and Debates of the Virginia State Convention*, 571, 760, 782, 783, 868.

28. Ibid., 492–93.

29. Ibid., 556.

30. Ibid., 573.

31. Munford, *The Two Parsons*, 571.

32. Gaines, "The Evening of Their Glory," 21.

33. *Proceedings and Debates of the Virginia State Convention*, 790.

34. Pleasants, "Sketches of the Virginia Convention," 303.

35. Garland 2: 332.

36. Andrew Jackson to JRR, September 16, 1829, JRR LC.

37. Martin Van Buren to JRR, September 17, 1829, Duke.

38. JRR to Andrew Jackson, September 24, 1829, JRR LC.

39. Van Buren, *Autobiography*, 418–19.

40. Ibid., 419.

41. Randolph's most sympathetic biographer writes that "Randolph, of course, should never have been appointed Minister to Russia, and he should not have accepted the appointment when tendered to him. His uncalculating candor of character, his impetuous temper, his eccentric deportment, and the proneness of his mind to occasional derangement tended to unfit him for a diplomatic post even at an earlier stage of his career." Bruce 1: 651.

42. "Col. Benton writes me that my nomination met with no opposition. . . . I congratulate you on the termination of a most tedious, expensive and unprofitable session of Congress." JRR to Martin Van Buren, June 1, 1830, JRR LC. "I got a letter yesterday from Col. Benton informing me that my nomination passed without opposition." JRR to J. R. Clay, June 1, 1830, JRR LC.

43. JRR to Andrew Jackson, June 8, 1830, JRR LC.

44. JRR to Nathaniel Macon, June 27, 1830, Duke; JRR to Andrew Jackson, June 28, 1830, JRR LC.

45. New York *American* 13, no. 4210, enclosed in JRR to Editor, New York *Evening Post*, September 2, 1832, TC UVA.

46. JRR to Martin Van Buren, August 3, 1830, JRR LC. Randolph noted that one crewmember was lost during the trip.

47. JRR to W. C. Rives, August 10, 22, 1830, JRR LC.

48. JRR to Nathan Loughborough, August 18, 1830, JRR UVA.

49. JRR to John Brockenbrough, [September 4, 1830], Shorey, 134.

50. Ibid., December 20, 1830, Shorey, 136–37.

51. Ibid.

52. Adams, *Randolph*, 302. Randolph denied the story. "Lies innumerable are circulating here," he wrote, "They relate to my reception by their Imperial Majesties and the Imperial Ministry, to my dress, etc. which are represented as being outré and ridiculous." JRR to J. R. Clay, November 23, 1830, JRR LC. Washington Irving supported Randolph's version. "The story of his kneeling to the Emperor must have arisen from what he relates himself; that, in advancing, as one of his legs is contracted, and somewhat shorter than the other, he limped with it in such a manner that he supposes the Emperor thought he was about to bend one knee, as he made a movement as if to prevent such a thing and said: No, No! Randolph, however, is too well informed on points of etiquette and too lofty a fellow to have made such a blunder." Washington Irving to Peter Irving, October 22, 1830, Irving, *Life of Washington Irving* 2: 439. See also Martin Van Buren to T. Ritchie, November 5, 1830, JRR LVA/UVA ("I have no reason to believe that the information in regard to Mr. Randolph's conduct at St. Petersburgh has the slightest foundation in truth"); J. R. Clay to [Editor, Richmond *Enquirer*], January 17, 1831, LVA/UVA (Accounts of JRR's conduct at court "are utterly devoid of truth").

53. JRR to John Brockenbrough, December 20, 1830, Shorey, 136.

54. Ibid.

55. JRR to J. R. Clay, August 1830, JRR LC; JRR to J. R. Clay, September 11, 23, 1830, JRR LC; JRR to Andrew Jackson, January 5, 1831, JRR UVA; JRR to William Leigh, December 16, 1830, JRR UVA.

56. JRR to John Brockenbrough, December 20, 1830, Shorey, 136.

57. Ibid., [September 4, 1830], Shorey, 134–35; JRR to Prince Lieven, August 19, 1830, JRR UVA.

58. JRR to Eliz. T. C. Bryan, September 14, 1830, Bryan.

59. JRR to Andrew Jackson, 10/22 August 1830, JRR LC.

60. "Randolph, who turns his diseases to commodity," John Quincy Adams wrote, "behaved for a few weeks at St. Petersburg like a crazy man." *Memoirs of John Quincy Adams* 8: 328.

61. JRR to Andrew Jackson, September 17, 29, 1830, JRR LC.

62. Ibid.; JRR to J. R. Clay, September 7, 19, 11, 23, 1830; November 23, 1830, JRR LC.

63. Regarding Randolph's efforts to return to Russia, see JRR to J. R. Clay, November 23, 1830, JRR LC ("If I hold out until May, you will see me in St. Petersburgh"); JRR to Andrew Jackson, January 5, 1831, JRR LC ("I confidently look back to a return to St. Petersburgh as soon as the Baltic shall be open"); JRR to J. R. Clay, January 15, 1831, JRR LC ("I shall repair to St. Petersburgh in May"); JRR to Mark Alexander, January 22, 1831, Garland 2: 341–42 ("I shall return as soon as the Baltic is open"); but see JRR to J. R. Clay, April 16, 1831, JRR LC ("My return to Russia is more than doubtful. I feel that it would almost be an act of suicide"). During moments of improved health, Randolph did attempt to manage treaty negotiations. "Before I left St. Petersburgh," he wrote to the president, "I had put the Imperial Ministry in full possession of all our views." JRR to Andrew Jackson, January 5, 1831, JRR LVA. He met in London with Prince Christoph Heinrich von Lieven, minister to Great Britain and brother of Prince Carl von Lieven, in an effort to reach a breakthrough. He was advised that "the present unsettled state of Europe" left the emperor no "leisure to attend to more distant and less important subjects." JRR to J. R. Clay, December 20, 1830, JRR LC. From St. Petersburg, Clay confirmed that while Russia "was in every way amicably disposed towards the United States . . . [and] the subject of navigation and commerce was one of great importance . . . it would be impossible to give an answer in time to meet the wishes of the President." Memorandum of J. R. Clay, in JRR to Andrew Jackson, September 17, 19, 1830. When James Buchanan, Randolph's successor as minister, arrived in Russia, he reported that Randolph "had applied himself with energy and dispatch, to accomplish the purposes of his mission." The Russians, Buchanan wrote, would give "no intimation" whether they "would be willing to treat with us." Moore, *Works of Buchanan* 2: 194. A modern study concludes that Randolph did not "contribute much to the furtherance of his countrymen's commercial aims." Kirchner, *Studies in Russian-American Commerce,* 17.

64. JRR to J. R. Clay, September 1, 1831, JRR LC.

65. Andrew Jackson to JRR, June 26, 1831, JRR LC; JRR to Andrew Jackson, June 28, 1831, JRR UVA.

66. JRR to Andrew Jackson, October 18, 1831, Bruce 1: 647.

67. Bruce 2: 190–95.

68. Ibid., 195–97.

69. JRR to William Wallace, March 17, 1831, Duke.

70. JRR to Andrew Jackson, March 1, 1832, JRR UVA.

71. JRR to J. R. Bryan, February 11, 1832, JRR UVA; JRR to Walter Holladay, January 1832, *American Heritage* 7, no. 5 (August 1956).

72. JRR to Andrew Jackson, January 3, [1832], JRR LVA. In one letter, Randolph requested Jackson appoint him minister to Great Britain. JRR to Andrew Jackson, March 18, 1832, Bruce 2: 14. In another letter, Randolph wrote that if "Alexander be satisfied of the friendship of Hephestus he will care little about his estimation of his Lieutenants. Now although you are not Alexander (that would be fulsome flattery) and I trust that I am something better than his minion (the nature of their connexion if I forget not was *Greek love*) yet if I could discern in your Lieutenants an Eumenes, or even an Antigonus, Lysimachus, Perdiccas, or Antipater, he should have my voice." JRR to Andrew Jackson, March 1, 1832, JRR UVA. The references are to Alexander the Great and his general staff. The reference to "Hephestus" is probably to "Hephaestion," Alexander's closest friend. It was historical rumor that Alexander and Hephaestion engaged in a homosexual relationship; hence Randolph's use of the term "Greek love." Jackson recorded no response to this strange analogy.

73. JRR to Timothy Pickering, April 24, 1828, MiH.

74. JRR to Neale Alexander, June 26, 1832, Kirk, *Randolph*, 94–95.

75. JRR to [unknown], December 6, 1832, Garland 2: 358.

76. JRR to Andrew Jackson, March 18, 1832, JRR UVA.

77. Ibid., March 27, 1832, JRR LC.

78. Ibid., March 28, 1832, JRR UVA. Randolph wrote that some of his friends were "very desirous to see me again in Congress, as it is understood that the V.P. [Calhoun] will take [Senator Robert] Hayne's place . . . where he can co-operate with the Godlike Man of the East [Webster] and the great orator of the West [Clay] . . . to the petty revenge of thwarting the measures of the Administration." JRR to Andrew Jackson, December 6, 1832, JRR LC.

79. JRR to Samuel P. Carson, January 27, 1833, JRR UVA.

80. Garland 2: 358.

81. JRR to Andrew Jackson, March 18, 1832, Bruce 1: 647; Devanny, "The Political Economy of John Randolph of Roanoke," 416.

82. JRR to Jacob Harvey, January 31, 1833, Garland 2: 360.

83. Bruce 2: 23.

84. Garland 2: 361–62.

85. Shorey, 146–47.

86. Bruce 2: 36; Remini, *Clay*, 433; Heidler, *Henry Clay*, 257.

87. JRR to Andrew Jackson, March 26, 1832, JRR LC.

88. Wiltse, *Calhoun* 2: 194.

89. JRR to John Brockenbrough, [April 23, 1833], Shorey, 145.

90. "Dr. Parrish's Deposition," 153.

91. Shorey, 148; "Dr. Parrish's Deposition," 153. .

92. "Dr. Parrish's Deposition," 153.

93. "Dr. Francis West's Reminiscences of the Last Moments of the Honorable John Randolph of Roanoke," JRR UVA.

94. "West's Reminiscences." Henry Adams, taking one last shot at Randolph, wrote: "Of his deathbed, it is as well not to attempt a description. It was grotesque—like his life." *Randolph*, 305.

95. "Dr. Parrish's Deposition." 154.

96. Ibid., 154–56.

97. Ibid. 155.

98. JRR to J. R. and Elizabeth T. C. Bryan, May 24, 1833, Bryan.

99. "West's Reminiscences."

EPILOGUE

1. Quincy, *Figures of the Past*, 216.

2. There are many sources for the "facing west" story. A contemporary account is recalled in Briscoe B. Bouldin to William C. Bruce, January 2, 1919, WCB (Roll 3, 223). When he was reinterred at Hollywood Cemetery, it was reported that he "was buried . . . like previously, with his head looking towards the west or the setting sun (as it was soon after his death) so that he could watch 'Harry of the West' [Henry Clay] in Kentucky." Richmond *Daily Dispatch*, December 15, 1879, 4.

3. *Register of Debates*, 23rd Cong., 1st sess., 2705.

4. Bruce 2: 57.

5. For a full account of the will dispute and Ohio settlement, see Mathias, "John Randolph's Freedmen: The Thwarting of a Will," 263; Bagby, "The Randolph Slave Saga," 104–11, 137–75.

6. Richmond *Daily Dispatch*, December 12, 1879, 1; December 14, 1879, 2; December 15, 1879, 3; *Richmond Daily Whig*, December 15, 1879, 1.

7. Richmond *Daily Dispatch*, December 12, 1879, 1.

8. Randolph "has been thoughtfully neglected in the textbooks of American history, this past half-century," Kirk writes, "or at best mentioned merely as a startling political eccentric." "Foreword," Shorey, xiv.

9. Malone, *Jefferson* 4: 443–46.

10. Brant, *Madison* 4: 322. Brant asserted that "peace with a man [Madison] who outstripped him politically was no more possible to Randolph than marriage." *Madison* 4: 232.

11. Jordan, *Political Leadership in Jefferson's Virginia*, 18–19; Dawidoff, *Education of Randolph*, 27; Adams, *Randolph*, 55.

12. Bowers, *Jefferson in Power*, 111. Henry Ammon wrote that Randolph was "warped by flaws which undermined his judgment and involved him in senseless squabbles." *Monroe*, 245. A recent take calls Randolph "mad, eloquent, imbibing." Wheelan, *Mr. Adams's Last Crusade*, 42.

13. Kirk, "A Composite Chronicle of His Life and Work in His Own Words," Panichas, ed., *The Essential Kirk*, xxix.

14. Kirk, *Randolph*, 19, 21, 25. Kirk's view resonated. "To compromise the self-evident principle upon which a free government is based," Norman Risjord wrote, "would be to compromise the whole structure." Accordingly, Randolph was "expressing no more that the general sentiments of the conservative wing of the party," and it should have surprised no one. *The Old Republicans*, 36–37. David Carson placed Randolph's actions squarely in the context of his principles. "He consistently called for a return to the

conservative principles of 1798, for a limited national government which recognized the sovereignty of each state, and for a strict separation-of-powers relationship between the President and Congress. . . . [I]f [he] seemed given to excesses in his opposition to Jefferson and Madison, it was because his passion was as strong as his principles." "That Ground Called Quiddism," 91–92. John Devanny wrote that Randolph "believed the primary end of any economic policy was the preservation of a patrimony of political and economic independence and virtue bequeathed by the Revolutionary generation to the nation. Any policy that threatened this patrimony . . . was anathema to [him]." "The Political Economy of John Randolph of Roanoke," 390. Noble Cunningham believed the reasons for Randolph's "violent, decisive, and irreparable" break with the administration "were less clear cut." *Jeffersonian Republicans*, 84.

15. Kirk, *Randolph*, 16.

16. Kirk, *The Conservative Mind*, 151.

17. Ibid., 151, 153, 154.

18. Ibid., 152, 158.

19. Ibid., 184.

20. Tate, *Conservatism and Southern Intellectuals*, 8.

21. Ibid., 20.

22. Devanny, "The Political Economy of John Randolph of Roanoke," 388–89, 416.

23. Kirk, *The Conservative Mind*, 150; Remini, *Henry Clay*, 78.

24. JRR to James Garnett, June 4, 1806, JMG.

25. JRR to John Brockenbrough, [December 23, 1821], Shorey, 40.

26. Ibid., September 22, 1826, Shorey, 77; JRR to James Garnett, April 24, 1811, JMG.

27. JRR to L. W. Tazewell, June 8, 1804, UNC; JRR to Theodore Dudley, August 30, 1807, Dudley, 34–35.

28. JRR to James M. Garnett, September 14, 1809, JMG.

29. JRR to William Thompson, May 13, 1804, Garland 1: 209–10. "Randolph and the other Old Republicans were men of private honesty, of economical and self-sufficient habits; they saw no reason why private morals should not be public morals or why the government should plunder, or be plundered, when the citizens should not." Kirk, *Randolph*, 133.

30. *AC*, 12th Cong., 2nd sess., 184–85.

31. JRR to Editor, Richmond *Enquirer*, January 7, 1815, Richmond *Enquirer*, April 1, 1815.

32. JRR to Edward Booker, February 9, 1816, JRR LC.

33. JRR to Jacob Harvey, January 31, 1833, Garland 2: 360.

APPENDIX 2: RANDOLPH'S CONTEMPORARIES

1. JRR to Richard Stanford, November 15, 1814, JRR UVA.

2. Garland 1: 261.

3. JRR to Theodore Dudley, September 3, 1811, Dudley, 101.

4. Ibid., February 5, 1822, Dudley, 250.

5. Oeste, *John Randolph Clay*.

6. JRR to Theodore Dudley, August 1818, Dudley, 203.

7. JRR to James Garnett, February 1, 1812, JMG.

8. JRR to Joseph Nicholson, February 17, 1811, JRR LC.

9. JRR to Henry M. Rutledge, August 2, 1817, JRR UVA.

10. JRR to George Logan, April 27, 1816, PaH.

11. JRR to Elizabeth T. Coalter, July 27, 1825, Bruce 2: 361.

Bibliography

PAPERS

Annals of Congress, 6th Congress (1st session)—18th Congress (1st session). *Register of Debates in Congress,* 1824–37.
Proceedings and Debates of the Virginia State Convention of 1829–1830. Richmond, Va.: Samuel Shepherd & Co., 1830.
Public Statutes at Large. Boston: Charles C. Little & James Brown.
American State Papers. Washington, D.C.: Gales & Seaton, 1832–1861.
Messages and Papers of the Presidents. New York: Bureau of National Literature, 1897.
Code of Virginia. Charlottesville: Michie Press, 1950.
Niles' Register. Washington, D.C.: Franklin Press, 1811–49.
American Turf & Sporting Magazine. Baltimore: J. S. Skinner, 1829–44.

ARTICLES

Ammon, Harry. "The Jeffersonian Republicans in Virginia." *Virginia Magazine of History and Biography* 71, no. 2 (April 1963): 153–67.
Biddle, Francis. "Scandal at Bizarre." *American Heritage* 12 (August 1961): 10–82.
Bouldin, Powhatan. "John Randolph of Roanoke." *Century Magazine* 51 (March 1896): 712–18.
Brant, Irving. "John W. Eppes, John Randolph, & Henry Adams." *Virginia Magazine of History and Biography* 63 (July 1955): 251–56.
Brookhiser, Richard. "Biographies" in "America Unabridged." *American Heritage* (November–December 2004): 27.
Brown, Dorothy M. "Embargo Politics in Maryland." *Maryland Historical Magazine* 58, no. 3 (September 1963): 193–210.

Carrington, R. W. "The Impeachment Trial of Samuel Chase." *Virginia Law Review* 9, no. 7 (May 1923): 485–500.

Carson, David A. "That Ground Called Quiddism: John Randolph's War with the Jefferson Administration." *Journal of American Studies* 20, no. 1 (April 1986): 71–92.

Coleman, Mary Haldane. "Whittier on John Randolph of Roanoke." *New England Quarterly* 8 (December 1935): 551–52.

Cunningham, Noble E. "Who Were the Quids?" *Mississippi Valley Historical Review* 50, no. 2 (September 1963): 252–63.

Cotts, Paul R. "Randolph v. Clay: A Duel of Words and Bullets." *Filson Club History Quarterly* 43 (April 1969): 151–57.

Crawford, Alan P. "A House Called Bizarre." *Washington Post,* November 26, 2000.

Cray, Robert E. "Remembering the USS Chesapeake: The Politics of Maritime Death and Impressment." *Journal of the Early Republic* 25, no. 3 (Fall 2005): 445–74.

Davis, Curtis C. "The Devil and John Randolph." *American Heritage* 7 (August 1956): 10–11.

D'Entremont, John. "John Randolph and the Field of Honor." *Lynch's Ferry* (Fall–Winter 2007): 4–10.

Devanny, John F., Jr. "A Loathing of Public Debt, Taxes, and Excises: The Political Economy of John Randolph of Roanoke." *Virginia Magazine of History and Biography* 109, no. 4 (2001): 387–416.

Doyle, Christopher L. "The Randolph Scandal in Early National Virginia, 1792–1815: New Voices in the 'Court of Honor.'" *Journal of Southern History* 69, no. 2 (May 2003): 283–318.

"Early Recollections of John Randolph." *Southern Literary Messenger* 28 (June 1859): 461–66.

"A Fig for the Constitution." In *The American Heritage Book of Presidents and Famous Americans* (New York: Dell Publishing Co.), vol. 3 (1967): 200–201.

Gaines, William H., Jr. "The Evening of Their Glory." *Virginia Cavalcade* 3, no. 1 (Summer 1953): 20–27.

Grigsby, Hugh B. "The Randolph Library." *Southern Literary Messenger* 20 (1854): 76–79.

———. "The Virginia Convention of 1829–30: A Discourse Delivered Before the Virginia Historical Society." Richmond, Va.: MacFarlane & Ferguson, 1854.

———. "Sketches of Members of the Constitutional Convention of 1829–30." *Virginia Magazine of History and Biography* 61, no. 3 (July 1953): 318–32.

Grinnan, Andrew Glassell. "The Prayer Book of Frances Bland, Mother of John Randolph of Roanoke." *William & Mary Quarterly* 17 (1909): 267–68.

Gutzman, Constantine. "The Randolph-Clay Duel." *Southern Partisan* 18 (4th Quarter 1998): 16–20.

Hart, Charles Henry. "An Affair of Honor: Daniel Webster and John Randolph." *The Magazine of American History* (New York: A. S. Barnes & Co.), vol. 4 (1880): 53–57.

Haskins, C. H. "The Yazoo Land Companies." *American Historical Association Papers* (New York, 1891), vol. 5: 61–103.

Haynes, George H., ed. "Letters of Samuel Taggart, Representative in Congress, 1805–1814." *Proceedings of American Antiquarian Society* 33 (April 1923): 113–226.

Hobson, Charles F. "The Marshall Court (1801–1835): Law, Politics, and the Emergence of the Federal Judiciary." In Christopher Tomlins, ed., *The United States Supreme Court: The Pursuit of Justice.* New York: Houghton Mifflin Co., 2005. 47–74.

Humphrey, Alexander. "The Impeachment of Samuel Chase." *American Lawyer* 8, no. 1 (January 1900): 57–62.

"John Randolph." *North American Review* 103, no. 212 (July 1866): 142–84.

"John Randolph." *United States Democratic Review* 28, no. 152 (February 1851): 119–27.

"John Randolph—A Personal Sketch." *Putnam's* 8, no. 44 (August 1856): 134–42.

"John Randolph of Roanoke." *Harper's Magazine* 5, no. 28 (September 1852): 531–37.

Johnson, Ludwell. "No Faith in Parchment." *Southern Partisan* 15 (4th Quarter 1995): 20–24.

Jordan, Daniel P. "John Randolph of Roanoke and the Art of Winning Elections in Jeffersonian Virginia." *Virginia Magazine of History and Biography* 86, no. 4 (October 1978): 389–407.

Kirk, Russell. "John Randolph of Roanoke on the Genius of Edmund Burke." *The Burke Newsletter* 4, no. 1 (Fall 1962): 167–69.

———. "Ten Exemplary Conservatives." Heritage Lecture 83, Heritage Foundation, December 18, 1986.

———. "Foreword." In Kenneth Shorey, ed., *Collected Letters of John Randolph to John Brockenbrough* (New Brunswick, N.J.: Transaction Books, 1988). xiii–xx.

———. "John Randolph of Roanoke: The Planter-Statesman." In George A. Panichas, ed., *The Essential Russell Kirk: Selected Essays.* Wilmington, Del.: ISI Books, 2007. 472–91.

Koenig, Louis. "Consensus Politics, 1800–1805." *American Heritage* 18 (February 1967): 4–7, 74–80.

"The Last Days of Randolph of Roanoke." *Southern Partisan* 9 (3rd Quarter 1989): 26–29.

"Letters of John Randolph of Roanoke to General Thomas Marsh Forman." *Virginia Magazine of History and Biography* 49, no. 3 (July 1941): 201–16.

Lewis, Charles Lee. "Decatur in Portraiture." *Maryland Historical Magazine* 35, no. 4 (December 1940): 365–73.

Lillich, Richard B. "The Chase Impeachment." *American Journal of Legal History* 4 (1960): 49–72.

Luconi, Stefano. "James Madison and Impeachment: Theory and Practice." In John R. Vile et al., eds., *James Madison: Philosopher, Founder, and Statesman.* Athens: Ohio University Press, 2008. 193–208.

Malone, Dumas. "John Randolph." *Dictionary of American Biography* 15.

Mathias, Frank F. "John Randolph's Freedmen: The Thwarting of a Will." *Journal of Southern History* 39, no. 2 (May 1973): 263–72.

Meade, Robert D. "John Randolph of Roanoke: Some New Information." *William & Mary Quarterly* 13, no. 2 (October 1933): 256–64.

Miller, F. Thornton. "John Marshall versus Spencer Roane: A Reevaluation of *Martin v. Hunter's Lessee." Virginia Magazine of History and Biography* 96, no. 3 (July 1988): 297–314.

Moncure, Thomas M., Jr. "The Court Decision that Nearly Destroyed the Episcopal Church." (Fredericksburg) *Free Lance-Star,* May 19, 2001.

O'Rourke, Kevin H. "War and Welfare: Britain, France, and the United States, 1807–1814." *Oxford Economic Papers* (Oxford: Oxford University Press), vol. 59 (2007): 8–30.

Pancake, John S. "The Invisibles: A Chapter in the Opposition to President Madison." *Journal of Southern History* 21 (February 1955): 17–37.

Parrish, Joseph. "John Randolph's Case. Dr. Parrish's Deposition." *Littell's Living Age* 15, no. 180 (October 23, 1847): 153–56.

Pleasants, Hugh R. "Sketches of the Virginia Convention of 1829–1830." *Southern Literary Messenger* (Richmond, Va.: MacFarlane and Ferguson, 1851), vol. 17: 147–54.

Presser, Stephen B. "A Tale of Two Judges." *Northwestern University Law Review* (1978–79): 88–91.

Radabaugh, John. "Spencer Roane and the Genesis of Virginia Judicial Review." *American Journal of Legal History* 6, no. 1 (January 1962): 63–70.

Risjord, Norman K. "1812: Conservatives, War Hawks, and the Nation's Honor." *William & Mary Quarterly* 18, no. 2 (April 1961): 196–210.

Sanford, William. "John Randolph of Roanoke." *Scott's Monthly Magazine* 2 (August 1866): 187–88.

Sheads, Scott S. "Joseph Hopper Nicholson: Citizen-Soldier of Maryland." *Maryland Historical Magazine* 98, no. 2 (Summer 2003): 133–51.

Spaulding, Thomas M. "Clay v. Randolph." *Michigan Quarterly Review* 1 (Winter 1962): 8–13.

Stanard, W. G. "The Randolph Family." *William & Mary Quarterly* 7: 122–24.

Stokes, William E., Jr. "Randolph of Roanoke." *American Heritage* (Spring 1952): 49–51.

Tate, Adam L. "Republicanism and Society: John Randolph of Roanoke, Joseph

Glover Baldwin, and the Quest for Social Order." *Virginia Magazine of History and Biography* 111 (Fall 2003): 263–98.

Tucker, John Randolph. "The Judges Tucker of the Court of Appeals of Virginia." *Virginia Law Register* 1, no. 11 (March 1896): 789–812.

Tucker, Nathaniel Beverley. "Garland's Life of Randolph." *Southern Quarterly Review* 4 (July 1851): 41–46.

Tyler, Lyon Gardiner. "Education in Colonial Virginia, Part II: Poor Children & Orphans." *William & Mary Quarterly* 6 (July 1897): 1–6.

———. "Education in Colonial Virginia, Part III: Free Schools." *William & Mary Quarterly* 6 (October 1897): 70–85.

Visootsak, Jeannie, and John M. Graham, Jr. "Klinefelter Syndrome and Other Sex Chromosomal Aneuploidies." *Orphanet Journal of Rare Diseases* 1 (October 24, 2006): 42.

Wattendorf, Daniel J., and Maximilian Muenke. "Klinefelter Syndrome." *American Family Physician* 72, no. 11 (December 1, 2005): 2259–62.

BOOKS

Abernethy, Thomas Perkins. *The Burr Conspiracy.* New York: Oxford University Press, 1954.

Adams, Charles Francis, ed. *Memoirs of John Quincy Adams.* Vol. 1. Philadelphia: J. B. Lippincott & Co., 1874.

Adams, Henry. *John Randolph.* Boston: Houghton, Mifflin & Co., 1882.

———. *History of the United States of America (During the Administrations of Jefferson and Madison).* 9 vols. New York: Charles Scribner's Sons, 1889–90.

———, ed. *Writings of Albert Gallatin.* 3 vols. Philadelphia: J. B. Lippincott, 1879.

Adams, Herbert B. *Life & Writings of Jared Sparks.* Boston: Houghton Mifflin and Co., 1893.

Adams, William H. *Gouverneur Morris: An Independent Life.* New Haven, Conn.: Yale University Press, 2003.

Ailsworth, Timothy S., Ann P. Keller, et al., eds. *Charlotte County: Rich Indeed.* Charlotte, Va.: Charlotte County Board, 1979.

Aitken, Thomas. *Albert Gallatin: Early America's Swiss-born Statesman.* New York: Vantage Press, 1985.

Allison, Robert J. *Stephen Decatur: American Naval Hero, 1779–1820.* Amherst: University of Massachusetts Press, 2005.

Ambler, Charles Henry. *Thomas Ritchie: A Study in Virginia Politics.* Richmond, Va.: Bell Books, 1913.

Ames, Seth, ed. *Works of Fisher Ames.* Vol. 1, *Correspondence.* Boston: Little, Brown and Co., 1854.

Ammon, Harry. *James Monroe: The Quest for National Identity.* New York: McGraw-Hill Book Co., 1971.

Anderson, Dice Robins. *William Branch Giles: A Study in the Politics of Virginia and the Nation from 1790 to 1830.* Menasha, Wis.: George Banta Publishing Co., 1914.

Baldwin, Joseph G. *Party Leaders.* New York: D. Appleton & Co., 1855.

Bauer, Elizabeth Kelley. *Commentaries on the Constitution, 1790–1860.* New York: Columbia University Press, 1952.

Benton, Thomas Hart. *Thirty Years' View.* 2 vols. New York: D. Appleton & Co., 1854.

Berger, Raoul. *Impeachment: The Constitutional Problems.* Cambridge, Mass.: Harvard University Press, 1973.

Beveridge, Albert J. *The Life of John Marshall.* 4 vols. Boston: Houghton Mifflin Co., 1916.

Bouldin, Powhatan. *Home Reminiscences of John Randolph of Roanoke.* Richmond, Va.: Clemmitt & Jones, 1878.

Bowers, Claude G. *Jefferson in Power.* Boston: Houghton, Mifflin & Co., 1936.

Boyd, Julian P., et al., eds. *The Papers of Thomas Jefferson.* 35 vols. (to date). Princeton: Princeton University Press, 1950–.

Bradshaw, Herbert Clarence. *History of Prince Edward County, Virginia.* Richmond, Va.: Dietz Press, 1955.

Brant, Irving. *James Madison: Father of the Constitution, 1787–1800.* New York: Bobbs-Merrill Co., Inc., 1950.

———. *James Madison: Secretary of State, 1800–1809.* New York: Bobbs-Merrill Co., Inc., 1953.

———. *James Madison: The President, 1809–1812.* New York: Bobbs-Merrill Co., Inc., 1956.

———. *James Madison: Commander-in-Chief.* New York: Bobbs-Merrill Co., Inc., 1961.

Brown, Everett Sommerville. *The Constitutional History of the Louisiana Purchase, 1803–1812.* Berkeley: University of California Press, 1920.

———, ed. *William Plumer's Memorandum of Proceedings in the United States Senate, 1803–1807.* New York: Macmillan Co., 1923.

Bruce, Dickson D., Jr. *The Rhetoric of Conservatism: The Virginia Convention of 1829–30 and the Conservative Tradition in the South.* San Marino, Calif.: Huntington Library Press, 1982.

Bruce, Philip A. *John Randolph.* Atlanta: Library of Southern Literature, vol. 10, 1907.

Bruce, William Cabell. *John Randolph of Roanoke.* 2 vols. New York: G. P. Putnam's Sons, 1922.

Buel, Richard, Jr. *America on the Brink: How the Political Struggle over the War of 1812 Almost Destroyed the Young Republic.* New York: Palgrave Macmillan, 2005.

Burns, James MacGregor. *Packing the Court: The Rise of Judicial Power and the Coming Crisis of the Supreme Court.* New York: Penguin Press, 2009.

Burstein, Andrew. *America's Jubilee: How in 1826 a Generation Remembered Fifty Years of Independence.* New York: Alfred A. Knopf, 2001.

Burstein, Andrew, and Nancy Isenberg. *Madison and Jefferson.* New York: Random House, 2010.

Callender, James. *The Prospect Before Us.* Richmond, Va.: Jones, Pleasants & Lyon, 1800.

Cappon, Lester J., ed., *The Adams-Jefferson Letters: The Complete Correspondence between Thomas Jefferson and John and Abigail Adams.* Chapel Hill: University of North Carolina Press, 1959.

Carpenter, T., ed., *The Trial of Col. Aaron Burr.* Washington: Westcott & Co., 1807.

Carter, Edward C., II, ed. *The Virginia Journals of Benjamin Henry Latrobe, 1795–1798.* Vol. 1. New Haven, Conn.: Yale University Press, 1977)

Cassell, Frank. *Merchant Congressman in the Young Republic: Samuel Smith of Maryland, 1752–1839.* Madison: University of Wisconsin Press, 1971.

Chernow, Ron. *Alexander Hamilton.* New York: Penguin Press, 2004.

Chitwood, Oliver P. *John Tyler: Champion of the Old South.* New York: D. Appleton–Century Co., 1939.

Clarkson, Paul S., and R. Samuel Jett. *Luther Martin of Maryland.* Baltimore: Johns Hopkins University Press, 1970.

Clarkson, Thomas. *An Essay on the Slavery and Commerce of the Human Species.* London: T. Cadell and J. Phillips, 1786.

Cleaves, Freeman. *Old Tippecanoe: William Henry Harrison and His Times.* New York: Charles Scribner's Sons, 1939.

Coit, Margaret. *John C. Calhoun: American Portrait.* Boston: Houghton Mifflin Co., 1950.

Combs, Jerald A. *The Jay Treaty: Political Battleground of the Founding Fathers.* Berkeley: University of California Press, 1970.

Conway, Moncure Daniel. *Omitted Chapters of History Disclosed in the Life and Papers of Edmund Randolph.* New York: G. P. Putnam's Sons, 1888.

Crawford, Alan Pell. *Unwise Passions.* New York: Simon & Schuster, 2000.

Cullen, Charles T., and Herbert A. Johnson, eds. *The Papers of John Marshall.* Vol. 2, *Correspondence and Papers.* Chapel Hill: University of North Carolina Press, 1977.

Cunningham, Noble E. *The Jeffersonian Republicans in Power: Party Operations, 1801–1809.* Chapel Hill: University of North Carolina Press, 1963.

Curtis, George M., and James J. Thompson Jr., eds. *The Southern Essays of Richard M. Weaver.* Indianapolis: Liberty Fund, 1987.

Curtis, George T. *Life of Daniel Webster.* New York: D. Appleton and Co., 1870.

Cutler, William Parker, and Julia Perkins Cutler. *Life, Journals and Correspondence of Rev. Manasseh Cutler.* 2 vols. Cincinnati: Robert Clarke & Co., 1888.

Dabney, Richard Heath. *John Randolph: A Character Sketch.* Dansville, N.Y.: Instructor Publishing Co., 1898.

Daniels, Jonathan. *The Randolphs of Virginia.* Garden City, N.Y.: Doubleday, 1972.

Dargo, George. *Jefferson's Louisiana: Politics and the Clash of Legal Traditions.* Cambridge, Mass.: Harvard University Press, 1975.

Dawidoff, Robert. *The Education of John Randolph.* New York: W. W. Norton & Co., 1979.

DeConde, Alexander. *This Affair of Louisiana.* New York: Charles Scribner's Sons, 1976.

de Kay, James Tertius. *A Rage for Glory: The Life of Commodore Stephen Decatur.* New York: Free Press, 2004.

Dodd, William E. *The Life of Nathaniel Macon.* Raleigh, N.C.: Edwards & Broughton, 1908.

Dudley, Theodore, ed. *Letters of John Randolph to a Young Relative: Embracing a Series of Years from Early Youth to Mature Manhood.* Philadelphia: Carey, Lee & Blanchard, 1834.

du Bellet, Louise Pecquet. *Some Prominent Virginia Families.* Lynchburg, Virginia: J. P. Bell Co., 1907.

Eckenrode, H. J. *The Randolphs: The Story of a Virginia Family.* New York: Bobbs-Merrill Co., 1946.

Egerton, Douglas R. *Gabriel's Rebellion: The Virginia Slave Conspiracies of 1800 and 1802.* Chapel Hill: University of North Carolina Press, 1993.

Elkins, Stanley, and Eric McKitrick. *The Age of Federalism.* New York: Oxford University Press, 1993.

Ellis, Joseph J. *Passionate Sage: The Character and Legacy of John Adams.* New York: W. W. Norton & Co., 1993.

———. *American Sphinx: The Character of Thomas Jefferson.* New York: Alfred A. Knopf, 1998.

———. *Founding Brothers: The Revolutionary Generation.* New York: Alfred A. Knopf, 2000.

Ellis, Richard E. *The Jeffersonian Crisis: Courts and Politics in the Young Republic.* New York: Oxford University Press, 1971.

Elsmere, Jane Shaffer. *Justice Samuel Chase.* Muncie: Janevar Publishing Co., 1980.

Foner, Phillip S., ed. *Basic Writings of Thomas Jefferson.* Garden City, N.Y.: Halcyon House, 1950.

Forbes, Robert Pierce. *The Missouri Compromise and Its Aftermath.* Chapel Hill: University of North Carolina Press, 2007.

Ford, Lacy K. *Deliver Us from Evil: The Slavery Question in the Old South.* New York: Oxford University Press, 2009.

Ford, Paul L., ed. *The Writings of Thomas Jefferson.* New York: G. P. Putnam's Sons.

Ford, Worthington C., ed. *Writings of John Quincy Adams.* Vol. 3, *1801–1810.* New York: Macmillan Co., 1914.

Frohnen, Bruce, ed. *The Anti-Federalists: Selected Writings & Speeches.* Washington, D.C.: Regnery Publishing, Inc., 1999.

Fuess, Claude Moore. *Daniel Webster.* Boston: Little, Brown and Co., 1930.

Gaines, William H., Jr. *Thomas Mann Randolph: Jefferson's Son-in-Law.* Baton Rouge: Louisiana State University Press, 1966.

Garland, Hugh A. *The Life of John Randolph of Roanoke.* 2 vols. New York: D. Appleton & Co., 1850.

Glenn, Thomas Allen. *Some Colonial Mansions and Those Who Lived in Them.* Philadelphia: Henry T. Coates & Co., 1899.

Grisby, Hugh B. *The Virginia Convention of 1829–30.* Richmond, Va.: MacFarlane & Fergusson, 1854.

Hall, Kermit L., and James W. Ely Jr., eds. *An Uncertain Tradition: Constitutionalism and the History of the South.* Athens: University of Georgia Press, 1989.

Hamilton, Phillip. *The Making and Unmaking of a Revolutionary Family: The Tuckers of Virginia, 1752–1830.* Charlottesville: University of Virginia Press, 2003.

Harding, Chester. *My Egotistigraphy.* Cambridge, Mass.: Press of John Wilson and Son, 1866.

Haskins, Charles H. *The Yazoo Land Companies.* New York: The Knickerbocker Press, 1891.

Heidler, David S., and Jeanne T. Heidler. *Henry Clay: The Essential American.* New York: Random House, 2010.

Heller, J. Roderick, III. *Democracy's Lawyer: Felix Grundy of the Old Southwest.* Baton Rouge: Louisiana State University Press, 2010.

Henry, William Wirt. *Patrick Henry: Life, Correspondence, and Speeches.* Harrisonburg, Va.: Sprinkle Publications, 1993.

Hickey, Donald R. *The War of 1812: A Forgotten Conflict.* Chicago: University of Illinois Press, 1989.

Hoffer, Peter Charles. *The Treason Trials of Aaron Burr.* Lawrence: University Press of Kansas, 2008.

Hoffer, Peter Charles, and N. E. H. Hull. *Impeachment in America, 1635–1805.* New Haven, Conn.: Yale University Press, 1984.

Hopkins, James C., ed. *The Papers of Henry Clay.* Lexington: University of Kentucky Press, 1959–.

Howe, Henry. *Historical Collections of Virginia.* Charleston, S.C.: Babcock & Co., 1845.

Huebner, Timothy S. *The Southern Judicial Tradition: State Judges and Sectional Distinctiveness, 1790–1890.* Athens: University of Georgia Press, 1999.

Irving, Pierre. *Life and Letters of Washington Irving.* New York: G. P. Putnam, 1864.

Isenberg, Nancy. *Fallen Founder: The Life of Aaron Burr.* New York: Viking, 2007.

Johnson, Gerald W. *Randolph of Roanoke: A Political Fantastic.* New York: Minton, Balch & Co., 1929.

Jordan, Daniel P. *Political Leadership in Jefferson's Virginia.* Charlottesville: University Press of Virginia, 1983.

Kastor, Peter J. *The Nation's Crucible: The Louisiana Purchase and the Creation of America.* New Haven, Conn.: Yale University Press, 2004.

Ketcham, Ralph. *James Madison: A Biography.* Charlottesville: University Press of Virginia, 1990.

Kierner, Cynthia A. *Scandal at Bizarre: Rumor and Reputation in Jefferson's America.* New York: Palgrave Macmillan, 2004.

King, Charles R., ed. *The Life and Correspondence of Rufus King.* New York: G. P. Putnam's Sons, 1897.

Kirchner, Walther. *Studies in Russian-American Commerce, 1820–1860.* Leiden, Netherlands: E. J. Brill, 1975.

Kirk, Russell. *The Conservative Mind.* Chicago: Regnery Books, 1953.

———. *John Randolph of Roanoke: A Study in American Politics with Selected Speeches and Letters,* 4th ed. Indianapolis: Liberty Fund, 1997.

Kirschke, James J. *Gouverneur Morris: Author, Statesman, and Man of the World.* New York: Thomas Dunne Books, 2005.

Knight, Lucian Lamar. *A Standard History of Georgia and Georgians.* Chicago: Lewis Publishing Co., 1917.

Kukla, Jon. *A Wilderness So Immense: The Louisiana Purchase and the Destiny of America.* New York: Alfred A. Knopf, 2003.

Langguth, A. J. *Union 1812.* New York: Simon & Schuster, 2006.

Lewis, Charles Lee. *The Romantic Decatur.* Philadelphia: University of Pennsylvania Press, 1937.

Lounsbury, Thomas R., ed. *Yale Book of American Verse.* New Haven, Conn.: Yale University Press, 1912.

MacKenzie, Alexander Slidell. *Life of Stephen Decatur.* Boston: Charles C. Little and James Brown, 1846.

Magrath, C. Peter. *Yazoo: Law and Politics in the Young Republic.* Providence, R.I.: Brown University Press, 1966.

Malone, Dumas. *Jefferson and His Time.* Vol. 1, *Jefferson the Virginian.* Boston: Little, Brown and Co., 1948.

———. *Jefferson and His Time.* Vol. 2, *Jefferson and the Rights of Man.* Boston: Little, Brown and Co., 1951.

———. *Jefferson and His Time.* Vol. 3, *Jefferson and the Ordeal of Liberty.* Boston: Little, Brown and Co., 1962.

———. *Jefferson and His Time*. Vol. 4, *Jefferson the President: First Term, 1801–1805*. Boston: Little, Brown and Co., 1970.

———. *Jefferson and His Time*. Vol. 5, *Jefferson the President: Second Term, 1805–1809*. Boston: Little, Brown and Co., 1974.

———. *Jefferson and His Time*. Vol. 6, *The Sage of Monticello*. Boston: Little, Brown and Co., 1981.

Mason, Matthew. *Slavery and Politics in the Early American Republic*. Chapel Hill: University of North Carolina Press, 2006.

Maxwell, William. *A Memoir of the Rev. John H. Rice*. Philadelphia: J. Whetham, 1835.

Mayo, Bernard. *Henry Clay: Spokesman of the West*. Boston: Houghton Mifflin Co., 1937.

McCaughey, Robert A. *Josiah Quincy, 1772–1864: The Last Federalist*. Cambridge, Mass.: Harvard University Press, 1974.

McDonald, Forrest. *The Presidency of Thomas Jefferson*. Lawrence: University Press of Kansas, 1976.

Meade, Robert Douthat. *Patrick Henry: Practical Revolutionary*. New York: J. B. Lippincott Co., 1969.

Meade, William. *Churches, Ministers and Families of Virginia*. Vol. 1. Philadelphia: J. B. Lippincott Co., 1900.

Melton, Buckner F., Jr. *Aaron Burr: Conspiracy to Treason*. New York: John Wiley & Sons, Inc., 2002.

Miller, F. Thornton. *Juries and Judges Versus the Law: Virginia's Provincial Legal Perspective, 1783–1828*. Charlottesville: University Press of Virginia, 1994.

Moore, John Basset, ed. *The Works of James Buchanan*. Vol. 2, *1830–1836*. Philadelphia: J. B. Lippincott Co., 1908.

Moore, Frank. *American Eloquence: A Collection of Speeches and Addresses*. Vol. 2. New York: D. Appleton and Co., 1857.

Moore, Glover. *The Missouri Controversy, 1819–1821*. Lexington: University of Kentucky Press, 1953.

Morrison, A. J. *The Beginnings of Public Education in Virginia, 1776–1860*. Richmond, Va.: Public Printing, 1917.

Morse, John T., Jr. *John Quincy Adams*. Boston: Houghton Mifflin and Co., 1882.

Munford, George Wythe. *The Two Parsons; Cupid's Sports; The Dream; the Jewels of Virginia*. Richmond, Va.: J. D. K. Sleight, 1884.

Newmyer, R. Kent. *John Marshall and the Heroic Age of the Supreme Court*. Baton Rouge: Louisiana State University Press, 2001.

Niven, John. *Martin Van Buren: The Romantic Age of American Politics*. New York: Oxford University Press, 1983.

Oeste, George Irvin. *John Randolph Clay: America's First Career Diplomat*. Philadelphia: University of Pennsylvania Press, 1966.

Panichas, George, ed. *The Essential Russell Kirk: Selected Essays.* Wilmington, Del.: ISI Books, 2007.

Parks, Joseph H. *Felix Grundy, Champion of Democracy.* Baton Rouge: Louisiana State University Press, 1940.

Parton, James. *Famous Americans of Recent Time.* Boston: Ticknor and Fields, 1867.

Perkins, Bradford. *Prologue to War: England and the United States, 1805–1812.* Berkeley: University of California Press, 1963.

Peterson, Merrill D. *The Great Triumvirate: Webster, Clay, and Calhoun.* New York: Oxford University Press, 1987.

Plumer, William, Jr. *Life of William Plumer.* Boston: Phillips, Sampson and Co., 1857.

Poore, Benjamin Perley. *Reminiscences of Sixty Years in the National Metropolis.* Philadelphia: Hubbard Brothers, 1886.

Quincy, Edmund. *Life of Josiah Quincy.* Boston: Ticknor and Fields, 1868.

Quincy, Josiah. *Figures of the Past.* Boston: Roberts Brothers, 1888.

Rehnquist, William H. *Grand Inquests: The Historic Impeachments of Justice Samuel Chase and President Andrew Johnson.* New York: William Morrow & Co., 1992.

Remini, Robert V. *Andrew Jackson and the Course of American Empire, 1767–1821.* New York: Harper & Row, 1977.

———. *Andrew Jackson and the Course of American Freedom, 1822–1832.* New York: Harper & Row, 1981.

———. *Andrew Jackson and the Course of American Democracy, 1833–1845.* New York: Harper & Row, 1984.

———. *Henry Clay: Statesman for the Union.* New York: W. W. Norton & Co., 1991.

———. *Daniel Webster: The Man and His Time.* New York: W. W. Norton & Co., 1997.

Risjord, Norman K. *The Old Republicans: Southern Conservatives in the Age of Jefferson.* New York: Columbia University Press, 1965.

Rush, Richard. *John Randolph at Home and Abroad.* Philadelphia: P. Force, 1828.

Rutland, Robert A., ed. *The Papers of James Madison, Presidential Series.* Charlottesville: University Press of Virginia, 1984.

Sargent, Nathan. *Public Men and Events from the Commencement of Mr. Monroe's Administration to the Close of Mr. Fillmore's Administration.* Vol. 1. Philadelphia: J. B. Lippincott & Co., 1875.

Sawyer, Lemuel. *A Biography of John Randolph.* New York: William Robinson, 1844.

Scott, Winfield. *Memoirs of Lieut. Gen. Scott, LLD, Written by Himself.* 2 vols. New York: Sheldon, 1864.

Sears, Louis M. *Jefferson and the Embargo.* Durham: Duke University Press, 1927.

Sharp, James Roger. *American Politics in the Early Republic: The New Nation in Crisis.* New Haven, Conn.: Yale University Press, 1993.

Shorey, Kenneth, ed. *Collected Letters of John Randolph of Roanoke to John Brocken-brough, 1812–1833.* New Brunswick, N.J.: Transaction Books, 1988.

Silbey, Joel H. *Martin Van Buren and the Emergence of American Popular Politics.* Lanham, Mo.: Rowman & Littlefield Publishers, Inc., 2002.

Sloan, Cliff, and David McKean. *The Great Decision: Jefferson, Adams, Marshall, and the Battle for the Supreme Court.* New York: PublicAffairs, 2009.

Smith, Jean Edward. *John Marshall: Definer of a Nation.* New York: Henry Holt and Co., 1996.

Smith, Margaret Bayard and Gaillard Hunt. *The First Forty Years of Washington Society.* New York: Charles Scribner's Sons, 1906.

Smith, Page. *John Adams.* 2 vols. New York: Doubleday & Co., 1962.

Smith, Samuel H., and Thomas Lloyd. *Trial of Samuel Chase.* Washington, D.C., 1805.

Sparks, W. H. *The Memoirs of Fifty Years.* Philadelphia: Claxton, Remsen & Haffelfin-ger, 1872.

Spivak, Burton. *Jefferson's English Crisis: Commerce, Embargo, and the Republican Revolution.* Charlottesville: University Press of Virginia, 1979.

Stokes, William E., Jr., and Francis L. Berkeley, Jr. *The Papers of John Randolph of Roanoke.* Charlottesville: University of Virginia Press, 1950.

Stone, Geoffrey R. *Perilous Times: Free Speech in Wartime.* New York: W. W. Norton & Co., 2004.

Tate, Adam L. *Conservatism and Southern Intellectuals, 1789–1861.* Columbia: University of Missouri Press, 2005.

Thomas, F. W. *John Randolph of Roanoke and Other Sketches of Characters.* Philadelphia: A. Hart, 1853.

Trent, William P. *Southern Statesmen of the Old Regime.* New York: Thomas Y. Crowell & Co., 1897.

Twohig, Dorothy, ed. *The Papers of George Washington, Retirement Series 3, September 1798–April 1799.* Charlottesville: University Press of Virginia, 1999.

Tyler, Lyon G., ed. *Encyclopedia of Virginia Biography.* New York: Lewis Historical Publishing Co., 1915.

Van Buren, Martin. *The Autobiography of Martin Van Buren.* In *Annual Report of the American Historical Association for the Year 1918.* Washington, D.C.: Government Printing Office, 1920.

Vipperman, Carl J. *William Lowndes and the Transition of Southern Politics.* Chapel Hill: University of North Carolina Press, 1989.

Walters, Raymond, Jr. *Albert Gallatin: Jeffersonian Financier & Diplomat.* New York: Macmillan Co., 1957.

Watkins, William J., Jr. *Reclaiming the American Revolution: The Kentucky and Virginia Resolutions and their Legacy.* New York: Palgrave Macmillan, 2004.

Wharton, Anne Hollingsworth. *Social Life in the Early Republic.* Philadelphia: J. B. Lippincott Co., 1903.

Wheelan, Joseph. *Jefferson's Vendetta: The Pursuit of Aaron Burr and the Judiciary.* New York: Carroll & Graf Publishers, 2005.

———. *Mr. Adams's Last Crusade.* New York: PublicAffairs, 2008.

Whittier, John Greenleaf. *The Writings of John Greenleaf Whittier.* Boston: Houghton Mifflin, 1892.

White, George. *Statistics of the State of Georgia.* Savannah: W. Thorne Williams, 1849.

Wilentz, Sean. *The Rise of American Democracy: Jefferson to Lincoln.* New York: W. W. Norton & Co., 2005.

Wilson, Clyde N. *From Union to Empire: Essays in the Jeffersonian Tradition.* Columbia, S.C.: Foundation for American Education, 2003.

Wilson, Clyde N., et al., eds. *The Papers of John C. Calhoun.* Columbia: University of South Carolina, 1959–.

Wilson, James Grant, and John Fiske, eds. *Appleton's Cyclopedia of American Biography.* Vol. 5. New York: D. Appleton and Co., 1900.

Wiltse, Charles M. *John C. Calhoun, Nationalist, 1782–1828.* New York: Bobbs-Merrill Co., 1944.

———. *John C. Calhoun, Nullifier, 1829–1839.* New York: Bobbs-Merrill Co., 1949.

———, ed. *The Papers of Daniel Webster.* 7 vols. Hanover, N.H.: University Press of New England, 1974–86.

Wirt, William. *Sketches of the Life and Character of Patrick Henry.* New York: Derby & Jackson, 1857.

Works of Stuart. Masters in Art, a Series of Illustrated Monographs. Boston: Bates & Guild Co., 1906.

DISSERTATIONS

Ammon, Harry. "The Republican Party in Virginia, 1789–1824." University of Virginia, 1948.

Bagby, Ross F. "The Randolph Slave Saga: Communities in Collision." Ohio State University, 1988.

Davy, Mason G. "The Political Oratory of John Randolph of Roanoke." Northwestern University, 1951.

Gelbach, Clyde C. "Spencer Roane of Virginia, 1762–1822: A Judicial Advocate of States' Rights." University of Pittsburgh, 1955.

Hines, Jack Wendell. "John Randolph and the Growth of Federal Power." University of Kansas, 1957.

Horsnell, Margaret E. "Spencer Roane: Judicial Advocate of Jeffersonian Principles." University of Minnesota, 1967.

Jordan, Daniel P. "John Randolph: Virginia Congressman, 1801–1825." University of Virginia, 1970.

Pawlett, Nathaniel Macon. "John Randolph of Roanoke: Virginia Senator, 1825–1827." University of Virginia, 1973.

Stokes, William E., Jr. "The Early Life of John Randolph of Roanoke, 1773–1794." University of Virginia, 1950.

———. "Randolph of Roanoke, A Virginia Portrait: The Early Career of John Randolph of Roanoke, 1773–1805." University of Virginia, 1955.

Wendelken, Daniel H. "The Rhetoric of John Randolph of Roanoke: A New Evaluation." Ohio University, 1984.

NEWSPAPERS

National Intelligencer.
New York Times.
Richmond *Daily Dispatch.*
Richmond *Daily Whig.*
Richmond *Enquirer.*
Virginia Gazette and General Advertiser.
Washington Post.

Index

Adams, Abigail, 46

Adams, Henry, 54, 64, 111, 131, 201, 249n22; describes JRR, 1, 2, 5, 10, 56, 103, 104, 106, 138; scorns JRR, 10, 314n94

Adams, John, 1, 38, 48, 50, 59, 76, 90, 213; JRR's disapproval of, 24, 207; and Playhouse incident, 45–46

Adams, John Quincy, 1, 81, 168, 187, 206, 207, 210; and Chase impeachment, 82, 83, 90, 91, 94, 96; and election of 1824, 201, 203

Alexandra, Empress of Russia, 223

Alien Act, 38, 39

Alston, Willis, 79, 112, 125; caned by JRR, 138–39; opposes JRR, 188

American Revolution, 5, 9, 12, 15–16, 151

American System, 192, 193

Ames, Fisher, 23, 82

Annals of Congress, 48, 57, 79, 132, 147, 152, 185

Annapolis Convention, 13

Antifederalists, 21

Appomattox River, 15, 20, 156

Arnold, Benedict, 15

Baker, Jerman, 11, 249n26

Bank of the United States, Second, 172–74, 183

Barbour, James, 122, 204

Bayard, James, 43, 47, 51, 53, 58, 60, 62

Beecher, Philemon, 130

Bentham, Jeremy, 2–3

Benton, Thomas Hart, 191; and friendship with JRR, 99, 104; and JRR-Clay duel, 211–12

Bidwell, Barnabas, 100, 104, 116; opposes JRR, 99, 104; serves on Florida committee, 101, 103

Bizarre (JRR's estate), 8, 9, 15, 29, 30, 31, 34, 36, 51, 64, 114, 161, 176, 251n60

Bland, Theodorick (JRR's grandfather), 9

Bland, Theodorick (JRR's uncle), 20, 36

Bleecker, Harmanus, 163, 167, 241

Bouldin, Thomas T., 229

Braddock, William, General, 15

Brant, Irving, 230

Brockenbrough, John, 155, 157, 158, 214, 215, 241

Bruce, William C., 38

Bryan, Elizabeth Coalter, 177, 180

Bryan, John Randolph, 176, 180, 230

Bryan, Joseph, 25, 26, 27, 84, 97, 116–17, 241

Bryan, Thomas, 176, 180

Buckingham County, Va., 140, 154, 169, 225

Burke, Edmund, 156–57, 158, 208

Burr, Aaron, 50, 81, 120–21; and Chase impeachment, 88, 91, 96; trial of, 122–24

Cabell, Joseph, 122

Calhoun, John C., 1, 140, 144, 149, 153, 173, 224, 226; debates JRR, 145–46, 148, 170, 230; influence of JRR on, 172, 200–201, 209; JRR's opinion of, 141, 147, 205, 224–25

Callender, James Thomson, 76

Cawsons (birthplace of JRR), 9, 97, 156

Charlotte County, Va., 40, 140, 150, 154, 169

Charlotte (Va.) Courthouse, 40, 114, 158, 197, 225

Chase, Samuel, 2, 76–77, 81, 82; impeachment trial of, 88–96, 97, 269n41, 272n54

Chesapeake, USS, 124–25

Chestnut Street Theatre, 44

Cheves, Langdon, 140

Clark, Christopher, 82, 91, 99

Clarkson, Thomas, 69, 70

Clay, Henry, 1, 140, 141–42, 148, 168, 174, 201, 203, 207, 209, 226; and "American System," 192–93, 195–98, 200; duel with JRR, 210–12; JRR's opinion of, 170, 196, 225, 229; and Missouri question, 184–86; removes JRR's dogs, 141; silences JRR, 149; and War Hawks, 141

Clay, John Randolph, 176–77, 178, 180, 223, 242

Coalter, Elizabeth Tucker, 176, 180

Cochrane, Humanities Professor, 21

Columbia College, 20, 21, 22, 24, 28

Commonwealth v. Richard Randolph, 32–33, 256n52

Constitution of the United States, 20, 24, 73, 75, 263n49; ratification of, 20, 21

Crawford, William, 188, 204, 206; runs for president, 201–2, 203; serves as JRR's second in duel, 139

Cumberland County, Va., 31, 154, 169

Cutler, Manasseh, 55, 79, 86, 90, 94, 108

Dawidoff, Robert, 167

Decatur, Stephen, 163, 187, 301n50

Decius letters, 115

Devanny, John, 231

Duane, William, 106

Dudley, Theodore, 105, 176, 177, 178, 179, 182, 242

election of 1800, 48–50, 51

election of 1808, 127–28

election of 1824, 201–3

Embargo Act (1807), 125–26, 134

Eppes, John Wayles, 66, 125; defeated by JRR, 140; defeats JRR, 150–51, 154; near duel with JRR, 139

Erskine, David, 125, 137

Federalists (political party), 34, 39, 43, 46, 47, 53, 54, 57, 59, 63, 84

Fletcher v. Peck, 86

Florida, 2, 100–104, 112, 113, 115

Ford, Lacy, 69, 70, 72

France, 35, 38; U.S. relations with, 100, 134–35, 138, 141

French Revolution, 33, 34

Fries, John, 76, 89

Gabriel's Revolt, 70

Gallatin, Albert, 1, 34, 58, 64, 78, 81, 98, 100, 102, 103, 126, 168; opinion of JRR, 132

Garland, Hugh, 38, 156

Garnett, James M., 113, 115, 118, 122, 135, 155, 156, 196, 242

Georgia, 34, 78, 79, 80

Giles, William Branch, 121, 137, 167, 204–5; and Chase impeachment, 83, 91; as majority leader of House, 54, 55, 261n9; replaced a majority leader by JRR, 63; serves on Burr grand jury, 122

Gilmer, Francis, 129

Glenlyvar, 30, 31, 32, 162, 167

Granger, Gideon, 84, 85

Great Britain: trade policy with, 107–10, 125–26, 134–35, 138; U.S. relations with, 99, 100, 137, 142–49

Great Seal of Virginia, 6

Greek independence, 193–95

Gregg, Andrew, 107

Gregg's Resolution, 107, 108, 110, 126, 190

Grigsby, Hugh, 218, 220
Griswold, Roger, 58, 60, 63, 65
Grundy, Felix, 140, 142, 144, 286n74
Guilford Court House, 12, 16
Gum Guiacum, 31

Hamilton, Alexander, 21, 51, 76, 78, 80, 81, 127, 269n38
Hargrave, Hester, 27, 38
Harper, Robert Goodloe, 88
Harrison, Mary, 30, 32
Harrison, Randolph, 30, 32, 163, 164
Harrison, William Henry, 68, 160
Hay, George, 103, 122
Henry, Patrick, 1, 17, 20, 24; debates JRR, 39–41, 259n107; defends Richard Randolph, 31–32; influence on JRR, 158, 197
Hogarth, William, 11, 249n29
Hooper, Edward, 129
Hopkinson, Joseph, 88, 92, 95
Huger, Benjamin, 57

Indiana Territory, 68
Irving, Washington, 122, 190
Islamic religion, 35–36, 194–95, 257n74

Jackson, Andrew, 1, 169, 206, 224; and Aaron Burr, 120, 122; appoints JRR Minister to Russia, 221–22; and election of 1824, 202–3
Jackson, James, 78
James River, 8, 9, 10, 15
Jay, John, 35
Jay's Treaty, 35
Jefferson Lottery, 209
Jefferson, Thomas, 1, 31, 35, 75, 81, 99, 111, 119, 126, 127, 184, 230; and attempt to purchase Florida, 2, 100–104, 115–16; break with JRR, 2, 86–87, 99, 101, 105–6, 110; and Burr trial, 120–22; and Chase impeachment, 77, 82, 98; election of 1800, 48, 50–53; first administration of, 53–56, 57–62; JRR's opinion of, 98, 188, 213; leader of Republican opposition, 35, 38–39, 45; and Louisiana purchase, 63, 64–66;

opinion of JRR, 2, 44, 47, 86, 100, 111, 115, 201; relationship with JRR, 55–56, 66–67, 86–87, 101, 105
Judiciary Act (1800), 1, 59
Judiciary Act (1801), 59

Kentucky Resolution (1798), 39
Key, Francis Scott, 1, 88, 154, 158, 168, 169, 183, 242
Key, Philip Barton, 88, 92
Kirk, Russell, 6, 7, 157, 184, 208–9, 230–31
Klinefelter Syndrome, 29

Lafayette, Marquis de, 11, 32
Latrobe, Benjamin, 122
Lee, Charles, 88, 92
Lincoln, Levi, 78
Livingston, Edward, 224
Livingston, Robert, 63, 64
Louisiana Purchase, 1, 64–66
Lowndes, William, 140

Macon, Nathaniel, 44, 45, 54, 55, 64, 77. 97. 99, 118, 125, 127, 137, 205, 231, 261n7; and Macon's Bill No. 1, 138; and Macon's Bill No. 2, 138; opinion of JRR, 132
Madison, Dolley, 112
Madison, James, 1, 13, 39, 63, 64, 103, 110, 134, 141, 168; election of 1808, 126–28; JRR's opinion of, 80, 98, 101, 104, 158–59, 188, 274n88; opinion of JRR, 148, 290n39; opposed by JRR, 101–2, 107–8, 111–12, 116; relationship with JRR, 23, 86–87, 96, 101–2, 274n88, 290n39; trade policies of, 136–38, 147–48; at Virginia Constitutional Convention, 217–19; and Yazoo controversy 2, 78, 80, 85
Malone, Dumas, 29, 230
Marbury v. Madison, 61, 75, 199, 267n2
Marshall, John, 1, 61, 162; and Burr trial, 121–23; and Chase impeachment, 81, 90–91; debates JRR, 42–34; defends Richard Randolph, 31–32; friendship with JRR, 1, 155–56, 188, 209, 213; JRR's opinion of, 155; and Marbury v. Madison, 75,

Marshall, John (*continued*)
  267n2; opinion of JRR, 155–56; at Virginia
  Constitutional Convention, 217
Martin, Luther, 92, 95; defends Aaron Burr,
  122; defends Justice Chase, 88, 92–93
Mason, George, 24, 216
Matoax (JRR's estate), 8, 9, 10, 13, 14, 15,
  20, 37
Maury, Walker, 16, 17, 18, 21; grammar
  school of, 16, 17, 18
McCulloch v. Maryland, 61, 263n49
McDonald, Forrest, 104
McKnight, James, 44, 45, 46
Merry, Anthony, 100, 120
Miller, Thornton, 5
Missouri compromise (1820), 184–87
Monroe, James, 1, 51, 63, 64, 65, 70, 82, 106,
  122, 192, 193, 201; election of 1816, 174;
  friendship with JRR, 102, 110, 151–52;
  JRR's opinion of, 128, 188; opinion of
  JRR, 128, 193; supported for president
  by JRR, 98, 110–11, 126–27; at Virginia
  Constitutional Convention, 217–20
Morris, Ann Cary Randolph (Nancy), 36, 62,
  180, 254n11; and Glenlyar events, 30–33;
  and Gouverneur Morris, 161; relationship
  with Richard Randolph, 32; relationship
  with Theodorick Randolph, 30; turned
  out of Bizarre, 98–99; vitriolic letters with
  JRR, 162–64, 165–67
Morris, Gouverneur, 161, 162, 163, 165
Mucius letters, 137, 285nn33–34

National Intelligencer, 170
Nicholas I, Emperor of Russia, 223
Nicholas, John, 42, 69
Nicholas, Wilson Cary, 122
Nicholson, Joseph H., 45, 47, 48, 49, 63, 103,
  110, 114, 115, 116, 127, 231, 242; and
  Chase impeachment, 77, 82, 91, 93–94,
  96; friendship with JRR, 44, 49, 55, 96–97,
  103, 110, 143; and Republican principles,
  50–51, 52, 64, 98, 138
Non-Intercourse Act, 134–35
nullification crisis, 224–25

Ogden, David, 162, 163

Page, Carter, 30, 32
Panama Congress, 209–10
Parrish, Joseph, 29, 226, 227, 228
Perry, Oliver, 160
Philadelphia *Aurora*, 106
Pickering, Timothy, 104
Pinckney, Charles Cotesworth, 128
Pitt, William, Earl of Chatham, 156, 177
Pitt, William, the younger, 55
Playhouse Incident, 44–48
Pleasants, Hugh, 217
Pleasants, James, 122
Plumer, William, 56, 63, 66, 79, 80, 85, 90, 91,
  92, 96, 101, 109, 243
Pocahontas, 8
Prince Edward County, Va., 128, 140, 150,
  151, 153, 154, 169, 182
Princeton University, 18, 19, 20

Quids. See *Tertium Quids*
Quincy, Josiah, 69, 100, 129, 131, 154, 158,
  159, 243

Randolph, Edmund, 11, 13, 24, 25, 27, 38, 122
Randolph family motto, 8, 9, 248n11
Randolph, Frances Bland (JRR's mother). *See*
  Tucker, Frances Bland Randolph (JRR's
  mother)
Randolph, John ("Possum Jack"), 136, 284n27
Randolph, John, of Roanoke
—characteristics of: alcohol use by, 33,
  94–95, 184, 307n11; bipolar disorder of,
  182–83; character and personality of,
  9, 17, 18, 22, 23, 28, 45, 47–48, 80, 89,
  100, 230, 232; debating skills of, 48, 56,
  57–58, 63–65, 104, 111–12, 171, 220–21;
  described, 2–4, 34, 36, 56–57, 63, 66, 100,
  106–7, 129, 279n25; and dogs, 129, 142,
  183, 286n68; drug use by, 91, 94, 135, 182,
  204, 214, 224, 247n29; "Dying, Sir, Dying"
  expression of, 175; equestrian interests of,
  16, 34, 62, 63, 81, 97, 114, 181, 206, 215;
  flair for dramatic, 12, 21, 38, 45, 56–57;

Gallophilia of, 34–35, 36, 46; health of 4, 9–10, 16, 28–29, 34, 36, 64, 83–84, 89, 91, 94, 97, 103, 135, 152, 153, 155, 174, 182–83, 186, 204, 214, 223, 226–27, 255n26, n28, 282n86, 310n74; as hunter, 10, 12, 34, 114, 135, 174–75, 183, 215; impotence of, 4, 27, 28–29, 38, 131; injuries to, 64, 135, 161, 162, 201; insomnia of, 34, 135; and Klinefelter syndrome, 29; mental and emotional health of, 22, 34, 36, 95–96, 135, 155, 174–75, 182–83, 187–88, 209, 224, 299n6; as naturalist, 10, 16, 18, 174–75, 181, 188, 191, 215; paternalistic ideal of, 70–72; popularity of, 64, 86, 97, 114, 169, 200–201, 221, 230; religious faith of, 11, 27, 70–71, 158, 168, 295n20; religious skepticism of, 35–36, 257n74; romances of, 26, 27, 29, 37–38; self-confidence of, 47–48, 52, 106; sense of duty, 12, 124, 143, 150; sense of justice, 34, 47, 115; sexuality of, 29; speaking ability of, 4, 19, 42, 57–58, 60, 64–65, 79, 84–86, 89, 94–95, 104, 107–9, 129–33, 144, 151, 171, 185, 218–19, 220, 282n101, 304n43; as sportsman, 10, 16, 34; styles himself "of Roanoke," 136, 284n27; temperament of, 9, 17, 38, 45–46, 66, 98, 100, 104
—defeat and return to the House: and election of 1816, 174; and internal improvements, 171; military service in War of 1812, 160; at Morrisania, 161–62; opposes Bank of the United States, 172–74
—early life: alleged marriage of, 26–27, 38, 255n13; and American Revolution, 12, 15; attends Washington's inauguration, 23; attends William & Mary, 31, 33, 256n42; in Bermuda, 17–18; birth and ancestry of, 8–9, 239; at Bizarre 9, 15, 29, 30, 34, 36, 51, 62, 64, 96, 153–54; and Cawsons (birthplace), 9, 156; in Charleston, S. C., 34–35; childhood and youth of, 9–18; at Columbia College, 20–23, 24, 28; and death of father, 9; and death of mother, 19–20, 21; and death of Richard Randolph, 36, 167–68; and death of Theodorick

Randolph, 28; descendant of Pocahontas, 8, 57; disciplined as youth, 13, 14, 17; dislike of formal schooling, 16–17, 19, 22, 24, 28; duel with Robert Taylor, 33; engaged to Maria Ward, 37–38, 255n13; "fit of passion," 9; flight from Benedict Arnold, 15; friendship with Joseph Bryan, 25, 26–27, 116–17; and Glenlyvar events, 30–33, 163–64; influence of culture on, 12; influence of land on, 10–11; influence of mother on, 11–12, 15; and influence of Randolph family, 8; "Keep your land" admonition to, 11, 16; law studies of, 24, 25, 27–28, 33, 34; Littleton Tazewell and, 17, 18, 20; "Macbeth has murdered sleep" exclamation of, 34; at Matoax, 9–10, 14, 15, 37; nicknamed "Jack Randle," 10; parochial life of, 9–10; in Philadelphia, 24, 25, 28, 33–34; at Princeton College, 19–20, 21–22, 252n95; at Princeton grammar school, 18–19; and Professor Cochrane, 21–22; relationship with brother, Richard, 19, 20, 30, 36; relationship with mother, 11–12; and Richard Randolph trial, 31, 32–33, 256n52; and St. George Tucker, 12, 13, 14, 15–16, 17, 20, 22, 26, 28, 33, 36, 51, 159–60, 250n49, 292n89; in Savannah, Ga., 34; and scarlet fever attack, 28–29; at Walker Maury's Grammar School, 16–18; in Williamsburg, 31, 33, 38; youthful misbehavior of, 18, 19, 22–23, 25–26, 27, 33–35
—early political career: and Alien and Sedition Acts 38–39; antifederalism of 21, 24, 33; "Ask my constituents" comment by, 42, 192; debates Patrick Henry 1, 40–41, 197, 259n107; elected to House of Representatives (1799) 39, 41; and French Revolution, 33, 34–35, 36; general political activity of, 23–24, 33, 35, 39, 41; and ratification of United States Constitution, 20–21
—education, 9, 11, 14, 16–19, 20–25, 27–28, 31, 34; attends William & Mary, 31, 33, 256n42; at Columbia College, 20–23, 24,

Randolph, John, of Roanoke (*continued*)
28; dislike of formal schooling, 16–17, 19,
22, 24, 28; law studies of, 24, 25, 27–28, 33,
34; at Princeton College, 19–20, 21–22,
252n95; at Princeton grammar school,
18–19; and Professor Cochrane, 21–22;
reading of 11, 14, 18, 25, 156–57, 177,
187; at Walker Maury's Grammar School,
16–18
—family and business affairs: advice to
family members, 176–81; break with
St. George Tucker, 13–14, 22, 159–60,
250n49, 292n89; engaged to Maria Ward,
37–38, 255n13; finances of, 11–12, 13–14,
22, 25–26, 33–34, 36–37, 97, 135–36,
155, 258n83; frees slaves in will, 229; and
Nancy Randolph Morris, 30, 33, 98–99,
161–64, 165–67, 168, 254n11, 294n114; as
planter and landowner, 36–37, 97, 135–36;
as slaveholder, 69, 70, 71, 72, 97, 131
—Jeffersonian leader in House: as Chairman
of Ways & Means, 54, 55, 66, 99–100;
and election of 1800, 48–50, 51; federal
judiciary, views on, 54, 58–62, 83,
96; fight with Willis Alston, 79; and
Gabriel's slave revolt, 70; and Indiana
Territory report, 68–69; and Jefferson's
first term, 1, 53–54, 55, 57–62, 63–64,
65–67; and Jefferson's secret attempt to
purchase Florida, 100–104, 115; John
Adams, scorn for, 24, 38; and Judiciary
Act, 60–62; and Louisiana Purchase, 61,
63–66, 264n76; as Majority Leader of
the House of Representatives 63–64, 66,
80, 99–100, 104, 111; as Majority Whip
of the House of Representatives, 54–55,
56–57, 58, 62; and national debt, 53, 54,
58; opposes James Madison, 98, 104;
"Playhouse incident" of, 44–48; proposed
as Commissioner to Great Britain, 99,
273n75; "Ragamuffin" speech of, 43–44; as
a Republican, 33, 34–35, 39, 41, 49, 53–54,
65; and Samuel Chase impeachment and
trial, 2, 77, 81, 82–83, 87, 88–92, 94–97;

scorn for Federalists, 36, 48–49, 50, 60–61,
63–64, 84–85, 170; "Western Reserve of
Connecticut" speech of, 48; and Yazoo
controversy, 2, 77–80, 81, 83–86, 97, 111;
and "Yazoo men," 79, 119
—last years: burial of, 229, 230; "Change is
not Reform" speech of, 218–20; death of,
227–28; frees slaves in will, 229; health
breaks in Russia, 223; as Minister to
Russia, 221–23, 312n52, 313n63; and
Nullification crisis, 224–26; opposes Force
Bill, 225; removal of remains of, 230;
views on Constitution of Virginia, 216,
218–20, 221; at Virginia Constitutional
Convention, 216–21
—opinions of: Aaron Burr, 121, 123; Daniel
Webster, 194; Edmund Burke, 156–57;
Edward Livingston, 224; Francis Scott
Key, 242; George Washington, 24, 34–35;
Henry Clay, 141, 169–70, 193, 225; James
Madison, 98, 101–2, 104, 116, 127; James
Monroe, 110, 188; James Wilkinson, 123–
24; John Adams, 24, 38; John C. Calhoun,
141, 147, 205, 224, 226; John Marshall,
155–56, 291n58; John Quincy Adams, 207;
Martin Van Buren, 207; Robert Smith,
137; St. George Tucker, 13–14; Spencer
Roane, 157–58, 291n74; Thomas Jefferson,
98, 129, 188; Walker Maury, 17–18, 21;
William Crawford, 202
—Quid leader in House: canes Willis
Alston, 138–39; as Chairman of Ways
& Means, 118, 125; defeated by Eppes
for re-election, 150–51, 153–55; defeats
Eppes for Congress, 140; and election of
1808, 127–28; foreman of Aaron Burr
Grand Jury, 121–24; France, and policies
toward, 108, 134–35; Great Britain, and
policies toward, 107–8, 124–25, 134–35,
137–38; "Great Britain Resolutions"
speech of, 142, 143–45, 147, 276n29; and
Gregg's Resolution, 107–8, 109–10; and
Henry Clay, 141, 148–49, 169–70, 185,
193, 196, 225, 226; and John C. Calhoun,

146–47, 148–49, 170, 172, 173–74, 200–201, 205, 209, 226; near-duel with James Wilkinson, 124, 280n47; near-duel with John W. Eppes, 139; near-duel with T. M. Randolph, 112–14, 115; and non-importation act, 134–35; opposes embargo, 126, 134; opposes war with Great Britain, 141, 143–45, 146–49, 151, 160; predicts civil war, 120; and "Protestor's letter" (Randolphia rescript), 127; removed from Ways & Means Committee, 125; silenced by Clay, 148–49; styles himself "of Roanoke," 136, 284n27; supports James Monroe, 110–11, 127; as the *Tertium Quid* (generally), 2, 105, 106, 107, 111, 119, 183–84, 188–89; and War Hawks, 141–42; writes "Decius" letters, 115–16; writes "Mucius" letters, 137, 285n33

—relationship with Jefferson, 1, 55–56, 64, 66, 67, 101, 105, 115–16, 128, 201, 262n22; breaks with Jefferson, 1–2, 66–67, 80, 85–87, 99–101, 105, 106; dubs Jefferson "St. Thomas of Cantingbury," 128, 308n27

—senator and opposition leader: "Blifil and Black George" speech of, 209–11; defeated for United States Senate, 212, 213–14; duel with Henry Clay, 1, 210–12; elected to United States Senate, 204–5; and Martin Van Buren, 206, 207–8; opposition leader to J. Q. Adams administration, 207–8, 209–10, 214–15

—southern conservative: and Apportionment bill, 188–90; and death of Stephen Decatur, 187, 301n50; debates Daniel Webster, 193–95; and election of 1824, 201–3; European travels, 190–91, 201–2, 212–13; "A Fig for the Constitution" speech of, 199–200; and Greek independence, 192, 193–95; and internal improvements, 192, 195–98; and Missouri question, 184–87; near-duel with Daniel Webster, 203–4, 305n88

—views on: abolitionists, 69, 73–74, 145,

184; abstractions and principles, 179, 184–85, 190, 219–20, 224; American Revolution, 15–16; aristocracy, 6–7, 178–179, 208–9; Bank of the United States, 172–74; Canada, 144; centralized power, 33, 61–62, 171, 197; change and reform, 2, 133, 218–19, 220; civic virtue, 6–7, 178–179; Clarkson's anti-slavery essay, 69–70; Constitution of the United States, 21, 24, 65, 73, 107, 132–33, 159, 173, 193, 196–97, 199–200; Constitution of Virginia, 216, 218–20, 221; decadence in Virginia, 179; dueling, 139–40, 167; embargo, 126, 134; equality, 6, 179, 190, 208–9, 231; federal judiciary, 54, 58–62, 83, 96; France, 108, 134–35; Gabriel's slave revolt, 70; Great Britain, 107–8, 124–25, 134–35, 137–38; Indians, 144; internal improvements, 171, 192, 195–98; Islamic religion, 35–36, 194–95, 257n74; liberty, 6, 34–35, 70, 132, 152, 159, 190, 231, 232–33; manumission of slaves, 69, 72; national debt, 53, 54, 58; nullification, 224–26; religion, 11, 27, 70–71, 158, 168, 257n74, 295n20; Republican betrayal of principles, 84–86, 98, 102, 103–4, 108–9, 116, 143–44, 145, 170; republican principles, 2, 33, 35, 39, 41, 46, 51, 52, 54, 65, 81, 97–98, 103–4, 108–9, 116, 141–44, 145, 152–53, 188–89, 230–31, 233; secession, 158, 200; slave emancipation, 69, 72, 197; slave insurrections, 70, 144–45; slave trade, 72, 120, 185; slavery, 69, 70, 72–73, 74, 131, 144–45, 158, 184, 197, 199, 264n4; slavery expansion, 68–69; sovereignty, 23–24, 78–79, 80, 132, 172; spending by federal government, 53, 54, 58, 66; standing armies, 43, 45, 47, 54, 138, 141; states' powers and rights, 33, 34, 72–73, 79, 80, 132, 144–45, 170, 172, 186–87; strict construction of Constitution, 61–62, 132, 196–97, 199–200; tariffs, 192, 198–200; taxation, 53, 54, 57–58, 111, 119, 171–72, 200; trade policies, 107–8, 119, 125–26,

Randolph, John, of Roanoke (*continued*)
128; tyranny, 34–35, 79; Virginia, 183; war
with Great Britain, 141, 143–45, 146–49,
151, 160

Randolph, John, Sr. (JRR's father), 9, 13, 20,
22, 36, 136, 248n9

Randolph, Judith (JRR's sister-in-law), 20,
29, 30, 32, 34, 36, 47, 62, 98, 155, 162, 164,
167, 170, 256n52

Randolph, Martha Jefferson (Patsy), 31, 32,
112

Randolph, Peyton, 38

Randolph, Richard (JRR's brother), 9,
19, 20, 22, 29, 34, 162, 252n99; alleged
relationship with Nancy Randolph
(Morris), 30; death of, 36, 167–68; and
events at Glenlyvar, 30–31, 163, 164, 167,
256n52; JRR's devotion to, 20; trial of,
31–33

Randolph, Richard, of Curles (JRR's
grandfather), 8, 248n5

Randolph, St. George (JRR's nephew), 29–30,
36, 102, 155, 176, 178

Randolph, Theodorick (JRR's brother), 9, 18,
19, 20, 21, 22, 23, 27, 28, 30, 33, 36, 163,
167, 253n113

Randolph, Thomas Mann, 112–14, 115

Randolph, Tudor (JRR's nephew), 36, 161,
162, 164, 178

Randolph, William, of Turkey Island (JRR's
great-grandfather), 8, 10, 248n1, n3

Randolphia rescript, 127

Reflections on the Revolution in France
(Burke), 156

Register of Debates, 207

Republicans (political party), 33, 34–35,
39, 40, 41, 42, 43, 49, 53, 53–54, 59, 65,
80, 106; and JRR, 84–86, 98, 102, 103–4,
108–9, 116, 143–44, 145, 170

Reynolds, Maria, 76

Reynolds, Michael, 44, 45, 46

Richmond *Enquirer*, 86, 90, 109, 111, 114,
115, 116, 128, 146, 150, 157, 169, 212,
213–14

Richmond Examiner, 76

Ritchie, Thomas, 114

Roane, Spencer, 5, 157–58, 291n74

Roanoke (JRR's estate), 8, 9, 16, 72, 97, 155,
176, 187

Rodney, Caesar, 82, 94, 104

Root, Erastus, 85

Rutledge, Henry, 26, 27, 243

Rutledge, John, 57

Scott, Winfield, 122

Sedgwick, Theodore, 42, 192

Sedition Act, 39

Sharp, James, 35

slavery, 68–74, 131, 144–45, 158, 184, 197,
199; and emancipation, 69, 72, 197; and
expansion, 68–69; and trade, 72, 120, 185

Smith, Robert, 137, 284n29

Smith, Samuel, 56

South Carolina Exposition (Calhoun), 324

Spencer, Gideon, 151

Stanford, Richard, 170, 243

Stuart, Gilbert, 106

Syphax (JRR's slave), 20

Tallmadge, Benjamin, 108

Tallmadge, James, 184

Tate, Adam, 5, 72, 145, 156, 157

Taylor, Creed, 39, 243

Taylor, John, of Caroline, 1, 5, 72, 125, 126,
231, 243

Taylor, Robert, 33

Tazewell, Littleton Waller, 17, 20, 122, 205,
243

Tertium Quids, 2, 105, 107, 110, 111, 114,
115, 119, 127

The Times (London), 191

Treaty of Ghent, 169

Treaty of Paris of 1783, 35

Treaty of Paris of 1795. *See* Jay's Treaty

Tucker, Frances Bland Randolph (JRR's
mother), 9, 11, 12, 13, 15, 19, 20, 159, 168,
249n32, 250n57

Tucker, Henry, Colonel, 18

Tucker, Henry St. George (JRR's half-
brother), 81, 88, 94, 204–5, 244

Tucker, Nathaniel Beverley (JRR's half-brother), 156, 157, 160

Tucker, St. George (JRR's step-father), 12–13, 16, 17, 18, 19, 21, 24, 28, 33, 51, 60, 83, 157; break with JRR, 13–14, 159–60, 250n49, 292n89; genealogical line of, 240; marries Frances Randolph, 12–13; relationship with JRR, 12–15, 19, 20, 22–23, 25–27, 36, 37

Tucker, Thomas Tudor (JRR's uncle), 20

Turkey Island, Va., 8

Tyler, John, 213, 214

Van Buren, Martin, 4, 188, 206, 207–8, 221–22, 307n4

Varnum, Joseph, 19, 125

"View of the Constitution of the United States" (Tucker), 13

Virginia Constitutional Convention of 1829, 2, 216, 217, 221

"Virginia Doctrine," 6

Virginia Gazette, 31

Virginia Ratification Convention (1788), 20, 21

Virginia Resolution (1798), 39

von Lieven, Carl Christoph, 223

War of 1812, 151–52, 160–61, 168–69; debate on, 142–47; declared, 149; ends, 169; U.S. policies prior to, 134, 136–39, 141, 147–48

Ward, Maria, 37–38

Washington, D.C., 49, 63, 152, 161–62, 169

Washington, George, 23, 24, 34–35, 39–40, 76, 84

Washington, Lawrence, 25

Ways and Means Committee, House of Representatives, 54, 55, 66, 100, 118

Webster, Daniel, 104, 108, 161, 203, 209, 226; debates JRR, 193–95; JRR opinion of, 194; near duel with JRR, 1, 203–4, 305n88; opinion of JRR, 207

West, Francis, Dr., 29, 227, 228

Whiskey Rebellion (1794), 76

Wilberforce, William, 191

Wilkinson, James, 120–21, 123, 124, 139

William & Mary, College of, 8, 12, 13, 16, 24, 31, 33

Williamsburg, Va., 17, 20, 28, 31, 33

Witherspoon, John, 19, 252n95

Wythe, George, 13, 24, 157

XYZ affair, 38–39

Yazoo land controversy, 1–2, 77–80, 83–86, 97, 111–12, 190, 193

Yorktown, siege of, 12, 16